The Growth of American Politics

Volume I

Through Reconstruction

The Growth of American Politics

Volume I

Through Reconstruction

A Modern Reader

edited by Frank Otto Gatell, Paul Goodman, and Allen Weinstein

New York
OXFORD UNIVERSITY PRESS · 1972

Library of Congress Catalogue Card Number: 78-182423
Printed in the United States of America

Contents

Introduction

Toward a New Political History

The student of politics has traditionally divided his attention between the art of gaining power and the craft of retaining it. Any dictionary definition of the term "politics" will recognize these dual functions: on the one hand, "policies or affairs of a government"; on the other, "the conducting of or engaging in political affairs, often professionally." When examined in tandem, they should provide a thorough understanding both of the way political power operates within a society, and some of its uses. Americans have been far from unique in asking questions of their political history that might help explain their contemporary society. In recent years, however, we have experienced a heightened sense of confusion concerning the directions of present-day America, and this lends special urgency to our desire for additional perspective through an understanding of our political past.

A century ago, even as recently as fifty years ago, United States political history seemed to most Americans (and to the country's historians) a refreshing and epic drama of expanding liberty and declining tyranny. This morality tale, pounded home in countless orations and sermons delivered on the Fourth of July and just about every other day, survived with hardly a phrase altered in the lectures of American history teachers from one-room grade schools to the universities. The United States, the story ran, had been founded in crisis by seventeenth-century North Europeans searching for religious and political freedom, created in revolution by eighteenth-century colonials struggling against imperial despotism, and consecrated in civil war by nineteenth-century

Unionists vindicating the national commitment to freedom by fighting against an aggressive slave power. Even in the nineteenth century, of course, there were dissents from this candy-coated version of political history. American Negroes (*after* Reconstruction), Socialists, utopian reformers, non-English-speaking immigrants, and Indians might be forgiven a dash of pardonable skepticism concerning the universality of America's reputed Mission to extend equally the boundaries of freedom. Nonetheless, for a majority of Americans, the prevailing image of libertarian nationalism, an "empire for liberty," seemed a reasonably adequate approximation of the realities of political life.

Growing doubts concerning the merits of this largely mythical and uncritical view of the American past emerged around 1900 as certain new perspectives began to take shape. Late nineteenth-century science had helped transform the way in which American history, along with other non-scientific disciplines, was studied in the universities. History became a profession, and historians became more exacting in their research techniques and increasingly more critical in their interpretations of the American past. When the historians of the first half of the nineteenth century did their work the American Revolution remained a still-vivid experience for many of their countrymen. Similarly, scholars in the latter half of the nineteenth century, both North and South, wrote under the lengthening and inhibiting shadow of a Civil War mythology. Historians who pioneered in critical assessments of their national past early in the twentieth century lived in a country fresh from easy yet disquieting imperial adventures and, moreover, touched everywhere by the ferment of a new reform wave.

The Progressive Era provided additional impetus, if any were needed, for historians to engage in a critical appraisal of the American past, if only to understand why industrialism and urbanization had brought in their wake so much political corruption, economic exploitation, and social misery. The hallmark of "Progressive history," as it came to be called, was a searching and present-minded view of contending forces within society. The American past seemed no longer the simple tale of freedom's triumph over oppression, but, instead, another simple tale—this one recounting a constant moral struggle of democratic against privileged elements. For Frederick Jackson Turner and others who saw the westward movement as the central interpretive clue to American development, conflicts between an expanding egalitarian frontier and stratified, older regions supplied the unifying theme. Shortly after Turner developed the frontier interpretation, another scholar, Charles A. Beard, presented another theory: he described American political history as a struggle among rival economic interest groups, a view that has remained powerful and influential among historians to this day. In Beard's analysis, class interests rather than sectional ties determined the fundamental lines of political cleavage in American history: farmers opposing merchants, workers opposing factory owners, Southern planters opposing Northern industrialists.

Progressivism had reflected the prevailing anxiety among Americans of most classes over "plutocracy," or unrestrained economic power, the threat posed to a democratic society by unsupervised business enterprise. Beard and his followers discovered similar threats at each stage in American political growth, which they interpreted as a constant struggle between competing economic classes for control of the government. Although these conflicts had sometimes produced positive advances in democratic government, such as the abolition of slavery, suffrage extension, and government regulation of business, Progressive historians still worried over what lay ahead. The past had been a struggle; the future would inevitably be shaped by struggle as well. Whether twentieth-century American democracy could survive such violent clashes in an era of giant cities, conglomerate industries, massive concentrations of economic power, and new techniques for manipulating the public will remained questionable. Largely due to the work of scholars such as Turner and Beard, American political history no longer seemed a providential story of liberty's demanding yet unstoppable triumph over tyranny. If anything, the Progressive historians made the outcome of the imminent struggle appear to be a fifty-fifty proposition.

Before Beard died in 1948, the United States had become engulfed in global conflicts, first with German and Japanese fascism in the early 1940's, and then, since 1945, with Russian and Chinese communism—foreign conflicts which forced serious reappraisals of the American past by political historians.

Increased attention to a comparison of American political history with the experiences of European and Asian nations led a number of younger scholars, in the wake of World War II, to challenge the assumption of Progressive historiography that conflict had been *the* dominant aspect of United States history. Both Beard's stress on class antagonisms and Turner's model of sectional hostility evoked growing, sometimes massive skepticism among historians who saw that, when compared with social struggles in other countries, American disputes appeared milder, less internecine, and more capable of compromise through existing institutional channels. Historians during the 1950's also stressed the comparatively high degree of individual freedom and material prosperity enjoyed in the United States, and for the first time since the turn of the century, most of the major innovative studies of American history bypassed the assumptions and visions of angry reformism.

Many factors helped produce this new burst of historical *un*-criticism, or "consensus" history—among them the stress on comparative history, the anxieties over national survival in an atomic age, and the growing body of scholarship which questioned numerous errors or oversimplifications in the work of the early masters such as Beard and Turner. For whatever reasons, the 1950's witnessed the brief heyday of consensus history, a bland yet often eloquent rewriting of American political history that accentuated the positive features while muting the importance of past conflicts.

An abrupt reversal of this "consensus" among American historians accompanied the growing economic, generational, and racial conflicts, in the 1960's. With the increase of social tension during the 1960's came a revival of the reform impulse among younger historians, a neo-Beardianism that owes far more to its originator's historical premises than its practitioners often recognize or care to admit. "New Left" akademicians, stressing class struggles as the determining factor in American political history, have yet to produce their own Beard or even a synthesis of our past equivalent to his. Yet they have voiced the disenchantment of liberal scholars, as well as radicals, with a political history based on "consensus" assumptions which, all too often, either whitewashed or neglected the ample record of political oppresion and social injustice in America.

Yet changes in American historiography do not result simply from altered climates of opinion, but often proceed from new methodology and new research within the historical profession itself. Thus, a procession of historians had scrutinized the Progressive historians' arguments for several decades, beginning long before World War II, and rejected many of them not because of changing values but because of conflicting evidence. Historians were trained and continue to be trained to examine new data and to question received explanations in an effort to achieve deeper understanding of the past. Thus, in analyzing frontier society in specific areas much more systematically than Turner alone was able to do, several historians discerned a highly stratified or, at the very least, contradictory social structure rather than the democratic fluidity which Turner theorized. Similarly, recent scholarship has exploded Beard's portrait of Confederation era politics as a clear-cut struggle between the mass of anti-Federalist farmers against a coalition of merchants, planters, and bondholders who favored the new frame of government. Later historians, studying a myriad of local economic and political groupings, exhumed a complex set of responses toward the Constitution absent from Beard's simple economic demonology. Beard's world portrayed a constant procession of clashing economic interests; Turner's, a welter of contending sectional interests. While not rejecting entirely either view of the American past, contemporary historians have shown greater interest than their major predecessors in evaluating other keys to American political history. Such factors as ethnic and religious ties, ideological commitments, and irrational drives have been isolated as powerful determinants of American political behavior by historians using a variety of new techniques borrowed from the social sciences.

Much of this scholarship—"the new political history" as some of its votaries dub it—cannot be explained merely through the recovery of vast bodies of data previously untapped by indolent historians, although new historical evidence has indeed proliferated of late. The primary influence behind recent major reinterpretations of American political history lies in the profound impact of the social sciences upon historians over the past several generations. The discipline of history has traditionally straddled the humanities and social sciences, pivoting toward the former in that it sometimes enjoys status as a literary art, yet eyeing enviously the claims for certitude and predictability made by the latter. Having grown restless with this half-caste intellectual classification, a growing number of scholars have struggled to introduce a more precise technical analysis of available data than has previously characterized historical generalizations. The "new political history" has attempted to apply methods of analysis perfected by the various social sciences—political science, psychology, sociology, economics, and anthropology—to the search for a more accurate rendering of America's political past.

Although influenced just as heavily by today's social climate of opinion as were their scholarly, "non-scientific" predecessors of previous eras, much of the best new work in political history at least makes an attempt to counter inevitable present-mindedness by rigorous, and hopefully fair-minded, application of techniques such as the systematic quantification of political data, the analysis of group ideology, and multivariate analysis of political behavior.

In the selections that follow, students will find samples of the older as well as of the new political history, sometimes blended in the same selection. Traditionally, political historians have formulated hypotheses to account for a historical development and then tested their theories against the available evidence through a wide-ranging yet frequently impressionistic and unsystematic examination of relevant data. The impressionistic method, and the intuition upon which it relies so heavily, will always remain among the historian's principal tools, if only because in most cases the data needed to answer with certainty many of the most significant historical questions are lacking, and will remain so.

But quantification, though no panacea, offers a valuable additional method, a precision tool for writing political history. Techniques of quantitative analysis have allowed for more accurate measurement of voting patterns among important groups in American life, both at the national and local levels. They have also allowed inept practitioners, those with a tendency to quantificate, to publish numerical gibberish; but then no methodology, traditional or super-modern, is any better than the people who apply it. Yet quantification permits historians to speculate more securely on the motivations behind group political attitudes and behavior. We can learn more easily, for example, what kinds of people voted for William Jennings Bryan or supported William McKinley in 1896; we can determine which groups were most likely to support the Democrat Andrew Jackson against his Whig opponents in the 1830's; we can guage the composition of the "ethnic vote" in 1860 (or in 1960); or evaluate similar voting behavior at other critical points in the American past.

Recent quantitative analysis of American political behavior has shown, for example, that United States politics cannot be understood solely in terms of economic class categories, although in their time such Beardian explanations represented a considerable advance in American historical writing. Today's historians must take into account equally powerful influences on political behavior, such as race, religion, ethnic background, cultural milieu, and ideology. Those who assume that people invariably vote their pocketbooks will find that a systematic culling of voting data does not always bear out that assumption. Variables other than economic class shape the complex manner in which people perceive and respond to political events. No discussion of the origins of the Civil War that fails to include the pathological elements in Southerners' fears over slavery, or the similarly irrational components in the anxieties of antebellum Northerners, can hope to explain that war's background adequately.

All of which is yet another way of saying that political history is more than the study of past politics. Recognizing the axiom that political behavior cannot be comprehended in isolation from other patterns of human behavior, political history has broadened its range. Such factors as group psychology, racism, ethnicity, economic development, immigration, nativism, and urban-rural conflicts have all become critically important (indeed, essential), to the study of American political history in recent years.

The analysis of American politics within broader social and cultural contexts has alerted historians to the influence of ideology, which is sometimes decisive for political action. The ideas and values which men believe in and sometimes die for are rarely accidental, and the forms they assume at any given time and place reflect the delicate adjustments made by individuals between their cultural beliefs and group interests. Yet ideas can become so powerful at critical moments in the history of a society as almost to assume a life of their own, exerting influences beyond the intellectual vanguard, often few in number, who transmit them. Thus the proto-revolutionaries of the 1760's and the Republicans of the 1850's both constructed ideologies that helped prepare their fellow countrymen for the impending realities of civil conflict. The natural rights doctrines of colonial dissidents during the Revolutionary era and the Republican party's free labor ideology nearly a century later both produced consequences that far exceeded their narrow class or group origins: American independence in the first instance, and the abolition of slavery in the second.

The newer political methodology, with its social analysis of politics and quantification of political behavior, along with the inconoclastic dismantling of the Progressive synthesis in recent decades, has left American political history in a state of confusion and disarray. Since World War II revisionist historians, using both new and traditional analytical techniques, have relentlessly and persuasively modified traditional views on almost every major question, often causing them to be discarded altogether. No alternative synthesis has yet emerged, however, to provide a coherent and systematic account of the growth of American politics. The story itself, an embarrassment of riches, was slighted by Progressive historians, and we are left with the difficulty of assimilating leads offered by the social sciences. Our bequest is a historical Tower of Babel that thus far defies synthetic reinterpretation.

Scholars also confront the compounding difficulties of the rapidly changing attitudes within the United States during the past decade—a growing loss of faith in progress, a profound skepticism over the worth of intellect, a reluctant recognition of the irrational and uncontrollable aspects of human behavior, and a fundamental loss of confidence in America's national destiny—all of which have denied to political historians a firm ground of current and universally accepted beliefs from which they could base a systematic treatment of the past.

In time, if our society can survive its present crises, a new overview of American political growth will emerge. We hope that at least some of the selections represented in this anthology will contribute to that synthesis. Certainly it is too soon to chart the exact contours of this new political history, but it will most likely rest on a more sophisticated understanding of the complexities of individual and social psychology than its predecessors did. It will also probably devote greater attention than did earlier twentieth-century political syntheses to explaining how geographic and vocational mobility, ethno-cultural and religious diversity, racial hostilities, and regional diversity have kept Americans from dividing along clear-cut economic class lines. It may examine in greater depth the manner in which American voters and their politicians have responded to constantly-changing urban and industrial patterns from the mid-nineteenth century to the present, and it may make more effective use of the quantitative method to sharpen our knowledge of how specific groups organize and act politically. The following selections should serve the student as a reliable and stimulating introduction to some of the work already done and to other larger projects yet in progress.

It is fairly safe to predict that no new synthesis can hope either to be accepted or long-lived unless it grapples with the past in all its puzzling complexity. That complexity, and the existing gaps in our knowledge which historians have recently become sensitized to, stand as formidable obstacles in the path of providing a revised, modern interpretation of the growth of American politics. But without such an interpretation, we shall not know where we came from—and in that blissful state of ignorance, we can hardly expect to know where we are headed.

I

Colonial Politics, 1607–1776

The Beginnings of American Politics

Politics and Social Structure in Virginia

by Bernard Bailyn

Politics and government in colonial America took its distinctive shape from circumstances in the New World that were unlike those in the Old. The political ideas and institutions brought from the Old World had been relied upon to establish order in the wilderness, but they did not, and for that reason they were changed. In every colony a ruling group sought at the outset to establish firm control for the few. In Massachusetts the leaders of the Massachusetts Bay Company, and in Virginia the officers of the Virginia Company, tried to monopolize power. In both cases elements that had been excluded challenged the ruling group, forcing them to broaden the terms of citizen participation. The Virginia House of Burgesses (1619) and the General Court of Massachusetts (1630) provided arenas in which more and more people could take part in decision-making. Similarly, when the Crown assumed direct control of these colonies, the king's officials discovered the necessity of reaching an accommodation with powerful local figures. In Virginia, Governor William Berkeley's attempt to resist any such accommodation resulted in rebellion and ended in the collapse of his regime.

From the beginning, traditional assumptions about government and politics ran afoul of American realities. In Europe, politics remained a privilege of the wealthy and well-born. In colonial America, however, the social structure lacked an entrenched hereditary elite to form a governing class. Instead, political leaders made their way to the top through trade, planting, and the professions. Political instability mirrored social instability. In a new society with abundant opportunities and with land accessible to many, new men and new families kept pushing their way forward to claim the status of gentlemen and the advantages of power.

Social instability had many and complex roots. Not only did an open social order and opportunities for acquiring wealth stir rivalries, but religious, sectional, and ethnic differences also served to foster competition among contending groups. Those living on the Virginia frontier had interests that clashed with those of Virginians from older settlements. In colonies with significant ethnic and religious minorities, such as New York, Maryland, and Pennsylvania, these minorities formed lines of division that generated conflict. In most cases stability came when disaffected groups gained recognition, re-establishing an equilibrium until new points of tension produced pressures that required new accommodations.

In the long run, the jockeying for position between established and aspiring elites weakened the authority of governing groups. With many competing for the right to rule, ordinary citizens, previously accustomed to deferring to the supposed wisdom of their social betters, became less deferential. This long, slow process turned Americans in the direction of expanded participation in politics and popular government.

In the following essay Bernard Bailyn analyzes the challenge and transformation of political structure in the important colony of Virginia. Virginia is especially interesting because it was the first British colony in America that altered its political structure. The process there became a blueprint: it repeated itself elsewhere in colonial America.

By the end of the seventeenth century the American colonists faced an array of disturbing problems in the conduct of public affairs. Settlers from England and Holland, reconstructing familiar institutions on American shores, had become participants in what would appear to have been a wave of civil disobedience. Constituted authority was confronted with repeated challenges. Indeed, a veritable anarchy seems to have prevailed at the center of colonial society, erupting in a series of insurrections that began as early as 1635 with the "thrusting out" of Governor Harvey in Virginia. Culpeper's Rebellion in Carolina, the Protestant Association in Maryland, Bacon's Rebellion in Virginia, Leisler's seizure of power in New York, the resistance to and finally the overthrow of Andros in New England—every colony was affected.

These outbursts were not merely isolated local affairs. Although their immediate causes were rooted in the particular circumstances of the separate colonies, they nevertheless had common characteristics. They were, in fact, symptomatic of a profound disorganization of European society in its American setting. Seen in a broad view, they reveal a new configuration of forces which shaped the origins of American politics.

In a letter written from Virginia in 1623, George Sandys, the resident treasurer, reported despondently on the character and condition of the leading settlers. Some of the councilors were "no more then Ciphers," he wrote; others were "miserablie poore"; and the few substantial planters lived apart, taking no responsibility for public concerns. There was, in fact, among all those "worthie the mencioninge" only one person deserving of full approval. Lieutenant William Peirce "refuses no labour, nor sticks at anie expences that may aduantage the publique." Indeed, Sandys added, Peirce was "of a Capacitie that is not to bee expected in a man of his breedinge."

The afterthought was penetrating. It cut below the usual complaints of the time that many of the settlers were lazy malcontents hardly to be preferred to the Italian glassworkers, than whom, Sandys wrote, "a more damned crew hell never vomited." What

From James Morton Smith (ed.), *Seventeenth-Century America: Essays in Colonial History* (Chapel Hill: University of North Carolina Press, for The Institute of Early American History and Culture, 1959), pp. 90–115. Reprinted by permission; most footnotes omitted.

lay behind Sandys's remark was not so much that wretched specimens were arriving in the shipments of servants nor even that the quality of public leadership was declining but that the social foundations of political power were being strangely altered.

All of the settlers in whatever colony presumed a fundamental relationship between social structure and political authority. Drawing on a common medieval heritage, continuing to conceive of society as a hierarchical unit, its parts justly and naturally separated into inferior and superior levels, they assumed that superiority was indivisible; there was not one hierarchy for political matters, another for social purposes. John Winthrop's famous explanation of God's intent that "in all times some must be rich some poore, some highe and eminent in power and dignitie; others meane and in subieccion" could not have been more carefully worded. Riches, dignity, and power were properly placed in apposition; they pertained to the same individuals.

So closely related were social leadership and political leadership that experience if not theory justified an identification between state and society. To the average English colonist the state was not an abstraction existing above men's lives, justifying itself in its own terms, taking occasional human embodiment. However glorified in monarchy, the state in ordinary form was indistinguishable from a more general social authority; it was woven into the texture of everyday life. It was the same squire or manorial lord who in his various capacities collated to the benefice, set the rents, and enforced the statutes of Parliament and the royal decrees. Nothing could have been more alien to the settlers than the idea that competition for political leadership should be open to all levels of society or that obscure social origins or technical skills should be considered valuable qualifications for office. The proper response to new technical demands on public servants was not to give power to the skilled but to give skills to the powerful. The English gentry and landed aristocracy remained politically adaptable and hence politically competent, assuming when necessary new public functions, eliminating the need for a professional state bureaucracy. By their amateur competence they made possible a continuing identification between political and social authority.

In the first years of settlement no one had reason to expect that this characteristic of public life would fail to transfer itself to the colonies. For at least a decade and a half after its founding there had been in the Jamestown settlement a small group of leaders drawn from the higher echelons of English society. Besides well-born soldiers of fortune like George Percy, son of the Earl of Northumberland, there were among them four sons of the West family—children of Lord de la Warr and his wife, a second cousin of Queen Elizabeth. In Virginia the West brothers held appropriately high positions; three of them served as governors. Christopher Davison, the colony's secretary, was the son of Queen Elizabeth's secretary, William Davison, M.P. and Privy Councilor. The troublesome John Martin, of Martin's Brandon, was the son of Sir Richard Martin, twice Lord Mayor of London, and also the brother-in-law of Sir Julius Caesar, Master of the Rolls and Privy Councilor. Sir Francis and Haute Wyatt were sons of substantial Kent gentry and grandsons of the Sir Thomas Wyatt who led the rebellion of 1554 against Queen Mary. George Sandys's father was the Archbishop of York; of his three older brothers, all knights and M.P.'s, two were eminent country gentlemen, and the third, Edwin, of Virginia Company fame, was a man of great influence in the city. George Thorpe was a former M.P. and Gentleman of the Privy Chamber.

More impressive than such positions and relationships was the cultural level represented. For until the very end of the Company period, Virginia remained to the literary and scientific an exotic attraction, its settlement an important moment in Christian history. Its original magnetism for those in touch with intellectual currents affected the early immigration. Of the twenty councilors of 1621, eight had been educated at Oxford, Cambridge, or the Inns of Court. Davison, like Martin trained in the law, was a poet in a family of poets. Thorpe was a "student of Indian views on religion and astronomy." Francis Wyatt wrote verses and was something of a student of political theory. Alexander Whitaker, M.A., author of *Good Newes from Virginia,* was the worthy heir "of a good part of the learning of his renowned father," the master of St. John's College and Regius Professor of Divinity at Cambridge. John Pory, known to history mainly as the speaker of the first representative assembly in America, was a Master of Arts, "protege and disciple of Hakluyt," diplomat, scholar, and traveler, whose writings from and about America have a rightful place in literary history. Above all there was George Sandys, "poet, traveller, and scholar," a member of Lord Falkland's literary circle; while in Jamestown he continued as a matter of course to work on his notable translation of Ovid's *Metamorphoses.*

There was, in other words, during the first years of settlement a direct transference to Virginia of the upper levels of the English social hierarchy as well as of the lower. If the great majority of the settlers were recruited from the yeoman class and below, there was nevertheless a reasonable representation from those upper groups acknowledged to be the rightful rulers of society.

It is a fact of some importance, however, that this governing elite did not survive a single generation, at least in its original form. By the thirties their number had declined to insignificance. Percy, for example, left in 1612. Whitaker drowned in 1617. Sandys and Francis Wyatt arrived only in 1621, but their enthusiasm cooled quickly; they were both gone by 1626. Of the Wests, only John was alive and resident in the colony a decade after the collapse of the Company. Davison, who returned to England in 1622 after only a year's stay, was sent back in 1623 but died within a year of his return. Thorpe was one of the six councilors slain in the massacre of 1622. Pory left for England in 1622; his return as investigating commissioner in 1624 was temporary, lasting only a few months. And the cantankerous Martin graced the Virginia scene by his absence after 1625; he is last heard from in the early 1630's petitioning for release from a London debtor's prison.

To be sure, a few representatives of important English families, like John West and Edmund Scarborough, remained. There were also one or two additions from the same social level. But there were few indeed of such individuals, and the basis of their authority had changed. The group of gentlemen and illuminati that had dominated the scene during the Company era had been dispersed. Their disappearance created a political void which was filled soon enough, but from a different area of recruitment, from below, from the toughest and most fortunate of the surviving planters whose eminence by the end of the thirties had very little to do with the transplantation of social status.[1]

The position of the new leaders rested on their ability to wring material gain from the wilderness. Some, like Samuel Mathews, started with large initial advantages, but more typical were George Menefie and John Utie, who began as independent landowners by right of transporting themselves and only one or two servants. Abraham Wood, famous for his explorations and like Menefie and Utie the future possessor of large estates and important offices, appears first as a servant boy on Mathews's plantation. Adam Thoroughgood, the son of a country vicar, also started in Virginia as a servant, aged fourteen. William Spencer is first recorded as a yeoman farmer without servants.

Such men as these—Spencer, Wood, Menefie, Utie, Mathews—

1. The difficulty of maintaining in Virginia the traditional relationship between social and political authority became in 1620 the basis of an attack by a group of "ancient planters," including Francis West, on the newly appointed governor, Sir George Yeardley. Although Yeardley had been knighted two years earlier in an effort to enhance his personal authority, the petitioners argued that his lack of eminence was discouraging settlement. "Great Actions," they wrote, "are carryed wth best successe by such Comanders who haue personall Aucthoritye & greatness answerable to the Action, Sithence itt is nott easye to swaye a vulgar and seruile Nature by vulgar & seruile Spiritts." Leadership should devolve on commanders whose "Eminence or Nobillitye" is such that "eueryе man subordinate is ready to yeild a willing submission wthowt contempt or repyning." The ordinary settlers, they said, would not obey the same authority "conferrd vpon a meane man . . . no bettar than selected owt of their owne Ranke." If, therefore, the Company hoped to attract and hold colonists, especially of "the bettar sorte," it should select as leaders in Virginia "some eythar Noble or little lesse in Honor or Dower . . . to maintayne & hold vp the dignitye of so Great and good a cawse." Susan M. Kingsbury (ed.), *The Records of the Virginia Company of London* (4 vols., Washington, D.C., 1906–35), III, 231–32.

were the most important figures in Virginia politics up to the Restoration, engrossing large tracts of land, dominating the Council, unseating Sir John Harvey from the governorship. But in no traditional sense were they a ruling class. They lacked the attributes of social authority, and their political dominance was a continuous achievement. Only with the greatest difficulty, if at all, could distinction be expressed in a genteel style of life, for existence in this generation was necessarily crude. Mathews may have created a flourishing estate and Menefie had splendid fruit gardens, but the great tracts of land such men claimed were almost entirely raw wilderness. They had risen to their positions, with few exceptions, by brute labor and shrewd manipulation; they had personally shared the burdens of settlement. They succeeded not because of, but despite, whatever gentility they may have had. William Claiborne may have been educated at the Middle Temple; Peirce could not sign his name; but what counted was their common capacity to survive and flourish in frontier settlements. They were tough, unsentimental, quick-tempered, crudely ambitious men concerned with profits and increased landholdings, not the grace of life. They roared curses, drank exuberantly, and gambled (at least according to deVries) for their servants when other commodities were lacking. If the worst of Governor Harvey's offenses had been to knock out the teeth of an offending councilor with a cudgel, as he did on one occasion, no one would have questioned his right to the governorship. Rank had its privileges, and these men were the first to claim them, but rank itself was unstable and the lines of class or status were fluid. There was no insulation for even the most elevated from the rude impact of frontier life.

As in style of life so in politics, these leaders of the first permanently settled generation did not re-create the characteristics of a stable gentry. They had had little opportunity to acquire the sense of public responsibility that rests on deep identification with the land and its people. They performed in some manner the duties expected of leaders, but often public office was found simply burdensome. Reports such as Sandys's that Yeardley, the councilor and former governor, was wholly absorbed in his private affairs and scarcely glanced at public matters and that Mathews "will rather hazard the payment of fforfeitures then performe our Injunctions" were echoed by Harvey throughout his tenure of office. Charles Harmar, justice of the peace on the Eastern Shore, attended the court once in eight years, and Claiborne's record was only slightly better. Attendance to public duties had to be specifically enjoined, and privileges were of necessity accorded provincial officeholders. The members of the Council were particularly favored by the gift of tax exemption.

The private interests of this group, which had assumed control of public office by virtue not of inherited status but of newly achieved and strenuously maintained economic eminence, were pursued with little interference from the traditional restraints imposed on a responsible ruling class. Engaged in an effort to establish themselves in the land, they sought as specific ends, autonomous local jurisdiction, an aggressive expansion of settlement and trading enterprises, unrestricted access to land, and, at every stage, the legal endorsement of acquisitions. Most of the major public events for thirty years after the dissolution of the Company—and especially the overthrow of Harvey—were incidents in the pursuit of these goals.

From his first appearance in Virginia, Sir John Harvey threatened the interests of this emerging planter group. While still in England he had identified himself with the faction that had successfully sought the collapse of the Company, and thus his mere presence in Virginia was a threat to the legal basis of land grants made under the Company's charter. His demands for the return as public property of goods that had once belonged to the Company specifically jeopardized the planters' holdings. His insistence that the governorship was more than a mere chairmanship of the Council tended to undermine local autonomy. His conservative Indian policy not only weakened the settlers' hand in what already seemed an irreconcilable enmity with the natives but also restricted the expansion of settlement. His opposition to

Claiborne's claim to Kent Island threatened to kill off the lucrative Chesapeake Bay trade, and his attempt to ban the Dutch ships from the colony endangered commerce more generally. His support of the official policy of economic diversification, together with his endorsement of the English schemes of tobacco monopoly, alienated him finally and completely from the Council group.

Within a few months of his assuming the governorship, Harvey wrote home with indignation of the "waywardnes and oppositions" of the councilors and condemned them for factiously seeking "rather for their owne endes then either seekinge the generall good or doinge right to particuler men." Before a year was out the antagonisms had become so intense that a formal peace treaty had to be drawn up between Harvey and the Council. But both sides were adamant, and conflict was inescapable. It exploded in 1635 amid comic opera scenes of "extreame coller and passion" complete with dark references to Richard the Third and musketeers "running with their peices presented." The conclusion was Harvey's enraged arrest of George Menefie "of suspicion of Treason to his Majestie"; Utie's response, "And wee the like to you sir"; and the governor's forced return to England.

Behind these richly heroic "passings and repassings to and fro" lies not a victory of democracy or representative institutions or anything of the sort. Democracy, in fact, was identified in the Virginians' minds with the "popular and tumultuary government" that had prevailed in the old Company's quarter courts, and they wanted none of it; the Assembly as a representative institution was neither greatly sought after nor hotly resisted. The victory of 1635 was that of resolute leaders of settlement stubbornly fighting for individual establishment. With the reappointment of Sir Francis Wyatt as governor, their victory was assured and in the Commonwealth period it was completely realized. By 1658, when Mathews was elected governor, effective interference from outside had disappeared and the supreme authority had been assumed by an Assembly which was in effect a league of local magnates secure in their control of county institutions.

One might at that point have projected the situation forward into a picture of dominant county families dating from the 1620's and 1630's, growing in identification with the land and people, ruling with increasing responsibility from increasingly eminent positions. But such a projection would be false. The fact is that with a few notable exceptions like the Scarboroughs and the Wormeleys, these struggling planters of the first generation failed to perpetuate their leadership into the second generation. Such families as the Woods, the Uties, the Mathews, and the Peirces faded from dominant positions of authority after the deaths of their founders. To some extent this was the result of the general insecurity of life that created odds against the physical survival in the male line of any given family. But even if male heirs had remained in these families after the death of the first generation, undisputed eminence would not. For a new emigration had begun in the forties, continuing for close to thirty years, from which was drawn a new ruling group that had greater possibilities for permanent dominance than Harvey's opponents had had. These newcomers absorbed and subordinated the older group, forming the basis of the most celebrated oligarchy in American history.

Most of Virginia's great eighteenth-century names, such as Bland, Burwell, Byrd, Carter, Digges, Ludwell, and Mason, appear in the colony for the first time within ten years either side of 1655. These progenitors of the eighteenth-century aristocracy arrived in remarkably similar circumstances. The most important of these immigrants were younger sons of substantial families well connected in London business and governmental circles and long associated with Virginia; family claims to land in the colony or inherited shares of the original Company stock were now brought forward as a basis for establishment in the New World.

Thus the Bland family interests in Virginia date from a 1618 investment in the Virginia Company by the London merchant John Bland, supplemented in 1622 by another in Martin's Hundred. The merchant never touched foot in America, but three of his sons did come to Virginia in the forties and fifties to exploit these investments. The Burwell fortunes derive from the early subscription to the Company of Edward Burwell, which was inherited in the late forties by his son, Lewis I. The first William Byrd arrived about 1670 to assume the Virginia properties of his mother's family, the Steggs, which dated back to the early days of the Company. The Digges's interests in Virginia stem from the original investments of Sir Dudley Digges and two of his sons in the Company, but it was a third son, Edward, who emigrated in 1650 and established the American branch of the family. Similarly, the Masons had been financially interested in Virginia thirty-two years before 1652, when the first immigrant of that family appeared in the colony. The Culpeper clan, whose private affairs enclose much of the history of the South in the second half of the seventeenth century, was first represented in Virginia by Thomas Culpeper, who arrived in 1649; but the family interests in Virginia had been established a full generation earlier: Thomas's father, uncle, and cousin had all been members of the original Virginia Company and their shares had descended in the family. Even Governor Berkeley fits the pattern. There is no mystery about his sudden exchange in 1642 of the life of a dilettante courtier for that of a colonial administrator and estate manager. He was a younger son without prospects, and his family's interests in Virginia, dating from investments in the Company made twenty years earlier, as well as his appointment held out the promise of an independent establishment in America.

Claims on the colony such as these were only one, though the most important, of a variety of forms of capital that might provide the basis for secure family fortunes. One might simply bring over enough of a merchant family's resources to begin immediately building up an imposing estate, as, presumably, did that ambitious draper's son, William Fitzhugh. The benefits that accrued from such advantages were quickly translated into landholdings in the development of which these settlers were favored by the chronology of their arrival. For though they extended the area of cultivation in developing their landholdings, they were not obliged to initiate settlement. They fell heirs to large areas of the tidewater region that had already been brought under cultivation. "Westover" was not the creation of William Byrd; it had originally been part of the De la Warr estate, passing, with improvements, to Captain Thomas Pawlett, thence to Theodorick Bland, and finally to Byrd. Lewis Burwell inherited not only his father's land, but also the developed estate of his stepfather, Wingate. Some of the Carters' lands may be traced back through John Utie to a John Jefferson, who left Virginia as early as 1628. Abraham Wood's entire Fort Henry property ended in the hands of the Jones family. The Blands' estate in Charles City County, which later became the Harrisons' "Berkeley" plantation, was cleared for settlement in 1619 by servants of the "particular" plantation of Berkeley's Hundred.

Favored thus by circumstance, a small group within the second generation migration moved toward setting itself off in a permanent way as a ruling landed gentry. That they succeeded was due not only to their material advantages but also to the force of their motivation. For these individuals were in social origins just close enough to establishment in gentility to feel the pangs of deprivation most acutely. It is not the totally but the partially dispossessed who build up the most propulsive aspirations, and behind the zestful lunging at propriety and status of a William Fitzhugh lay not the narcotic yearnings of the disinherited but the pent-up ambitions of the gentleman *manqué*. These were neither hard-handed pioneers nor dilettante romantics, but ambitious younger sons of middle-class families who knew well enough what gentility was and sought it as a specific objective.

The establishment of this group was rapid. Within a decade of their arrival they could claim, together with a fortunate few of the first generation, a marked social eminence and full political authority at the county level. But their rise was not uniform. Indeed, by the seventies a new circumstance had introduced an effective principle of social differentiation among the colony's leaders. A hierarchy of position within the newly risen gentry was created by the Restoration government's efforts to extend its control more effectively over its mercantile empire. Demanding of its colonial executives and their advisors closer supervision over the external aspects of the economy, it offered a measure of patronage necessary for enforcement. Public offices dealing with matters that profoundly affected the basis of economic life—tax collection, customs regulation, and the bestowal of land grants—fell within the gift of the governor and tended to form an inner circle of privilege. One can note in Berkeley's administration the growing importance of this barrier of officialdom. Around its privileges there formed the "Green Spring" faction, named after Berkeley's plantation near Jamestown, a group bound to the governor not by royalist sympathies so much as by ties of kinship and patronage.

Thus Colonel Henry Norwood, related to Berkeley by a "near affinity in blood," was given the treasurership of the colony in 1650, which he held for more than two decades. During this time Thomas Ludwell, a cousin and Somerset neighbor of the governor, was secretary of state, in which post he was succeeded in 1678 by his brother Philip, who shortly thereafter married Berkeley's widow. This Lady Berkeley, it should be noted, was the daughter of Thomas Culpeper, the immigrant of 1649 and a cousin of Thomas Lord Culpeper who became governor in 1680. Immediately after her marriage to Berkeley, her brother Alexander requested and received from the governor the nomination to the surveyor-generalship of Virginia, a post he filled for twenty-three years while resident in England, appointing as successive deputies the brothers Ludwell, to whom by 1680 he was twice related by marriage. Lady Berkeley was also related through her mother to William Byrd's wife, a fact that explains much about Byrd's prolific office-holding.[2]

2. Colonel [Henry] Norwood, A *Voyage to Virginia* (1649), in Peter Force (ed.), *Tracts, and Other Papers Relating Principally to the Origin, Settlement, and Progress of the Colonies in North America* (4 vols., Washington, D.C., 1836–46), III, 49, 50; *Virginia Magazine of History and Biography*, 33 (1925), 5, 8; Fairfax Harrison, "A Key Chart of the . . . Culpepers," *ibid.*,

The growing distinctiveness of provincial officialdom within the landed gentry may also be traced in the transformation of the Council. Originally, this body had been expected to comprise the entire effective government, central and local; councilors were to serve, individually or in committees, as local magistrates. But the spread of settlement upset this expectation, and at the same time as the local offices were falling into the hands of autonomous local powers representing leading county families, the Council, appointed by the governor and hence associated with official patronage, increasingly realized the separate, lucrative privileges available to it.

As the distinction between local and central authority became clear, the county magistrates sought their own distinct voice in the management of the colony, and they found it in developing the possibilities of burgess representation. In the beginning there was no House of Burgesses; representation from the burghs and hundreds was conceived of not as a branch of government separate from the Council but as a periodic supplement to it. Until the

351–55, 348; *William and Mary Quarterly*, 1st ser., 19 (1910–11), 209–10. It was after Culpeper's appointment to the governorship that Byrd was elevated to the Council and acquired the auditor- and receiver-generalships. William G. and Mary N. Stanard, comps., *The Colonial Virginia Register* (Albany, N. Y., 1902), 22–23.

The Berkeley-Norwood connection may be followed out in other directions. Thus the Colonel Francis Moryson mentioned by Norwood as his friend and traveling companion and whom he introduced to the governor was given command of the fort at Point Comfort upon his arrival in 1649, replacing his brother, Major Richard Moryson, whose son Charles was given the same post in the 1660's. Francis, who found the command of the fort "profitable to him," was elevated by Berkeley to the Council and temporarily to the deputy-governorship, "wherein he got a competent estate"; he finally returned to England in the position of colony agent. Norwood, *Voyage*, 50; *Virginia Magazine of History and Biography*, 9 (1900–1901), 122–23; Ella Lonn, *The Colonial Agents of the Southern Colonies* (Chapel Hill, 1945), 21 ff.

The inner kinship core of the group enclosed the major provincial positions mentioned above. But the wider reaches of the clique extended over the Council, the collectorships, and the naval offices as well as minor positions within the influence of the governor. On these posts and their holders, see Stanard and Stanard, comps., *Va. Register*, 38–40; Philip A. Bruce, *Institutional History of Virginia in the Seventeenth Century* (2 vols., New York, 1910), II, Chaps. XXXVIII–XLII. On the limitations of the gubernatorial influence after 1660, see Wesley Frank Craven, *The Southern Colonies in the Seventeenth Century, 1607–1689* (Baton Rouge, La., 1949), 293.

fifties the burgesses, meeting in the Assemblies with the councilors, felt little need to form themselves into a separate house, for until that decade there was little evidence of a conflict of interests between the two groups. But when, after the Restoration, the privileged status of the Council became unmistakable and the county magnates found control of the increasingly important provincial administration pre-empted by this body, the burgess part of the Assembly took on a new meaning in contrast to that of the Council. Burgess representation now became vital to the county leaders if they were to share in any consistent way in affairs larger than those of the counties. They looked to the franchise, hitherto broad not by design but by neglect, introducing qualifications that would ensure their control of the Assembly. Their interest in provincial government could no longer be expressed in the conglomerate Assembly, and at least by 1663 the House of Burgesses began to meet separately as a distinct body voicing interests potentially in conflict with those of the Council.

Thus by the eighth decade the ruling class in Virginia was broadly based on leading county families and dominated at the provincial level by a privileged officialdom. But this social and political structure was too new, too lacking in the sanctions of time and custom, its leaders too close to humbler origins and as yet too undistinguished in style of life, to be accepted without a struggle. A period of adjustment was necessary, of which Bacon's Rebellion was the climactic episode.

Bacon's Rebellion began as an unauthorized frontier war against the Indians and ended as an upheaval that threatened the entire basis of social and political authority. Its immediate causes had to do with race relations and settlement policy, but behind these issues lay deeper elements related to resistance against the maturing shape of a new social order. These elements explain the dimensions the conflict reached.

There was, first, resistance by substantial planters to the privileges and policies of the inner provincial clique led by Berkeley and composed of those directly dependent on his patronage. These dissidents, among whom were the leaders of the Rebellion, represented neither the down-trodden masses nor a principle of opposition to privilege as such. Their discontent stemmed to a large extent from their own exclusion from privileges they sought. Most often their grievances were based on personal rebuffs they had received as they reached for entry into provincial officialdom. Thus—to speak of the leaders of the Rebellion—Giles Bland arrived in Virginia in 1671 to take over the agency of his late uncle in the management of his father's extensive landholdings, assuming at the same time the lucrative position of customs collector which he had obtained in London. But, amid angry cries of "*pittyfull fellow, puppy* and *Sonn of a Whore*," he fell out first with Berkeley's cousin and favorite, Thomas Ludwell, and finally with the governor himself; for his "Barbarous and Insolent Behaviors" Bland was fined, arrested, and finally removed from the collectorship. Of the two "chiefe Incendiarys," William Drummond and Richard Lawrence, the former had been quarreling with Berkeley since 1664, first over land claims in Carolina, then over a contract for building a fort near James City, and repeatedly over lesser issues in the General Court; Lawrence "some Years before . . . had been partially treated at Law, for a considerable Estate on behalfe of a Corrupt favorite." Giles Brent, for his depredations against the Indians in violation of official policy, had not only been severely fined but barred from public office. Bacon himself could not have appeared under more favorable circumstances. A cousin both of Lady Berkeley and of the councilor Nathaniel Bacon, Sr., and by general agreement "a Gent:man of a Liberall education" if of a somewhat tarnished reputation, he had quickly staked out land for himself and had been elevated, for reasons "best known to the Governour," to the Council. But being "of a most imperious and dangerous hidden Pride of heart . . . very ambitious and arrogant," he wanted more, and quickly. His alienation from and violent opposition to Berkeley were wound in among the animosities created by the Indian problem and were further complicated by his own unstable personality; they were related also to the fact that Berkeley finally turned down the secret offer Bacon and Byrd made in 1675 for the purchase from the governor of a monopoly of the Indian trade.

These specific disputes have a more general aspect. It was three decades since Berkeley had assumed the governorship and begun rallying a favored group, and it was over a decade since the Restoration had given this group unconfined sway over the provincial government. In those years much of the choice tidewater land as well as the choice offices had been spoken for, and the tendency of the highly placed was to hold firm. Berkeley's Indian policy—one of stabilizing the borders between Indians and whites and protecting the natives from depredation by land-hungry settlers—although a sincere attempt to deal with an extremely difficult problem, was also conservative, favoring the established. Newcomers like Bacon and Bland and particularly landholders on the frontiers felt victimized by a stabilization of the situation or by a controlled expansion that maintained on an extended basis the existing power structure. They were logically drawn to aggressive positions. In an atmosphere charged with violence, their interests constituted a challenge to provincial authority. Bacon's primary appeal in his "Manifesto" played up the threat of this challenge:

> Let us trace these men in Authority and Favour to whose hands the dispensation of the Countries wealth has been commited; let us observe the sudden Rise of their Estates [compared] with the Quality in wch they first entered this Country. . . . And lett us see wither their extractions and Education have not bin vile, And by what pretence of learning and vertue they could [enter] soe soon into Imployments of so great Trust and consequence, let us . . . see what spounges have suckt up the Publique Treasure and wither it hath not bin privately contrived away by unworthy Favourites and juggling Parasites whose tottering Fortunes have bin repaired and supported at the Publique chardg.

Such a threat to the basis of authority was not lost on Berkeley or his followers. Bacon's merits, a contemporary wrote, "thretned an eclips to there riseing gloryes . . . (if he should continue in the

Governours favour) of Seniours they might becom juniours, while there younger Brother . . . might steale away that blessing, which they accounted there owne by birthright."

But these challengers were themselves challenged, for another main element in the upheaval was the discontent among the ordinary settlers at the local privileges of the same newly risen county magnates who assailed the privileges of the Green Spring faction. The specific Charles City County grievances were directed as much at the locally dominant family, the Hills, as they were at Berkeley and his clique. Similarly, Surry County complained of its county court's highhanded and secretive manner of levying taxes on "the poore people" and of setting the sheriffs' and clerks' fees; they petitioned for the removal of these abuses and for the right to elect the vestry and to limit the tenure of the sheriffs. At all levels the Rebellion challenged the stability of newly secured authority.

It is this double aspect of discontent behind the violence of the Rebellion that explains the legislation passed in June, 1676, by the so-called "Bacon's Assembly." At first glance these laws seem difficult to interpret because they express disparate if not contradictory interests. But they yield readily to analysis if they are seen not as the reforms of a single group but as efforts to express the desires of two levels of discontent with the way the political and social hierarchy was becoming stabilized. On the one hand, the laws include measures designed by the numerically predominant ordinary settlers throughout the colony as protests against the recently acquired superiority of the leading county families. These were popular protests and they relate not to provincial affairs but to the situation within the local areas of jurisdiction. Thus the statute restricting the franchise to freeholders was repealed; freemen were given the right to elect the parish vestrymen; and the county courts were supplemented by elected freemen to serve with the regularly appointed county magistrates.

On the other hand, there was a large number of measures

expressing the dissatisfactions not so much of the ordinary planter but of the local leaders against the prerogatives recently acquired by the provincial elite, prerogatives linked to officialdom and centered in the Council. Thus the law barring office-holding to newcomers of less than three years' residence struck at the arbitrary elevation of the governor's favorites, including Bacon; and the acts forbidding councilors to join the county courts, outlawing the governor's appointment of sheriffs and tax collectors, and nullifying tax exemption for councilors all voiced objections of the local chieftains to privileges enjoyed by others. From both levels there was objection to profiteering in public office.

Thus the wave of rebellion broke and spread. But why did it subside? One might have expected that the momentary flood would have become a steady tide, its rhythms governed by a fixed political constellation. But in fact it did not; stable political alignments did not result. The conclusion to this controversy was characteristic of all the insurrections. The attempted purges and counterpurges by the leaders of the two sides were followed by a rapid submerging of factional identity. Occasional references were later made to the episode, and there were individuals who found an interest in keeping its memory alive. Also, the specific grievances behind certain of the attempted legal reforms of 1676 were later revived. But of stable parties or factions around these issues there were none.

It was not merely that in the late years of the century no more than in the early was there to be found a justification for permanently organized political opposition or party machinery, that persistent, organized dissent was still indistinguishable from sedition; more important was the fact that at the end of the century as in 1630 there was agreement that some must be "highe and eminent in power and dignitie; others meane and in subieccion." Protests and upheaval had resulted from the discomforts of discovering who was, in fact, which, and what the particular consequences of "power and dignitie" were.

But by the end of the century the most difficult period of

adjustment had passed and there was an acceptance of the fact that certain families were distinguished from others in riches, in dignity, and in access to political authority. The establishment of these families marks the emergence of Virginia's colonial aristocracy.

It was a remarkable governing group. Its members were soberly responsible, alive to the implications of power; they performed their public obligations with notable skill. Indeed, the glare of their accomplishments is so bright as occasionally to blind us to the conditions that limited them. As a ruling class the Virginian aristocracy of the eighteenth century was unlike other contemporary nobilities or aristocracies, including the English. The differences, bound up with the special characteristics of the society it ruled, had become clear at the turn of the seventeenth century.

Certain of these characteristics are elusive, difficult to grasp and analyze. The leaders of early eighteenth-century Virginia were, for example, in a particular sense, cultural provincials. They were provincial not in the way of Polish *szlachta* isolated on their estates by poverty and impassable roads, nor in the way of sunken *seigneurs* grown rustic and old-fashioned in lonely Norman chateaux. The Virginians were far from uninformed or unaware of the greater world; they were in fact deeply and continuously involved in the cultural life of the Atlantic community. But they knew themselves to be provincials in the sense that their culture was not self-contained; its sources and superior expressions were to be found elsewhere than in their own land. They must seek it from afar; it must be acquired, and once acquired be maintained according to standards externally imposed, in the creation of which they had not participated. The most cultivated of them read much, purposefully, with a diligence the opposite of that essential requisite of aristocracy, uncontending ease. William Byrd's diary with its daily records of stints of study is a stolid testimonial to the virtues of regularity and effort in maintaining standards of civilization set abroad.

In more evident ways also the Virginia planters were denied an uncontending ease of life. They were not *rentiers*. Tenancy, when it appeared late in the colonial period, was useful to the landowners mainly as a cheap way of improving lands held in reserve for future development. The Virginia aristocrat was an active manager of his estate, drawn continuously into the most intimate contacts with the soil and its cultivation. This circumstance limited his ease, one might even say bound him to the soil, but it also strengthened his identity with the land and its problems and saved him from the temptation to create of his privileges an artificial world of self-indulgence.

But more important in distinguishing the emerging aristocracy of Virginia from other contemporary social and political elites were two very specific circumstances. The first concerns the relationship between the integrity of the family unit and the descent of real property. "The English political family," Sir Lewis Namier writes with particular reference to the eighteenth-century aristocracy,

> is a compound of "blood," name, and estate, this last . . . being the most important of the three. . . . The name is a weighty symbol, but liable to variations. . . . The estate . . . is, in the long run, the most potent factor in securing continuity through identification. . . . Primogeniture and entails psychically preserve the family in that they tend to fix its position through the successive generations, and thereby favour conscious identification.

The descent of landed estates in eighteenth-century England was controlled by the complicated device known as the strict settlement, which provided that the heir at his marriage received the estate as a life tenant, entailing its descent to his unborn eldest son and specifying the limitations of the encumbrances upon the land that might be made in behalf of his daughters and younger sons.

It was the strict settlement, in which in the eighteenth century perhaps half the land of England was bound, that provided continuity over generations for the landed aristocracy. This permanent identification of the family with a specific estate and with the status and offices that pertained to it was achieved at the cost of sacrificing the younger sons. It was a single stem of the family only that retained its superiority; it alone controlled the material basis for political dominance.

This basic condition of aristocratic governance in England was never present in the American colonies, and not for lack of familiarity with legal forms. The economic necessity that had prompted the widespread adoption of the strict settlement in England was absent in the colonies. Land was cheap and easily available, the more so as one rose on the social and political ladder. There was no need to deprive the younger sons or even daughters of landed inheritances in order to keep the original family estate intact. Provision could be made for endowing each of them with plantations, and they in turn could provide similarly for their children. Moreover, to confine the stem family's fortune to a single plot of land, however extensive, was in the Virginia economy to condemn it to swift decline. Since the land was quickly worn out and since it was cheaper to acquire new land than to rejuvenate the worked soil by careful husbandry, geographical mobility, not stability, was the key to prosperity. Finally, since land was only as valuable as the labor available to work it, a great estate was worth passing intact from generation to generation only if it had annexed to it a sufficient population of slaves. Yet this condition imposed severe rigidities in a plantation's economy —for a labor force bound to a particular plot was immobilized— besides creating bewildering confusions in law.

The result, evident before the end of the seventeenth century, was a particular relationship between the family and the descent of property. There was in the beginning no intent on the part of the Virginians to alter the traditional forms; the continued vitality of the ancient statutes specifying primogeniture in certain cases was assumed. The first clear indication of a new trend came in the third quarter of the century, when the leading gentry, rapidly accumulating large estates, faced for the first time the problem of the transfer of property. The result was the subdivision of the great holdings and the multiplication of smaller plots while the net amount of land held by the leading families continued to rise.

This trend continued. Primogeniture neither at the end of the seventeenth century nor after prevailed in Virginia. It was never popular even among the most heavily endowed of the tidewater families. The most common form of bequest was a grant to the eldest son of the undivided home plantation and gifts of other tracts outside the home county to the younger sons and daughters. Thus by his will of 1686 Robert Beverley, Sr., bequeathed to his eldest son, Peter, all his land in Gloucester County lying between "Chiescake" and "Hoccadey's" creeks (an unspecified acreage); to Robert, the second son, another portion of the Gloucester lands amounting to 920 acres; to Harry, 1,600 acres in Rappahannock County; to John, 3,000 acres in the same county; to William, two plantations in Middlesex County; to Thomas, 3,000 acres in Rappahannock and New Kent counties; to his wife, three plantations including those "whereon I now live" for use during her lifetime, after which they were to descend to his daughter Catherine, who was also to receive £200 sterling; to his daughter Mary, £150 sterling; to "the childe that my wife goeth with, be it male or female," all the rest of his real property; and the residue of his personal property was "to be divided and disposed in equall part & portion betwix my wife and children." Among the bequests of Ralph Wormeley, Jr., in 1700 was an estate of 1,500 acres to his daughter Judith as well as separate plantations to his two sons.

Entail proved no more popular than primogeniture. Only a small minority of estates, even in the tidewater region, were ever entailed. In fact, despite the extension of developed land in the course of the eighteenth century, more tidewater estates were docked of entails than were newly entailed.

Every indication points to continuous and increasing difficulty in reproducing even pale replicas of the strict settlement. In 1705 a law was passed requiring a special act of the Assembly to break an entail; the law stood, but between 1711 and 1776 no fewer than 125 such private acts were passed, and in 1734 estates of under £200 were exempted from the law altogether. The labor problem alone was an insuperable barrier to perpetuating the traditional forms. A statute of 1727, clarifying the confused legislation of earlier years, had attempted to ensure a labor force on entailed land by classifying slaves as real property and permitting them to be bound together with land into bequests. But by 1748 this stipulation had resulted in such bewildering "doubts, variety of opinions, and confusions" that it was repealed. The repeal was disallowed in London, and in the course of a defense of its action the Assembly made vividly clear the utter impracticality of entailment in Virginia's economy. Slaves, the Assembly explained, were essential to the success of a plantation, but "slaves could not be kept on the lands to which they were annexed without manifest prejudice to the tenant in tail. . . . often the tenant was the proprietor of fee simple land much fitter for cultivation than his intailed lands, where he could work his slaves to a much greater advantage." On the other hand, if a plantation owner did send entailed slaves where they might be employed most economically the result was equally disastrous:

> the frequent removing and settling them on other lands in other counties and parts of the colony far distant from the county court where the deeds or wills which annexed them were recorded and the intail lands lay; the confusion occasioned by their mixture with fee simple slaves of the same name and sex and belonging to the same owner; the uncertainty of distinguishing one from another after several generations, no register of their genealogy being kept and none of them having surnames, were great mischiefs to purchasers, strangers, and creditors, who were often unavoidably deceived in their purchases and hindered in the recovery of their just debts. It also lessened the credit of the country; it being dangerous for the merchants of Great Britain to trust possessors of many slaves for fear the slaves might be intailed.

A mobile labor force free from legal entanglements and a rapid turnover of lands, not a permanent hereditary estate, were prerequisites of family prosperity. This condition greatly influenced social and political life. Since younger sons and even daughters inherited extensive landed properties, equal often to those of the eldest son, concentration of authority in the stem family was precluded. Third generation collateral descendants of the original immigrant were as important in their own right as the eldest son's eldest son. Great clans like the Carters and the Lees, though they may have acknowledged a central family seat, were scattered throughout the province on estates of equal influence. The four male Carters of the third generation were identified by contemporaries by the names of their separate estates, and, indistinguishable in style of life, they had an equal access to political power.

Since material wealth was the basis of the status which made one eligible for public office, there was a notable diffusion of political influence throughout a broadening group of leading families. No one son was predestined to represent the family interest in politics, but as many as birth and temperament might provide. In the 1750's there were no fewer than seven Lees of the same generation sitting together in the Virginia Assembly; in the Burgesses they spoke for five separate counties. To the eldest, Philip Ludwell Lee, they conceded a certain social superiority that made it natural for him to sit in the Council. But he did not speak alone for the family; by virtue of inheritance he had no unique authority over his brothers and cousins.

The leveling at the top of the social and political hierarchy, creating an evenness of status and influence, was intensified by continuous intermarriage within the group. The unpruned branches of these flourishing family trees, growing freely, met and intertwined until by the Revolution the aristocracy appeared to be one great tangled cousinry.

As political power became increasingly diffused throughout the upper stratum of society, the Council, still at the end of the seventeenth century a repository of unique privileges, lost its effective superiority. Increasingly through the successive decades its authority had to be exerted through alignments with the Burgesses—alignments made easier as well as more necessary by the crisscrossing network of kinship that united the two houses. Increasingly the Council's distinctions became social and ceremonial.

The contours of Virginia's political hierarchy were also affected by a second main conditioning element, besides the manner of descent of family property. Not only was the structure unusually level and broad at the top, but it was incomplete in itself. Its apex, the ultimate source of legal decision and control, lay in the quite different society of England, amid the distant embroilments of London, the court, and Parliament. The levers of control in that realm were for the most part hidden from the planters; yet the powers that ruled this remote region could impose an arbitrary authority directly into the midst of Virginia's affairs.

One consequence was the introduction of instabilities in the tenure and transfer of the highest offices. Tenure could be arbitrarily interrupted, and the transfer to kin of such positions at death or resignation—uncertain in any case because of the diffusion of family authority—could be quite difficult or even impossible. Thus William Byrd II returned from England at the death of his father in 1704 to take over the family properties, but though he was the sole heir he did not automatically or completely succeed to the elder Byrd's provincial offices. He did, indeed, become auditor of Virginia after his father, but only because he had carefully arranged for the succession while still in London; his father's Council seat went to someone else, and it took three years of patient maneuvering through his main London contact, Micajah Perry, to secure another; he never did take over the receivership. Even such a power as "King" Carter, the reputed owner at his death of 300,000 acres and 1,000 slaves, was rebuffed by the resident deputy governor and had to deploy forces in England in order to transfer a Virginia naval office post from one of his sons to another. There was family continuity in public office, but at the highest level it was uncertain, the result of place-hunting rather than of the absolute prerogative of birth.

Instability resulted not only from the difficulty of securing and transferring high appointive positions but also and more immediately from the presence in Virginia of total strangers to the scene, particularly governors and their deputies, armed with extensive jurisdiction and powers of enforcement. The dangers of this element in public life became clear only after Berkeley's return to England in 1677, for after thirty-five years of residence in the colony Sir William had become a leader in the land independent of his royal authority. But Howard, Andros, and Nicholson were governors with full legal powers but with at best only slight connections with local society. In them, social leadership and political leadership had ceased to be identical.

In the generation that followed Berkeley's departure, this separation between the two spheres created the bitterest of political controversies. Firmly entrenched behind their control of the colony's government, the leading families battled with every weapon available to reduce the power of the executives and thus to eliminate what appeared to be an external and arbitrary authority. Repeated complaints by the governors of the intractable opposition of a league of local oligarchs marked the Virginians' success. Efforts by the executives to discipline the indigenous leaders could only be mildly successful. Patronage was a useful weapon, but its effectiveness diminished steadily, ground down between a resistant Assembly and an office-hungry bureaucracy in England. The possibility of exploiting divisions among the resident powers also declined as kinship lines bound the leading families closer together and as group interests became clearer with the passage of time. No faction built around the gubernatorial power could survive independently; ultimately its adherents would fall away and it would weaken. It was a clear logic of the situation that led the same individuals who had promoted Nicholson as a replacement for Andros to work against him once he assumed office.

Stability could be reached only by the complete identification of external and internal authority through permanent commitment by the appointees to local interests. Commissary Blair's extraordinary success in Virginia politics was based not only on his excellent connections in England but also on his marriage into the

Harrison family, which gave him the support of an influential kinship faction. There was more than hurt pride and thwarted affection behind Nicholson's reported insane rage at being spurned by the highly marriageable Lucy Burwell; and later the astute Spotswood, for all his success in imposing official policy, fully quieted the controversies of his administration only by succumbing completely and joining as a resident Virginia landowner the powers aligned against him.

But there was more involved than instability and conflict in the discontinuity between social and political organization at the topmost level. The state itself had changed its meaning. To a Virginia planter of the early eighteenth century the highest public authority was no longer merely one expression of a general social authority. It had become something abstract, external to his life and society, an ultimate power whose purposes were obscure, whose direction could neither be consistently influenced nor accurately plotted, and whose human embodiments were alien and antagonistic.

The native gentry of the early eighteenth century had neither the need nor the ability to fashion a new political theory to comprehend their experience, but their successors would find in the writings of John Locke on state and society not merely a reasonable theoretical position but a statement of self-evident fact.

I have spoken exclusively of Virginia, but though the histories of each of the colonies in the seventeenth century are different, they exhibit common characteristics. These features one might least have expected to find present in Virginia, and their presence there is, consequently, most worth indicating.

In all of the colonies the original transference of an ordered European society was succeeded by the rise to authority of resident settlers whose influence was rooted in their ability to deal with the problems of life in wilderness settlements. These individuals attempted to stabilize their positions, but in each case they were challenged by others arriving after the initial settlements, seeking to exploit certain advantages of position, wealth, or influence. These newcomers, securing after the Restoration governmental appointments in the colonies and drawn together by personal ties, especially those of kinship and patronage, came to constitute colonial officialdom. This group introduced a new principle of social organization; it also gave rise to new instabilities in a society in which the traditional forms of authority were already being subjected to severe pressures. By the eighth decade of the seventeenth century the social basis of public life had become uncertain and insecure, its stability delicate and sensitive to disturbance. Indian warfare, personal quarrels, and particularly the temporary confusion in external control caused by the Glorious Revolution became the occasions for violent challenges to constituted authority.

By the end of the century a degree of harmony had been achieved, but the divergence between political and social leadership at the topmost level created an area of permanent conflict. The political and social structures that emerged were by European standards strangely shaped. Everywhere as the bonds of empire drew tighter the meaning of the state was changing. Herein lay the origins of a new political system.

The Power of Colonial Assemblies

The Role of the Lower Houses of Assembly in Eighteenth-Century Politics

by Jack P. Greene

When American Revolutionaries took their stand against Parliament on the principle of "no taxation without representation," they were defending the authority of colonial legislative bodies, the principal instruments of self-government in America. Jack P. Greene here describes how the Southern assemblies exercised extensive power and became almost sovereign, with the powers, among others, to tax and to appoint local officials.

It had taken generations for these bodies to accumulate the authority that by the eighteenth century made them the most important centers of authority in the colonies. Representative government was not even planned for by the founders of Virginia or Massachusetts. American conditions and the English parliamentary tradition forced concessions in the direction of a more broadly based government. Although early assemblies, designed to act as advisory bodies rather than legislative centers, had limited roles, by the time the colonists challenged the parliamentary right of taxation in the 1760's they insisted that only their own assemblies could tax. The colonial assemblies, argued the British, derived their authority from the king and Parliament, and therefore were subordinate to those higher authorities. For over a century, however,

London had allowed the power of the colonial assemblies to grow. It was easier and cheaper to permit the Americans to govern themselves than to impose on them a complex and expensive bureaucracy.

Taking advantage of the superficiality of royal rule—the absence of a British army in America in peacetime, and the venality of crown officials—colonial politicians steadily eroded the authority of the Crown. Royal officials, especially the governors, learned that if they wanted co-operation from the assemblies they would have to go along with the colonials who controlled them. The British executive, the king, controlled an enormous patronage list, and he could ordinarily count on support from the largest parliamentary bloc, the independent country gentlemen. The colonial governor, on the other hand, had neither adequate patronage nor the prestige and mystique surrounding the throne in England. Moreover, he had no solidly reliable group in the colonial assemblies on whom he could count. Support had be to earned or purchased from the assemblies, and when received it was often at the expense of imperial authority.

The rise of the representative assemblies was perhaps the most significant political and constitutional development in the history of Britain's overseas empire before the American Revolution. Crown and proprietary authorities had obviously intended the governor to be the focal point of colonial government with the lower houses merely subordinate bodies called together when necessary to levy taxes and ratify local ordinances proposed by the executive. Consequently, except in the New England charter colonies, where the representative bodies early assumed a leading role, they were dominated by the governors and councils for most of the period down to 1689. But beginning with the Restoration and intensifying their efforts during the years following the Glorious

From *The Journal of Southern History*, XXVII (November 1961), 451–74. footnotes omitted. (This version has been revised by the author.)

Revolution, the lower houses engaged in a successful quest for power as they set about to restrict the authority of the executive, undermine the system of colonial administration laid down by imperial and proprietary authorities, and make themselves paramount in the affairs of their respective colonies.

Historians have been fascinated by this phenomenon. For nearly a century after 1776 they interpreted it as a prelude to the American Revolution. In the 1780's the pro-British historian George Chalmers saw it as the early manifestation of a latent desire for independence, an undutiful reaction to the mild policies of the Mother Country. In the middle of the nineteenth century the American nationalist George Bancroft, although more interested in other aspects of colonial history, looked upon it as the natural expression of American democratic principles, simply another chapter in the progress of mankind. The reaction to these sweeping interpretations set in during the last decades of the nineteenth century, when Charles M. Andrews, Edward Channing, Herbert L. Osgood, and others began to investigate in detail and to study in context developments from the Restoration to the end of the Seven Years' War. Osgood put a whole squadron of Columbia students to work examining colonial political institutions, and they produced a series of institutional studies in which the evolution of the lower houses was a central feature. These studies clarified the story of legislative development in each colony, but this necessarily piecemeal approach, as well as the excessive fragmentation that characterized the more general narratives of Osgood and Channing, tended to emphasize the differences rather than the similarities in the rise of the lower houses and failed to produce a general analysis of the common features of their quest for power. Among later scholars, Leonard W. Labaree in his excellent monograph *Royal Government in America* presented a comprehensive survey of the institutional development of the lower houses in the royal colonies and of the specific issues involved in their struggles with the royal governors, but he did not offer any systematic interpretation of the general process and pattern of legislative development. Charles Andrews promised to tackle this problem and provide a synthesis in the later volumes of his magnum opus, *The Colonial Period of American History,* but he died before completing that part of the project.

As a result, some fundamental questions have never been fully answered, and no one has produced a comprehensive synthesis. No one has satisfactorily worked out the basic pattern of the quest; analyzed the reasons for and the significance of its development; explored its underlying assumptions and theoretical foundations; or assessed the consequences of the success of the lower houses, particularly the relationship between their rise to power and the coming of the American Revolution. This essay is intended to suggest some tentative conclusions about these problems, not to present ultimate solutions. My basic research on the lower houses has been in the Southern royal colonies and in Nova Scotia. One of the present purposes is to test the generalizations I have arrived at about the Southern colonies by applying them to what scholars have learned of the legislatures in the other colonies. This procedure has the advantage of providing perspective on the story of Southern developments. At the same time, it may serve as one guidepost for a general synthesis in the future.

Any student of the eighteenth-century political process will sooner or later be struck by the fact that, although each of the lower houses developed independently and differently, their stories were similar. The elimination of individual variants, which tend to cancel out each other, discloses certain basic regularities, a clearly discernible pattern—or what the late Sir Lewis Namier called a morphology—common to all of them. They all moved along like paths in their drives for increased authority, and although their success on specific issues differed from colony to colony and the rate of their rise varied from time to time, they all ended up at approximately the same destination. They passed successively through certain vaguely defined phases of political development. Through most of the seventeenth century the lower houses were still in a position of subordination, slowly groping for the power to tax and the right to sit separately from the council and initiate laws. Sometime during the early eighteenth century most of them advanced to a second stage at which they could battle on equal terms with the governors and councils and challenge even the powers in London if necessary. At that point the lower houses began their bid for political supremacy. The violent eruptions that followed usually ended in an accommodation with the governors and councils which paved the way for the ascendancy of the lower houses and saw the virtual eclipse of the colonial executive. By the end of the Seven Years' War, and in some instances considerably earlier, the lower houses had reached the third and final phase of political dominance and were in a position to speak for the colonies in the conflict with the imperial government which ensued after 1763.

By 1763, with the exception of the lower houses in the corporate colonies of Rhode Island and Connecticut, which had virtually complete authority, the Pennsylvania and Massachusetts houses of representatives were probably most powerful. Having succeeded in placing its election on a statutory basis and depriving the Council of direct legislative authority in the Charter of Privileges in 1701, the Pennsylvania House under the astute guidance of David Lloyd secured broad financial and appointive powers during the administrations of Daniel Gookin and Sir William Keith. Building on these foundations, it gained almost complete dominance in the 1730's and 1740's despite the opposition of the governors, whose power and prestige along with that of the Council declined rapidly. The Massachusetts House, having been accorded the unique privilege of sharing in the selection of the Council by the royal charter of 1691, already had a strong tradition of legislative supremacy inherited from a half-century of corporate experience. During the first thirty years under the new charter first the benevolent policies of Sir William Phips and William Stoughton and then wartime conditions during the tenures of Joseph Dudley and Samuel Shute enabled the House, led by Elisha Cooke, Jr., to extend its authority greatly. It emerged from the conflicts over the salary question during the 1720's with firm control over finance, and the Crown's abandonment of its demand for a permanent revenue in the early 1730's paved the way for an accommodation with subsequent governors and the eventual dominance of the House under Governor William Shirley after 1740.

The South Carolina Commons and New York House of Assembly were only slightly less powerful. Beginning in the first decade of the eighteenth century, the South Carolina lower house gradually assumed an ironclad control over all aspects of South Carolina government, extending its supervision to the minutest details of local administration after 1730 as a succession of governors, including Francis Nicholson, Robert Johnson, Thomas Broughton, the elder William Bull, and James Glen offered little determined opposition. The Commons continued to grow in stature after 1750 while the Council's standing declined because of the Crown policy of filling it with placemen from England and the Common's successful attacks upon its authority. The New York House of Assembly began to demand greater authority in reaction to the mismanagement of Edward Hyde, Viscount Cornbury, during the first decade of the eighteenth century. Governor Robert Hunter met the challenge squarely during his ten-year administration beginning in 1710, but he and his successors could not check the rising power of the House. During the seven-year tenure of George Clarke beginning in 1736, the House advanced into the final stage of development. Following Clarke, George Clinton made a vigorous effort to reassert the authority of the executive, but neither he nor any of his successors was able to challenge the power of the House.

The lower houses of North Carolina, New Jersey, and Virginia developed more slowly. The North Carolina lower house was fully capable of protecting its powers and privileges and competing on equal terms with the executive during the last years of proprietary rule and under the early royal governors, George Burrington and Gabriel Johnston. But it was not until Arthur Dobbs's tenure in the 1750's and 1760's that, meeting more regularly, it assumed the upper hand in North Carolina politics under the astute guidance of Speaker Samuel Swann and treasurers John Starkey and Thomas Barker. In New Jersey the lower house was partially thwarted in its spirited bid for power during the 1740's under the leadership of John Kinsey and Samuel Nevill by the determined opposition of Governor Lewis Morris, and it did not gain superiority until the administrations of Jonathan Belcher, Thomas Pownall, Francis Bernard, and Thomas Boone during the Seven Years' War. Similarly, the Virginia Burgesses vigorously sought to establish its control in the second decade of the century under Alexander Spotswood, but not until the administrations of Sir William Gooch and Robert Dinwiddie, when first the expansion of the colony and then the Seven Years' War required more regular sessions, did the Burgesses finally gain the upper hand under the effective leadership of Speaker John Robinson.

Among the lower houses in the older colonies, only the Maryland House of Delegates and the New Hampshire House of Assembly failed to reach the final level of development in the period before 1763. The Maryland body made important advances early in the eighteenth century while under the control of the Crown and aggressively sought to extend its authority in the 1720's under the leadership of the older Daniel Dulany and again in the late 1730's and early 1740's under Dr. Charles Carroll. But the proprietors were usually able to thwart these attempts, and the Delegates failed to pull ahead of the executive despite a concerted effort during the last intercolonial war under the administration of Horatio Sharpe. In New Hampshire, the House had exercised considerable power through the early decades of the eighteenth century, but Governor Benning Wentworth effectively challenged its authority after 1740 and prevented it from attaining the extensive power exercised by its counterparts in other colonies. It should be emphasized, however, that neither the Maryland nor the New Hampshire lower house was in any sense impotent and along with their more youthful equivalent in Georgia gained dominance during the decade of debate with Britain after 1763. Of the lower houses in the continental colonies with pre-1763 political experience, only the Nova Scotia Assembly had not reached the final phase of political dominance by 1776.

The similarities in the process and pattern of legislative development from colony to colony were not entirely accidental. The lower houses faced like problems and drew upon common traditions and imperial precedents for solutions. They all operated in the same broad imperial context and were affected by common historical forces. Moreover, family, cultural, and commercial ties often extended across colony lines, and newspapers and other printed materials, as well as individuals, often found their way from one colony to another. The result was at least a general awareness of issues and practices in neighboring colonies, and occasionally there was even a conscious borrowing of precedents and traditions. Younger bodies such as the Georgia Commons and Nova Scotia Assembly were particularly indebted to their more mature counterparts in South Carolina and Massachusetts Bay. On the executive side, the similarity in attitudes, assumptions, and policies among the governors can be traced in large measure to the fact that they were all subordinate to the same central authority in London, which pursued a common policy in all the colonies.

Before the Seven Years' War the quest was characterized by a considerable degree of spontaneity, by a lack of awareness that activities of the moment were part of any broad struggle for power. Rather than consciously working out the details of some master plan designed to bring them liberty or self-government, the lower houses moved along from issue to issue and from situation to situation, primarily concerning themselves with the problems at hand and displaying a remarkable capacity for spontaneous action, for seizing any and every opportunity to enlarge their own influence at the executive's expense and for holding tenaciously to powers they had already secured. Conscious of the issues involved in each specific conflict, they were for the most part unaware of and uninterested in the long-range implications of their actions. Virginia Governor Francis Fauquier correctly judged the matter in 1760. "Whoever charges them with acting upon a premeditated concerted plan, don't know them," he wrote of the Virginia Burgesses, "for they mean honestly, but are Expedient Mongers in the highest Degree." Still, in retrospect it is obvious that throughout the eighteenth century the lower houses were engaged in a continuous movement to enlarge their sphere of influence. To ignore that continuity would be to miss the meaning of eighteenth-century colonial political development.

One is impressed with the rather prosaic manner in which the lower houses went about the task of extending their authority, with the infrequency of dramatic conflict. They gained much of their power in the course of routine business, quietly and simply extending and consolidating their authority of passing laws and establishing practices the implications of which escaped both colonial executives and imperial authorities and were not always fully recognized even by the lower houses themselves. In this way they gradually extended their financial authority to include the powers to audit accounts of all public officers, to share in disbursing public funds, and eventually even to appoint officials concerned in collecting and handling local revenues. Precedents thus established soon hardened into fixed principles, "undoubted rights" or "inherent powers," changing the very fabric of their respective constitutions. The notable absence of conflict is perhaps best illustrated by the none too surprising fact that the lower houses made some of their greatest gains under those governors with whom they enjoyed the most harmony, in particular Keith in Pennsylvania, Shirley in Massachusetts, Hunter in New York, and the elder and younger Bull in South Carolina. In Virginia the House of Burgesses made rapid strides during the 1730's and 1740's under the benevolent government of Gooch, who discovered early in his administration that the secret of political success for a Virginia governor was to reach an accord with the plantation gentry.

One should not conclude that the colonies had no exciting legislative–executive conflicts, however. Attempts through the middle decades of the eighteenth century by Clinton to weaken the financial powers of the New York House, Massachusetts governors

Samuel Shute and William Burnet to gain a permanent civil list, Benning Wentworth to extend unilaterally the privilege of representation to new districts in New Hampshire, Johnston to break the extensive power of the Albemarle Counties in the North Carolina lower house, Dinwiddie to establish a fee for issuing land patents without the consent of the Virginia Burgesses, and Boone to reform South Carolina's election laws each provided a storm of controversy that brought local politics to a fever pitch. But such conflicts were the exception and usually arose not out of the lower houses' seeking more authority but from the executives' attempts to restrict powers already won. Impatient of restraint and jealous of their rights and privileges, the lower houses responded forcefully and sometimes violently when executive action threatened to deprive them of those rights. Only a few governors, men of the caliber of Henry Ellis in Georgia and to a lesser extent William Henry Lyttelton in South Carolina and Bernard in New Jersey, had the skill to challenge established rights successfully without raising the wrath of the lower houses. Clumsier tacticians—Pennsylvania's William Denny, New York's Clinton, Virginia's Dinwiddie, North Carolina's Dobbs, South Carolina's Boone, Georgia's John Reynolds—failed when pursuing similar goals.

Fundamentally, the quest for power in both the royal and the proprietary colonies was a struggle for political identity, the manifestation of the political ambitions of the leaders of emerging societies within each colony. There is a marked correlation between the appearance of economic and social elites produced by the growth in colonial wealth and population on the one hand and the lower houses' demand for increased authority, dignity, and prestige on the other. In the eighteenth century a group of planters, merchants, and professional men had attained or were rapidly acquiring within the colonies wealth and social position. The lower houses' aggressive drive for power reflects the determination of this new elite to attain through the representative assemblies political influence as well. In another but related sense, the lower houses' efforts represented a movement for autonomy in local affairs, although it is doubtful that many of the members recognized them as such. The lower houses wished to strengthen their authority within the colonies and to reduce to a minimum the amount of supervision, with the uncertainties it involved, that royal or proprietary authorities could exercise. Continuously nourished by the growing desire of American legislators to be masters of their own political fortunes and by the development of a vigorous tradition of legislative superiority in imitation of the imperial House of Commons, this basic principle of local control over local affairs in some cases got part of its impetus from an unsatisfactory experience early in the lower houses' development with a despotic, inefficient, or corrupt governor such as Thomas, Lord Culpeper, or Francis, Lord Howard or Effingham, in Virginia, Lionel Copley in Maryland, Sir Edmund Andros in Massachusetts, Seth Sothell in North Carolina, or the infamous Cornbury in New York and New Jersey.

With most of their contemporaries in Great Britain, colonial Americans were convinced that men were imperfect creatures, perpetually self-deluded, enslaved by their passions, vanities, and interests, confined in their vision and understanding, and incapable of exercising power over each other without abusing it. This cluster of assumptions with the associated ideals of a government of laws rather than of men and of a political structure that restrained the vicious tendencies of man by checking them against each other was at the heart of English constitutionalism. In Britain and in the colonies, wherever Englishmen encountered a seeming abuse of power, they could be expected to insist that it be placed under legal and constitutional restraints. Because the monarchy had been the chief offender in seventeenth-century England, it became conventional for the representative branch to keep an especially wary eye on the executive, and the Glorious Revolution tended to institutionalize this pattern of behavior. The necessity to justify the Revolution ensured both that the specter of Stuart despotism would continue to haunt English political arenas throughout the eighteenth century and that representative bodies and representatives would be expected—indeed obliged—to be constantly on the lookout for any signs of that excess of gubernatorial power that would perforce result in executive tyranny. When colonial lower houses demanded checks on the prerogative and sought to undermine executive authority, they were, then, to some extent, playing out roles created for them by their predecessors in the seventeenth-century English House of Commons and using a rhetoric and a set of ground rules that grew out of the revolutionary conditions of Stuart England. In every debate, and in every political contest, each American legislator was a potential Coke, Pym, or Hampden, and each governor, at least in legislators' minds, a potential Charles I or James II.

But the lower houses' quest for power involved more than the extension of legislative authority within the colonies at the expense of the colonial executives. After their initial stage of evolution, the lower houses learned that their real antagonists were not the governors but the proprietors or Crown officials in London. Few governors proved to be a match for the representatives. A governor was almost helpless to prevent a lower house from exercising powers secured under his predecessors, and even the most discerning governor could fall into the trap of assenting to an apparently innocent law that would later prove damaging to the royal or proprietary prerogative. Some governors, for the sake of preserving amicable relations with the representatives or because they thought certain legislation to be in the best interest of a colony, actually conspired with legislative leaders to present the actions of the lower houses in a favorable light in London. Thus, Jonathan Belcher worked with Massachusetts leaders to parry the Crown's demand for a permanent revenue in the 1730's, and Fauquier joined with Speaker John Robinson in Virginia to prevent the separation of the offices of speaker and treasurer during the closing years of the Seven Years' War.

Nor could imperial authorities depend upon the colonial councils to furnish an effective check upon the representatives' advancing influence. Most councilors were drawn from the rising social and economic elites in the colonies. The duality of their role is obvious. Bound by oath to uphold the interests of the Crown or the proprietors, they were also driven by ambition and a variety of local pressures to maintain the status and power of the councils as well as to protect and advance their own individual interests and those of their group within the colonies. These two objectives were not always in harmony, and the councils frequently sided with the lower houses rather than with the governors. With a weakened governor and an unreliable council, the task of restraining the representative assemblies ultimately devolved upon the home government. Probably as much of the struggle for power was played out in Whitehall as in Williamsburg, Charleston, New York, Boston, or Philadelphia.

Behind the struggle between colonial lower houses and the imperial authorities were two divergent, though on the colonial side not wholly articulated, concepts of the constitutions of the colonies and in particular of the status of the lower houses. To the very end of the colonial period, imperial authorities persisted in the views that colonial constitutions were static and that the lower houses were subordinate governmental agencies with only temporary and limited lawmaking powers—in the words of one imperial official, merely "so many Corporations at a distance, invested with an Ability to make Temporary By Laws for themselves, agreeable to their respective Situations and Climates." In working out a political system for the colonies in the later seventeenth century, imperial officials had institutionalized these views in the royal commissions and instructions. Despite the fact that the lower houses were yearly making important changes in their respective constitutions, the Crown never altered either the commissions or instructions to conform with realities of the colonial political situation and continued to maintain throughout the eighteenth century that they were the most vital part of the constitutional structure of the royal colonies. The Pennsylvania and to a lesser extent the

Maryland proprietors were less rigid, although they also insisted upon their theoretical constitutional and political supremacy over the lower houses.

Colonial lower houses had little respect for and even less patience with such a doctrinaire position, and whether or not royal and proprietary instructions were absolutely binding upon the colonies was the leading constitutional issue in the period before 1763. As the political instruments of what was probably the most pragmatic society in the eighteenth-century Western World, colonial legislators would not likely be restrained by dogma divorced from reality. They had no fear of innovations and welcomed the chance to experiment with new forms and ideas. All they asked was that a thing work. When the lower houses found that instructions from imperial authorities did not work in the best interests of the colonies, that they were, in fact, antithetic to the very measures they as legislatures were trying to effect, they openly refused to submit to them. Instructions, they argued, applied only to officials appointed by the Crown.

> Instructions from his majesty, to his governor, or the council, are binding to them, and esteemed as laws or rules; because if either should disregard them, they might immediately be displaced,

declared a South Carolina writer in 1756 while denying the validity of an instruction that stipulated colonial councils should have equal rights with the lower houses in framing money bills. "But, if instructions should be laws and rules to the people of this province, then there would be no need of assemblies, and all our laws and taxes might be made and levied by an instruction." Clearly, then, instructions might bind governors, but never the elected branch of the legislature.

Even though the lower houses, filled with intensely practical politicians, were concerned largely with practical political considerations, they found it necessary to develop a body of theory with which to oppose unpopular instructions from Britain and to support their claims to greater political power. In those few colonies that had charters, the lower houses relied upon the guarantees in them as their first line of defense, taking the position that the stipulations of the charters were inviolate, despite the fact that some had been invalidated by English courts, and could not be altered by executive order. A more basic premise which was equally applicable to all colonies was that the constituents of the lower houses, as inhabitants of British colonies, were entitled to all the traditional rights of Englishmen. On this foundation the colonial legislatures built their ideological structure. In the early charters the Crown had guaranteed the colonists "all privileges, franchises and liberties of this our kingdom of England . . . any Statute, act, ordinance, or provision to the contrary thereof, notwithstanding." Such guarantees, colonials assumed, merely constituted recognition that their privileges as Englishmen were inherent and unalterable and that it mattered not whether they stayed on the home islands or migrated to the colonies. "His Majesty's Subjects coming over to America," the South Carolina Commons argued in 1739 while asserting its exclusive right to formulate tax laws, "have no more forfeited this their most valuable Inheritance than they have withdrawn their Allegiance." No "Royal Order," the Commons declared, could "qualify or any wise alter a fundamental Right from the Shape in which it was handed down to us from our Ancestors."

One of the most important of these rights was the privilege of representation, on which, of course, depended the very existence of the lower houses. Imperial authorities always maintained that the lower houses existed only through the consent of the Crown, but the houses insisted that an elected assembly was a fundamental right of a colony arising out of an Englishman's privilege to be represented and that they did not owe their existence merely to the king's pleasure.

> Our representatives, agreeably to the general sense of their constituents [wrote New York lawyer William Smith in the 1750's] are tenacious in their opinion, that the inhabitants of this colony are entitled to all the privileges of Englishmen; that they have a right to participate

in the legislative power, and that the session of assemblies here, is wisely substituted instead of a representation in parliament, which, all things considered, would, at this remote distance, be extremely inconvenient and dangerous.

The logical corollary to this argument was that the lower houses were equivalents of the House of Commons and must perforce in their limited spheres be entitled to all the privileges possessd by that body in Great Britain. Hence, in cases where an invocation of fundamental rights was not appropriate, the lower houses frequently defended their actions on the grounds that they were agreeable to the practice of the House of Commons. Thus in 1775 the North Carolina Lower House denied the right of the Council to amend tax bills on the grounds that it was "contrary to Custom and Usage of Parliament." Unintentionally, Crown officials encouraged the lower houses to make this analogy by forbidding them in the instructions to exercise "any power or privilege whatsoever which is not allowed by us to the House of Commons . . . in Great Britain."

Because neither fundamental rights nor imperial precedents could be used to defend practices that were contrary to customs of the mother country or to the British constitution, the lower houses found it necessary to develop still another argument: that local precedents, habits, traditions, and statutes were important parts of their particular constitutions and could not be abridged by a royal or proprietary order. The assumptions were that the legislatures could alter colonial constitutions by their own actions without the active consent of imperial officials and that once the alterations were confirmed by usage they could not be countermanded by the British government. They did not deny the power of the governor to veto or of the Privy Council to disallow their laws but argued that imperial acquiescence over a long period of time was tantamount to consent and that precedents thus established could not be undone without their approval. The implication was that the American colonists saw their constitutions as living, growing, and constantly changing organisms, a theory which was directly opposite to the imperial view. To be sure, precedent had always been an important element in shaping the British constitution, but Crown officials were unwilling to concede that it was equally so in determining the fundamental law of the colonies. They willingly granted that colonial statutes, once formally approved by the Privy Council, automatically became part of the constitutions of the colonies, but they officially took the position that both royal instructions and commissions, as well as constitutional traditions of the mother country, took precedence over local practice or unconfirmed statutes. This conflict of views persisted throughout the period after 1689, becoming more and more of an issue in the decades immediately preceding the American Revolution.

In the last analysis it was the imperial denial of the validity of the constitutional defenses of the lower houses that drove colonial lawmakers to seek to extend the power of the lower houses at the very time they were insisting—and, in fact, deeply believed—that no one individual or institution should have a superiority of power in any government. No matter what kind of workable balance of power might be attained within the colonies, there was always the possibility that the home government might unleash the unlimited might of the parent state against the colonies. The chief fear of colonial legislators, then, was not the power of the governors, which they could control, but that of the imperial government, which in the circumstances they could never hope to control, and the whole movement for legislative authority in the colonies can be interpreted as a search for a viable constitutional arrangement in which the rights of the colonists would be secured against the preponderant power of the mother country. The failure of imperial authorities to provide such an arrangement or even to formalize what small concessions they did make, meant, of course, that the search could never be fulfilled, and the resulting anxiety, only partly conscious and finding expression through the classic arguments and ringing phrases of English political struggles of the seventeenth century, impelled the lower houses and the men who composed them relentlessly through the colonial period and was perhaps the most important single factor in the demand of patriot leaders for explicit, written constitutions after the Declaration of Independence.

It is nonetheless true that, if imperial authorities did not grant the validity of the theoretical arguments of the lower houses, neither did they make any systematic or concerted effort to force a rigid compliance with official policies for most of the period after 1689. Repressive measures, at least before 1763, rarely went beyond the occasional disallowance of an offending statute or the official reprimand of a rambunctious lower house. General lack of interest in the routine business of colonial affairs and failure to recognize the potential seriousness of the situation may in part account for this leniency, but it is also true that official policy under both Walpole and the Pelhams called for a light rein on the colonies on the assumption that contented colonies created fewer problems for the administration. "One would not Strain any point," Charles Delafaye, secretary to the lords justices, cautioned South Carolina's Governor Francis Nicholson in 1722, "where it can be of no Service to our King or Country." "In the Plantations," he added, "the Government should be as Easy and Mild as possible to invite people to Settle under it." Three times between 1734 and 1749 the ministry failed to give enthusiastic support to measures introduced into Parliament to ensure the supremacy of instructions over colonial laws. Though the Calverts were somewhat more insistent upon preserving their proprietary prerogatives, in general the proprietors were equally lax as long as there was no encroachment upon their land rights or proprietary dues.

Imperial organs of administration were in fact inadequate to deal effectively with all the problems of the empire. Since no special governmental bodies were created in England to deal exclusively with colonial affairs, they were handled through the regular machinery of government—a maze of boards and officials whose main interests and responsibilities were not the supervision of overseas colonies. The only body sufficiently informed and interested to deal competently with colonial matters was the Board of Trade, and it had little authority, except for the brief period from 1748 to 1761 under the presidency of George Dunk, Earl of Halifax. The most useful device for restraining the lower houses was the Privy Council's right to review colonial laws, but even that was only partly effective, because the mass of colonial statutes annually coming before the Board of Trade made a thorough scrutiny impossible. Under such arrangements no vigorous colonial policy was likely. The combination of imperial lethargy and colonial aggression virtually guaranteed the success of the lower houses' quest for power. An indication of a growing awareness in imperial circles of the seriousness of the situation was Halifax's spirited, if piecemeal, effort to restrain the growth of the lower houses in the early 1750's. Symptomatic of these efforts was the attempt to make Georgia and Nova Scotia model royal colonies at the institution of royal government by writing into the instructions to their governors provisions designed to insure the continued supremacy of the executive and to prevent the lower houses from going the way of their counterparts in the older colonies. However, the outbreak of the Seven Years' War forced Halifax to suspend his activities and prevented any further reformation until the cessation of hostilities.

Indeed, the war saw a drastic acceleration in the lower houses' bid for authority, and its conclusion found them in possession of many of the powers held less than a century before by the executive. In the realm of finance they had imposed their authority over every phase of raising and distributing public revenue. They had acquired a large measure of independence by winning control over their compositions and proceedings and obtaining guarantees of basic English parliamentary privileges. Finally, they had pushed their power even beyond that of the English House of Commons by gaining extensive authority in handling executive affairs, including the right to appoint executive officers and to share in formulating executive policy. These specific gains were symptoms of developments of much greater significance. To begin with, they were symbolic of a fundamental shift of the constitutional center of power in the colonies from the executive to the elected branch of the legislature. With the exception of the Georgia and Nova Scotia bodies, both of which had less than a decade of political experience behind them, the houses had by 1763 succeeded in attaining a new status, raising themselves from dependent lawmaking bodies to the center of political authority in their respective colonies.

But the lower houses had done more than simply acquire a new status in colonial politics. They had in a sense altered the structure of the constitution of the British empire itself by asserting colonial authority against imperial authority and extending the constitutions of the colonies far beyond the limitations of the charters, instructions, or fixed notions of imperial authorities. The time was ripe for a re-examination and redefinition of the constitutional position of the lower houses. With the rapid economic and territorial expansion of the colonies in the years before 1763 had come a corresponding rise in the responsibilities and prestige of the lower houses and a growing awareness among colonial representatives of their own importance, which had served to strengthen their long-standing, if still imperfectly defined, impression that colonial lower houses were the American counterparts of the British House of Commons. Under the proper stimuli, they would carry this impression to its logical conclusion: that the lower houses enjoyed an equal status under the Crown with Parliament. Here, then, well beyond the embryonic stage, was the theory of colonial equality with the mother country, one of the basic constitutional principles of the American Revolution, waiting to be nourished by the series of crises that beset imperial–colonial relations between 1763 and 1776.

The psychological implications of this new political order were profound. By the 1750's the phenomenal success of the lower houses had generated a soaring self-confidence, a willingness to take on all comers. Called upon to operate on a larger stage during the Seven Years' War, they emerged from that conflict with an increased awareness of their own importance and a growing consciousness of the implication of their activities. Symptomatic of these developments was the spate of bitter controversies that characterized colonial politics during and immediately after the war. The Gadsden election controversy in South Carolina, the dispute over judicial tenure in New York, and the contests over the pistole fee and the two-penny act in Virginia gave abundant evidence of both the lower houses' stubborn determination to preserve their authority and the failure of Crown officials in London and the colonies to gauge accurately their temper or to accept the fact that they had made important changes in the constitutions of the colonies.

With the shift of power to the lower houses also came the development in each colony of an extraordinarily able group of politicians. The lower houses provided excellent training for the leaders of the rapidly maturing colonial societies, and the recurring controversies prepared them for the problems they would be called upon to meet in the dramatic conflicts after 1763. In the decades before Independence there appeared in the colonial statehouses John and Samuel Adams and James Otis in Massachusetts Bay; William Livingston in New York; Benjamin Franklin and John Dickinson in Pennsylvania; Daniel Dulany the younger in Maryland; Richard Bland, Richard Henry Lee, Thomas Jefferson, and Patrick Henry in Virginia; and Christopher Gadsden and John Rutledge in South Carolina. Along with dozens of others, these men guided their colonies through the debate with Britain, assumed direction of the new state governments after 1776, and played conspicuous roles on the national stage as members of the Continental Congress, the Confederation, and, after 1787, the new federal government. By the 1760's, then, almost every colony had an imposing group of native politicians thoroughly schooled in the political arts and primed to meet any challenge to the power and prestige of the lower houses.

Britain's "new colonial policy" after 1763 provided just such a challenge. It precipitated a constitutional crisis in the empire, creating new tensions and setting in motion forces different from those that had shaped earlier developments. The new policy was based upon concepts both unfamiliar and unwelcome to the colonists such as centralization, uniformity, and orderly development. Yet it was a logical culmination of earlier trends and, for the most part, an effort to realize old aspirations. From Edward Randolph in the last decades of the seventeenth century to the Earl of Halifax in the 1750's colonial officials had envisioned a highly centralized empire with a uniform political system in each of the colonies and with the imperial government closely supervising the subordinate governments. But, because they had never made any sustained or systematic attempt to achieve these goals, there had developed during the first half of the eighteenth century a working arrangement permitting the lower houses considerable latitude in shaping colonial constitutions without requiring crown and proprietary officials to give up any of their ideals. That there had been a growing divergence between imperial theory and colonial practice mattered little so long as each refrained from challenging the other. But the new policy threatened to upset this arrangement by implementing the old ideals long after the conditions that produced them had ceased to exist. Aimed at bringing the colonies more closely under imperial control, this policy inevitably sought to curtail the influence of the lower houses, directly challenging many of the powers they had acquired over the previous century. To American legislators accustomed to the lenient policies of Walpole and the Pelhams and impressed with the rising power of their own lower houses, the new program seemed a radical departure from precedent, a frontal assault upon the several constitutions they had been forging over the previous century. To protect gains they had already made and to make good their pretensions to greater political significance, the lower houses thereafter no longer had merely to deal with weak governors or casual imperial administrators; they now faced an aggressive group of officials bent upon using every means at their disposal, including the legislative authority of Parliament, to gain their ends.

Beginning in 1763 one imperial action after another seemed to threaten the position of the lower houses. Between 1764 and 1766 Parliament's attempt to tax the colonists for revenue directly challenged the colonial legislatures' exclusive power to tax, the cornerstone of their authority in America. A variety of other measures, some aimed at particular colonial legislatures and others at general legislative powers and practices, posed serious threats to powers that the lower houses had either long enjoyed or were trying to attain. To meet these challenges, the lower houses had to spell out the implications of the changes they had been making, consciously or not, in the structures of their respective governments. That is, for the first time they had to make clear in their own minds and then to verbalize what they conceived their respective constitutions in fact were or should be. In the process, the spokesmen of the lower houses laid bare the wide gulf between imperial theory and colonial practice. During the Stamp Act crisis in 1764–1766 the lower houses claimed the same authority over taxation in the colonies as Parliament had over that matter in England, and a few of them even asserted an equal right in matters of internal policy. Although justified by the realities of the colonial situation, such a definition of the lower houses' constitutional position within the empire was at marked variance with imperial ideals and only served to increase the determination of the home government to take a stricter tone. This determination was manifested after the repeal of the Stamp Act by Parliament's claim in the Declaratory Act of 1766 to "full power and authority" over the colonies "in all cases whatsoever."

The pattern over the next decade was on the part of the home government one of increasing resolution to deal firmly with the colonies and on the part of American lawmakers a heightened consciousness of the implications of the constitutional issue and a continuously rising level of expectation. In addition to their insistence upon the right of Parliament to raise revenue in the colonies, imperial officials also applied, in a way that was increasingly irksome to American legislators, traditional instruments of royal control like restrictive instructions, legislative review, the governors' power to dissolve the lower houses and the suspending clause requiring prior approval of the Crown before laws of an "extraordinary nature" could go into effect. Finally Parliament threatened the very existence of the lower houses by a measure suspending the New York Assembly for refusing to comply with the Quartering Act in 1767 and by another altering the substance of the Massachusetts constitution in the Massachusetts Government Act in 1774. In the process of articulating and defending their constitutional position, the lower houses acquired aspirations well beyond any they had had in the years before 1763. American representatives became convinced in the decade after 1766 not only that they knew best what to do for their constituents and the colonies and that anything interfering with their freedom to adopt whatever course seemed necessary was an intolerable and unconstitutional restraint but also that the only security for their political fortunes was in the abandonment of their attempts to restrict and define parliamentary authority in America and instead to deny Parliament's jurisdiction over them entirely by asserting their equality with Parliament under the Crown. Suggested by Richard Bland as early as 1766, such a position was openly advocated by James Wilson and Thomas Jefferson in 1774 and was officially adopted by the First Continental Congress when it claimed for Americans in its declarations and resolves "a free and exclusive power of legislation in their several provincial legislatures, where their right of representation can alone be preserved, in all cases of taxation and internal polity."

Parliament could not accept this claim without giving up the principles it had asserted in the Declaratory Act and, in effect, abandoning the traditional British theory of empire and accepting the colonial constitutional position instead. The First Continental Congress professed that a return to the *status quo* of 1763 would satisfy the colonies, but Parliament in 1774–1776 was unwilling even to go that far, much less to promise them exemption from parliamentary taxation. Besides, American legislators now aspired to much more. James Chalmers, Maryland planter and later loyalist who was out of sympathy with the proceedings of American patriots between 1774 and 1776, correctly charged that American leaders had "been constantly enlarging their views, and stretching them beyond their first bounds, till at length they have wholly changed their ground." Edward Rutledge, young delegate from South Carolina to the First Continental Congress, was one who recognized that the colonies would not "be satisfied with a restoration of such rights only, as have been violated since the year '63, when we have as many others, as clear and indisputable, that will even then be infringed." The simple fact was that American political leaders, no matter what their professions, would not have been content to return to the old inarticulated and ambiguous pattern of accommodation between imperial theory and colonial practice that had existed through most of the period between 1689 and 1763. They now sought to become masters of their own political fortunes. Rigid guarantees of colonial rights and precise definitions of the constitutional relationship between the mother country and the colonies and between Parliament and the lower houses on American terms—that is, imperial recognition of the autonomy of the lower houses in local affairs and of the equality of the colonies with the mother country—would have been required to satisfy them.

No analysis of the charges in the Declaration of Independence can fail to suggest that the preservation and consolidation of the rights and powers of the lower houses were central in the struggle with Britain from 1763 to 1776, just as they had been the most important issue in the political relationship between Britain and the colonies over the previous century and a half. Between 1689 and 1763 the lower houses' contests with royal governors and imperial officials had brought them political maturity, a considerable measure of control over local affairs, capable leaders, and a rationale to support their pretensions to political power within the colonies and in the empire. The British challenge after 1763 threatened to render their accomplishments meaningless and drove them to demand equal rights with Parliament and autonomy in local affairs and eventually to declare their independence. At issue was the whole political structure forged by the lower houses over the previous century. In this context the American Revolution becomes in form, if not in essence, a war for political survival, a conflict involving not only individual rights as traditionally emphasized by historians of the event but assembly rights as well.

2

The Revolutionary Struggle, 1776–1789

The Revolutionary Colonial Elites

The Ward-Hopkins Controversy and the American Revolution in Rhode Island

by Mack E. Thompson

One clue to understanding the origins of the American Revolution lies in knowledge of the motives of those who led the resistance to Great Britain in the 1760's and 1770's. During the century and a half that followed the first settlements, the colonists had been loyal subjects of the mother country. Then, in less than fifteen years, conflict between the Americans and the British escalated into revolution as the colonists resisted, first peacefully and then with force, British attempts to reform relations with their American colonies by imposing new taxes and trade regulations. Standing at the head of the American resistance were the native-born colonial elites—Boston merchants, New York lawyers, and Virginia planters. For generations these and other like groups had enjoyed virtual freedom to carve out large areas of self-government and unregulated economic enterprise. When Parliament in the 1760's sought to strengthen imperial control by taxing Americans and by making British officials immune from manipulation by colonial elites, these groups reacted violently to the threat of subordination. They rallied popular support by convincing many other Americans that if Parliament were allowed to tax them without their consent, then the liberty of all Americans stood in jeopardy.

The supreme crisis of 1776 forced Americans to choose sides. Many of them, leaders included, remained loyal to the king, but the bulk of the native ruling groups supported Independence and provided leadership in the Revolutionary War. Nowhere was the unity of colonial leaders revealed more clearly than in Rhode Island. As Mack E. Thompson shows, Rhode Island in the mid-eighteenth century was torn by internal factionalism between two groups of merchants and their allies, one group centered in Providence, the other in Newport. Yet when external challenges from Britain threatened basic American interests in the 1760's both sides, at each other's throats for a generation, formed a united front. Thus, unlike other great revolutions of modern history—in France, Russia, or China—the American Revolution began largely as a defense of the power of entrenched elites. Even so, as the essays in this section demonstrate, the Revolution also contained an inner logic and momentum that set in motion forces which profoundly reshaped American politics, pushing it in non-elitist directions.

From 1755 to 1770 the colony of Rhode Island was torn by an internal political struggle that historians usually refer to as the Ward–Hopkins controversy, since the two factions contending for political supremacy were led by Samuel Ward from Westerly and Newport and Stephen Hopkins from Providence. Those who consider the American Revolution as an internal social and political conflict as well as a revolt from political obedience to England seem to see their thesis substantiated by the Ward–Hopkins controversy. Their assumption is that in pre-Revolutionary Rhode Island the people were sharply divided politically along economic class lines. One author states that Rhode Island was "a battleground for conservative merchants and radical farmers," and that

From *The William and Mary Quarterly,* 3rd ser., XVI (July 1959), 363–75. Reprinted by permission; footnotes omitted.

"radicalism won victories earlier than in the other colonies." "When the break with England came," this author concludes, "Newport and the Narragansett country remained loyal, whereas the agrarian north, which was in control of the government, declared Rhode Island's independence of Britain two months before the radical party was able to achieve that end in the Continental Congress. Throughout the revolutionary period the Rhode Islanders were staunch defenders of democracy and state sovereignty." In other words, the colony was taken into the Revolution by northern agrarian radicals who had earlier won a victory for democratic rights against southern conservative merchants. The purpose of this paper is to offer an alternative interpretation of the Ward–Hopkins controversy and the Revolution in Rhode Island.

It is true that Rhode Island was split politically along geographic lines. Hopkins's supporters were located in the northern towns and Ward's in the southern. But to view the north's rise to political power as a victory for agrarian radicalism is to miss entirely the significance of Stephen Hopkins's political success. Fundamental to an understanding of domestic politics in Rhode Island is a clear picture of the colony's economic growth during the middle half of the eighteenth century.

To speak of the north as "agrarian" and the south as "mercantile" is a fairly accurate description of Rhode Island in 1720, if we mean that commercial activity was confined largely to Newport and the Narragansett country in the south. Before that date, and for some years after, only in Newport, on Aquidneck Island in Narragansett Bay, did there exist in Rhode Island an urban community with a fairly sizable population employed in commerce and manufacturing. And only in the southern part of the colony, in the Narragansett country, were there substantial numbers of capitalistic farmers. In the rest of the colony an overwhelming majority of the people were engaged in subsistence agriculture, and commercial activity was relatively unimportant.

Until the 1750's the agrarian interests managed to have a decisive voice in the formation of public policy because the architects of the colony's government in the seventeenth century had fashioned a system to serve the needs of an agricultural population, and their charter had placed control of the central government in the hands of men residing in small farming communities. As long as Rhode Island's economic base remained predominantly that of subsistence agriculture the most important unit of government was town, not colony, government. With few exceptions the problems of these people could be solved by the town council. For decades the powers of the General Assembly were neither numerous nor vigorously exercised except in the area of monetary policy. From 1710 to 1751 Rhode Island farmers passed nine paper money bills or "banks" in an attempt to solve their monetary problems. They were forcefully but unsuccessfully opposed by the commercial interests in Newport.

But the Rhode Island economy was not static. During the half-century preceding the Revolution, external as well as internal events caused a remarkable economic growth that profoundly altered long existing political conditions. Newport, already one of the five leading ports in America by 1720, continued to grow. As the West India market expanded and the number of trading ships to Newport increased, Narragansett planters geared their production to meet the demands of agricultural exporters. Increasingly these planters turned from subsistence to capitalistic farming, sending their surpluses to Newport for distribution. Opportunities in manufacturing, particularly distilling, shipbuilding, and rope-making, caused many farmers to diversify their activities and in some cases to leave the land altogether. Long existing cultural, religious, and family affinities between the Newport and Narragansett residents were strengthened by intimate economic association, and the planters of Narragansett drifted slowly into political alliance with merchant, mechanic, and professional classes of Newport. Newporters or men closely identified with the interests of that town began to monopolize the governorship and other important offices in the colonial government. They also tried to run the General Assembly in their own interests but were never quite able to wrest control from the grip of the small farmers.

While Newport was expanding its commercial activities and extending its economic and political influence into the southern agricultural communities, in the north, on the banks of the Seekonk and Providence Rivers, another commercial center was rising. For almost a century Providence, the oldest town in the colony, had remained an agricultural community, but in the second quarter of the eighteenth century it responded to the same influences that were making Newport one of the leading ports in British North America. By the mid 1750's Providence was a thriving port with a young and enterprising group of merchants.

Providence's economic growth is not surprising. In some respects that city was more advantageously located than Newport. Providence not only had a protected outlet to the sea, but her merchants could draw on a larger hinterland for their cargoes than could Newport's. In response to increased demand for exports, several Providence merchants began to manufacture candles, chocolate, barrel hoops, rum, and rope and to serve as middlemen, supplying Newport merchants with cargo they could not find on the island or in the Narragansett country across the bay. By the early 1750's Providence was prepared to challenge Newport for economic leadership of the colony.

It is against this background of economic change that Rhode Island politics must be projected. Newport's continued expansion and Providence's rise as an important commercial center were both cause and effect of the violent political controversy that erupted in 1755 and continued for over a decade. In that year the freemen elected Stephen Hopkins, one of Providence's leading merchants, to the governorship, an office he held for nine of the next thirteen years. His election shows that a realignment of political forces had taken place—the hitherto fairly unified agrarian interest had disintegrated, and two composite factions, one in the north and another in the south, had appeared. The new factions were made up of cross sections of society—large and small farmers, merchants and tradesmen, professional men and other freeman. The previous division of political forces along agrarian–commercial lines was no more. Hopkins's election also shows that political leadership had finally passed from the agrarian–small town interests to commercial and manufacturing groups and that the chief instrument for the promotion of economic growth was likely to be the General Assembly rather than the town council. Although rural towns continued to exert considerable influence in the political life of the colony, thirty years passed before they again consolidated to seize control of the government.

With the disintegration of agrarian solidarity and the growth of two factions composed of men from both the urban and rural areas, political success went to the man who could reconcile conflicting interests within his own section and attract a majority of the few uncommitted freemen. As the contest between the north and south developed, leaders of both sides realized that the voters holding the balance of power were concentrated most heavily in the farming communities in the central part of the colony, equidistant from the two commercial centers of Newport and Providence. Stephen Hopkins, one of the most accomplished politicians in colonial America, was more successful in appealing to these freemen and better able to prevent any serious defections in his party than was his opponent, Samuel Ward.

The climax to the prolonged struggle came in the election of 1767, when Hopkins decisively defeated Ward for the governorship and dealt the southern party a shattering blow from which it never recovered. Hopkins's success was the result of a combination of factors. By 1767, after controlling the government for two consecutive years, Ward and his followers in Newport had alienated the Narragansett planters and farmers by refusing to support a measure to regulate interest rates, and some of the latter began to look elsewhere for political leadership. Ward's party was further discredited by the gerrymandering activities of Elisha Brown, the deputy governor.

Hopkins helped his cause by collecting a large election fund and conducting an energetic campaign. Personal influence, money, and liberal amounts of rum were brought to bear, and where possible, the old, the sick, and the infirm were carried to the polls to cast their ballots for Hopkins-party men. Freemen were not only paid to vote for Hopkins and his supporters but "many persons that is stranious for Mr. Ward who may be agreed with for a Small Sum to Lay Still," were also approached. One Hopkins-party campaign worker, "Clostly Engaged in the Grand Cause" in Cumberland, reported that he would "be short with Regard to the Necessary argument (haveing Last Evening fell into Company with Two men who was against us Last year, who was hard to Convince of their Error, but I over come them) shall want five Dollars more which I must have; for I must meat the above two men. To morror morning almost up to Woonsoketfalls where I expect to Settle Some things very favourable To the Campaign. . . . ." He ended his urgent letter with the candid remark: "am Engaged Clostly in makeing freemen and hope I shall merrit the Beaver Hat."

Hopkins's success in 1767 was materially aided by the growing identification of outlying towns with Providence as a result of the economic opportunities that flourishing port offered. Providence's economic growth may be compared to an expanding whirlpool; when it began slowly to spin in the second quarter of the century, it drew nearby agricultural communities into its vortex. In the next decades, as its force increased, it slowly but inexorably sucked more distant towns into its center. Political sympathies apparently were swept along with economic interests, for these towns eventually supported Stephen Hopkins and the northern party. Southern response to this economic and political alignment was what triggered the Ward-Hopkins controversy and kept it alive for over a decade.

Stephen Hopkins's elections to the governorship in 1755 and in subsequent years was not a victory for social and political radicalism. On issues commonly associated with radicalism there was little discussion and almost no discussion at all directly relating to internal political controversies. During Hopkins's numerous administrations no new laws were passed or even introduced in the General Assembly abolishing or lowering the property qualifications for the vote. The people were apparently not concerned with such issues. And ironically, on the most important problem of the period, currency, the men who assumed the leadership in solving it were not the southern "conservative merchants" but the northern "radical farmers." Stephen Hopkins, one of Providence's leading merchants, and the Browns of Providence, Obadiah and his four nephews, Nicholas, Joseph, John, and Moses, who operated one of the largest shipping firms in the colony, led the fight for currency reform. By the early 1760's Stephen Hopkins's northern followers were committed to a program of sound money and in 1763 they were able to push through the assembly the first bill to regulate currency in the history of the colony. While some southerners supported currency reform, the Browns would never have been able to pass the bill without the support of representatives from the nearby agricultural towns, a fact which points up the composite nature of the northern faction. Subsequent legislation provided Rhode Island with a stable currency until the Revolution.

To see in Rhode Island's political controversy a class struggle—agrarian radicals fighting conservative merchants—is to see something that did not exist. That came only in the post-Revolutionary years and had its roots in the changes brought about by the war and the success of the Revolution. This is not to say that before 1776 there were no class distinctions or that members of the lower classes did not resent advantages enjoyed by the upper classes; but there is little evidence that such distinctions or sentiments resulted in social tensions serious enough to label revolutionary.

Briefly stated, then, the chief cause for the intense political struggle in Rhode Island before the Revolution was the desire of men in the north and the south to gain control of the government to promote private and public interests. When the southern and northern economies expanded, and merchants, tradesmen, and capitalistic farmers emerged whose needs could no longer be satisfied by the town meeting, they began to compete with one another for control of the colonial government. The General Assembly could bestow many profitable favors on deserving citizens; it could issue flags of truce to merchants authorizing them to exchange French prisoners and provisions in the West Indies; it could determine which merchants could outfit privateers; it could grant monopolies to enterprising businessmen; it could vote funds to build or repair lighthouses, bridges, schools, and to make other local public improvements; it could alter the apportionment of taxes to the benefit of towns in particular sections. These and other powers only the General Assembly had. The section that controlled the government could use the assembly as an instrument to promote its economic and cultural growth.

A good illustration of this interpretation of domestic politics in Rhode Island occurs in the struggle that took place in 1769 and 1770 over the permanent location of the College of Rhode Island. After considerable discussion, the choice of sites for the college narrowed to Providence and Newport. The contestants considered the controversy one more episode, and perhaps the last, in the long drawn-out competition for economic and political leadership between the north and the south. In a letter to the town councils of Scituate and Glocester, Stephen Hopkins and Moses Brown of Providence wrote:

When we consider that the building the College here will be a means of bringing great quantities of money into the place, and thereby of greatly increasing the markets for all kinds of the countries produce; and, consequently, of increasing the value of all estates to which this town is a market; and also that it will much promote the weight and influence of this northern part of the Colony in the scale of government in all times to come, we think every man that hath an estate in this County who duly weighs these advantages, with many others that will naturally occur to his mind, must, for the bettering of his own private interest, as well as for the public good, become a contributor to the College here, rather than it should be removed from hence. . . .

We are more zealous in this matter as we have certain intelligence that the people in Newport, who are become sinsible of the importance of this matter, are very deligently using every method in their power to carry the prize from us, and as the few remaining days of this month is the whole time in which we can work to any purpose, we hope none will slumber or sleep. We think ourselves in this matter wholly engaged for the public good; and therefore hope to be borne with when we beg of you and all our neighbors, to seriously consult their own interest and pursue it with unremitted zeal.

The governing body of the College of Rhode Island eventually voted to make Providence the permanent home of the institution. In the 1770 election, Samuel Ward, his brother Henry, who was the colony secretary, and a few other southern politicians made a determined effort to capture control of the government in order to get a charter for a college in Newport. They failed and their bill to charter a second college was defeated by deputies committed to northern leadership.

To say that the central theme of the Ward-Hopkins controversy was the political struggle between similar interests in two different sections does not necessarily assume a uniformity of motives on the part of the participants. Undoubtedly some men on both sides were propelled above all else by the financial rewards public office afforded, by personal animosities, and by desire for social prestige, while others devoted their time and money to politics because of a sense of public responsibility or simply because they enjoyed the game of politics. But what bound the men of each party together was their recognition that the promotion of their own section, and thus their own interests, could best be done through control of the government. Social and economic classes could co-operate for this purpose in the two sections. In fact, co-operation, not dissension, between classes is the distinctive characteristic of pre-Revolutionary political life in Rhode Island.

If we turn now to consider the claim that Rhode Island split into radical and conservative camps over British attempts to extend parliamentary authority to America, we find that the facts do not bear out this claim. Rhode Island was one of the first colonies to react to the Sugar Act of 1764 and to the Stamp Act of the following year. In the General Assembly, members of the two factions united to petition the Lords Commissioners for Trade and Plantations for their repeal. This early response set the tone for resistance to subsequent parliamentary legislation and ministerial attempts to enforce customs regulations.

The political leaders of both factions opposed British policy with equal vigor. Stephen Hopkins made a strong defense of American rights in *The Rights of the Colonies Examined,* and the General Assembly sent this pamphlet to the colony's agent in England for use in the move for repeal of the Stamp Act. Hopkins's subsequent service for the cause of American independence is too well known to necessitate further comment. His political opponent, Samuel Ward, was no less a patriot. In fact, Ward held the governorship during the Stamp Act crisis when the colony successfully prevented the use of stamps. He made every effort to frustrate attempts of the king's officers to enforce the Acts of Trade and was an outspoken critic of British trade regulations. When the First Continental Congress met in Philadelphia in September 1774, Ward and Hopkins attended as delegates from Rhode Island.

Stout resistance by these key figures to Parliament's attempts to extend its authority to the American colonies was emulated by the second rank of leaders of both factions and strongly supported by the freemen. The only person of importance in the north who attempted to abide by the Stamp Act was John Foster, a justice of the peace and clerk of the Inferior Court of Common Pleas for Providence County, who refused to open his court and transact business without stamps. A crowd of angry people gathered before his house and threatened to ride him out of town on a rail unless he changed his mind. This was enough to convince Foster of his error. In 1769 after the Townshend Acts were passed and again in 1772, royal officials trying to perform their duties were roughly treated by the northerners; and in 1773, when British naval vessels were patrolling Narragansett Bay in an effort to stop contraband trade, John Brown, the leading merchant in Providence, and a number of citizens, burned the revenue vessel, the *Gaspee,* to the water's edge. Royal investigators could get no assistance from Rhode Islanders in their search for the culprits. In the south, in Newport, throughout the period 1765–75, the people frequently demonstrated their hostile attitude toward British policy and supporters of the Crown.

One of the striking things about anti-British leadership in Rhode Island is its continuity. The same people who successfully organized the opposition to the Stamp Act and the Townshend Acts led the resistance to the Tea Act and the Intolerable Acts and declared Rhode Island's independence. For the most part these leaders were not radical agrarians but members of the commercial and professional classes of both Providence and Newport. This does not mean that the farmers were pro-British. There was stronger loyalist sentiment among the merchants in Newport than among the farmers in the agricultural communities. What it does mean is that the farmers were content to follow the lead of men like Hopkins and Ward. The merchants, shipowners, and lawyers who were the leaders in domestic politics were also the leaders in the Revolutionary movement.

Articulate supporters of Parliament supremacy in Rhode Island during the 1760's were almost without exception royal government employees. They constituted an infinitesimal percentage of the population and exerted no influence within the colonial government and very little outside it. And when they did speak out, they made every effort to hide their identity and to cloak their real intentions. If discovered, they were either forced into silence or hounded out of the colony. During the five years before the outbreak of violence, supporters of British policy were even less noticeable than during the earlier period. Even Joseph Wanton, Rhode Island's Episcopalian governor who eventually went over to the British, was a strong defender of American liberties throughout these years. When Rhode Island declared its independence, the few citizens who could not accept the decision either withdrew from active participation in public affairs or left the colony.

The colony's vigorous, continuous opposition to British policy proves that Rhode Islanders were trying to preserve a system with which they were well satisfied, rather than to change it. The struggle for home rule in Rhode Island was not paralleled by any fight between agrarian and commercial classes to determine who should rule at home. The transition from colony to commonwealth was made with practically no changes in the existing institutions, leadership, or social structure. And there were few demands for any changes. The struggle for democratic rights came in the postwar decade and its origins must be sought in the changes produced by the war and Independence and not in the Ward–Hopkins controversy.

Political Consequences of The Revolution

Government By the People: The American Revolution and the Democratization of the Legislatures

by Jackson Turner Main

American politics had been in flux since the first settlements, and the Revolution caused still more alterations. Independence shifted the locus of all authority from England to America, making Americans masters of their political destinies. Effective new state regimes, and a weak national government, replaced the Crown. New principles of government, forged during the resistance to Britain and elaborated after 1776, shaped the conduct of politics. In some ways the changes were obvious and immediate. Royal governors gave way to executives chosen in the states either by popular election or by the legislatures. Vital matters of public policy, such as laws regulating economic activity, which were once the prerogative of Parliament, now fell within the exclusive jurisdiction of American lawmakers. Citizens accustomed to playing a passive role in public affairs and deferring to rule by local elites found themselves mobilized by those same elites to defend American liberty against Britain.

Some historians, including Jackson Turner Main, argue that the Revolution did more than modify American forms of government, that it also significantly democratized the recruitment of new men within the power structure. Comparing the social status of colonial assemblymen with those serving in the now independent legislatures, Main finds that farmers and artisans—the common people—were much better represented than they had been earlier, when the wealthy occupied commanding positions. By opening doors to newcomers, by retiring many of the older leaders, and also by legitimizing popular sovereignty and encouraging challenges to established authority, the Revolution added considerable democratic potential to American politics. Many of the former undemocratic leaders were Tories—thus now discredited. Many positions, then, were left open by default—not by a process of democratization.

Yet despite Main's impressive evidence, it may be that after the Revolution the elites continued to enjoy power all out of proportion to their numbers. Before we can assess the significance of this shift in recruitment, we must know how farmers and artisans used power when members of those classes gained office. Did they still defer to the leadership of lawyers, merchants, and planters? Or did they form a distinctive, organized bloc, determined to advance the interests of their own social classes? It is certain that the Revolution created fresh opportunities in politics for middling but ambitious individuals, because many established leaders were swept aside and traditional lines of authority became blurred. Yet it is also likely that the deference tendered the upper classes by the lower declined but did not disappear.

An article with "democracy" in its title, these days, must account for itself. This essay holds that few colonials in British North America believed in a government by the people, and that they were content to be ruled by local elites; but that during the Revolution two interacting developments occurred simultaneously: ordinary citizens increasingly took part in politics, and American political theorists began to defend popular government. The ideological shift can be traced most easily in the newspapers,

From *The William and Mary Quarterly*, 3rd ser., XXIII (July 1966), 391–407. Reprinted by permission; most footnotes omitted.

while evidence for the change in the structure of power will be found in the make-up of the lower houses during the revolutionary years.

Truly democratic ideas, defending a concentration of power in the hands of the people, are difficult to find prior to about 1774. Most articulate colonials accepted the Whig theory in which a modicum of democracy was balanced by equal parts of aristocracy and monarchy. An unchecked democracy was uniformly condemned. For example, a contributor to the *Newport Mercury* in 1764 felt that when a state was in its infancy, "when its members are few and virtuous, and united together by some peculiar ideas of freedom or religion; the whole power may be lodged with the people, and the government be purely democratical"; but when the state had matured, power must be removed from popular control because history demonstrated that the people "have been incapable, collectively, of acting with any degree of moderation or wisdom." Therefore, while colonial theorists recognized the need for some democratic element in the government, they did not intend that the ordinary people—the *demos*—should participate. The poorer men were not allowed to vote at all, and that part of the populace which did vote was expected to elect the better sort of people to represent them. "Fabricus" defended the "democratic principle," warned that "liberty, when once lost, is scarce ever recovered," and declared that laws were "made for the people, and not people for the laws." But he did not propose that ordinary citizens should govern. Rather, "it is right that men of *birth and fortune*, in every government that is free, should be invested with power, and enjoy higher honours than the people." According to William Smith of New York, offices should be held by "the better Class of People" in order that they might introduce that "Spirit of Subordination essential to good Government." A Marylander urged that members of the Assembly should be "ABLE in ESTATE, ABLE in KNOWLEDGE AND LEARNING," and mourned that so many "little upstart insignificant Pretenders" tried to obtain an office. "The *Creature* that is able to keep a little Shop, rate the Price of an Ell of Osnabrigs, or, at most, to judge of the Quality of a Leaf of Tobacco" was not a fit statesman, regardless of his own opinion. So also in South Carolina, where William Henry Drayton warned the artisans that mechanical ability did not entitle them to hold office. This conviction that most men were incompetent to rule, and that the elite should govern for them, proved a vital element in Whig thought and was its most antidemocratic quality. The assumption was almost never openly challenged during the colonial period.

Whether the majority whose capacity was thus maligned accepted the insulting assumption is another question. They were not asked, and as they were unable to speak or write on the subject, their opinions are uncertain. But the voters themselves seem to have adhered, in practice at least, to the traditional view, for when the people were asked to choose their representatives they seldom elected common farmers and artisans. Instead they put their trust in men of the upper class. In the colonies as a whole, about 30 per cent of the adult white men owned property worth £500 or more. About two-thirds of these colonials of means had property worth £500 to £2,000; their economic status is here called *moderate*. The other third were worth over £2,000. Those worth £2,000 to £5,000 are called *well-to-do*, and those whose property was valued at more than £5,000 are called *wealthy*. The overwhelming majority of the representatives belonged to that 10 per cent who were well-to-do or wealthy. Government may have been for the people, but it was not administered by them. For evidence we turn to the legislatures of New Hampshire, New York, New Jersey, Maryland, Virginia, and South Carolina.

In 1765 New Hampshire elected thirty-four men to its House of Representatives. Practically all of them lived within a few miles of the coast; the frontier settlements could not yet send deputies, and the Merrimack Valley towns in the south-central part of the colony, though populous, were allotted only seven. New Hampshire was not a rich colony. Most of its inhabitants were small farmers with property enough for an adequate living but no more.

There were a few large agricultural estates, and the Portsmouth area had developed a prosperous commerce which supported some wealthy merchants and professional men; but judging from probate records not more than one man in forty was well-to-do, and true wealth was very rare. Merchants, professional men, and the like comprised about one-tenth of the total population, though in Portsmouth, obviously, the proportion was much larger. Probably at least two-thirds of the inhabitants were farmers or farm laborers and one in ten was an artisan. But New Hampshire voters did not call on farmers or men of average property to represent them. Only about one-third of the representatives in the 1765 House were yeomen. Merchants and lawyers were just as numerous, and the rest followed a variety of occupations: there were four doctors and several millers and manufacturers. One-third of the delegates were wealthy men and more than two-thirds were at least well-to-do. The relatively smaller upper class of the colony, concentrated in the southeast, furnished ten of the members. They did not of course, constitute a majority, and the family background of most of the representatives, like that of most colonials, was undistinguished. Probably nearly one-half had acquired more property and prestige than their parents. In another age New Hampshire's lower house would have been considered democratic—compared with England's House of Commons it certainly was—but this was a new society, and the voters preferred the prosperous urban upper class and the more substantial farmers.

New York was a much richer colony than New Hampshire. Although most of its population were small farmers and tenants, there were many large landed estates and New York City was incomparably wealthier than Portsmouth. In general the west bank of the Hudson and the northern frontier were usually controlled by the yeomanry, as was Suffolk County on Long Island, but the east bank from Albany to the City was dominated by great "manor lords" and merchants. The great landowners and the merchants held almost all of the twenty-eight seats in the Assembly. In 1769 the voters elected only seven farmers. Five others, including Frederick Philipse and Pierre Van Cortland, the wealthy manor lords from Westchester, were owners of large tenanted estates. But a majority of New York's legislators were townspeople. Merchants were almost as numerous as farmers, and together with lawyers they furnished one-half of the membership. The legislators were no more representative in their property than in their occupation. At most, five men, and probably fewer, belonged to the middle class of moderate means. At least 43 per cent were wealthy and an equal number were well-to-do. The members' social background was also exceptional. Ten came from the colony's foremost families who had, for the times, a distinguished ancestry, and two-thirds or more were born of well-to-do parents. Taken as a whole, the legislators, far from reflecting New York's social structure, had either always belonged to or had successfully entered the colony's economic and social upper class.

New Jersey's Assembly was even smaller than that of New York. The body chosen in 1761, and which sat until 1769, contained but twenty men. Half of these represented the East Jersey counties (near New York City) which were in general occupied by small farmers, but only three of the ten members came from that class. The others were merchants, lawyers, and large proprietors. Although several of these had started as yeomen they had all acquired large properties. West Jersey, which had a greater number of sizable landed estates, especially in the Delaware Valley region, sent the same sort of men as did East Jersey: three farmers, an equal number of large landowners, and an even larger number of prosperous townsmen, some of whom also owned valuable real estate. Merchants and lawyers made up one-half of the membership. As usual, a considerable proportion—perhaps 40 per cent—were self-made men, but the colony's prominent old families furnished at least 30 per cent of the representatives. Four out of five members were either well-to-do or wealthy.

In contrast to the legislatures of New Hampshire, New York, and New Jersey, Maryland's House of Delegates was a large body and one dominated by the agricultural interest. Like its northern equivalents, however, its members belonged to the upper class of the colony—in Maryland, the planter aristocracy. The 1765 House supposedly contained over sixty members, but only fifty-four appear in the records. About one-half of these came from the Eastern Shore, an almost entirely rural area. Except for Col. Thomas Cresap, who lived on Maryland's small frontier, the remainder came from the Potomac River and western Chesapeake Bay counties, where agriculture was the principal occupation but where a number of towns also existed. About one-sixth of the Delegates belonged to the yeoman farmer class. Most of these lived on the Eastern Shore. Incidentally they did not vote with the antiproprietary, or "popular," party, but rather followed some of the great planters in the conservative "court" party. As in the northern colonies, a number of the Delegates were *nouveaux riches*, but in Maryland's stable and primarily "Tidewater" society, fewer than one-fifth had surpassed their parents in wealth. The overwhelming majority came from the lesser or the great planter class, and probably one-third belonged to the colony's elite families. Four-fifths were well-to-do or wealthy. Lawyers and merchants (among whom were several of the self-made men) furnished about one-sixth of the principally rural membership.

Virginia's Burgesses resembled Maryland's Delegates, but they were even richer and of even more distinguished ancestry. The Old Dominion's much larger west helped to make the House of Burgesses twice as large a body, with 122 members in 1773. Small property holders, though they formed a great majority of the voters, held only one out of six seats. Half of the Burgesses were wealthy and four-fifths were at least well-to-do. Merchants and lawyers contributed one-fifth of the members, much more than their proper share, but most of them were also large landholders and the legislature was firmly in control of the great planters. Indeed the median property owned was 1,800 acres and 40 slaves. Virginia's social structure was quite fluid, especially in the newly settled areas, but between five-sixths and seven-eighths of the delegates had inherited their property. A roll call of the Burgesses would recite the names of most of the colony's elite families, who held nearly one-half of the seats.

The planters of South Carolina, unlike the Virginians, were unwilling to grant representation to the upcountry, and its House of Commons was an exclusively eastern body. The colony was newer and its society may have been more fluid, for in 1765 between 20 and 40 per cent of the representatives were self-made men. The legislature also differed from its southern equivalents in Maryland and Virginia in that nearly half of its members were merchants, lawyers, or doctors. But these figures are deceptive, for in reality most of these men were also great landowners, as were almost all of the representatives; and prominent old families contributed one half of the members of the House. All were at least well-to-do and over two-thirds were wealthy. The rich planters of South Carolina's coastal parishes held a monopoly of power in the Assembly.

These six legislatures, from New Hampshire to South Carolina, shared the same qualities. Although farmers and artisans comprised probably between two-thirds and three-fourths of the voters in the six colonies, they seldom selected men from their own ranks to represent them. Not more than one out of five representatives were of that class. Fully one-third were merchants and lawyers or other professionals, and most of the rest were large landowners. Although only about 10 per cent of the colonials were well-to-do or wealthy, this economic elite furnished at least 85 per cent of the assemblymen. The mobile character of colonial society meant that perhaps 30 per cent had achieved their high status by their own efforts; but an even larger percentage were from prominent, long-established families.

Collectively these "representatives of the people" comprised not a cross section of the electorate but a segment of the upper class. Although the colonials cherished the democratic branch of their governments, and although a majority may have hoped to make the lower house all-powerful, they did not yet conceive that the *demos* should actually govern. The idea of a government by as well as for the people was a product of the Revolution. It should be noted here that Rhode Island and Connecticut are exceptions to this general pattern, though the upper house of Connecticut was composed entirely of well-to-do men. As for Massachusetts, the number of representatives with moderate properties exceeded that in the royal and proprietary colonies; but the Massachusetts legislature was still controlled by the well-to-do. Of the 117 men in the House in 1765, at least fifty-six were not farmers and thirteen were large landowners; of the remaining forty-eight, thirty-seven were ordinary farmers and the occupations of eleven are unknown. Among those representatives whose economic status can be discovered (about nine-tenths), well over one-half were well-to-do or wealthy and two-fifths of these had inherited their property.

Widespread popular participation in politics began during 1774 with the various provincial congresses and other extralegal organizations. Although the majority of these bodies seem to have been made up of men of standing, both artisans and farmers appeared in greater numbers than they had in the colonial legislatures. There were several reasons for this. Whereas heretofore the more recently settled areas of most colonies had been underrepresented—at times seriously so—the legal prohibitions on their sending representatives to the colonial assemblies did not apply to the extralegal congresses, and they chose delegates when they wished. Moreover, the congresses were much larger than the colonial assemblies, and consequently the over-all number of men who could be elected was greatly increased. For instance, South Carolina's House of Commons contained forty-eight men in 1772, but almost twice that number attended the first Provincial Congress in December 1774 and four times as many were present in January 1775. By 1775 the western districts were sending about one-third of the members. Similarly, nothing now prevented New Hampshire's country villages from choosing representatives, and they seized the opportunity. By the time the fourth Provincial Congress met in New Hampshire, four times as many men attended as had been admitted to the 1773 legislature, and nearly one-half of them came from the inland counties.

Perhaps an even more important reason for the greater participation in politics by men of moderate means than simply the enlarged and broadened membership of the Provincial Congresses was that the interior areas often contained no real upper class. They had no choice but to send men of moderate property. Furthermore, many men of the upper classes who had previously held political power were not sympathetic with the resistance movement and either withdrew from politics or did not participate in the extralegal Congresses. At the same time events thrust new men forward, as for example in Charleston where the artisans became increasingly active. As the Revolution ran its course, many new men came to fill the much larger number of civil offices, and new men won fame in battle. These developments were quickly reflected in the composition of the legislatures, and by the time the war ended the legislatures were far different bodies from what they had been in colonial days. At the same time democratic ideas spread rapidly, justifying and encouraging the new order.

With the overthrow of royal government, the previously unrepresented New Hampshire villages hastened to choose representatives to the state legislature. The number of men present in the lower house varied considerably, for some smaller communities were too poor to send a man every year, while others combined to finance the sending of a single delegate; but during the 1780's between two and three times as many attended as before the war. The House chosen in 1786 had eighty-eight members. The balance of power had shifted into the Merrimack Valley, for fewer than half of the delegates came from the two counties near the coast, and even these included frontier settlements.

The socio-economic composition of the New Hampshire legislature also changed. All but four of the 1765 legislators can be identified, but more than one-fifth of the postwar representatives are obscure, and the parentage of very few can be established despite the existence of many town histories, genealogies, and published records. Before the war fewer than one-third were farmers, exclusive of large landowners but including the men whose occupation is doubtful; by 1786 at least 50 per cent were yeomen and of those whose occupations are unknown are added, as most of them should be, the proportion rises to over 70 per cent. Merchants and lawyers, who had furnished about one-third of the members of the 1765 legislature, now comprised only one-tenth of the membership. Similarly, men of wealth totaled one-third of the former legislature but less than one-tenth of the latter. The well-to-do element who had dominated the prewar Assembly with 70 per cent of the seats were now reduced to a minority of about 30 per cent. Thus a very large majority of the new legislature consisted of ordinary farmers who had only moderate properties. Ten members of the prominent old families had seats in the 1765 house; by 1786 there were only four in a body two and one-half times as large. Even if the newly represented towns are eliminated, the trend toward the election of less wealthy and less distinguished representatives remains the same, though the degree of change is less. If only the towns which sent men to both legislatures are considered, one finds that whereas farmers formed between 20 and 30 per cent in 1765, they accounted for 55 to 67 per cent twenty years later. Similarly, in these towns the proportion of representatives having moderate properties rose from 30 per cent to more than twice that. Thus the economic and social character of the members in the lower house had been radically changed.

The pattern of change was much the same in other states. New York's society was fundamentally less egalitarian than that of New Hampshire, having more men with large estates and proportionately fewer areas dominated by small farmers. The agricultural upcountry had not yet extended much beyond Albany to the north and Schenectady to the west, so that most New Yorkers still lived in the older counties. As might be expected, the changes which occurred in New York were not as striking as in New Hampshire, but they were still obvious. By 1785 the counties west of the Hudson, together with those north of Westchester, increased their representation from about one-third to nearly two-thirds of the total. That fact alone might not have guaranteed a social or economic change in the composition of the Assembly, for every county had its upper class, but the new legislature differed from the old in many respects. The voters selected far fewer townspeople. In the 1769 Assembly some 57 per cent of the members had been engaged primarily in a nonagricultural occupation; by 1785 the proportion had been halved. Farmers, exclusive of large landowners, had made up 25 per cent of the total in 1769; now they furnished about 42 per cent.[1] In contrast, one-half of the 1769 legislators had been merchants and lawyers, but now such men held less than one-third of the seats. Similarly, the proportion of wealthy members dropped from 43 per cent to 15 per cent, whereas the ratio of men of moderate means increased from probably one-seventh to nearly one-half. New York's elite families, which had contributed ten out of twenty-eight Assemblymen in 1769, contributed the same number in 1785, but in a House twice as large. Meanwhile the number of men who had started without any local family background, newcomers to New York, increased from two to twenty-three. In general, the yeoman-artisan "middle class," which in colonial days had furnished a half-dozen members, now actually had a majority in the legislature. Under the leadership of George Clinton and others of higher economic and social rank, they controlled the state during the entire decade of the eighties.[2] In New York, as in New Hampshire, the trend was the

1. So many men in the 1785 legislature are obscure that the figure cannot be exact, but it is a safe assumption that those who lived in the country and whose occupations are not given in local histories, genealogies, or other published sources, were farmers. Ordinarily, men of importance, or business and professional men, are discussed in such sources, so that if one conscientiously searches the published materials, including, of course, the wills, most of those men who remain unidentified can be confidently termed farmers of moderate property.

2. As far as the fathers of these legislators could be identified, 12 of the prewar 28 were merchants, lawyers, and large landowners, as were 12 or possibly 13 of the postwar 66.

same even within those counties which had been represented before the Revolution. If Washington and Montgomery counties are eliminated, the proportion of delegates who were well-to-do declined from 86 per cent to 60 per cent.

New Jersey's lower house, the size of which had increased in stages from twenty members to thirty-nine after the Revolution, retained equal distribution of seats between East and West Jersey. As in New Hampshire and New York, the economic upper class of well-to-do men, which in New Jersey had held three-fourths of the seats before the war, saw its control vanish; indeed, two-thirds of the states' representatives in 1785 had only moderate properties. The typical legislator before the war held at least 1,000 acres; in 1785 the median was about 300 acres. Merchants and lawyers were all but eliminated from the legislature, retaining only a half-dozen seats. The colonial elite, once controlling one-third of the votes of the house, now had one-eighth; the overwhelming majority of the new legislators were men who had been unknown before the war and whose ancestry, where ascertainable, was uniformly undistinguished. Fully two-thirds of the representatives were ordinary farmers, presumably men of more than average ability and sometimes with military experience, but clearly part of the common people. Again these changes occurred not just because new areas were represented but because the counties which had sent delegates in the prewar years now chose different sorts of men. In New Jersey, the counties of Cumberland, Salem, Hunterdon, Morris, and Sussex had previously been underrepresented. If these are eliminated, we find that the proportion of men of moderate property rose from 20 per cent to 73 per cent and of farmers (exclusive of large landowners) from 23.5 per cent to 60 per cent.

Southern legislatures were also democratized. Maryland's House of Delegates expanded to seventy-four by 1785, with the addition of a few members from the western counties. As had been true before the war, most of the representatives were engaged in agriculture, the proportion of those with a nonfarm occupation remaining constant at about 20 per cent. The most obvious change in economic composition was the replacement of planters by farmers, of large property owners by men with moderate estates. If the planter is defined as one who held at least twenty slaves or 500 acres, then they formed 57 per cent of the House in 1765 and only 36.5 per cent in 1785, while the farmers increased from 18.5 to 28 per cent. Wealthy men occupied about two-fifths of the seats in the pre-Revolutionary period, one-sixth after the war, while delegates with moderate property, who had previously formed only one-fifth of the total, now comprised one-third. The yeoman farmer class, though still lacking a majority, had doubled in numbers, while members of the old ruling families, in turn, saw their strength halved. By comparison with the northern states the shift of power was decidedly less radical, but the change was considerable. It was made more obvious, incidentally, by the great contrast between the postwar House of Delegates and the postwar Senate, for the large majority of the Senators were wealthy merchants, lawyers, and planters, who fought bitterly with the popular branch.

The planter class of Virginia, like that of Maryland, did not intend that the Revolution should encourage democracy, but it was unable to prevent some erosion of its power. The great landowners still controlled the lower house, though their strength was reduced from 60 per cent to 50 per cent, while that of ordinary farmers rose from perhaps 13 per cent in 1773 to 26 per cent in 1785. An important change was the decline in the number of wealthy members, who now held one-quarter instead of one-half of the seats. Power thus shifted into the hands of the lesser planters, the well-to-do rather than the wealthy. Meanwhile, men with moderate properties doubled their share, almost equaling in number the wealthy Burgesses. Similarly the sons of the First Families lost their commanding position, while an even larger fraction of delegates were of humble origins. The general magnitude of the change is suggested by the decline in the median property held from 1,800 acres to about 1,100, and from forty slaves to twenty.

Thus, although the planter class retained control of the Burgesses, the people were now sending well-to-do rather than wealthy men, and at least one out of four representatives was an ordinary citizen. A roll call of the House would still recite the familiar names of many elite families, but it would also pronounce some never heard before. The alteration in the composition of the Virginia legislature undoubtedly sprang in part from the growing influence of westerners, for counties beyond the Blue Ridge sent many more representatives in 1785 than before the war, while the representation from the Piedmont also increased in size. However, the same shift downward also occurred within the older counties, those which had been represented in 1773. If we eliminate from consideration all of the newly formed counties, we find that delegates with moderate property increased from 13.5 per cent to 23 per cent, and that wealthy ones declined from 48 to 30 per cent, while the proportion of farmers rose from 13 to about 25 per cent.

The South Carolina constitution of 1778 is noted as an expression of conservatism. Its conservatism, however, was much more evident with respect to the Senate than to the House of Representatives, which was now nearly four times as large. Although the eastern upper class refused to grant westerners as many seats in the House as were warranted by their population, the upcountry did increase its share from not more than 6 or 8 per cent (depending on one's definition of where the upcountry started) to nearly 40 per cent. The urban upper class of merchants, lawyers, and doctors dropped to 20 per cent of the total membership in 1785, as compared to 36 per cent in 1765. The agricultural interest greatly increased its influence, the principal gain being made by farmers rather than by planters. A significant change was a reduction in the strength of wealthy representatives, who made up four-fifths of those whose property is known in 1765 and but one-third twenty years later. The pre-Revolutionary House of Commons seems to have contained not a single man of moderate property, but the postwar representatives included more than fifty such—probably over 30 per cent of the membership. The median acreage held by the 1765 members was certainly over 2,000 and probably a majority owned over 100 slaves each. The lack of tax records makes it impossible to determine what land the 1785 representatives held, but they obviously owned much less; while the median number of slaves was about twenty-five. The scarcity of such records as well as of genealogies and other historical materials also makes it exceedingly difficult to identify any but fairly prominent men. This situation in itself lends significance to the fact that whereas before the Revolution the desired information is available for seven out of eight representatives and even for over two-thirds of their parents, data are incomplete concerning 30 per cent of the postwar delegates and most of their parents. Equally significant is the different social make-up of the two bodies. The long-established upper class of the province controlled half of the 1765 house, but less than one-fourth of the 1785 legislature. Although most of the representatives were well-to-do, the house was no longer an exclusively aristocratic body, but contained a sizable element of democracy. It should be pointed out that South Carolina was peculiar in that the change in the House was due almost entirely to the admission of new delegates from the west. In those parishes which elected representatives both before and after the war, the proportion of wealthy delegates decreased very slightly, while that of men with moderate property rose from zero to between 7 and 14 per cent.

All of the six legislatures had been greatly changed as a result of the Revolution. The extent of that change varied from moderate in Virginia and Maryland to radical in New Hampshire and New Jersey, but everywhere the same process occurred. Voters were choosing many more representatives than before the war, and the newly settled areas gained considerably in representatives. The locus of power had shifted from the coast into the interior. Voters were ceasing to elect only men of wealth and family. The proportion of the wealthy in these legislatures dropped from 46 per cent to 22 per cent; members of the prominent old families declined from 40 per cent to 16 per cent. Most of these came from the long-established towns or commercial farm areas. Of course many men who were well-to-do or better continued to gain office, but their share decreased from four-fifths to just one-half. Even in Massachusetts the percentage of legislators who were wealthy or well-to-do dropped from 50 per cent in 1765 to 21.5 per cent in 1784.[3]

Table 1

Economic Status of the Representatives[4]

	N.H., N.Y., and N.J.		Md., Va., and S.C.	
	Prewar (*percentages*)	*Postwar* (*percentages*)	*Prewar* (*percentages*)	*Postwar* (*percentages*)
Wealthy	36	12	52	28
Well-to-do	47	26	36	42
Moderate	17	62	12	30
Merchants & lawyers	43	18	22.5	17
Farmers	23	55	12	26

3. Economic Status of Massachusetts Representatives (percentages)

	1765	1784 *duplicate towns*	1784 *total*
wealthy	17	8	6.5
well-to-do	33	17	15
moderate	40	55	51.5
unknown	10	20	27

Probably most of those whose property is unknown had only moderate incomes. Similarly, the proportion of men from prominent old families dropped from 22 per cent to 6 per cent, college-educated delegates from 27 per cent to 9 per cent, and representatives whose fathers were well-to-do from 30 per cent to 10 per cent, the change being greatest in the new towns but occurring everywhere.

4. This table analyzes the property of about 900 representatives. The economic status of 85 per cent was discovered with reasonable certainty. Most of the rest were dealt with by informed guesswork. No one was admitted to the wealthy category unless their property was certainly known. Lawyers were

Significantly, the people more and more often chose ordinary yeomen or artisans. Before the Revolution fewer than one out of five legislators had been men of that sort; after Independence they more than doubled their strength, achieving in fact a majority in the northern houses and constituting over 40 per cent generally. The magnitude of the change is suggested by the fact that the legislators of the postwar South owned only about one-half as much property as their predecessors. Also suggestive is the great increase in the proportion of men of humble origin, which seems to have more than doubled. Therefore men who were or had once been a part of the *demos* totaled about two-thirds of the whole number of representatives. Clearly, the voters had ceased to confine themselves to an elite, but were selecting instead men like themselves. The tendency to do so had started during the colonial period, especially in the North, and had now increased so dramatically as almost to revolutionize the legislatures. The process occurred also in those areas which were represented both before and after the Revolution, as compared with those which were allowed to choose delegates for the first time after the war. Although a similar change may not have taken place in Connecticut or Rhode Island, it surely did so in the states of Pennsylvania, Delaware, North Carolina, and Georgia, which have not been analyzed here.

assumed to be well-to-do, for almost all of them were. Merchants were also considered well-to-do if they lived in an important urban center, but inland shopkeepers were not. Doctors and judges were distributed on similar principles. Artisans were almost always of moderate property. Farmers and those whose occupation was unknown composed the two largest groups. Those who came from the inland, semi-subsistence communities were almost never well-to-do, the exceptions being conspicuous men, so that if nothing was discovered about them they were almost certainly of moderate means. On the other hand, those who lived in the well-developed commercial farm areas were often well-to-do, so they were not assigned to any category unless other information was available. The basis for this procedure was derived from extensive study of property holdings as discussed in my *Social Structure of Revolutionary America*. By such an analysis the proportion of unknowns was reduced to 3.33 per cent, most of whom were probably of moderate property. They are eliminated in the table. Percentages for occupation are less accurate, especially those for the postwar South.

Table 2

Economic Status of the Representatives from Pre-Revolutionary Districts

	N.H., N.Y., and N.J.		Md., Va., and S.C.	
	Prewar	*Postwar*	*Prewar*	*Postwar*
Wealthy	35	18	50	38
Well-to-do	45	37	38	42
Moderate	20	45	12	20
Merchants & lawyers	41	24	22	18.5
Farmers	25	50	12	22

The significance of the change may be more obvious to historians than it was to men of the Revolutionary era. Adherents of the Whig philosophy deplored the trend. They continued to demand a government run by the elite in which the democratic element, while admitted, was carefully checked. Such men were basically conservatives who conceived themselves as struggling for liberty against British tyranny, and who did not propose to substitute a democratical tyranny for a monarchical one. The states, observed a philosophical New Englander in 1786, were "worse governed" than they had been because "men of sense and property have lost much of their influence by the popular spirit of the war." The people had once respected and obeyed their governors, senators, judges, and clergy. But "since the war, blustering ignorant men, who started into notice during the troubles and confusion of that critical period, have been attempting to push themselves into office."

On the other hand, democratic spokesmen now rose to defend this new government by the people. A writer in a Georgia newspaper rejoiced in 1789 that the state's representatives were "taken from a class of citizens who hitherto have thought it more for their interest to be contented with a humbler walk in life," and hoped that men of large property would not enter the state, for Georgia had "perhaps the most *compleat* democracy in the known world," which could be preserved only by economic equality. In Massachusetts as early as 1775 "Democritus" urged the voters to "choose men that have learnt to get their living by honest industry, and that will be content with as small an income as the generality of those who pay them for their service. If you would be well represented," he continued, "choose a man in middling circumstances as to worldly estate, if he has got it by his industry so much the better, he knows the wants of the poor, and can judge pretty well what the community can bear of public burdens, if he be a man of good common understanding." "A Farmer" in Connecticut boldly declared it a maxim that the people usually judged rightly, insisted that politics was not so difficult but that common sense could comprehend it, and argued that every freeman could be a legislator.

The change in men might be deprecated or applauded, but it could not be denied, and some found it good. To Jedidiah Morse the government of Virginia still seemed to be "oligarchical or aristocratical," but to a Virginian a revolution had taken place. The newly chosen House of Burgesses, wrote Roger Atkinson in 1776, was admirable. It was "composed of men not quite so well dressed, nor so politely educated, nor so highly born as some Assemblies I have formerly seen," yet on the whole he liked it better. "They are the People's men (and the People in general are right). They are plain and of consequence less disguised, but I believe to the full as honest, less intriguing, more sincere. I wish the People may always have Virtue enough and Wisdom enough to chuse such plain men." Democracy, for a moment at least, seemed to have come to Virginia.

Foundations of the American Republic

The American Science of Politics

by Gordon S. Wood

Almost two hundred years ago, at a time when kings and nobles ruled everywhere else, Americans founded the first great republic of modern history. The idea of a nation conceived on the basis of popular sovereignty was perilously novel for its time, and has yet to prove its practicability in most parts of today's world. Here, in a chapter from his larger study, The Creation of the American Republic, *Gordon S. Wood describes the new science of politics and government as it evolved in the Revolutionary and post-Revolutionary eras.*

The Revolution had not transformed America's economic system—that had to wait for the Industrial Revolution of the nineteenth century—nor did it turn the social structure upside down. The most creative consequences of the Revolution were political—the reconstruction of authority in the states and the creation of an effective national government. British withdrawal forced Americans to think critically about appropriate forms of government. First, each of the new states adopted republican constitutions, acts which in themselves proved profoundly revolutionary. They established new rules for politics which officeholders and other citizens would thereafter have to observe. As colonists,

Americans had discovered that the British constitution offered no protection from tyranny, since Parliament enjoyed unlimited authority. Before 1776, a constitution was simply a description of the laws and forms of government that existed in a nation at any given time, and those laws and forms could be altered with ease. But Americans saw in a constitution a higher law, deriving its legitimacy from the people who sanctioned it, and placing limitations on the rulers. Moreover, they were convinced that a constitution should not be easily changed.

Just as Americans groped toward new conceptions of constitutionality, so too they worked out through trial and error new forms of government they hoped would provide a fair chance to reconcile liberty with public order. At first, legislatures dominated the new state governments, but Americans quickly discovered the dangers of legislative despotism and erected safeguards against it through a complex series of checks and balances. Similarly, Americans initially identified the preservation of liberty with political power lodged close to the people, in state and local governments. But a decade's experience under weak central government and the Articles of Confederation convinced many of the need to shift some authority away from the states to a strengthened national government.

The ultimate aim, Wood argues, was to guarantee a maximum of meaningful liberty to the individual. A critical study of the American political experience since 1789 will allow students to decide whether the Founding Fathers were justified in their belief that by fragmenting power, by placing limits on government, and by freeing individuals to pursue private interests, citizens would be able to attain the goal of ordered liberty.

1. *Democratic Republics*

Undoubtedly John Taylor was right about the source of the new principles of politics discovered during the Revolutionary era.

From *The Creation of the American Republic, 1776–1787* (Chapel Hill: University of North Carolina Press, for The Institute of Early American History and Culture, 1969), pp. 593–615. Reprinted by permission; footnotes omitted.

The creation of a new political theory was not as much a matter of deliberation as it was a matter of necessity. The blending of diverse views and clashing interests into the new federal system, Madison told Jefferson in October 1787, was nothing "less than a miracle." Although no one person had done so much to create the Constitution, Madison generously but rightly stressed to the end of his life that it was not "the offspring of a single brain" but "the work of many heads and many hands." The formation of the new government, as Franklin observed to a European correspondent in 1788, was not like a game of chess, methodically and consciously played. It was more like a game of dice, with so many players, "their ideas so different, their prejudices so strong and so various, and their particular interests, independent of the general, seeming so opposite, that not a move can be made that is not contested." Yet somehow out of all these various moves the Constitution had emerged, and with it had emerged not only "a wonder and admiration" among the members of the Convention themselves, but also a growing awareness among all Americans that the Constitution had actually created a political system "so novel, so complex, and intricate" that writing about it would never cease. The Constitution had become the climax of a great revolution. "Till this period," declared Aaron Hall of New Hampshire in a 1788 oration, "the revolution in America has never appeared to me to be completed; but this is laying on the cap-stone of the great American Empire." It was not the revolution that had been intended but it was a real revolution nonetheless, marked by a momentous upheaval in the understanding of politics where the "collected wisdom of ages" was "interwoven in this form of government." "The independence of America considered merely as a separation from England, would have been a matter but of little importance," remarked Thomas Paine, "had it not been accompanied by a revolution in the principles and practise of governments." "There are some great eras," said James Wilson, "when important and very perceptible alterations take place in the situation of men and things." And America, added David Ramsay, was in the midst of one of those great eras.

Americans now told themselves with greater assurance than ever that they had created something remarkable in the history of politics. "The different constitutions which have been adopted by these states," observed John Stevens in 1787, "are experiments in government entirely new; they are founded upon principles peculiar to themselves." Admittedly they had not fully understood politics at the outset of the Revolution; but within a decade they believed that most of the defects of their early state constitutions had been discovered and were on the way to being remedied. And the new federal Constitution expressed all they had learned. "The government of the United States," wrote Nathaniel Chipman of Vermont in 1793, "exhibits a new scene in the political history of the world, . . . exhibits, in theory, the most beautiful system, which has yet been devised by the wisdom of man." With their governments the Americans had placed the science of politics on a footing with the other great scientific discoveries of the previous century. Their governments, said William Vans Murray, represented "the most finished political forms" in history and had "deservedly attracted the attention of all speculative minds." It was therefore important for "the cause of liberty all over the world, that they should be understood." And by the end of the 1780's and the early nineties Americans increasingly felt compelled to explain to themselves and to the world the uniqueness of what they had discovered.

Their governments were so new and so distinctive that they groped for political terms adequate to describe them. By the late 1780's Americans generally were calling their governments democracies, but peculiar kinds of democracies. America, said Murray, had established governments which were "in their principles, structure, and whole mass, purely and unalterably Democratic." The American republics, remarked John Stevens, approached "nearer to perfect democracies" than any other governments in the world. Yet democracy, as eighteenth-century political scientists generally understood the term, was not, they realized, a wholly accurate description of their new governments. They were "Democratic Republics," as Chipman called them, by which was "meant, a Representative Democracy." In *The Federalist*, Number 10, Madison called the American governments republics, as distinct from a "pure democracy" in which a small number of citizens assembled and administered the government in person. For Madison a republic had become a species of government to be classed alongside aristocracy or democracy, a distinctive form of government "in which the scheme of representation takes place." Representation—that was the key conception in unlocking an understanding of the American political system. America was, as Hamilton said, "a *representative democracy*." Only the American scheme, wrote Thomas Paine, was based "wholly on the system of representation," and thus it was "the only real republic in character and practise, that now exists." The American polity was "representation ingrafted upon democracy," creating "a system of government capable of embracing and confederating all the various interests and every extent of territory and population."

2. *The Pervasiveness of Representation*

It was representation then—"the delegation of the government . . . ," said Madison, "to a small number of citizens elected by the rest"—that explained the uniqueness of the American polities. "The *principle* on which all the American governments are founded," wrote Samuel Williams of Vermont, "is *representation*." No other nation, said Charles Pinckney of South Carolina, so enjoyed the right of self-government, "where the true principles of representation are understood and practised, and where all authority flows from and returns at stated periods to, the people." Representation, said Edmund Randolph, was "a thing not understood in its full extent till very lately." Neither the Israelites nor the ancients had properly comprehended the uses of representation—"a very excellent modern improvement in the management of republics," said Samuel Langdon of New Hampshire. "It is surprising, indeed," said Wilson, "how very imperfectly, at this day, the doctrine of representation is understood in Europe. Even Great Britain, which boasts a superior knowledge of the subject, and is generally supposed to have carried it into practice, falls far short of its true and genuine principles." Representation, remarked Wilson, barely touched the English constitution, since it was not immediately or remotely the source of executive or judicial power. Even in the legislature representation was not "a pervading principle," but actually was only a check, confined to the Commons. The Lords acted either under hereditary right or under an authority granted by the prerogative of the Crown and hence were "not the representatives of the people." The world, it seemed, had "left to America the glory and happiness of forming a government where representation shall at once supply the basis and the cement of the superstructure." "In America," said Williams, "every thing tended to introduce, and to complete the system of representation." America, wrote Madison, had created the first example of "a government wholly popular, and founded at the same time, wholly on that principle [of representation]." Americans had made their entire system from top to bottom representative, "diffusing," in Wilson's words, "this vital principle throughout all the different divisions and departments of the government." Since Americans, influenced by the implications of the developing conception of actual representation, now clearly believed that "the right of representing is conferred by the act of electing," every part of the elective governments had become representative of the people. In truth, said Madison, representation was "the pivot" on which the whole American system moved.

Although the members of the houses of representatives were perhaps the more "immediate representatives," no longer were they the full and exclusive representatives of the people. "The Senators," said Nathaniel Chipman, "are to be representatives of the people, no less, in fact, than the members of the other house."

Foreigners, noted William Vans Murray, had mistaken the division of the legislatures in America as some sort of an embodiment of an aristocracy. Even in Maryland and in the federal Constitution where the senates were indirectly elected, the upper house was derived mediately from the people. "It represents the people. It represents no particular order of men or of ranks." To those who sought to comprehend fully the integrity of the new system the senate could only be a weight in the powers of legislative deliberation, not a weight of property, of privileges, or of interests. Election by the people, not the number of chambers in the legislature, declared John Stevens, had made "our governments the most democratic that ever existed anywhere." "With us," concluded Wilson, "the power of magistrates, call them by whatever name you please, are the grants of the people."

Therefore all governmental officials, including even the executive and judicial parts of the government, were agents of the people, not fundamentally different from the people's nominal representatives in the lower houses of the legislatures. The Americans of 1776, observed Wilson, had not clearly understood the nature of their executives and judiciaries. Although the authority of their governors and judges became in 1776 as much "the child of the people" as that of the legislatures, the people could not forget their traditional colonial aversion to the executive and judiciary, and their fondness for their legislatures, which under the British monarchy had been the guardians of their rights and the anchor of their political hopes. "Even at this time," Wilson noted with annoyance, "people can scarcely devest themselves of those opposite prepossessions." The legislatures often were still called "the *people's representatives*," implying, "though probably, not avowed upon reflection," that the executive and judicial powers were not so strongly or closely connected with the people. "But it is high time," said Wilson, "that we should chastise our prejudices." The different parts of the government were functionally but not substantively different. "The executive and judicial powers are now drawn from the same source, are now animated by the same principles, and are now directed to the same ends, with the legislative authority: they who execute, and they who administer the laws, are so much the servants, and therefore as much the friends of the people, as those who make them." The entire government had become the limited agency of the sovereign people.

The pervasive Whig mistrust of power had in the years since Independence been increasingly directed not only against the traditional rulers, but also against the supposed representatives of the people, who now seemed to many to be often as distant and unrepresentative of the people's interests as Parliament once had been. "The representatives of the people, in a popular assembly," said Hamilton, "seem sometimes to fancy that they are the people themselves." The constitutional reformers seized on the people's growing suspicion of their own representatives and reversed the perspective: the houses of representatives, now no more trusted than other parts of the government, seemed to be also no more representative of the people than the other parts of the government. They had lost their exclusive role of embodying the people in the government. In fact the people did not actually participate in the government any more, as they did, for example, in the English House of Commons. The Americans had taken the people out of the government altogether. The "true distinction" of the American governments, wrote Madison in *The Federalist,* "lies *in the total exclusion of the people, in their collective capacity,* from any share" in the government. Or from a different point of view the Americans could now argue that the people participated in all branches of the government and not merely in their houses of representatives. "The whole powers of the proposed government," said Hamilton in *The Federalist,* "is to be in the hands of the representatives of the people." All parts of the government were equally responsible but limited spokesmen for the people, who remained as the absolute and perpetual sovereign, distributing bits and pieces of power to their various agents.

Confrontation with the Blackstonian concept of legal sovereignty had forced American theorists to relocate it in the people-at-large, a transference that was comprehensible only because of the peculiar experience of American politics. "Sovereignty," said James Sullivan, "must in its nature, be absolute and uncontrolable by any civil authority. . . . A subordinate sovereignty is nonsense: A subordinate, uncontrolable power is a contradiction in terms." In America this kind of sovereignty could only exist in the people themselves, who "may invest the exercise of it in whom they please; but where the power delegated by them is subordinate, or controlable by any other delegated civil power, it is not a sovereign power." Thus it was obvious that in America "there is no supreme power but what the people themselves hold." "The supreme power," said Wilson, "is in them; and in them, even when a constitution is formed, and government is in operation, the supreme power still remains." The powers of the people were thus never alienated or surrendered to a legislature. Representation, in other words, never eclipsed the people-at-large, as apparently it did in the English House of Commons. In America the people were never really represented in the English sense of the term. "A portion of their authority they, indeed, delegate; but they delegate that portion in whatever manner, in whatever measure, for whatever time, to whatever persons, and on whatever conditions they choose to fix." Such a delegation, said Sullivan, was necessarily fragmentary and provisional; "it may extend to some things and not to others or be vested for some purposes, and not for others." Only a proper understanding of this vital principle of the sovereignty of the people could make federalism intelligible. The representation of the people, as American politics in the Revolutionary era had made glaringly evident, could never be virtual, never inclusive; it was acutely actual, and always tentative and partial. "All power whatever," said John Stevens, "is vested in, and immediately derived from, the people only; the rulers are their deputies merely, and at certain short periods are removable by them: nay," he added, "the very government itself is a creature formed by themselves, and may, whenever they think it necessary, be at any time new modelled."

3. *The Equation of Rulers and Ruled*

This conception of the sovereignty of the people used to create the new federal government had at last clarified the peculiar American idea of a constitution. A constitution, as James Iredell said, was "a declaration of particular powers by the people to their representatives, for particular purposes. It may be considered as a great power of attorney, under which no power can be exercised but what is expressly given." A constitution for Americans, said Thomas Paine, was "not a thing in name only; but in fact. . . . It is the body of elements, to which you can refer, and quote article by article; and which contains . . . every thing that relates to the complete organization of a civil government, and the principles on which it shall act, and by which it shall be bound." A constitution was thus a "thing *antecedent* to a government, and a government is only the creature of a constitution." It was truly, said Wilson, the act of the people, and "in their hands it is clay in the hands of the potter: they have the right to mould, to preserve, to improve, to refine, and to furnish it as they please." Only by conceiving of a constitution as a written delimitation of the grant of power made by the people to the government was "the important distinction so well understood in America, between a Constitution established by the people and unalterable by the government, and a law established by the government and alterable by the government" rendered truly comprehensible.

In America a constitution had become, as Madison pointed out, a charter of power granted by liberty rather than, as in Europe, a charter of liberty granted by power. Magna Carta and the English Bill of Rights were not constitutions at all. They "did not," said Paine, "create and give powers to Government in the manner a constitution does." They were really only "restrictions on assumed power," bargains "which the parts of the government made with each other to divide powers, profits and privileges." "The far famed social compact between the people and their rulers," declared David Ramsay, "did not apply to the United States." "To suppose that any government can be a party in a compact with the whole people," said Paine, "is to suppose it to have existence before it can have a right to exist." In America, said Ramsay, "the sovereignty was in the people," who "deputed certain individuals as their agents to serve them in public stations agreeably to constitutions, which they prescribed for their conduct." Government, concluded Paine, "has of itself no rights; they are altogether duties."

Yet if the ancient notion of a contract was to be preserved in American thinking, then it must be a Lockean contract, one formed by the individuals of the society with each other, instead of a mutual arrangement between rulers and ruled. In most countries, declared Charles Backus in 1788, the people "have obtained a partial security of their liberties, by extorted concessions from their nobles or kings. But in America, the *People* have had an opportunity of forming a compact *betwixt themselves;* from which alone, their rulers derive all their authority to govern." This image of a social contract formed by isolated and hostile individuals was now the only contractual metaphor that comprehended American social reality. Since an American constitution could no longer be regarded as a contract between rulers and people, representing distinct and unified interests, considerations like protection and allegiance lost their relevance. "Writers on government have been anxious on the part of the people," observed Nathaniel Chipman in 1793, "to discover a consideration given for the right of protection. . . . While government was supposed to depend on a compact, not between the individuals of a people, but between the people and the rulers, this was a point of great consequence." But not any longer in America, where government was based on a compact only among the people. Obedience to the government in America followed from no such traditional consideration. The flow of authority itself was reversed, and "*consent*," which had not been the basis of magisterial authority in the past, now became "the sole obligatory principle of human government and human laws." Because of the pervasiveness of representational consent through all parts of the government, "the judgments of our courts, and the commissions constitutionally given by our governor," said John Jay, "are as valid and as binding on all our persons whom they concern, as the laws passed by our legislature." The once important distinction between magisterial authority and representative legislative authority was now obliterated. "All constitutional acts of power, whether in the executive or in the judicial department, have as much legal validity and obligation as if they proceeded from the legislature." No more revolutionary change in the history of politics could have been made: the rulers had become the ruled and the ruled the rulers.

4. *The Parceling of Power*

The American governments, wrote Samuel Williams in his *Natural and Civil History of Vermont* of 1794, "do not admit of sovereignty, nobility, or any kind of hereditary powers; but only of powers granted by the people, ascertained by written constitutions, and exercised by representation for a given time." Hence such governments "do not admit of monarchy or aristocracy; nor do they admit of what was called democracy by the ancients." The old classification of politics by the number and character of the rulers no longer made sense of American practice where "all is transacted by representation" expressed in different ways. The government in the several states thus "varies in its form; committing more or less power to a governor, senate, or house of representatives, as the circumstances of any particular state may require. As each of these branches derive their whole power from the people, are accountable to them for the use and exercise they make of it, and may be displaced by the election of others," the liberty and security of the people, as Americans had thought in

1776, no longer came from their participation in one part of the government, as the democracy balanced against the monarchy and aristocracy, "but from the responsibility, and dependence of each part of the government, upon the people."

In slightly more than two decades of polemics the Americans had destroyed the age-old conception of mixed government and had found new explanations for their polities created in 1776, explanations that rested on their expansion of the principle of representation. America had not discovered the idea of representation, said Madison, but it could "claim the merit of making the discovery the basis of unmixed and extensive republics." And their republics were now peculiarly unmixed, despite the presence of senates and governors. They could in fact intelligibly be considered to be democracies, since, as James Wilson said, "in a democracy" the supreme power "is inherent in the people, and is either exercised by themselves or their representatives." Perhaps no one earlier or better described the "new and rich discoveries in jurisprudence" Americans had made than did Wilson. The British constitution, he said, had attempted to combine and to balance the three different forms of government, but it had obviously failed. And it was left to the Americans to realize that it was "not necessary to intermix the different species of government" in order to attain perfection in politics. "We have discovered, that one of them—the best and purest—that, in which the supreme power remains with the people at large, is capable of being formed, arranged, proportioned, and organized in such a manner, as to exclude the inconveniences, and to secure the advantages of all three." The federal Constitution, said Wilson, was therefore "purely democratical," even though in its outward form it resembled the conventional mixed government: "all authority of every kind *is derived by* REPRESENTATION *from the* PEOPLE *and the* DEMOCRATIC *principle is carried into every part of the government*." The new government was in fact, incongruous as it sounded, a mixed or balanced democracy.

Americans had retained the forms of the Aristotelian schemes of government but had eliminated the substance, thus divesting the various parts of the government of their social constituents. Political power was thus disembodied and became essentially homogeneous. The division of this political power now became (in Jefferson's words) "the first principle of a good government," the "distribution of its powers into executive, judiciary, and legislative, and a sub-division of the latter into two or three branches." Separation of powers, whether describing executive, legislative, and judicial separation or the bicameral division of the legislature (the once distinct concepts now thoroughly blended), was simply a partitioning of political power, the creation of a plurality of discrete governmental elements, all detached from yet responsible to and controlled by the people, checking and balancing each other, preventing any one power from asserting itself too far. The libertarian doctrine of separation of powers was expanded and exalted by the Americans to the foremost position in their constitutionalism, premised on the belief, in John Dickinson's words, that "government must never be lodged in a single body." Enlightenment and experience had pointed out "the propriety of government being committed to such a number of great departments"—three or four, suggested Dickinson—"as can be introduced without confusion, distinct in office, and yet connected in operation." Such a "repartition" of power was designed to provide for the safety and ease of the people, since "there will be more obstructions interposed" against errors and frauds in the government. "The departments so constituted," concluded Dickinson, "may therefore be said to be balanced." But it was not a balance of "any intrinsic or constitutional properties," of any social elements, but rather only a balance of governmental functionaries without social connections, all monitored by the people who remained outside, a balanced government that worked, "although," said Wilson, "the materials, of which it is constructed, be not an assemblage of different and dissimilar kinds."

Abuse of governmental power, especially from the legislature, was now best prevented, as Madison put it in *The Federalist*,

Number 51, one of the most significant expressions of the new political thinking, "by so contriving the interior structure of the government as that its several constituent parts may, by their mutual relations, be the means of keeping each other in their proper places." Perhaps the most rigorous separation of powers could be attained, suggested Madison in a revelation of the assumptions behind the new conception of government, by having all the departments of government drawn directly from the same fountain of authority, the people, "through channels having no communication whatever with one another." However, since such a plan was probably impractical, some deviations from "the principle" were necessary. Yet every effort, emphasized Madison, should be made to keep the separate departments independent, or else they could not effectively check and balance each other. The legislature must be divided and the executive fortified with a veto in order to distribute power and guard against encroachments. Moreover, continued Madison with mounting enthusiasm, the new federal government—with its new kind of "mixed character"—possessed an immense advantage over the conventional single republics which were limited in the amount of separating and dividing of powers they could sustain. "In the compound republic of America," said Madison, "the power surrendered by the people is first divided between two distinct governments, and then the portion allotted to each subdivided among distinct and separate departments." Furthermore, the partitioning of power in America would be intensified by "the extent of country and number of people comprehended under the same government," so that "the society itself will be broken into so many parts, interests and classes of citizens, that the rights of individuals, or of the minority, will be in little danger from interested combinations of the majority."

It was an imposing conception—a kinetic theory of politics—such a crumbling of political and social interests, such an atomization of authority, such a parceling of power, not only in the governmental institutions but in the extended sphere of the society itself, creating such a multiplicity and a scattering of designs and passions, so many checks, that no combination of parts could hold, no group of evil interests could long cohere. Yet out of the clashing and checking of this diversity Madison believed the public good, the true perfection of the whole, would somehow arise. The impulses and passions would so counteract each other, so neutralize their potencies, as America's contending religious sects had done, that reason adhering in the natural aristocracy would be able to assert itself and dominate.

5. *The End of Classical Politics*

The Americans had reversed in a revolutionary way the traditional conception of politics: the stability of government no longer relied, as it had for centuries, upon its embodiment of the basic social forces of the state. Indeed, it now depended upon the prevention of the various social interests from incorporating themselves too firmly in the government. Institutional or governmental politics was thus abstracted in a curious way from its former associations with the society. But at the same time a more modern and more realistic sense of political behavior in the society itself, among the people, could now be appreciated. This revolution marked an end of the classical conception of politics and the beginning of what might be called a romantic view of politics. The eighteenth century had sought to understand politics, as it had all of life, by capturing in an integrated, ordered, changeless ideal the totality and complexity of the world—an ideal that the concept of the mixed constitution and the proportioned social hierarchy on which it rested perfectly expressed. In such an ideal there could be only potential energy, no kinetic energy, only a static equilibrium among synthetic orders, and no motion among the particular, miscellaneous parts that made up the society. By destroying this ideal Americans placed a new emphasis on the piecemeal and the concrete in politics at the expense of order and completeness. The Constitution represented both the climax and the finale of the American Enlightenment, both the fulfillment and the end of the belief that the endless variety and perplexity of society could be reduced to a simple and harmonious system. By attempting to formulate a theory of politics that would represent reality as it was, the Americans of 1787 shattered the classical Whig world of 1776.

Americans had begun the Revolution assuming that the people were a homogeneous entity in society set against the rulers. But such an assumption belied American experience, and it took only a few years of independence to convince the best American minds that distinctions in the society were "various and unavoidable," so much so that they could not be embodied in the government. Once the people were thought to be composed of various interests in opposition to one another, all sense of a graduated organic chain in the social hierarchy became irrelevant, symbolized by the increasing emphasis on the image of a social contract. The people were not an order organically tied together by their unity of interest but rather an agglomeration of hostile individuals coming together for their mutual benefit to construct a society. The Americans transformed the people in the same way that Englishmen a century earlier had transformed the rulers: they broke the connectedness of interest among them and put them at war with one another, just as seventeenth-century Englishmen had separated the interests of rulers and people and put them in opposition to each other.

As Joel Barlow noted in 1792, the word "*people*" in America had taken on a different meaning from what it had in Europe. In America it meant the whole community and comprehended every human creature in the society; in Europe, however, it meant "something else more difficult to define." "Society," said Enos Hitchcock in 1788, "is composed of individuals—they are parts of the whole." And such individuals in America were the entire society: there could be nothing else—no orders, no lords, no monarch, no magistrates in the traditional sense. "Without the distinctions of titles, families, or nobility," wrote Samuel Williams, "they acknowledged and reverenced only those distinctions which nature had made, in a diversity of talents, abilities, and virtues. There were no family interests, connexions, or estates, large enough to oppress them. There was no excessive wealth in the hands of a few, sufficient to corrupt them." The Americans were thus both equal and unequal at the same time.

> They all feel that nature has made them equal in respect to their rights; or rather that nature has given to them a common and an equal right to liberty, to property, and to safety; to justice, government, laws, religion, and freedom. They all see that nature has made them very unequal in respect to their original powers, capacities, and talents. They become united in claiming and in preserving the equality, which nature has assigned to them; and in availing themselves of the benefits, which are designed, and may be derived from the inequality, which nature has also established.

Politics in such a society could no longer be simply described as a contest between rulers and people, between institutionalized orders of the society. The political struggles would in fact be among the people themselves, among all the various groups and individuals seeking to create inequality out of their equality by gaining control of a government divested of its former identity with the society. It was this disembodiment of government from society that ultimately made possible the conception of modern politics and the eventual justification of competing parties among the people. Those who criticized such divisive jealousy and opposition among the people, said William Hornby of South Carolina in 1784, did not understand "the great change in politics, which the revolution must have necessarily produced. . . . In *these* days we are equal citizens of a DEMOCRATIC REPUBLIC, in which *jealousy* and *opposition* must naturally exist, while there exists a difference in the minds, interests, and sentiments of mankind." While few were as yet willing to justify factionalism so blatantly, many now realized with Madison that "the regulation of these various and interfering interests forms the principal task of modern legislation, and involves the spirit of party and faction in the necessary and ordinary operations of the government." Legislation in such a society could not be the transcending of the different interests but the reconciling of them. Despite Madison's lingering hope, the public good could not be an entity distinct from its parts; it was rather "the general combined interest of all the state put together, as it were, upon an average."

Under the pressure of this transformation of political thought old words and concepts shifted in emphasis and took on new meanings. Tyranny was now seen as the abuse of power by any branch of the government, even, and for some especially, by the traditional representatives of the people. "The accumulation of all powers," said Madison, "legislative, executive, and judiciary, in the same hands, whether of one, a few, or many, and whether hereditary, self-appointed, or elective, may justly be pronounced the very definition of tyranny." The separation of this governmental power, rather than simply the participation of the people in a part of the government, became the best defense of liberty. Therefore liberty, as the old Whigs had predominantly used the term—public or political liberty, the right of the people to share in the government—lost its significance for a system in which the people participated throughout.

The liberty that was now emphasized was personal or private, the protection of individual rights against all governmental encroachments, particularly by the legislature, the body which the Whigs had traditionally cherished as the people's exclusive repository of their public liberty and the surest weapon to defend their private liberties. Such liberties, like that of freedom of the press, said both Madison and Paine, were now in less danger from "any direct attacks of Power" than they were from "the silent awe of a predominant party" or "from a fear of popular resentment." The assumptions behind such charges were radically new and different from those of the Whigs of 1776: men now began to consider "the interests of society and the rights of individuals as distinct," and to regard public and private liberty as antagonistic rather than complementary. In such circumstances the aim of government, in James Iredell's words, became necessarily twofold: to provide "for the security of every individual, as well as a fluctuating majority of the people." Government was no longer designed merely to promote the collective happiness of the people, but also, as the Tories had urged in the early seventies, "to protect citizens in their personal liberty and their property" even against the public will. Indeed, Madison could now say emphatically, "Justice is the end of government. It is the end of civil society." Unless individuals and minorities were protected against the power of majorities no government could be truly free.

Because of this growing sense of discrepancy between the rights of the society and the rights of individuals and because the new federal government was designed to prevent the emergence of any "common passion" or sense of oneness among large numbers of persons "on any other principles than those of justice and the general good," comprehensible only by a natural elite, the older emphasis on public virtue existing throughout the society lost some of its thrust; and men could now argue that "*virtue*, patriotism, or love of country, never was nor never will be till men's natures are changed, a fixed, permanent principle and support of government." The problem was, as Charles Thompson lamented in 1786, that most Americans had no other "Object" than their own "individual happiness." While Thompson still hoped that the people would eventually become "sufficiently impressed with a sense of what they owe to their national character," others began recasting their thinking. As early as 1782 Jefferson told Monroe that it was ridiculous to suppose that a man should surrender himself to the state. "This would be slavery, and not that liberty which the bill of rights has made inviolable, and for the preservation of which our government has been changed." Freedom, said Jefferson, would be destroyed by "the establishment of the opinion that the state has a *perpetual* right to the services of all it's members." The aim of instilling a spartan creed in America thus began to seem more and more nonsensical. By 1785 Noah Webster was directly challenging Montesquieu's opinion that public virtue was a necessary foundation for democratic republics. Such virtue or patriotism, said Webster, could never predominate. Local attachments would always exist, self-interest was all there ever was. But under a democracy, argued Webster, a self-interested man must court the people, thus tending to make self-love coincide with the people's interest.

William Vans Murray devoted an entire chapter of his *Political Sketches,* published in 1787, to a denial of the conventional view that republicanism was dependent upon virtue. The compulsion for such arguments was obvious. America, as Murray admitted, was "in a state of refinement and opulence," and was increasingly being permeated by "luxurious habits"—characteristics which time-honored writers on politics had declared incompatible with republican virtue and simplicity, and thus foreboding signs of an inevitable declension of the state. Yet the political scientists who spouted these maxims of republicanism had never known America. "The truth is," said Murray, "Montesquieu had never study'd a free Democracy." All the notions of these "refining speculists" had come from impressions of the ancient republics which possessed only "undefined constitutions, . . . constructed in days of ignorance." The republics of antiquity had failed because they had "attempted to force the human character into distorted shapes." The American republics, on the other hand, said Murray, were built upon the realities of human nature. They were free and responsive to the people, framed so as to give "fair play" to the actions of human nature, however unvirtuous. They had been created rationally and purposefully—for the first time in history—without attempting to pervert, suppress, or ignore the evil propensities of all men. Public virtue—the "enthusiasm," as Murray called it, of a rude and simple society, the public proscription of private pursuits for luxury—had at last "found a happy substitution in the energy of true freedom, and in a just sense of civil liberty." The American governments possessed "the freedom of Democracy, without its anarchy."

Although they were "so extremely popular," wrote John Stevens, "yet the checks which have been invented (particularly in some of them) have rendered these governments capable of a degree of stability and consistency beyond what could have been expected, and which will be viewed with surprise by foreigners." Undoubtedly virtue in the people had been an essential substitute for the lack of good laws and the indispensable remedy for the traditional defects of most democratic governments. But in America where the inconveniences of the democratic form of government had been eliminated without destroying the substantial benefits of democracy—where there was introduced, said James Wilson, "into the very form of government, such particular checks and controls, as to make it advantageous even for bad men to act for the public good"—the need for a society of simple, equal, virtuous people no longer seemed so critical. America alone, wrote Murray, had united liberty with luxury and had proved "the consistency of the social nature with the political happiness of man."

Such depreciations of public virtue were still sporadic and premature, yet they represented the beginnings of a fundamental shift in thought. In place of individual self-sacrifice for the good of the state as the bond holding the republican fabric together, the Americans began putting an increasing emphasis on what they called "public opinion" as the basis of all governments. Montesquieu in his *Spirit of the Laws,* wrote Madison in 1792, had only opened up the science of politics. Governments could not be divided simply into despotisms, monarchies, and republics sustained by their "operative principles" of fear, honor, and virtue. Governments, suggested Madison, were better divided into those which derived their energy from military force, those which operated by corrupt influence, and those which relied on the will and interest of the society. While nearly all governments, including the British monarchy, rested to some extent on public opinion, only in America had public consent as the basis of government attained its greatest perfection. No government, Americans told themselves over and over, had ever before so completely set its roots in the sentiments and aims of its citizens. All the power of America's governments, said Samuel Williams, was "derived from the public opinion." America would remain free not because of any quality in its citizens of spartan self-sacrifice to some nebulous public good, but in the last analysis because of the concern each individual would have in his own self-interest and personal freedom. The really great danger to liberty in the extended republic of America, warned Madison in 1791, was that each individual may become insignificant in his own eyes—hitherto the very foundation of republican government.

Such a total grounding of government in self-interest and consent had made old-fashioned popular revolutions obsolete. Establishments whose foundations rest on the society itself, said Wilson, cannot be overturned by any alteration of the government which the society can make. The decay and eventual death of the republican body politic now seemed less inevitable. The prevailing opinion of political writers, noted Nathaniel Chipman, had been "that man is fatally incapable of forming any system which shall endure without degeneration," an opinion that appeared "to be countenanced by the experience of ages." Yet America had lighted the way to a reversal of this opinion, placing, as David Ramsay put it, "the science of politics on a footing with the other sciences, by opening it to improvements from experience, and the discoveries of future ages." Governments had never been able to adjust continually to the operations of human nature. It was "impossible," said Chipman, "to form any human institution, which should accommodate itself to every situation in progress." All previous peoples had been compelled to suffer with the same forms of government—probably unplanned and unsuitable in the first place—despite extensive changes in the nature of their societies. "The confining of a people, who have arrived at a highly improved state of society, to the forms and principles of a government, which originated in a simple, if not barbarous state of men and manners," was, said Chipman, like Chinese foot-binding, a "perversion of nature," causing an incongruity between the form of government and the character of the society that usually ended in a violent eruption, in a forceful effort to bring the government into accord with the new social temperament of the people.

However, the American republics possessed what Thomas Pownall called "a *healing principle*" built into their constitutions. Each contained "within itself," said Samuel Williams, "the means of its own *improvement*." The American governments never pretended, said Chipman, to perfection or to the exclusion of future improvements. "The idea of incorporating, in the constitution itself, a plan of reformation," enabling the people periodically and peacefully to return to first principles, as Machiavelli had urged, the Americans realized, was a totally new contribution to politics. The early state constitutions, David Ramsay admitted, possessed many defects. "But in one thing they were all perfect. They left the people in the power of altering and amending them, whenever they pleased." And the Americans had demonstrated to the world how a people could fundamentally and yet peaceably alter their forms of government. "This revolution principle—that, the sovereign power residing in the people, they may change their constitution and government whenever they please—is," said James Wilson, "not a principle of discord, rancour, or war: it is a principle of melioration, contentment, and peace." Americans had in fact institutionalized and legitimized revolution. Thereafter, they believed, new knowledge about the nature of government could be converted into concrete form without resorting to violence. Let no one, concluded Chipman, now rashly predict "that this beautiful system is, with the crazy empires of antiquity, destined to a speedy dissolution; or that it must in time, thro' the degeneracy of the people, and a corruption of its principles, of necessity give place to a system of remediless tyranny and oppression." By actually implementing the old and trite conception of the sovereignty of the people, by infusing political and even legal life into the people, Americans had created, said Wilson, "the great panacea of human politics." The illimitable progress of mankind promised by the Enlightenment could at last be made coincident with the history of a single nation. For the Americans at least, and for others if they followed, the endless cycles of history could finally be broken.

The Americans of the Revolutionary generation believed that they had made a momentous contribution to the history of politics. They had for the first time demonstrated to the world how a people could diagnose the ills of its society and work out a peaceable process of cure. They had, and what is more significant they knew they had, broken through the conceptions of political theory that had imprisoned men's minds for centuries and brilliantly reconstructed the framework for a new republican polity, a reconstruction that radically changed the future discussion of politics. The Federalists had discovered, they thought, a constitutional antidote "wholly popular" and "strictly republican" for the ancient diseases of a republican polity—an antidote that did not destroy the republican vices, but rather accepted, indeed endorsed and relied upon them. The Federalist image of a public good undefinable by factious majorities in small states but somehow capable of formulation by the best men of a large society may have been a chimera. So too perhaps was the Federalist hope for the filtration of the natural social leaders through a federal sieve into political leadership. These were partisan and aristocratic purposes that belied the Federalists' democratic language. Yet the Federalists' intellectual achievement really transcended their particular political and social intentions and became more important and more influential than they themselves anticipated. Because their ideas were so popularly based and embodied what Americans had been groping towards from the beginning of their history, the Federalists' creation could be, and eventually was, easily adopted and expanded by others with quite different interests and aims at stake, indeed, contributing in time to the destruction of the very social world they had sought to maintain. The invention of a government that was, in James Sullivan's words, "perhaps without example in the world" could not long remain a strictly Federalist achievement. "As this kind of government," wrote

Samuel Williams, "is not the same as that, which has been called monarchy, aristocracy, or democracy; as it had a conspicuous origin in America, and has not been suffered to prevail in any other part of the globe, it would be no more than just and proper, to distinguish it by its proper name, and call it, *The American System of Government*."

So piecemeal was the Americans' formulation of this system, so diverse and scattered in authorship, and so much a simple response to the pressures of democratic politics was their creation, that the originality and the theoretical consistency and completeness of their constitutional thinking have been obscured. It was a political theory that was diffusive and open-ended; it was not delineated in a single book; it was peculiarly the product of a democratic society, without a precise beginning or an ending. It was not political theory in the grand manner, but it was political theory worthy of a prominent place in the history of Western thought.

Making The Constitution

The Founding Fathers: A Reform Caucus In Action

by John P. Roche

"O Marvellous Constitution! Magic Parchment! Transforming Word! Maker, Monitor, Guardian of Mankind!"—in such poetic effusions did otherwise sober judges, lawyers, and politicians once invoke the Federal Constitution. If the Constitution was Holy Writ, as many nineteenth-century Americans seemed to believe, then the Founding Fathers who met in Philadelphia in 1787 to draft the document had done no less than put on paper God's design for governance. When a new generation of critical historians challenged the cult of constitution-worship during the Progressive Era (1900–1920) and labeled the Constitution the work of a wealthy elite determined to protect its investments, their heresy produced derision, outrage, and charges of un-Americanism. Nevertheless, Progressive historians argued that the Framers had acted out of class interests, that profit-seeking public security holders had played the "dynamic" role in the movement for the Constitution, and that the common people, unconsulted at the convention, had opposed ratification.

In the following essay John P. Roche re-examines the history of the Philadelphia meeting, steering a course between uncritical hero-worship and historical muckraking. Roche sees the Framers as practical politicians who designed a national government with which Americans might grapple effectively with major problems—defending national interests overseas, promoting growth at home, and guaranteeing security to a multiplicity of interests. At the same time, Roche insists, the Framers kept an eye on the average citizen outside the convention hall. They knew that any workable constitution would have to receive widespread public support. Acknowledging that the Framers were an elite group, Roche maintains that they were also a responsible elite, sensitive above all to the American commitment to popular government. As neither demigods nor moneygrubbers, many felt that the fate of America's republican experiment depended on whether a central government could be devised that would be strong enough to promote "the general welfare," yet not so powerful as to jeopardize either states' rights or individual liberty. It was no easy task, and the duration of their handiwork provides the best evidence of their success.

Over the last century and a half, the work of the Constitutional Convention and the motives of the Founding Fathers have been analyzed under a number of different ideological auspices. To one generation of historians, the hand of God was moving in the assembly; under a later dispensation, the dialectic (at various levels of philosophical sophistication) replaced the Deity: "relationships of production" moved into the niche previously reserved for Love of Country. Thus in counterpoint to the Zeitgeist, the Framers have undergone miraculous metamorphoses: at one time acclaimed as liberals and bold social engineers, today they appear in the guise of sound Burkean conservatives, men who in our time would subscribe to *Fortune*, look to Walter Lippmann for political theory, and chuckle patronizingly at the antics of Barry Goldwater. The implicit assumption is that if James Madison were among us, he would be President of the Ford Foundation,

From the *American Political Science Review*, LV (December 1961), 799–816. Reprinted by permission; footnotes omitted.

while Alexander Hamilton would chair the Committee for Economic Development.

The "Fathers" have thus been admitted to our best circles; the revolutionary ferocity which confiscated all Tory property in reach and populated New Brunswick with outlaws has been converted by the "Miltown School" of American historians into a benign dedication to "consensus" and "prescriptive rights." The Daughters of the American Revolution have, through the ministrations of Professors Boorstin, Hartz, and Rossiter, at last found ancestors worthy of their descendants. It is not my purpose here to argue that the "Fathers" were, in fact, radical revolutionaries; that proposition has been brilliantly demonstrated by Robert R. Palmer in his *Age of the Democratic Revolution.* My concern is with the further position that not only were they revolutionaries, but also they were democrats. Indeed, in my view, there is one fundamental truth about the Founding Fathers that *every* generation of Zeitgeisters has done its best to obscure: they were first and foremost superb democratic politicians. I suspect that in a contemporary setting, James Madison would be Speaker of the House of Representatives and Hamilton would be the *éminence grise* dominating (*pace* Theodore Sorenson or Sherman Adams) the Executive Office of the President. They were, with their colleagues, *political men*—not metaphysicians, disembodied conservatives, or Agents of History—and as recent research into the nature of American politics in the 1780s confirms, they were committed (perhaps willy-nilly) to working within the democratic framework, within a universe of public approval. Charles Beard *and* the filiopietists to the contrary notwithstanding, the Philadelphia Convention was not a College of Cardinals or a council of Platonic guardians working within a manipulative, pre-democratic framework; it was a *nationalist* reform caucus which had to operate with great delicacy and skill in a political cosmos full of enemies to achieve the one definitive goal—popular approbation.

Perhaps the time has come, to borrow Walton Hamilton's fine

phrase, to raise the Framers from immortality to mortality, to give them credit for their magnificent demonstration of the art of democratic politics. The point must be re-emphasized; they *made* history and did it within the limits of consensus. There was nothing inevitable about the future in 1787; the *Zeitgeist,* that fine Hegelian technique of begging causal questions, could only be discerned in retrospect. What they did was to hammer out a pragmatic compromise which would both bolster the "National interest" and be acceptable to the people. What inspiration they got came from their collective experience as professional politicians in a democratic society. As John Dickinson put it to his fellow delegates on August 13, "Experience must be our guide. Reason may mislead us."

In this context, let us examine the problems they confronted and the solutions they evolved. The Convention has been described picturesquely as a counterrevolutionary junta and the Constitution as a *coup d'état,* but this has been accomplished by withdrawing the whole history of the movement for constitutional reform from its true context. No doubt the goals of the constitutional elite were "subversive" to the existing political order, but it is overlooked that their subversion could only have succeeded if the people of the United States endorsed it by regularized procedures. Indubitably they were "plotting" to establish a much stronger central government than existed under the Articles, but only in the sense in which one could argue equally well that John F. Kennedy was, from 1956 to 1960, "plotting" to become President. In short, on the fundamental *procedural* level, the Constitutionalists had to work according to the prevailing rules of the game. Whether they liked it or not is a topic for spiritualists—and is irrelevant: one may be quite certain that had Washington agreed to play the De Gaulle (as the Cincinnati once urged), Hamilton would willingly have held his horse, but such fertile speculation in no way alters the actual context in which events took place.

I

When the Constitutionalists went forth to subvert the Confederation, they utilized the mechanisms of political legitimacy. And the roadblocks which confronted them were formidable. At the same time, they were endowed with certain potent political assets. The history of the United States from 1786 to 1790 was largely one of a masterful employment of political expertise by the Constitutionalists as against bumbling, erratic behavior by the opponents of reform. Effectively, the Constitutionalists had to induce the states, by democratic techniques of coercion, to emasculate themselves. To be specific, if New York had refused to join the new Union, the project was doomed; yet before New York was safely in, the reluctant state legislature had *sua sponte* to take the following steps: (1) agree to send delegates to the Philadelphia Convention; (2) provide maintenance for these delegates (these were distinct stages: New Hampshire was early in naming delegates, but did not provide for their maintenance until July); (3) set up the special *ad hoc* convention to decide on ratification; and (4) concede to the decision of the *ad hoc* convention that New York should participate. New York admittedly was a tricky state, with a strong interest in a *status quo* which permitted her to exploit New Jersey and Connecticut, but the same legal hurdles existed in every state. And at the risk of becoming boring, it must be reiterated that the *only* weapon in the Constitutionalist arsenal was an effective mobilization of public opinion.

The group which undertook this struggle was an interesting amalgam of a few dedicated nationalists with the self-interested spokesmen of various parochial bailiwicks. The Georgians, for example, wanted a strong central authority to provide military protection for their huge, underpopulated state against the Creek Confederacy; Jerseymen and Connecticuters wanted to escape from economic bondage to New York; the Virginians hoped to establish a system which would give that great state its rightful place in the councils of the republic. The dominant figures in the politics of these states therefore cooperated in the call for the Convention. In other states, the thrust towards national reform was taken up by opposition groups who added the "national interest" to their weapons system; in Pennsylvania, for instance, the group fighting to revise the Constitution of 1776 came out four-square behind the Constitutionalists, and in New York, Hamilton and the Schuyler *ambiance* took the same tack against George Clinton. There was, of course, a large element of personality in the affair: there is reason to suspect that Patrick Henry's opposition to the Convention and the Constitution was founded on his conviction that Jefferson was behind both, and a close study of local politics elsewhere would surely reveal that others supported the Constitution for the simple (and politically quite sufficient) reason that the "wrong" people were against it.

To say this is not to suggest that the Constitution rested on a foundation of impure or base motives. It is rather to argue that in politics there are no immaculate conceptions and that in the drive for a stronger general government, motives of all sorts played a part. Few men in the history of mankind have espoused a view of the "common good" or "public interest" that militated against their private status; even Plato with all his reverence for disembodied reason managed to put philosophers on top of the pile. Thus it is not surprising that a number of diversified private interests joined to push the nationalist public interest; what would have been surprising was the absence of such a pragmatic united front. And the fact remains that, however motivated, these men did demonstrate a willingness to compromise their parochial interests in behalf of an ideal which took shape before their eyes and under their ministrations.

As Stanley Elkins and Eric McKitrick have suggested in a perceptive essay, what distinguished the leaders of the Constitutionalist caucus from their enemies was a "Continental" approach to political, economic, and military issues. To the extent that they shared an institutional base of operations, it was the Continental

Congress (thirty-nine of the delegates to the Federal Convention had served in Congress), and this was hardly a locale which inspired respect for the state governments. Robert de Jouvenal observed French politics half a century ago and noted that a revolutionary Deputy had more in common with a non-revolutionary Deputy than he had with a revolutionary non-Deputy; similarly one can surmise that membership in the Congress under the Articles of Confederation worked to establish a continental frame of reference, that a Congressman from Pennsylvania and one from South Carolina would share a universe of discourse which provided them with a conceptual common denominator *vis à vis* their respective state legislatures. This was particularly true with respect to external affairs: the average state legislator was probably about as concerned with foreign policy then as he is today, but Congressmen were constantly forced to take the broad view of American prestige, were compelled to listen to the reports of Secretary John Jay and to the dispatches and pleas from their frustrated envoys in Britain, France, and Spain. From considerations such as these, a "Continental" ideology developed which seems to have demanded a revision of our domestic institutions primarily on the ground that only by invigorating our general government could we assume our rightful place in the international arena. Indeed, an argument with great force—particularly since Washington was its incarnation—urged that our very survival in the Hobbesian jungle of world politics depended upon a reordering and strengthening of our national sovereignty.

Note that I am not endorsing the "Critical Period" thesis; on the contrary, Merrill Jensen seems to me quite sound in his view that for most Americans, engaged as they were in self-sustaining agriculture, the "Critical Period" was not particularly critical. In fact, the great achievement of the Constitutionalists was their ultimate success in convincing the elected representatives of a majority of the white male population that change was imperative. A small group of political leaders with a Continental vision and essentially a consciousness of the United States' *inter-*

national impotence, provided the matrix of the movement. To their standard other leaders rallied with their own parallel ambitions. Their great assets were (1) the presence in their caucus of the one authentic American "father figure," George Washington, whose prestige was enormous; (2) the energy and talent of their leadership (in which one must include the towering intellectuals of the time, John Adams and Thomas Jefferson, despite their absence abroad), and their communications "network," which was far superior to anything on the opposition side; (3) the preemptive skill which made "their" issue The Issue and kept the locally oriented opposition permanently on the defensive; and (4) the subjective consideration that these men were spokesmen of a new and compelling credo: *American* nationalism, that ill-defined but nonetheless potent sense of collective purpose that emerged from the American Revolution.

Despite great institutional handicaps, the Constitutionalists managed in the mid-1780's to mount an offensive which gained momentum as years went by. Their greatest problem was lethargy, and paradoxically, the number of barriers in their path may have proved an advantage in the long run. Beginning with the initial battle to get the Constitutional Convention called and delegates appointed, they could never relax, never let up the pressure. In practical terms, this meant that the local "organizations" created by the Constitutionalists were perpetually in movement building up their cadres for the next fight. (The word organization has to be used with great caution: a political organization in the United States—as in contemporary England—generally consisted of a magnate and his following, or a coalition of magnates. This did not necessarily mean that it was "undemocratic" or "aristocratic," in the Aristotelian sense of the word: while a few magnates such as the Livingstons could draft their followings, most exercised their leadership without coercion on the basis of popular endorsement. The absence of organized opposition did not imply the impossibility of competition any more than low public participation in elections necessarily indicated an undemocratic suffrage.)

The Constitutionalists got the jump on the "opposition" (a collective noun: oppositions would be more correct) at the outset with the demand for a Convention. Their opponents were caught in an old political trap: they were not being asked to approve any specific program of reform, but only to endorse a meeting to discuss and recommend needed reforms. If they took a hard line at the first stage, they were put in the position of glorifying the *status quo* and of denying the need for *any* changes. Moreover, the Constitutionalists could go to the people with a persuasive argument for "fair play"—"How can you condemn reform before you know precisely what is involved?" Since the state legislatures obviously would have the final say on any proposals that might emerge from the Convention, the Constitutionalists were merely reasonable men asking for a chance. Besides, since they did not make any concrete proposals at that stage, they were in a position to capitalize on every sort of generalized discontent with the Confederation.

Perhaps because of their poor intelligence system, perhaps because of over-confidence generated by the failure of all previous efforts to alter the Articles, the opposition awoke too late to the dangers that confronted them in 1787. Not only did the Constitutionalists manage to get every state but Rhode Island (where politics was enlivened by a party system reminiscent of the "Blues" and the "Greens" in the Byzantine Empire) to appoint delegates to Philadelphia, but when the results were in, it appeared that they dominated the delegations. Given the apathy of the opposition, this was a natural phenomenon: in an ideologically nonpolarized political atmosphere those who get appointed to a special committee are likely to be the men who supported the movement for its creation. Even George Clinton, who seems to have been the first opposition leader to awake to the possibility of trouble, could not prevent the New York legislature from appointing Alexander Hamilton—though he did have the foresight to send two of his henchmen to dominate the delegation. Incidentally, much has been made of the fact that the delegates to

Philadelphia were not elected by the people; some have adduced this fact as evidence of the "undemocratic" character of the gathering. But put in the context of the time, this argument is wholly specious: the central government under the Articles was considered a creature of the component states and in all the states but Rhode Island, Connecticut and New Hampshire, members of the national Congress were chosen by the state legislatures. This was not a consequence of elitism or fear of the mob; it was a logical extension of states' rights doctrine to guarantee that the national institution did not end-run the state legislatures and make direct contact with the people.

II

With delegations safely named, the focus shifted to Philadelphia. While waiting for a quorum to assemble, James Madison got busy and drafted the so-called Randolph or Virginia Plan with the aid of the Virginia delegation. This was a political masterstroke. Its consequence was that once business got underway, the framework of discussion was established on Madison's terms. There was no interminable argument over agenda; instead the delegates took the Virginia Resolutions—"just for purposes of discussion"—as their point of departure. And along with Madison's proposals, many of which were buried in the course of the summer, went his major premise: a new start on a Constitution rather than piecemeal amendment. This was not necessarily revolutionary—a little exegesis could demonstrate that a new Constitution might be formulated as "amendments" to the Articles of Confederation—but Madison's proposal that this "lump sum" amendment go into effect after approval by nine states (the Articles required unanimous state approval for any amendment) was thoroughly subversive.

Standard treatments of the Convention divide the delegates into "nationalists" and "states' righters" with various improvised shadings ("moderate nationalists," etc.), but these are *a posteriori* categories which obfuscate more than they clarify. What is striking to one who analyzes the Convention as a case-study in democratic politics is the lack of clear-cut ideological divisions in the Convention. Indeed, I submit that the evidence—Madison's *Notes*, the correspondence of the delegates, and debates on ratification—indicates that this was a remarkably homogeneous body on the ideological level. Yates and Lansing, Clinton's two chaperones for Hamilton, left in disgust on July 10. (Is there anything more tedious than sitting through endless disputes on matters one deems fundamentally misconceived? It takes an iron will to spend a hot summer as an ideological *agent provocateur.*) Luther Martin, Maryland's bibulous narcissist, left on September 4 in a huff when he discovered that others did not share his self-esteem; others went home for personal reasons. But the hard core of delegates accepted a grinding regimen throughout the attrition of a Philadelphia summer precisely because they shared the Constitutionalist goal.

Basic differences of opinion emerged, of course, but these were not ideological; they were *structural*. If the so-called "states' rights" group had not accepted the fundamental purposes of the Convention, they could simply have pulled out and by doing so have aborted the whole enterprise. Instead of bolting, they returned day after day to argue and to compromise. An interesting symbol of this basic homogeneity was the initial agreement on secrecy: these professional politicians did not want to become prisoners of publicity; they wanted to retain that freedom of maneuver which is only possible when men are not forced to take public stands in the preliminary stages of negotiation. There was no legal means of binding the tongues of the delegates: at any stage in the game a delegate with basic principled objections to the emerging project could have taken the stump (as Luther Martin did after his exit) and denounced the convention to the skies. Yet Madison did not even inform Thomas Jefferson in Paris of the course of the deliberations and available correspondence indicates that the delegates generally observed the injunction.

Secrecy is certainly uncharacteristic of any assembly marked by strong ideological polarization. This was noted at the time: the *New York Daily Advertiser*, August 14, 1787, commented that the ". . . profound secrecy hitherto observed by the Convention [we consider] a happy omen, as it demonstrates that the spirit of party on any great and essential point cannot have arisen to any height."

Commentators on the Constitution who have read *The Federalist* in lieu of reading the actual debates have credited the Fathers with the invention of a sublime concept called "Federalism." Unfortunately *The Federalist* is probative evidence for only one proposition: that Hamilton and Madison were inspired propagandists with a genius for retrospective symmetry. Federalism as the theory is generally defined, was an improvisation which was later promoted into a political theory. Experts on "federalism" should take to heart the advice of David Hume, who warned in his *Of the Rise and Progress of the Arts and Sciences* that ". . . there is no subject in which we must proceed with more caution than in [history], lest we assign causes which never existed and reduce what is merely contingent to stable and universal principles." In any event the final balance in the Constitution between the states and the nation must have come as a great disappointment to Madison, while Hamilton's unitary views are too well known to need elucidation.

It is indeed astonishing how those who have glibly designated James Madison the "father" of Federalism have overlooked the solid body of fact which indicates that he shared Hamilton's quest for a unitary central government. To be specific, they have avoided examining the clear import of the Madison–Virginia Plan, and have disregarded Madison's dogged inch-by-inch retreat from the bastions of centralization. The Virginia Plan envisioned a unitary national government effectively freed from and dominant over the states. The lower house of the national legislature was to be elected directly by the people of the states with membership proportional to population. The upper house was to be selected by the lower and the two chambers would elect the executive and choose the judges. The national government would be thus cut completely loose from the states.

The structure of the general government was freed from state control in a truly radical fashion, but the scope of the authoirty of the national sovereign as Madison initially formulated it was breathtaking—it was a formulation worthy of the Sage of Malmesbury himself. The national legislature was to be empowered to disallow the acts of state legislatures, and the central government was vested, in addition to the powers of the nation under the Articles of Confederation, with plenary authority wherever ". . . the separate States are incompetent or in which the harmony of the United States may be interrupted by the exercise of individual legislation." Finally, just to lock the door against state intrusion, the national Congress was to be given the power to use military force on recalcitrant states. This was Madison's "model" of an ideal national government, though it later received little publicity in *The Federalist*.

The interesting thing was the reaction of the Convention to this militant program for a strong autonomous central government. Some delegates were startled, some obviously leery of so comprehensive a project of reform, but nobody set off any fireworks and nobody walked out. Moreover, in the two weeks that followed, the Virginia Plan received substantial endorsement *en principe;* the initial temper of the gathering can be deduced from the approval "without debate or dissent," on May 31, of the Sixth Resolution which granted Congress the authority to disallow state legislation ". . . contravening *in its opinion* the Articles of Union." Indeed, an amendment was included to bar states from contravening national treaties.

The Virginia Plan may therefore be considered, in ideological terms, as the delegates' Utopia, but as the discussions continued and became more specific, many of those present began to have second thoughts. After all, they were not residents of Utopia or guardians in Plato's Republic who could simply impose a philosophical ideal on subordinate strata of the population. They were practical politicians in a democratic society, and no matter what their private dreams might be, they had to take home an acceptable package and defend it—and their own political futures—against predictable attack. On June 14 the breaking point between dream and reality took place. Apparently realizing that under the Virginia Plan, Massachusetts, Virginia, and Pennsylvania could virtually dominate the national government—and probably appreciating that to sell this program to "the folks back home" would be impossible—the delegates from the small states dug in their heels and demanded time for a consideration of alternatives. One gets a graphic sense of the inner politics from John Dickinson's reproach to Madison: "You see the consequences of pushing things too far. Some of the members from the small States wish for two branches in the General Legislature and are friends to a good National Government; but we would sooner submit to a foreign power than . . . be deprived of an equality of suffrage in both branches of the Legislature, and thereby be thrown under the domination of the large States."

The bare outline of the *Journal* entry for Tuesday, June 14, is suggestive to anyone with extensive experience in deliberative bodies. "It was moved by Mr. Patterson [*sic*, Paterson's name was one of those consistently mispelled by Madison and everybody else] seconded by Mr. Randolph that the further consideration of the report from the Committee of the whole House [endorsing the Virginia Plan] be postponed til tomorrow. and before the question for postponement was taken. It was moved by Mr. Randolph seconded by Mr. Patterson that the House adjourn." The House adjourned by obvious prearrangement of the two principals: since the preceding Saturday when Brearley and Paterson of New Jersey had announced their fundamental discontent with the representational features of the Virginia Plan, the informal pressure had certainly been building up to slow down the steamroller. Doubtless there were extended arguments at the Indian Queen between Madison and Paterson, the latter insisting that events were moving rapidly towards a probably disastrous conclusion, towards a political suicide pact. Now the process of accommodation was put into action smoothly—and wisely, given the character and strength of the doubters. Madison had the votes, but this was one of those situations where the enforcement of mechanical majoritarianism could easily have destroyed the objectives of the majority: the Constitutionalists were in quest of a qualitative as well as a quantitative consensus. This was hardly from deference to local Quaker custom; it was a political imperative if they were to attain ratification.

III

According to the standard script, at this point the "states' rights" group intervened in force behind the New Jersey Plan, which has been characteristically portrayed as a reversion to the *status quo* under the Articles of Confederation with but minor modifications. A careful examination of the evidence indicates that only in a marginal sense is this an accurate description. It is true that the New Jersey Plan put the states back into the institutional picture, but one could argue that to do so was a recognition of political reality rather than an affirmation of states' rights. A serious case can be made that the advocates of the New Jersey Plan, far from being ideological addicts of states' rights, intended to substitute for the Virginia Plan a system which would both retain strong national power and have a chance of adoption in the states. The leading spokesman for the project asserted quite clearly that his views were based more on counsels of expediency than on principle; said Paterson on June 16: "I came here not to speak my own sentiments, but the sentiments of those who sent me. Our object is not such a Governmt. as may be best in itself, but such a one as our Constituents have authorized us to prepare, and as they will approve." This is Madison's version; in Yates's transcription, there is a crucial sentence following the remarks above: "I believe that a little practical virtue is to be preferred to the finest theoretical principles, which cannot be carried into effect." In his preliminary speech on June 9, Paterson had stated ". . . to the public mind we must accommodate ourselves," and in his notes for this and his later effort as well, the emphasis is the same. The *structure* of government under the Articles should be retained:

2. Because it accords with the Sentiments of the People

   [Proof:]
   1. Coms. [Commissions from state legislatures defining the jurisdiction of the delegates]
   2. News-papers—Political Barometer. Jersey never would have sent Delegates under the first [Virginia] Plan—

   Not here to sport Opinions of my own. Wt. [What] can be done. A little practicable Virtue preferrable to Theory.

This was a defense of political acumen, not of states' rights. In fact, Paterson's notes of his speech can easily be construed as an argument for attaining the substantive objectives of the Virginia Plan by a sound political route, *i.e.*, pouring the new wine in the old bottles. With a shrewd eye, Paterson queried:

Will the Operation and Force of the [central] Govt. depend upon the mode of Representn.—No—it will depend upon the Quantum of Power lodged in the leg. ex. and judy. Departments—Give [the existing] Congress the same Powers that you intend to give the two Branches, [under the Virginia Plan] and I apprehend they will act with as much Propriety and more Energy. . . .

In other words, the advocates of the New Jersey Plan concentrated their fire on what they held to be the *political liabilities* of the Virginia Plan—which were matters of institutional structure—rather than on the proposed scope of national authority. Indeed, the Supremacy Clause of the Constitution first saw the light of day in Paterson's Sixth Resolution; the New Jersey Plan contemplated the use of military force to secure compliance with national law; and finally Paterson made clear his view that under either the Virginia or the New Jersey systems, the general government would ". . . act on individuals and not on states." From the states' rights viewpoint, this was heresy: the fundament of that doctrine was the proposition that any central government had as its constituents the states, not the people, and could only reach the people through the agency of the state government.

Paterson then reopened the agenda of the Convention, but he did so within a distinctly nationalist framework. Paterson's position was one favoring a strong central government in principle, but opposing one which in fact *put the big states in the saddle.* (The Virginia Plan, for all its abstract merits, did very well by Virginia.) As evidence for this speculation there is a curious and intriguing proposal among Paterson's preliminary drafts of the New Jersey Plan:

> Whereas it is necessary in Order to form the People of the U. S. of America in to a Nation, that the States should be consolidated, by which means all the Citizens thereof will become equally intitled to and will equally participate in the same Privileges and Rights . . . it is therefore resolved, that all the Lands contained within the Limits of each state individually, and of the U. S. generally be considered as constituting one Body or Mass, and be divided into thirteen or more integral parts.
>
> Resolved, That such Divisions or integral Parts shall be styled Districts.

This makes it sound as though Paterson was prepared to accept a strong unified central government along the lines of the Virginia Plan if the existing states were eliminated. He may have gotten the idea from his New Jersey colleague Judge David Brearley, who on June 9 had commented that the only remedy to the dilemma over representation was ". . . that a map of the U. S. be spread out, that all the existing boundaries be erased, and that a new partition of the whole be made into 13 equal parts." According to Yates, Brearley added at this point, ". . . then a government on the present [Virginia Plan] system will be just."

This proposition was never pushed—it was patently unrealistic—but one can appreciate its purpose: it would have separated the men from the boys in the large-state delegations. How attached would the Virginians have been to their reform principles if Virginia were to disappear as a component geographical unit (the largest) for representational purposes? Up to this point, the the Virginians had been in the happy position of supporting high ideals with that inner confidence born of knowledge that the "public interest" they endorsed would nourish their private interest. Worse, they had shown little willingness to compromise. Now the delegates from the small states announced that they were unprepared to be offered up as sacrificial victims to a "national interest" which reflected Virginia's parochial ambition. Caustic Charles Pinckney was not far off when he remarked sardonically that ". . . the whole [conflict] comes to this": "Give N. Jersey an equal vote, and she will dismiss her scruples, and concur in the Natil. system." What he rather unfairly did not add was that the Jersey delegates were not free agents who could adhere to their private convictions; they had to take back, sponsor and risk their reputations on the reforms approved by the Convention—and in New Jersey, not in Virginia.

Paterson spoke on Saturday, and one can surmise that over the weekend there was a good deal of consultation, argument, and caucusing among the delegates. One member at least prepared a full length address: on Monday Alexander Hamilton, previously mute, rose and delivered a six-hour oration. It was a remarkably apolitical speech; the gist of his position was that *both* the Virginia and New Jersey Plans were inadequately centralist, and he detailed a reform program which was reminiscent of the Protectorate under the Cromwellian *Instrument of Government* of 1653. It has been suggested that Hamilton did this in the best political tradition to emphasize the moderate character of the Virginia Plan, to give the cautious delegates something *really* to worry about; but this interpretation seems somehow too clever. Particularly since the sentiments Hamilton expressed happened to be completely consistent with those he privately—and sometimes publicly—expressed throughout his life. He wanted, to take a striking phrase from a letter to George Washington, a "strong well mounted government"; in essence, the Hamilton Plan contemplated an elected life monarch, virtually free of public control, on the Hobbesian ground that only in this fashion could strength and stability be achieved. The other alternatives, he argued, would put policy-making at the mercy of the passions of the mob; only if the sovereign was beyond the reach of selfish influence would it be possible to have government in the interests of the whole community.

From all accounts, this was a masterful and compelling speech, but (aside from furnishing John Lansing and Luther Martin with ammunition for later use against the Constitution) it made little impact. Hamilton was simply transmitting on a different wave length from the rest of the delegates; the latter adjourned after his great effort, admired his rhetoric, and then returned to business. It was rather as if they had taken a day off to attend the opera. Hamilton, never a particularly patient man or much of a negotiator, stayed for another ten days and then left, in considerable disgust, for New York. Although he came back to Philadelphia sporadically and attended the last two weeks of the Convention, Hamilton played no part in the laborious task of hammering out the Constitution. His day came later when he led the New York Constitutionalists into the savage imbroglio over ratification—an arena in which his unmatched talent for dirty political infighting may well have won the day. For instance, in the New York Ratifying Convention, Lansing threw back into Hamilton's teeth the sentiments the latter had expressed in his June 18 oration in the Convention. However, having since retreated to the fine defensive positions immortalized in *The Federalist*, the Colonel flatly denied that he had ever been an enemy of the states, or had believed that conflict between states and nation was inexorable! As Madison's authoritative *Notes* did not appear until 1840, and there had been no press coverage, there was no way to verify his assertions, so in the words of the reporter, ". . . a warm personal altercation between [Lansing and Hamilton] engrossed the remainder of the day [June 28, 1788]."

IV

On Tuesday morning, June 19, the vacation was over. James Madison led off with a long, carefully reasoned speech analyzing the New Jersey Plan which, while intellectually vigorous in its criticisms, was quite conciliatory in mood. "The great difficulty," he observed, "lies in the affair of Representation; and if this could be adjusted, all others would be surmountable." (As events were to demonstrate, this diagnosis was correct.) When he finished, a vote was taken on whether to continue with the Virginia Plan as the nucleus for a new constitution: seven states voted "Yes"; New York, New Jersey, and Delaware voted "No"; and Maryland, whose position often depended on which delegates happened to be on the floor, divided. Paterson, it seems, lost decisively; yet in a fundamental sense he and his allies had achieved their purpose: from that day onward, it could never be forgotten that the state governments loomed ominously in the background and that no verbal incantations could exorcise their power. Moreover, nobody bolted the convention: Paterson and his colleagues took their defeat in stride and set to work to modify the Virginia Plan, particularly with respect to its provisions on representation in the national legislature. Indeed, they won an immediate rhetorical bonus; when Oliver Ellsworth of Connecticut rose to move that the word "national" be expunged from the Third Virginia Resolution ("Resolved that a *national* Government ought to be established consisting of a *supreme* Legislative, Executive and Judiciary"), Randolph agreed and the motion passed unanimously. The process of compromise had begun.

For the next two weeks, the delegates circled around the problem of legislative representation. The Connecticut delegation appears to have evolved a possible compromise quite early in the debates, but the Virginians and particularly Madison (unaware that he would later be acclaimed as the prophet of "federalism") fought obdurately against providing for equal representation of states in the second chamber. There was a good deal of acrimony and at one point Benjamin Franklin—of all people—proposed the institution of a daily prayer; practical politicians in the gathering, however, were meditating more on the merits of a good committee than on the utility of Divine intervention. On July 2, the ice began to break when through a number of fortuitous events—and one that seems deliberate—the majority against equality of representation was converted into a dead tie. The Convention had reached the stage where it was "ripe" for a solution (presumably all the therapeutic speeches had been made), and the South Carolinians proposed a committee. Madison and James Wilson wanted none of it, but with only Pennsylvania dissenting, the body voted to establish a working party on the problem of representation.

The members of this committee, one from each state, were elected by the delegates—and a very interesting committee it was. Despite the fact that the Virginia Plan had held majority support up to that date, neither Madison nor Randolph was selected (Mason was the Virginian) and Baldwin of Georgia, whose shift in position had resulted in the tie, was chosen. From the composition, it was clear that this was not to be a "fighting" committee: the emphasis in membership was on what might be described as "second-level political entrepreneurs." On the basis of the discussions up to that time, only Luther Martin of Maryland could be described as a "bitter-ender." Admittedly, some divination enters into this sort of analysis, but one does get a sense of the mood of the delegates from these choices—including the interesting selection of Benjamin Franklin, despite his age and intellectual wobbliness, over the brilliant and incisive Wilson or the sharp, polemical Gouverneur Morris, to represent Pennsylvania. His passion for conciliation was more valuable at this juncture than Wilson's logical genius, or Morris's acerbic wit.

There is a common rumor that the Framers divided their time between philosophical discussions of government and reading the classics in political theory. Perhaps this is as good a time as any to note that their concerns were highly practical, that they spent little time canvassing abstractions. A number of them had some acquaintance with the history of political theory (probably gained from reading John Adams's monumental compilation A *Defense of the Constitutions of Government*, the first volume of which appeared in 1786), and it was a poor rhetorician indeed who could not cite Locke, Montesquieu, or Harrington *in support* of a desired goal. Yet up to this point in the deliberations, no one had expounded a defense of states' rights or the "separation of powers" on anything resembling a theoretical basis. It should be reiterated that the Madison model had no room either for the states or for the "separation of powers": effectively *all* governmental power was vested in the national legislature. The merits of Montesquieu did not turn up until *The Federalist;* and although a perverse argument could be made that Madison's ideal was truly in the tradition of John Locke's *Second Treatise of Government*, the Locke whom the American rebels treated as an honorary president was a pluralistic defender of vested rights, not of parliamentary supremacy.

It would be tedious to continue a blow-by-blow analysis of the work of the delegates; the critical fight was over representation of the states and once the Connecticut Compromise was adopted on July 17, the Convention was over the hump. Madison, James Wilson, and Gouverneur Morris of New York (who was there representing Pennsylvania!) fought the compromise all the way in a last-ditch effort to get a unitary state with parliamentary supremacy. But their allies deserted them and they demonstrated after their defeat the essentially opportunist character of their objections—using "opportunist" here in a non-pejorative sense, to indicate a willingness to swallow their objections and get on with the business. Moreover, once the compromise had carried (by five states to four, with one state divided), its advocates threw themselves vigorously into the job of strengthening the general government's substantive powers—as might have been predicted, indeed, from Paterson's early statements. It nourishes an increased respect for Madison's devotion to the art of politics, to realize that this dogged fighter could sit down six months later and prepare essays for *The Federalist* in contradiction to his basic convictions about the true course the Convention should have taken.

V

Two tricky issues will serve to illustrate the later process of accommodation. The first was the institutional position of the Executive. Madison argued for an executive chosen by the National Legislature and on May 29 this had been adopted with a provision that after his seven-year term was concluded, the chief magistrate should not be eligible for re-election. In late July this was reopened and for a week the matter was argued from several different points of view. A good deal of desultory speech-making ensued, but the gist of the problem was the opposition from two sources to election by the legislature. One group felt that the states should have a hand in the process; another small but influential circle urged direct election by the people. There were a number of proposals: election by the people, election by state governors, by electors chosen by state legislatures, by the National Legislature (James Wilson, perhaps ironically, proposed at one point that an Electoral College be chosen by lot from the National Legislature!), and there was some resemblance to three-dimensional chess in the dispute because of the presence of two other variables, length of tenure and re-eligibility. Finally, after opening, reopening, and re-reopening the debate, the thorny problem was consigned to a committee for resolution.

The Brearley Committee on Postponed Matters was a superb aggregation of talent and its compromise on the Executive was a masterpiece of political improvisation. (The Electoral College, its creation, however, had little in its favor as an *institution*—as the delegates well appreciated.) The point of departure for all discussion about the presidency in the Convention was that in immediate terms, the problem was non-existent; in other words, everybody present knew that under any system devised, George Washington would be President. Thus they were dealing in the future tense and to a body of working politicians the merits of the Brearley proposal were obvious: everybody got a piece of cake. (Or to put it more academically, each viewpoint could leave the Convention and argue to its constituents that it had *really* won the day.) First, the state legislatures had the right to determine the mode of selection of the electors; second, the small states received a bonus in the Electoral College in the form of a guaranteed minimum of three votes while the big states got acceptance of the principle of proportional power; third, if the state legislatures agreed (as six did in the first presidential election), the people could be involved directly in the choice of electors; and finally, if no candidate received a majority in the College, the right of decision passed to the National Legislature with each state exercising equal strength. (In the Brearley recommendation, the election went to the Senate, but a motion from the floor substituted the House; this was accepted on the ground that the Senate already had enough authority over the Executive in its treaty and appointment powers.)

This compromise was almost too good to be true, and the Framers snapped it up with little debate or controversy. No one seemed to think well of the College as an *institution;* indeed, what evidence there is suggests that there was an assumption that once Washington had finished his tenure as President, the electors would cease to produce majorities and the chief executive would usually be chosen in the House. George Mason observed casually that the selection would be made in the House nineteen times in twenty and no one seriously disputed this point. The vital aspect of the Electoral College was that it got the Convention over the hurdle and protected everybody's interests. The future was left to cope with the problem of what to do with this Rube Goldberg mechanism.

In short, the Framers did not in their wisdom endow the United States with a College of Cardinals—the Electoral College was neither an exercise in applied Platonism nor an experiment in indirect government based on elitist distrust of the masses. It was merely a jerry-rigged improvisation which has subsequently been endowed with a high theoretical content. When an elector from Oklahoma in 1960 refused to cast his vote for Nixon (naming Byrd and Goldwater instead) on the ground that the Founding Fathers intended him to exercise his great independent wisdom, he was indulging in historical fantasy. If one were to indulge in counter-fantasy, he would be tempted to suggest that the Fathers would be startled to find the College still in operation—and perhaps even dismayed at their descendants' lack of judgment or inventiveness.

The second issue on which some substantial practical bargaining took place was slavery. The morality of slavery was, by design, not at issue; but in its other concrete aspects, slavery colored the arguments over taxation, commerce, and representation. The "Three-Fifths Compromise," that three-fifths of the slaves would be counted both for representation and for purposes of direct taxation (which was drawn from the past—it was a formula of Madison's utilized by Congress in 1783 to establish the basis of state contributions to the Confederation treasury) had allayed some Northern fears about Southern over-representation (no one then foresaw the trivial role that direct taxation would play in later federal financial policy), but doubts still remained. The Southerners, on the other hand, were afraid that Congressional control over commerce would lead to the exclusion of slaves or to their excessive taxation as imports. Moreover, the Southerners were disturbed over "navigation acts," *i.e.*, tariffs, or special legislation providing, for example, that exports be carried only in American ships; as a section depending upon exports, they wanted protection from the potential voracity of their commercial brethren of the Eastern states. To achieve this end, Mason and others urged that the Constitution include a proviso that navigation and commercial laws should require a two-thirds vote in Congress.

These problems came to a head in late August and, as usual, were handed to a committee in the hope that, in Gouverneur Morris's words, ". . . these things may form a bargain among the Northern and Southern states." The Committee reported its measures of reconciliation on August 25, and on August 29 the package was wrapped up and delivered. What occurred can best be described in George Mason's dour version (he anticipated Calhoun in his conviction that permitting navigation acts to pass by majority vote would put the South in economic bondage to the North—it was mainly on this ground that he refused to sign the Constitution):

> The Constitution as agreed to till a fortnight before the Convention rose was such as one as he would have set his hand and heart to. . . . [Until that time] The 3 New England States were constantly with us in all questions . . . so that it was these three States with the 5 Southern ones against Pennsylvania, Jersey and Delaware. With respect to the importation of slaves, [decision-making] was left to Congress. This disturbed the two Southernmost States who knew that Congress would immediately suppress the importation of slaves. Those two States therefore struck up a bargain with the three New England States. If they would join to admit slaves for some years, the two Southernmost States would join in changing the clause which required the ⅔ of the Legislature in any vote [on navigation acts]. It was done.

On the floor of the Convention there was a virtual love-feast on this happy occasion. Charles Pinckney of South Carolina attempted to overturn the committee's decision, when the compromise was reported to the Convention, by insisting that the South needed protection from the imperialism of the Northern states. But his Southern colleagues were not prepared to rock the boat and General C. C. Pinckney arose to spread oil on the suddenly ruffled waters; he admitted that:

> It was in the true interest of the S[outhern] States to have no regulation of commerce; but considering the loss brought on the commerce

of the Eastern States by the Revolution, their liberal conduct towards the views of South Carolina [on the regulation of the slave trade] and the interests the weak Southn. States had in being united with the strong Eastern states, he thought it proper that no fetters should be imposed on the power of making commercial regulations; *and that his constituents, though prejudiced against the Eastern States, would be reconciled to this liberality*. He had himself prejudices agst the Eastern States before he came here, but would acknowledge that he had found them as liberal and candid as any men whatever. (Italics added.)

Pierce Butler took the same tack, essentially arguing that he was not too happy about the possible consequences, but that a deal was a deal. Many Southern leaders were later—in the wake of the "Tariff of Abominations"—to rue this day of reconciliation; Calhoun's *Disquisition on Government* was little more than an extension of the argument in the Convention against permitting a congressional majority to enact navigation acts.

VI

Drawing on their vast collective political experience, utilizing every weapon in the politician's arsenal, looking constantly over their shoulders at their constituents, the delegates put together a Constitution. It was a makeshift affair; some sticky issues (for example, the qualification of voters) they ducked entirely; others they mastered with that ancient instrument of political sagacity, studied ambiguity (for example, citizenship), and some they just overlooked. In this last category, I suspect, fell the matter of the power of the federal courts to determine the constitutionality of acts of Congress. When the judicial article was formulated (Article III of the Constitution), deliberations were still in the stage where the legislature was endowed with broad power under the Randolph formulation, authority which by its own terms was scarcely amenable to judicial review. In essence, courts could hardly determine when ". . . the separate States are incompetent or . . . the harmony of the United States may be interrupted";

the National Legislature, as critics pointed out, was free to define its own jurisdiction. Later the definition of legislative authority was changed into the form we know, a series of stipulated powers, *but the delegates never seriously re-examined the jurisdiction of the judiciary under this new limited formulation.* All arguments on the intention of the Framers in this matter are thus deductive and *a posteriori,* though some obviously make more sense than others.

The Framers were busy and distinguished men, anxious to get back to their families, their positions, and their constituents, not members of the French Academy devoting a lifetime to a dictionary. They were trying to do an important job, and do it in such a fashion that their handiwork would be acceptable to very diverse constituencies. No one was rhapsodic about the final document, but it was a beginning, a move in the right direction, and one they had reason to believe the people would endorse. In addition, since they had modified the impossible amendment provisions of the Articles (the requirement of unanimity which could always be frustrated by "Rogues Island") to one demanding approval by only three-quarters of the states, they seemed confident that the gaps in the fabric which experience would reveal could be rewoven without undue difficulty.

So with a neat phrase introduced by Benjamin Franklin (but devised by Gouverneur Morris) which made their decision sound unanimous, and an inspired benediction by the Old Doctor urging doubters to doubt their own infallibility, the Constitution was accepted and signed. Curiously, Edmund Randolph, who had played so vital a role throughout, refused to sign, as did his fellow Virginian George Mason and Elbridge Gerry of Massachusetts. Randolph's behavior was eccentric, to say the least—his excuses for refusing his signature have a factitious ring even at this late date; the best explanation seems to be that he was afraid that the Constitution would prove to be a liability in Virginia politics, where Patrick Henry was burning up the countryside with impassioned denunciations. Presumably, Randolph wanted to check the temper of the populace before he risked his reputation, and perhaps his job, in a fight with both Henry and Richard Henry Lee. Events lend some justification to this speculation: after much temporizing and use of the conditional subjunctive tense, Randolph endorsed ratification in Virginia and ended up getting the best of both worlds.

Madison, despite his reservations about the Constitution, was the campaign manager in ratification. His first task was to get the Congress in New York to light its own funeral pyre by approving the "amendments" to the Articles and sending them on to the state legislatures. Above all, momentum had to be maintained. The anti-Constitutionalists, now thoroughly alarmed and no novices in politics, realized that their best tactic was attrition rather than direct opposition. Thus they settled on a position expressing qualified approval but calling for a second Convention to remedy various defects (the one with the most demagogic appeal was the lack of a Bill of Rights). Madison knew that to accede to this demand would be equivalent to losing the battle, nor would he agree to conditional approval (despite wavering even by Hamilton). This was an all-or-nothing proposition: national salvation or national impotence with no intermediate positions possible. Unable to get congressional approval, he settled for second best: a unanimous resolution of Congress transmitting the Constitution to the states for whatever action they saw fit to take. The opponents then moved from New York and the Congress, where they had attempted to attach amendments and conditions, to the states for the final battle.

At first the campaign for ratification went beautifully: within eight months after the delegates set their names to the document, eight states had ratified. Only in Massachusetts had the result been close (187–168). Theoretically, a ratification by one more state convention would set the new government in motion, but in fact until Virginia and New York acceded to the new Union, the latter was a fiction. New Hampshire was the next to ratify; Rhode Island was involved in its characteristic political convulsions (the

Legislature there sent the Constitution out to the towns for decision by popular vote and it got lost among a series of local issues); North Carolina's convention did not meet until July and then postponed a final decision. This is hardly the place for an extensive analysis of the conventions of New York and Virginia. Suffice it to say that the Constitutionalists clearly outmaneuvered their opponents, forced them into impossible political positions, and won both states narrowly. The Virginia Convention could serve as a classic study in effective floor management: Patrick Henry had to be contained, and a reading of the debates discloses a standard two-stage technique. Henry would give a four- or five-hour speech denouncing some section of the Constitution on every conceivable ground (the federal district, he averred at one point, would become a haven for convicts escaping from state authority!); when Henry subsided, "Mr. Lee of Westmoreland" would rise and literally poleaxe him with sardonic invective (when Henry complained about the militia power, "Lighthorse Harry" really punched below the belt: observing that while the former Governor had been sitting in Richmond during the Revolution, *he* had been out in the trenches with the troops and thus felt better qualified to discuss military affairs). Then the gentlemanly Constitutionalists (Madison, Pendleton, and Marshall) would pick up the matters at issue and examine them in the light of reason.

Indeed, modern Americans who tend to think of James Madison as a rather dessicated character should spend some time with this transcript. Probably Madison put on his most spectacular demonstration of nimble rhetoric in what might be called "The Battle of the Absent Authorities." Patrick Henry in the course of one of his harangues alleged that Jefferson was known to be opposed to Virginia's approving the Constitution. This was clever: Henry hated Jefferson, but was prepared to use any weapon that came to hand. Madison's riposte was superb: First, he said that with all due respect to the great reputation of Jefferson, he was not in the country and therefore could not formulate an adequate judgment; second, no one should utilize the reputation of an outsider—the

Virginia Convention was there to think for itself; third, if there were to be recourse to outsiders, the opinions of George Washington should certainly be taken into consideration; and finally, he knew from privileged personal communications from Jefferson that in fact the latter *strongly favored* the Constitution. To devise an assault route into this rhetorical fortress was literally impossible.

VII

The fight was over; all that remained now was to establish the new frame of government in the spirit of its framers. And who were better qualified for this task than the Framers themselves? Thus victory for the Constitution meant simultaneous victory for the Constitutionalists; the anti-Constitutionalists either capitulated or vanished into limbo—soon Patrick Henry would be offered a seat on the Supreme Court and Luther Martin would be known as the Federalist "bull-dog." And irony of ironies, Alexander Hamilton and James Madison would shortly accumulate a reputation as the formulators of what is often alleged to be our political theory, the concept of "federalism." Also, on the other side of the ledger, the arguments would soon appear over what the Framers "really meant"; while these disputes have assumed the proportions of a big scholarly business in the last century, they began almost before the ink on the Constitution was dry. One of the best early ones featured Hamilton versus Madison on the scope of presidential power, and other Framers characteristically assumed positions in this and other disputes on the basis of their political convictions.

Probably our greatest difficulty is that we know so much more about what the Framers *should have meant* than they themselves did. We are intimately acquainted with the problems that their Constitution should have been designed to master; in short, we have read the mystery story backwards. If we are to get the right "feel" for their time and their circumstances, we must in Maitland's phrase, ". . . think ourselves back into a twilight." Obviouly, no one can pretend completely to escape from the solipsistic web of his own environment, but if the effort is made, it is possible to appreciate the past roughly on its own terms. The first step in this process is to abandon the academic premise that because we can ask a question, there must be an answer.

Thus we can ask what the Framers meant when they gave Congress the power to regulate interstate and foreign commerce, and we emerge, reluctantly perhaps, with the reply that (Professor Crosskey to the contrary notwithstanding) they may not have known what they meant, that there may not have been any semantic consensus. The Convention was not a seminar in analytic philosophy or linguistic analysis. Commerce was *commerce*—and if different interpretations of the word arose, later generations could worry about the problem of definition. The delegates were in a hurry to get a new government established; when definitional arguments arose, they characteristically took refuge in ambiguity. If different men voted for the same proposition for varying reasons, that was politics (and still is); if later generations were unsettled by this lack of precision, that would be their problem.

There was a good deal of definitional pluralism with respect to the problems the delegates did discuss, but when we move to the question of extrapolated intentions, we enter the realm of spiritualism. When men in our time, for instance, launch into elaborate talmudic exegesis to demonstrate that federal aid to parochial schools is (or is not) in accord with the intentions of the men who established the Republic and endorsed the Bill of Rights, they are engaging in historical Extra-Sensory Perception. (If one were to join this E. S. P. contingent for a minute, he might suggest that the hard-boiled politicians who wrote the Constitution and Bill of Rights would chuckle scornfully at such an invocation of authority: obviously a politician would chart his course on the intentions of the living, not of the dead, and count the number of Catholics in his constituency.)

The Constitution, then, was not an apotheosis of "constitutionalism," a triumph of architectonic genius; it was a patch-work sewn together under the pressure of both time and events by a group of extremely talented democratic politicians. They refused to attempt the establishment of a strong, centralized sovereignty on the principle of legislative supremacy for the excellent reason that the people would not accept it. They risked their political fortunes by opposing the established doctrines of state sovereignty because they were convinced that the existing system was leading to national impotence and probably foreign domination. For two years, they worked to get a convention established. For over three months, in what must have seemed to the faithful participants an endless process of give-and-take, they reasoned, cajoled, threatened, and bargained amongst themselves. The result was a Constitution which the people, in fact, by democratic processes, did accept, and a new and far better national government was established.

Beginning with the inspired propaganda of Hamilton, Madison, and Jay, the ideological build-up got under way. *The Federalist* had little impact on the ratification of the Constitution, except perhaps in New York, but this volume had enormous influence on the image of the Constitution in the minds of future generations, particularly on historians and political scientists who have an innate fondness for theoretical symmetry. Yet, while the shades of Locke and Montesquieu *may* have been hovering in the background, and the delegates *may* have been unconscious instruments of a transcendent *telos*, the careful observer of the day-to-day work of the Convention finds no over-arching principles. The "separation of powers" to him seems to be a by-product of suspicion, and "federalism" he views as a *pis aller*, as the farthest point the delegates felt they could go in the destruction of state power without themselves inviting repudiation.

To conclude, the Constitution was neither a victory for abstract theory nor a great practical success. Well over half a million men had to die on the battlefields of the Civil War before certain constitutional principles could be defined—a baleful consideration which is somehow overlooked in our customary tributes to the farsighted genius of the Framers and to the supposed American talent for "constitutionalism." The Constitution was, however, a vivid demonstration of effective democratic political action, and of the forging of a national elite which literally persuaded its countrymen to hoist themselves by their own boot straps. American pro-consuls would be wise not to translate the Constitution into Japanese, or Swahili, or treat it as a work of semi-Divine origin; but when students of comparative politics examine the process of nation-building in countries newly freed from colonial rule, they may find the American experience instructive as a classic example of the potentialities of a democratic elite.

3

Foundations for a New Politics, 1789–1824

The Emergence of Political Parties

The First American Party System

by Paul Goodman

Today, as in the past, American politics is on trial. Because political parties—private, voluntary institutions not mentioned in the Constitution—conduct much of the vital business of government in America, deciding who gets what, when, and how, politics in America has largely been the history of political parties. Yet that was not always so. Modern political parties emerged in the United States only as late as the 1790's, and not until much later in Western Europe. America gave birth to political parties after it rediscovered popular government.

As revolutionaries, Americans repudiated the sovereignty of king and Parliament and proclaimed instead the sovereignty of the people. The first American parties, however, did not spring up suddenly in the wake of the Revolution or because of increasing democratization of politics produced in that era. As in the colonial past, so in revolutionary America, many citizens were inclined to defer to the leadership of elites which traditionally claimed the right and enjoyed the power to govern. Groups of ambitious politicians, both in and out of office, jockeyed for control and occasionally appealed to voters for public support. In time of great voter apathy, the factious politics of a few had ample room in which to flourish. The Revolution, however, increased the potential for change. Since independent Americans, no longer owing allegiance to a distant Crown, had become theoretical masters of their own republican fate, they began to show more interest in government as a vehicle through which they could advance their well-being.

The Revolution politicized the citizenry, lowered obstacles to political participation, and heightened expectations. The adoption of the Constitution in 1789 created, in addition, a national political arena—the presidency and Congress—in which rival interests in a large, complex republic competed for advantage. Cliques accustomed to running things in their own states often found their will thwarted on the national scene. Only by forming coalitions with others whose votes might dominate Congress or elect a President could any single group hope to exert influence at the national capital. Political parties appeared to fulfill this and other needs. By nominating candidates and gathering behind them a broad base of support committed to programs and policies that appealed to the party's constituency, the first parties provided Americans with instruments for capturing power and making government serve their interests.

Paul Goodman analyzes the complex process through which the first modern political parties arose in the United States. Created by men who professed to abhor "parties"—any organized groups seeking power—the first political parties rescued popular government from the realm of theory and helped to mold it into a practical, political system.

The fears that haunted Americans in the decades preceding the Revolution continued to trouble the Revolutionary generation as it reconstructed political authority on "pure" republican foundations. No longer feeling themselves subjects of a corrupt kingdom,

Americans were free at last to devise political arrangements that would reconcile the competing claims of liberty and authority, protecting them from the aggressive and tyrannical propensities of power, and yet restraining those forces which threatened to disrupt communal order.

The solution was expected to come from a diligent study of politics, "the divine science." For two decades Americans wrote and rewrote constitutions, confident that appropriate constitutional mechanisms would tame faction, enable diverse and conflicting interests to secure justice, and lay the foundations of a great republic which was strong yet free. These high hopes, elaborately expounded during the formation of the federal Constitution, generated expectations that the young nation would avoid the rivalry and corruption, the tumult and violence that had infected and doomed earlier experiments in free government. The new frame of government was supposed to deliver Americans from the squabbling petty interests whose representatives schemed for the immediate, selfish advantage of their parochial constituencies.

The first decade's experience under the new regime was profoundly disillusioning. In the eyes of many the republic seemed to split into warring factions as dangerous as citizens had feared; as they saw it, forces lurked everywhere bent on subverting the carefully wrought structure of 1787 and overturning the social order. Networks of aristocrats, monarchists, and Jacobins, financial manipulators, "wild Irishmen," clerical bigots and blaspheming *Illuminati*, paid foreign agents and sowers of sedition and treason, they thought, roamed the republic plotting its destruction. In the decade preceding the Revolution, and recurrently throughout their history, Americans believed that sinister elements threatened their existence.

These perceptions of experience and the actual realities of public affairs were disturbingly incongruent. Those who built the first political party system in the 1790's mistook parties for factions, assuming that those with whom they differed were disloyal to the nation and its ideals. Though vastly different in structure and function from earlier forms of political organization, the first parties were confused with factions because the modern political party was outside the range of this generation's experience as well as its historical consciousness. Federalists and Republicans alike regarded themselves not as parties but as embodiments of the nation's will. When out of office, their duty was to recapture power from those temporarily and illegitimately exercising it; when in office, their task was to keep it from those ready to usurp and misuse it. Unconscious builders of political parties, Federalists and Republicans were prisoners of inherited political assumptions which distorted their understanding of the innovations stemming from the creation of a strong central government in a federal system. Viewing the political parties of the 1790's as alliances of factious elements, many Americans believed that factions had achieved cohesiveness, organization, and unity which made them more dangerous than ever, capable of overwhelming the consitutional mechanisms designed to restrain them.

Yet Americans were slowly learning from experience to accept the legitimacy of organized political activity in support of or in opposition to those who exercised the powers of government. In time political parties came to be recognized as institutions essential to the survival of free government, providing an orderly means of articulating the majority's wishes and settling differences among contending groups. The acceptance of parties, and their incorporation into the structure of American politics, constituted a recognition that the forces which generated them were inherent in an open society.

Unlike later nation-builders, the Americans had no contemporary models for guidance; nor were the lessons of history useful except as they helped them avoid the errors of others. Though unaware that they were experiencing political modernization, the necessities of circumstance forced them to change their ways of managing public business.

If crises in participation promote the growth of political parties, the contours of such crises in America differed noticeably from similar phenomena in other times and places. No fundamental social or economic transformation preceded the emergence of the early party system, nor was "the extension of the suffrage," as LaPalombara and Weiner, and others, have suggested, "the real impetus for the creation of some form of party organization at the local level." The Revolution did not radically alter the productive system or the social structure, and suffrage had not been monopolized by a few even before independence. The absence of a native hereditary aristocracy, the superficiality of royal control, the great instability in the fortunes of leading men, and the constant need to recruit additional leadership to govern a new and rapidly expanding society, made it difficult to exclude the most talented and persistent elements which sought to participate in public affairs. The colonists did not experience full-scale democracy, but those who exercised power had never been as secure as their counterparts in the Old World were.

The movement for independence which expressed the Americans' determination to preserve self-government had failed to generate parties such as those which appeared in the 1790's. The Revolutionary leaders did not, as later ones did, need to create a party to mobilize support outside the government, because they already dominated much of the existing political structure. They were not conspirators forced to operate outside the framework of established authority, but parliamentary leaders, accustomed to exercise power and able to work through established institutions. . . . The Revolutionary forces thus always enjoyed the legitimacy of being part of constituted authority. Accustomed to authority, the revolutionary leaders did not depend primarily on mass movements to organize resistance.

When political parties did emerge in the 1790's, they did not effect radical change in the *formal* terms of participation in government. Rather they mobilized previously inactive elements, bringing into the political arena citizens and groups that had had the right but not the desire or incentive to participate. Far more important in broadening the base of popular government than liberalization of the suffrage was erosion of the habits of deference which had enabled those claiming social superiority to command the respect and support of their inferiors. The decline of deference had its roots in the social disorganization accompanying the transplantation of traditional English institutions and attitudes to America. Because the American social order lacked either a nobility or other familiar ruling elements, its leadership strata was self-made and recruited from the middle and lower strata; and because abundant resource opportunities enabled the shrewd and enterprising to rise, the composition of the leading strata lacked permanence, as newcomers edged their way to prominence. The Revolution intensified the degree of social disorganization, as established elements were swept away by war, and further undermined the capacity of leaders to lead, making it harder than ever for citizens to know to whom they should defer when so many, often new faces, competed for their favor. Political parties hastened the decline of deference by legitimizing and institutionalizing competition for the electorate's favor and by enhancing the likelihood that challengers might succeed in ousting established elements. Thus instead of being the product of an enlarged franchise, the first American party system generally sharply increased the level of voter participation.

In addition to resolving crises of participation, political parties, as LaPalombara and Weiner suggest, emerge during crises of legitimacy. By proclaiming themselves instruments of the majority, parties authenticate a regime's claim to represent the popular will. The new Revolutionary regimes in America, following the Declaration of Independence, enjoyed legitimacy from the outset without the aid of modern parties to express majority will. The Revolutionary cause never became a party cause because it was seen as a defense of established units of local government against the usurpations of king and parliament. The colonists believed they were upholding the British constitution against those who sought to subvert it, and with relatively little difficulty the new regimes quickly assumed the right to exercise all the functions of government. These regimes suffered few doubts about their legitimacy, for the logic of the Revolutionary argument left no other conceivable claimant to sovereign power. Those Americans who opposed the Revolutionary movement either went into exile or quietly submitted, so the new republic was spared the challenges of potentially disloyal elements receptive to opportunities for restoring the old regime. . . .

The most troublesome problem of authority arose over the establishment of the national government. Those who favored strengthening the Confederation at the expense of the states, and who later wanted to scrap the Articles entirely, attacked the adequacy rather than the legitimacy of existing arrangements. And those who unsuccessfully but vigorously fought adoption of the new federal Constitution quietly and rapidly submitted to the new regime, without entirely abandoning their doubts. In the 1790's also, Americans often divided over the course the new government was steering, but few wished to undo the settlement of 1787. From time to time the disaffected lost hope that their interests could be advanced within the established political framework. Some of these elements joined the Whisky Rebellion in 1793 or Fries's Rebellion in 1799, or toyed with separating from the Union, as did some Republicans in the Old Southwest in the 1790's and some Federalists in New England after 1800. On the whole, however, while political activists professed to believe that their opponents plotted their downfall and endangered the social order, they argued that the evil stemmed from a perversion of legitimate authority which could be cured not by rejecting authority as such but by changing the men who held the reins of power. No *Putsch* could hope to succeed as long as most citizens had faith in peaceful change, and hence no group, however alienated, could reasonably expect to get its way through violence. Even hopelessly discouraged minorities, such as the later Federalists, became resigned to their fate.

The establishment of a national center of decision-making generated greater tensions than the framers had foreseen. Many feared for the stability of the social order or doubted that the new framework of government would enable Americans to master the forces that threatened survival. By 1815, however, these fears and doubts had subsided. The nation experienced a series of internal and external challenges but emerged with its constitutional fabric intact and its citizens more nearly united than ever. By providing orderly means of determining the majority's will and enabling conflicting forces to settle their differences peacefully, the first political parties authenticated government's claim to represent the people. Yet in the early years of party development their functions were obscured because no one had anticipated how difficult it would be to articulate the national will in a republic that was larger in territory, and more diverse in its social components, than any in the past. The new government immediately faced a series of decisions on problems whose specific outlines and complex dimensions could not be foreseen in 1787, and whose solutions were likely to lead to disagreements. Though nearly all agreed that public policy must be based on the majority's wishes, no one could authoritatively know or interpret the majority's wishes because the people themselves often had no opinion, and when they did, it was hopelessly divided or fragmented. The task of the early political parties was to attempt to clarify, to articulate and channel, the majority's preferences. Though the clash of parties helped to give legitimacy to the policies adopted by government, citizens often found it difficult to accept this mode of decision-making because the deferential style of politics lingering from the past assumed that a disinterested, virtuous, and wise few were to be entrusted with power. But party politics assumed that no group had either a prescriptive right to govern or an inherent monopoly of wisdom or competence.

Like the crisis in participation and legitimacy, the American version of the crisis of national integration also diverged from the experience of many other new nations. In certain critical respects, a large measure of integration had been achieved before the 1790's.

From the beginning the republic enjoyed territorial integration, with territorial limits defined by the boundaries of the colonies which the new nation automatically incorporated. Predominantly English in nationality and Protestant in religion, the colonists had also long shared a common culture inherited from Britain. Even more important were experiences which shaped a new sense of identity, transforming Britons into Americans. "What is an American?," Crèvecœur asked, and announced that "a new race of men" had appeared whose ideas and institutions distinguished them from those they had left behind in Europe. Long before Americanness was embodied in a sovereign state, the colonists had sensed that they shared a common nationality born of their unique experiences—the product not simply of a common language, culture, religion, or long identification with place, but of being uprooted and replanted in the wilderness. The Americans assumed that they were unique and superior because they assumed that their society was enlightened beyond any other. . . .

Yet integration was incomplete; like the crises of participation and legitimacy, the crisis of integration was subdued and prolonged. At first Americans misjudged the extent to which independence required the centralization of authority. They believed that by locating sovereignty in the states, power would be less dangerous to liberty; diversity, they thought, was not inconsistent with national prosperity and survival. The experiment in decentralization foundered when citizens discovered that their well-being required a redistribution of power. The new federal Constitution attempted to achieve a greater degree of national integration, sufficient to promote "the general welfare" without eliminating local authority but limiting its scope. The Constitution created a new locus of power which promoted greater integration by requiring the articulation of a national will to decide those policy questions which had become the responsibility of all the people, the voters in the Union. But it provided no mechanism for focusing national attention on the pressing issues of the day or for collecting popular sentiment. The first political parties, offsprings of a national center of decision-making, performed that task.

As long as the states had been sovereign during the Confederation, conflicts of interest were played out within the arenas of state politics. The members of Congress in the Confederation were ambassadors from their states, and in most matters local perspectives were decisive. The new Constitution shifted the locus of decision-making, and for the first time citizens elected a Congress and President to grapple with problems on a scale and in a context that were new. Whether the nation survived and prospered now depended on what happened at the national capital. Federal power was not distant and abstract but could reach into a citizen's pocketbook, hale him before the courts, and determine whether he lived at peace or war with other nations. Centralization also vastly multiplied the numbers and complexity of the groups competing for advantage. By throwing representatives of diverse elements together under one jurisdiction, the Constitution heightened the sense of group differences and local senses of identity. Frustrated Virginians became exploited planters and Southerners; disappointed Massachusetts men became aggrieved merchants and Easterners. The multiplication of heterogeneous elements, each prone to identify its own interests with what it regarded as the national welfare, certain that anything threatening its special interests jeopardized the common good, increased the intensity of political life. Groups used to getting their way at home were unused to being thwarted in the new arena. But there they repeatedly encountered frustration and discouragement, which aroused suspicions that "the general welfare" was being sacrificed to faction.

The only way to resist was to find new methods of arousing the electorate to the presumed dangers and to forge a national coalition to install in the legislative and executive branches men devoted to "the common good." To do this, electoral alliances among elements in the various states were indispensable, especially in the organization of Congress and the choice of a President. Paradoxically, though centralization promoted national integration, it also led to the polarization of the nation into parties by generating conflicts which required new institutions for their management and resolution. The parties divided people as they united them. Each party brought together diverse elements previously little known to one another, elements whose common fears and interests dictated their union and required the formulation of an ideology which defined their purpose and could claim to represent the national ideals. To form an effective party coalition, the diverse social materials were forced to accommodate to one another and to formulate a program and ideology vague and broad enough to carry a wide appeal. Once in power, parties learned that the compromises that had brought them into office could help keep them there by accommodating the opposition when feasible. Thus parties organized conflict and in doing so intensified it, but they also instituted an orderly means of settling differences without resorting to violence. Parties offered hope to the threatened or discouraged that the next election would bring a change in fortune and the restoration of virtue to the seats of power. And when that happened, the Union once more would be whole: "We are all republicans, we are all federalists," as Jefferson put it.

The first American party system made leadership and policy formulation sensitive to the conflicting demands of diverse elements scattered across an extensive republic and thereby helped to reconcile these heterogeneous elements to the Union. It did not, however, resolve the crisis in integration for the long run; by the middle of the nineteenth century, altered circumstances intensified the long smoldering crisis of national integration beyond the capacity of the party system of that time to resolve.

The course of party development in the 1790's was slow, uneven, and incomplete. Parties appeared earlier in some communities than elsewhere, and though they eventually spread into most states, they barely took root in some. In some states a strong two-party system developed and persisted; in others it did not survive much beyond the election of 1800, and one party dominated thereafter. In some of the two-party states the contending forces were evenly balanced, but elsewhere they were unevenly matched. Some second parties became, after a struggle, the major party; others never achieved power. The peculiar circumstances of each state shaped the timing, direction, and precise course of party development.

Party evolution in the states was determined by conditions that preceded the appearance of stimuli to party growth and influenced the extent to which competitive politics flourished. The most important were the political infra-structure—the constitutional mechanisms and procedures, formal and informal, which defined the rules of the game—and the social structure, which influenced the range and intensity of group conflict. Both determined the strength with which habits of deference endured.

Some social structures nourished competitive politics while others discouraged it. States with a high degree of social differentiation and social change experienced tensions that weakened habits of deference and generated rivalry which promoted party development. Demographic patterns and shifts were one persistent important source of conflict. The influx of new population into an area was an index of the opportunities that attracted settlers to a region. The older and more densely settled areas, often the smaller states, exerted less pull on prospective emigrants because there was little good land left, and the few that might venture into such communities found it much harder to penetrate the established order. Unsettled areas not only offered land to newcomers but, since there was no pre-existing social structure, permitted settlers to fashion one themselves. All positions of influence were up for grabs where no established groups controlled them. Yet the unsettled areas were not the only ones experiencing high rates of population growth. Rapidly developing urban areas with expanding commercial economies, such as Baltimore, offered considerable opportunity to newcomers. Whatever reasons pulled men, the rapid influx of population into western Pennsylvania, up-country South Carolina and Georgia, Maine, and central and western New York introduced disruptive elements that required assimilation into the social structure; in turn, this usually meant a redistribution of power. Differential rates of growth within a state gave a sectional or regional pattern to politics as new groups concentrated in certain areas and challenged the authority of those situated in older, more stable communities.

Population growth often brought increased demographic heterogeneity. Some states already had highly differentiated populations before the Revolution. Pennsylvania had large numbers of Germans, fragmented into a variety of Protestant denominations, with the Lutherans the largest and most active; Scots-Irish who were also Presbyterians; and English and Welsh who were generally Quakers or Episcopalians. These ethnic and religious groups were concentrated in certain parts of the state which gave them a greater degree of self-consciousness, cohesiveness, and political force than they would have had were they distributed more evenly throughout the colonies or within the state. Similarly, in the 1790's a highly visible and often vocal influx of English and French *émigrés* from the tyranny and turmoil of Europe added troublesome new elements.

Memberships in ethnic and religious groups mediated an individual's relationships with authority. . . . Sometimes objective interests appear to explain partisan choice, as when religious dissenters supported the Republicans because they were opposed to religious bigotry and establishments. In other instances a group's party preference seemed to depend on its leaders' personal ambitions and antagonisms. These could, however, be reconciled with the group's interests, since support of its leaders was a way of asserting the group's dignity and expressing its desire for proper recognition in the community. Ethnic and religious influences on party preference were also complicated by the looseness of party identifications, which could easily be altered. Thus Pennsylvania Germans generally voted Federalist until the late 1790's, when the direct tax, reminding them of the hated hearth tax in

Europe which went to fill the coffers of Rome, turned them toward Jeffersonian Republicanism in 1800. A further complication was that individuals were subjected to multiple pressures, such as occupational and regional ones, which might reinforce or conflict with ethnic and religious ones.

Conflict rooted in competitive economic interests has traditionally become a primary focus of political history. The difficulty with the conventional economic interpretation is that economic or occupational groups in America did not form homogeneous classes and were usually deeply divided. Men differed on the best ways to advance their material well-being; but more importantly, their political preference was colored by the totality of their social situation, which included other roles besides occupational ones. Thus a Quaker merchant might have thought Federalist foreign policy was good for business, but his view might also have been shaped by his desire to harmonize his role as a merchant with his cultural ties with England, or with his fear of those who challenged his position through the Republican party. Though the conventional picture that the early parties stemmed from conflicts between agrarian, commercial, financial, and manufacturing interests is no longer persuasive, economic development was an important source of social differentiation. Some states and certain regions within a state experienced much less economic growth than other areas. Where rapid growth did occur, it generated rivalries that contributed to party development. Thus the emergence of Baltimore as a leading commercial center produced a powerful, ambitious group of Republican merchants, revolving around Robert and Samuel Smith and their connections, who successfully challenged the power of an old-line Federalist leadership entrenched in the rural counties. . . .

Sectional and provincial loyalties further complicated the political picture. Whether one left one's native region or stayed behind, place of birth was a source of pride. People thought of themselves as Virginians or Massachusetts men, Northerners or Southerners, as well as Americans. Presidential ticket makers knew this when they balanced George Washington with John Adams, Adams with Charles C. Pinckney of South Carolina, Thomas Jefferson with Aaron Burr, James Madison with Elbridge Gerry of Massachusetts. "How shall we conjure down this damnable rivalry between Virginia and Massachusetts?" John Adams asked Jefferson some years after they had done battle as representatives of their beloved rival commonwealths and regions.

Whatever its sources, diversity produced tensions in the social structure that undermined habits of deference, fostered competition, and promoted party growth. The variety of groups produced many different perceptions of self-interest and attitudes toward public policy, gave individuals an incentive to participate in public affairs to further their own group interests, and threw up leaders who expressed different perspectives. Wherever social diversity was greatest, it was most difficult for leadership to exercise power unchecked or to continue to receive uncritical deference from the citizenry. Where many competed for advantage in an open society, few could long resist pressures from the excluded. Hence states with highly differentiated social structures were likely to exhibit a more competitive politics than states with a low degree of differentiation. Since aristocracy also ran afoul of republican ideology, thwarted or endangered interests conventionally sought to discredit opponents by denouncing them as "aristocrats." Resistance to change was taken as proof that some Americans presumed illegitimately to possess a superior right to govern and sought to perpetuate temporary advantage, recently acquired, by transforming it into permanent privilege. The result, presumably, would be an hereditary aristocracy, without the birth, blood, or antiquity with which such groups traditionally justified their position. The father of Jeffersonian Republicanism proclaimed the party faith by demanding "equal rights for all, special privileges for none," a theme that reappeared in Republican rhetoric in endlessly different forms like a Wagnerian leitmotif. Here was a doctrine that, theoretically at least, tolled the death knell for the politics of deference.

Diversity of political interests and perspectives not only increased the desire of people to participate politically; it also created obstacles to national integration. The great range of varying interests competing for influence made the achievement of a national consensus no easy task. The first American party system played a critical role, not only in providing a means for various groups to influence decision-making through alliances with others which gave them effective political striking power, but also in promoting trust and a willingness to compromise among disparate forces separated by parochial perspectives and preferences. As the first parties integrated diverse social materials into effective institutions, they provided an instrument by which the nation could accommodate rivalries. For these reasons, not only was a heterogeneous social structure a precondition for the development of political parties in general, but the special form party development took in a particular community reflected in addition its own configuration of social forces. . . .

For almost a generation Americans engaged in a great deal of constitution-making. The particular arrangement agreed upon was the product of colonial experiences and existing power relationships, as well as historical investigation and philosophical reflection. Each state's constitution influenced the extent to which its politics was competitive, for the rules of the game usually shaped patterns of political expression. Thus, in states where informal procedures had traditionally played an important role, inferiors customarily deferred to their superiors; politics was likely to be less competitive than it was in states where leadership recruitment and decision-making were formalized as the result of open rivalry. Formalization promoted political polarization on a statewide basis, sharpened divisions between contending forces, and stimulated coalitions among those with common interests. Where local offices were largely appointive rather than elective, informal arrangements were likely to prevail. Self-perpetuating town and country cliques took turns in office with each member getting an opportunity to enjoy the perquisites and profits of office, as long as he demonstrated appropriate loyalty and patience. Ambitious newcomers were neutralized by admitting them to the favored circle, placing them at the bottom of the ladder but assuring them of eventual ascent. Since disaffected members of the group or excluded elements had no recourse to the electorate to gain access to office, it was nearly hopeless to fight the system, especially since the dominant loyal group easily controlled the county's only elected official, the representative in the legislature. Where local office was elective, on the other hand, political procedures were usually more formalized and open and the opportunities of electoral choice encouraged competition for office. The excluded and disaffected had a more reasonable chance to unseat an entrenched group, which found it much harder to monopolize patronage and office.

A deferential style of politics was strongest where informal procedures and appointive office went together with a constitution which dispersed decision-making in the towns and counties. The more the political structure was decentralized, the more difficult it was to organize on a colony-wide or statewide basis. A strong executive with patronage and the veto, independent of the legislature because he owed his election not to its favor but to a popular vote in a statewide constituency, and who could succeed himself repeatedly, was a centralizing force which promoted political competition. . . .

The political infra-structure of each state was the product of its own peculiar historical development. Whether a state relied on formal or informal procedures, recruited its leaders through election or appointment, centralized or decentralized power, or had a strong or a weak executive, was not entirely fortuitous but reflected the distribution of forces and power in the community and the way citizens thought it best to manage their public affairs. The shaping force in making constitutions was not logic but experience and expectations.

A competitive social and political structure was a necessary precondition for party growth, but not a precipitant. Before 1789 rivalries generally involved provincial interests within the states.

The federal Constitution, however, pushed citizens into a national political arena since the locus of decision-making was now divided between central and local governments. This change rendered inadequate the older methods by which public affairs were managed and stimulated the invention of new ones.

The parties which emerged in the 1790's were distinguished from the factions and *ad hoc* interest groups that had competed for advantage in the colonial and Revolutionary years by their elaboration of structures and functions. Parties systematically organized electoral processes by developing techniques for nominating candidates and persuading the citizens to vote for them on election day. The elaboration of ideologies and party structure, the recruitment of party leadership at different levels, the enlistment of a faithful cadre of party workers, and the development of party loyalty within the electorate gave the first American party system an institutional complexity and stability that earlier political forms lacked. As alliances of heterogeneous elements within a state and among groups in different states, parties also developed a territorial range and social density that made them national in scope and function.

The struggle over centralization during the 1780's, culminating in the federal Constitution, polarized the nation, as widely dispersed and diverse citizens collectively decided how best to manage the affairs of the republic. The newly established national government was also a potential source of continued polarization. The problems confronting the country and the policy choices adopted would affect citizens wherever they lived, and recognition of this fact worked against traditional parochial outlooks. The developing national perspectives of farmers, merchants, manufacturers, mechanics and artisans, holders of public securites, and others were now sharpened and deepened as they sought to shape public policy at the national capital after 1789. As the new government chose between competing courses, it won increased favor among some but disappointed others. Groups learned that they could effectively promote their interests only through national authority, but that rival groups could also thwart their desires through that same authority. Conflicts, compromises, bargains, and deals with distant and often unfamiliar elements were necessary before decisions could be reached. The first American party system became the principal means by which the complex array of interests and local perspectives sorted themselves out and joined together in electoral alliances to promote their welfare.

In the early 1790's Congress became a dramatic arena within which rival groups quarreled over policy questions. Should the state debts be assumed by the federal government, how should the federal debt be funded, how should the tax burden be distributed, should a national bank be established, how should the public domain be managed—these were some of the many vexing questions facing the new government. As a consequence of repeated clashes in the legislative chambers there was an increasing polarization within Congress around particular leaders and issues. As members of Congress articulated differences inherent in the electorate and fought to gain their way, newspapers and other communications media made citizens more aware than ever of the differences that divided them. As divisions emerged in Congress, legislative leaders became keenly interested in the outcome of congressional elections which would determine the strength of their troops at the next session. In this way, national leaders came to take a growing interest in the politics of the various states, while at the same time voters now were making choices that would influence, and were influenced by, national perspectives.

Presidential elections had a similar effect. The obvious preference for George Washington in the first two presidential elections delayed the nationalizing and polarizing impact of a contest for the presidency, and hence its contribution to political party development. The absence of consensus over the succession in 1796, however, encouraged leaders in the capital to form alliances and make arrangements with the various elements that influenced the choice of presidential electors in the states in order to mobilize support behind particular candidates. The previous divisions in the Congress, in the executive branch, and in the states simplified the task of presidential ticket-makers, since lines of opposition had been drawn more and more clearly in many communities before the intrusion of the presidential question.

Thus differences over policy produced national perspectives among interests and voters, splits in the Congress, and rivalry over the presidency, and in turn promoted party development. So too did personal rivalries and conflicts of interest within the states, many of which preceded party development but nonetheless fed the flames of party battle in the 1790's. In many states persisting antagonisms influenced the way people chose sides in the controversies which began to erupt in the capital. The Washington administration could not appoint all those who desired recognition, and those who were disappointed added to the numbers of the disgruntled. . . .

Yet none of these divisions aroused an often lethargic electorate in the way the ideological and diplomatic crisis generated by the French Revolution did. The outbreak of war in Europe in 1793 between Revolutionary France and the coalition of old regimes which were determined to crush republicanism agitated Americans profoundly. The Revolution in France forced them to choose between peace and war, between a French or a British alliance, between lining up with "the party of humanity" or backing "the forces of reaction." Determined to remain neutral in deed, if not in thought, Americans could not escape a choice. Their prosperity was closely bound to ties of trade with the belligerents, and their security and sense of destiny deeply involved in the fate of French republicanism.

At the center of party conflict in the mid-1790's, moreover, was a widespread belief that the future of the republic was threatened. Those who considered themselves Republicans had believed even earlier that the decisions made by the early, Federalist-dominated Congresses had departed from republican principles by benefiting the few at the expense of the many. But Federalists were equally convinced that those measures, denounced as anti-republican by their critics, actually promoted the stability and prosperity of the nation and thereby helped to assure the success of the republican experiment. When Federalists moved to prevent British interference with American trade with France from precipitating war, they confirmed Republican suspicions that they were aristocrats with British sympathies. When Republicans in turn sought to block ratification of Jay's Treaty in 1795 and thereby risk war with Britain, Federalists were confirmed in their suspicions that the Republicans were Jacobins with French sympathies. The crisis of the mid-1790's affected people wherever they lived and whatever their local circumstances, and had a saliency that earlier issues had lacked. By arousing widespread, deep, and fierce partisan sentiments, it simplified and dramatized electoral choice.

The Republican party continued to attract many of those who had already been alienated by the policies of the federal government. Now it also came to encompass others who had once supported Federalist domestic policy but would not support Federalist foreign policy, and still others who had previously taken little interest in public affairs but were aroused by what they saw as new dangers. Although most Republicans prudently wished to avoid involvement in foreign wars, they could not hide their sympathies, and now perceived their own Revolution as the first act in the drama of mankind's regeneration through the American example. Should the votaries of superstition and oppression crush republicanism in Europe, they thought, it could not long survive in America. Moreover, French defeat would bring into question the universality of America's own Revolutionary example and strike a mortal blow at the party of humanity. The Jeffersonians, along with many European *philosophes*, saw the American Revolution as the most important event in human affairs since the coming of Christ. As Jesus had delivered mankind from the tyranny of sin and death, so republicanism, inspired by the American model, promised to free mankind from civic inequality and slavery.

Other Americans, of course, disagreed. Most had welcomed the French Revolution in its early years, but as it became violent and expansionist, and threatened to disrupt peaceful and profitable ties with the rest of the world, the consensus dissolved. Federalism expressed the fears and disillusionment of those who believed that France discredited republicanism by its inability to reconstruct a stable fabric of government at home and by its insatiable lust for conquest abroad. The future of republicanism rested not on the outcome of events abroad but on the establishment of a strong and stable republic at home, they thought, and the export of Jacobinism to the United States was now the most serious threat to the survival of the republic since the crisis of the 1780's. Thus the Federalist and Republican parties, both devoted to republicanism, each believed that the other threatened its survival at home. For the Republicans, those who favored a protective alliance with Britain and were willing to join the war against France betrayed the country's ideals and its mission. In turn, Federalists believed that men who were incapable of distinguishing between genuine republicanism and Gallic tyranny were at bottom American Jacobins who endangered the social order.

Whether citizens chose Federalism or Republicanism depended on their attitudes toward national authority and the way in which they thought it affected their vital interests. Federalist leadership was mainly drawn from elites who had achieved positions of prominence before or during the Revolution, but who were insecure because of challenges from below. These challenges they perceived as attacks on constituted authority, and thus they looked to the national government to protect them from disorder and the spread of "French principles." Republican leaders were more often ambitious newcomers, outsiders who had been excluded by dominant groups from positions of prestige and power. Denied equal access to government, they believed that they were the victims of an erstwhile aristocracy; and thus they regarded national authority as a potential instrument of local aristocracy and identified emotionally with French Revolutionary attacks on entrenched privilege. These alienated elements were galvanized, organized, made self-conscious through the leadership of elites in other states which did not feel threatened within and hence felt no fear of Jacobinism at home, but were disaffected from national authority because they believed they were denied their rightful place in the national councils. For them, the necessities of the national political arena required that they enlist support from among discontented elements in other states even though such allies might be their social inferiors. . . .

Even where conditions were most favorable to party growth, the first American party system failed to survive. In some states where the Republicans won majorities in 1800, Federalists perceived only the dimmest hopes of making a comeback, and many simply gave up the fight. Others invested new energies in party activity, though often with disappointing results. The crisis in foreign affairs after 1805, culminating in the unpopular Embargo of 1807 and the divisive decision to go to war in 1812, caused dissension among Republicans and led to a brief revival of Federalist strength, which, however, fell far short of enabling the party to recapture national power or even to regain it for long in many states. By 1815 Federalism and Republicanism no longer divided the nation into rival political formations. Party organizations decayed, ideological and programmatic differences were blurred, and many Federalists in search of office joined their erstwhile enemies. With each passing year, Jefferson's vision was increasingly coming to pass—"We are all republicans, we are all federalists"—although the emphasis fell on the former term.

Most explanations of the first party system's arrested development have focused on the Federalist decline. Some have argued that the party was deeply divided in the late 1790's between Hamiltonian war Federalists and Adams peace Federalists, and that this division cost the party dearly in the election of 1800 and unity was never restored. But why not? Why didn't the necessities of defeat, the experience of being a minority, force discordant elements to bury their differences sufficiently to form an effective opposition and regain power? Another analysis suggests that the Federalists were doomed by their conservative, aristocratic ideology, which was increasingly incongruous in a society of ongoing democratization. But why didn't the Federalists make a greater effort to adjust their ideology to political realities, as politicians usually do if they desire to regain power? And why were Republican elites so successful in building a party whose *raison d'être* was the destruction of aristocracy? Some have argued that Federalist principles made them loath to resort to the political methods and machinery which the Jeffersonians used so successfully to win office. But why should Federalist gentlemen have been less willing to innovate than Republican gentlemen? Moreover, recent studies suggest that younger Federalists did build elaborate party organizations in many states after 1800 without abandoning their basic ideology. Yet despite such efforts, the party failed to arrest decay.

Another course of explanation seems to be in order. It might begin with the fact that the first political parties were new and fragile institutions, lacking deep roots in political experience, and that party identification and loyalty was recent and weak. It is often difficult to fix clearly a politician's partisan identity in the 1790's and early 1800's, and shifts from one party to another occurred frequently. Party organization was also new and often rudimentary, falling short of stable institutional foundations; thus the early parties were not autonomous institutions, but hastily formed, loose alliances of individuals and groups. Should disaffection or apathy overtake these groups the party would wither away, because the party structure, as such, had only a weak claim to citizen support. Before the 1790's no one had been born a Federalist or Republican, and thus most ordinary citizens and voters did not inherit an ancestral party loyalty. The superficiality of party development helps explain why so many party leaders, especially Federalists, retired from battle, and why still others defected to the Republicans.

Party growth had thrived on the tensions of the 1790's, but

those tensions ebbed in the years that followed Jefferson's election. As the Republicans took power, most Federalists learned that, after all, their old fears of Jacobinism were unfounded. In office the Republicans left many important Federalist policies undisturbed, carefully cultivated support from moderate Federalists they hoped to convert, retained many Federalist jobholders and made removals covertly and piecemeal, so as not to alarm the opposition. Victory was also sobering for the Republicans. Their assumption of power reduced their fears of monarchy and restored their faith in peaceful means of effecting change. Controlling the presidency and Congress, Republicans were no longer hostile to national authority; and power gave them confidence, especially as their continued rule became assured. The more secure and dominant they became, the more they were prone to split into warring factions, especially in states where Federalists no longer effectively challenged them. On this count too, men of virtually all persuasions came to think less and less in party terms.

In this situation, the first party system withered away because most of its builders did not regard themselves as professional party politicians. Such leaders as Washington, Jefferson, and Hamilton had seen themselves as disinterested statesmen, not as political brokers among competing interests or as election managers, even when necessity forced them to behave as though they were. Confidence in their rectitude and the wisdom of their policies made Federalists insensitive and indifferent to the political dangers their rhetoric and programs entailed. In a social order where habits of deference still persisted, a statesman was accustomed to doing what he thought right regardless of personal risk, whereas a professional politician typically calculates risks and maneuvers accordingly within the mainstream of popular currents. The Federalists claimed to be statesmen, not professionals. To most early Republican as well as Federalist leaders too, politics was not a profession. It was rather a duty, a responsibility of gentlemen whose primary commitment was to planting, or trade, or law, or medicine, and the good life. Most hated to stand for or serve in public office. Party leaders often had to plead with popular vote-getters to run for office and with men of special talent to accept major appointments. Despite grave fears for the future of the republic, Thomas Jefferson fled public life in 1793 for Monticello, and not to build an opposition party, as mythology tells it. While President, John Adams spent so much time at home amid comfortable surroundings, neglecting affairs of state, that he temporarily lost control of his own administration. Men unaccustomed to the stinging shafts of political attack, thin-skinned, unused to the rough and tumble of political warfare, preferred to retreat to their firesides rather than remain as targets for mudslingers. If a man was disappointed or defeated, he gracefully retired; one's career did not revolve around winning and holding office. Once again, this was particularly the case among Federalist leaders. For the professional whose occupation is politics, there is nothing else to do but plan, work, wait, and hope for the next election. He knows that there is rhythm in political life and that eventually his fortunes will improve; tomorrow's possible victory makes it easier to accept today's defeat and inspires new energies to hasten the time of his return to office. But for defeated Federalists there could be no such expectation, if only because they had no experience with the cyclical alternation of parties in and out of power. Defeat, when it came, was total.

The Revolutionary generation did produce some prototypes of the political professional, men like Aaron Burr and DeWitt Clinton of New York, whose careers revolved around the pursuit of office. But such individuals inspired distrust and contempt even among those temporarily allied with them, those who needed and used their skills and strength. One could never quite trust men who were governed exclusively by selfish desires, devoid of principle, willing to resort to almost any means to gain their ends. During the deadlocked presidential election of 1800 that ended in the House of Representatives, Alexander Hamilton urged Federalists to support Jefferson over Burr because he thought that the Virginia gentleman, for all his faults, was far less dangerous than the unscrupulous Manhattan politician. In the eyes of the patrician leaders of the first party system, men like Burr lacked the essential moral qualities political leadership demanded. Only those recruited from among the "real" interests of the republic—merchants, farmers, and planters—could understand and would serve the people's needs. Lawyers, the occupation from whom professional politicians were to be recruited, were suspect since they were widely viewed as social parasites, producing no wealth but prospering off the miseries of those who did. To keep public life pure, officials should receive small salaries that would discourage service by any except virtuous men motivated by civic responsibility. A hireling political leadership was as unacceptable in a republic, they thought, as a hireling clergy in a reformed church, and equally dangerous.

One day the republic would need the services and skills of professional politicians. The Revolutionary generation had already discovered that the tasks of governance were far more difficult and complex than they had at first realized. As nation-builders the Americans were amateurs who sailed into rough and uncharted waters, only vaguely aware of the difficult storms ahead. At each step of the journey, none could quite see where it all would lead; but each decision confronted citizens with pressing new problems and choices. Winning independence did not so much create a nation as give men a chance to discover arrangements by which power could be harnessed in the service of liberty and the common good, so that a republic justified by the principles of the Declaration would be more than a short-lived utopian dream. The first efforts to reconstruct political authority in the Confederation by centering power in the states proved incomplete, but the new federal system invented by the Constitution-makers of 1787 was likewise no magic solution. Neither was the first American party system, although it did offer new hope and provide experience on which the organizers of later party systems could draw.

Expanding the Vote

Hard Feelings about the Suffrage

by Chilton Williamson

Most students reading this essay will be eligible to vote in federal elections. But until 1971, in nearly all states, only persons twenty-one and over could go to the polls. This latest extension of the suffrage is one more step in the broadening of the terms of voluntary participation in United States politics. Now vocal, restless younger voters, previously excluded, have the vote, generating apprehensions among some older Americans. In the following essay, Chilton Williamson, using the history of three Northeastern states in the early nineteenth century as test cases, describes a far more fundamental democratization of American voting rights which aroused conservative fears long ago—the elimination of property qualifications.

Property qualifications had long existed in England, and the American colonists simply adapted English practice to their own circumstances. The property requirement disenfranchised the great mass of adult males in England and assured the continuation of aristocratic rule. But in America, where land was abundant and easily accessible, a much higher percentage of the white, adult male population—in many colonies well over the majority—could vote. The Revolution, with its appeal to popular sovereignty, brought the justice of requiring that a man own property before he could vote into question, so a few states extended the franchise to all who paid some taxes. Yet most states maintained the property test on the theory that only those with property, those who had a tangible stake in society, could be trusted to vote independently and responsibly.

In practice, despite the liberal franchise, voter turnout remained low, both in state elections and, after 1789, in national elections. The poor turnouts resulted from apathy, the absence of meaningful choices on election days, and the ingrained willingness of many common people to defer to the wisdom and expertise of their better educated and richer neighbors.

The development of political parties in the 1790's produced a notable surge in the number of voters. First, parties competed vigorously, aroused the electorate, and made sure that the faithful trooped to the polls. And electioneering, newspaper wars, and campaign promises gave people an incentive to vote. Parties transformed government from something remote and distant into an institution that appeared to affect their welfare directly. Each party claimed that the country would prosper under its guidance, and its guidance alone.

At the same time that partisan rivalry increased voter participation, a broadening of the electorate took place, as Chilton Williamson demonstrates. In Connecticut, New York, Massachusetts, and elsewhere, astute politicians saw in a wider franchise a way to gain office, first by championing a popular cause and then by securing credit for achieving a democratic reform. The campaign to eliminate property qualifications ran into much less opposition in America than in Europe because in the New World most people either owned some property or expected to own some as the result of individual enterprise. The wealthy, therefore, felt less threatened than did European elites, fearful of being engulfed, once the barriers went down, by a mass of propertyless farmers and urban laborers.

In Britain and in Europe, the Napoleonic Wars were followed by a period of reaction against war and revolution, and against the democratic principles which many thought were responsible for both. British historians have long agreed that the sequence of events from 1789 to 1815 postponed the reform of British suffrage and representation until 1832, when the great Reform Bill was passed. The conservative reaction was reflected here and there in America but it made little or no impression upon majority opinion in Connecticut, Massachusetts, and New York, where constitutional revision reopened the issue of the suffrage. Conservatives thought they had the better of the arguments, but they did not have the votes to sustain them.

The reasons for the further attrition of suffrage conservatism differed somewhat from state to state. Federalism in Connecticut, for example, had been dealt a series of blows since about 1812 from which it never recovered. Firstly, the Federalists' lack of patriotism during the war was widely condemned; secondly, they failed to appease the religious grievances of a large number of citizens and, in general, showed themselves incapable of adjusting their thought to the changing times. Federalism was weakened further as the result of criticism within the party of the power of Congregational ministers in state affairs. Lay Federalists were less disposed to accept without question the advice, so freely tendered, of leading Congregational ministers on nominations to office and on other secular matters. Lyman Beecher asserted that the refusal of Federalist laymen to accept the nominees of the ministers for governor in 1811 "shook the stability of the standing order and the Federal Party in the state" and, in effect, broke the charm which the ministers had held for generations over laymen.

Demands for reform increased to the point where it was possible to unite all the elements which had grievances against the standing order. The fusion of the reform elements took place at a meeting of Republicans and Episcopalians at New Haven in

February 1816. Reformers agreed to a program which included pledges to separate church and state, reform the suffrage, repeal the Stand Up Law, shift the incidence of taxation from polls to real property, and achieve full publicity for legislative debates and proceedings, a practice conceded in Britain only shortly before the American Revolution and by the United States Congress as late as 1793.

Oliver Wolcott, ex-Federalist, farmer, manufacturer, and Congregationalist, assumed the leadership of a more heterogeneous Republican party than that of Abraham Bishop's time. To appeal to all reformers, it was called the Toleration Party or the Union Reform Ticket. The party exerted all its efforts in 1817 to win control of the state government in order to assure the calling of a constitutional convention which would carry through reform.

The first order of business for Republicans after their success in the elections of 1817 was the repeal of the Stand Up Law. A friend of Oliver Wolcott strongly advised him to attack the law because it was outrageous that men "called freemen" had to vote publicly before the civil authorities and established clergy, both of whom were active in elections. Connecticut would not know true freedom, he said, until it enjoyed the secret ballot in all elections. Much to the point was Republican conviction that the law cost them about one-fourth of their potential voting strength. The property tests, the failure of Federalist-dominated towns to qualify as many Republican freemen as they did Federalists, and the "criminal neglect" of voting were responsible, according to Connecticut Republicans, for the fact that only about one person in ten voted in their state, whereas about one in six voted in Massachusetts, New Hampshire, and Vermont.

Federalists defended the old order, particularly the Stand Up Law, saying that its repeal would force the return to the cumbersome methods of nominating the assistants which had been abandoned by some towns in favor of those of the Stand Up Law long before it had been passed. Republicans remained unconvinced and, in the fall of 1817, it was repealed.

Another reform adopted in 1817 increased Republican strength.

Believing that the most important element of the population unable to qualify under existing legislation were young men, reformers gave the vote to all free males over twenty-one who paid taxes or served in the militia. Although this act was in part an electoral stratagem, it also stemmed from the conviction that in any act so fundamental as the writing of a constitution virtually all adult males should have a say. It was because of this conviction that all adult males had been permitted to vote for members of the state convention to ratify the Federal Constitution. Federalists opposed the act publicly as much as they dared. They denounced it as a wicked device of Connecticut Jacobinism, adopted only when Republicans suspected that a majority of qualified freemen would not vote for reform.

Federalists tried to discredit reform not only by associating it with Jacobinism but also by confounding it with the British reform movement. Commenting upon the Union and Reform Ticket of 1817, the *Connecticut Mirror* said that this "charming name appears to be of English origin, and is thought will inherit all the virtues of its family relations in that country." Agreeing with Lyman Beecher that Connecticut Republicans included nearly all the smaller sects, "besides the Sabbath-breakers, rum-selling tippling folk, infidels and ruff-scuff generally," Federalists spokesmen were certain that the Republic had degenerated under the leadership of Jefferson. Cromwell's military dictatorship was as much the inevitable outcome of English democracy as Napoleon's dictatorship was the outcome of French democracy, declared the *Connecticut Courant*, and asserted that both Englishmen and Frenchmen preferred a military dictatorship to the "plague of democracy, from which they had escaped." A dictatorship, it implied, would be preferable to democracy in Connecticut.

Here, as elsewhere, Federalists appealed to the writings of Thomas Jefferson when it suited their purposes. They tried to infer from what he had written that all was well in Connecticut, quoting his alleged statement that Connecticut was "the Athens of America." Some Federalists introduced the argument that their state was basically a democracy in the true sense of the word because the people, rightly conceived, already comprised the majority of the voters. Drawing a distinction between *the people* and *the populace*, the *Courant* declared that *the people* were actually the middle class. In Connecticut, this middle class was descended from Englishmen who had triumphed at the time of the Glorious Revolution. It was midway between "the great ones" and the populace, which elsewhere in the world, particularly in Africa and Asia, was alarmingly large.

In reply, Republicans revived the arguments of Abraham Bishop, but they recognized also that changing times had produced new problems, all of which had a bearing upon the suffrage reform movement. One of these was the result of the growth of manufacturing which had been stimulated by the Embargo and War of 1812 and now sought protection by federal tariff legislation. Henry Clay, sponsor of the American system, advocated a protective tariff not only to help small manufacturers struggling against British competition but also to create a home market in the east for the surplus farm products of the west. In Philadelphia, Matthew Carey, fresh from reading Richard Malthus's *Essay on Population,* supported tariff protection as the means by which American manufacturers could pay higher wages to their working people than were paid in Europe, thereby forestalling Malthus's gloomy predictions concerning the future of an industrial society.

Connecticut's suffrage reformers were sensitive to this problem and aware of its bearing upon the suffrage because Connecticut was becoming a center of manufacturing. Hitherto, the Blackstonian argument that employees of manufacturing establishments should not be allowed to vote because they were overly dependent upon their employers had been a theoretical one for Americans in general. This argument was relevant only in an industrial society such as Britain or in certain societies on the European continent. The debates in America over the tariff showed, however, that the tempo of industrialism in the United States was quickening. The fears of suffrage conservatives for the future had, for the first time, real substance. The Connecticut legislature listened with attention, no doubt, to Matthew Griswold when he described in Blackstonian terms how manufacturing would in time change the face of America and produce a shock to the electoral system.

In an important development in suffrage thought, Republicans, some of whom were engaged like Wolcott in manufacturing, repudiated the Blackstonian argument and advocated a taxpaying qualification. *Niles' Register*, a national spokesman for the manufacturing interest, said that property tests themselves led to an aristocracy while a personal-property test or universal suffrage led to election frauds. Only a taxpaying qualification was free of these undesirable accompaniments. A proper and just handling of the suffrage, it maintained, was the bulwark against social instability and radicalism. Industrialism, in effect, was incompatible neither with order nor a broad suffrage. "If the suffrage is rightfully considered," *Niles' Register* said in 1820, "it is hardly possible that any serious contention can arise among the people of a free state." Needless to say, the journal approved the repeal of the Stand Up Law, declaring that Connecticut needed a constitution to secure "equal rights."

At this time, Connecticut was not only undergoing changes resulting from the growth of manufacturing but was also being affected by the growth of the New West. Young men and others had already left Connecticut to help found Vermont and had contributed greatly to the peopling of the Western Reserve. One suffrage reformer argued that political reform at home might prevent further emigration. The *Connecticut Register* declared that, if men continued victims of the Stand Up Law and other injustices, they would "emigrate to the west and your state would lose its name in the nation."

Lastly, Republicans were aware of the necessity for the reform of the militia. In Washington, John C. Calhoun, as Secretary of War, was endeavoring to create a militia system which would prove more effective in future wars. Reformers in Connecticut thought that the militia of their state had been ineffective in the

War of 1812 because young men were not very concerned about protecting a state in whose government they had no share, and they argued that at least all adult males active in the militia should be allowed to vote. A New Haven paper declared in 1816 that it was as honorable to qualify a man as a freeman as it was to equip him to fight, as honorable to assist him in getting to the polls as in getting him to a military review.

In one particular only were proponents and opponents of reform in agreement. Both had had considerable acquaintaince with the abuse of the franchise by illegal voting and they wanted a realistic and enforceable election law. The elections of 1817 and 1818 had witnessed extraordinary exertions on both sides to win by fair means or foul. One observer declared, in view of the practices of those elections, that Connecticut had a corrupt version of universal suffrage and that almost any change would be for the better. Partly for this reason, the suffrage clause of the constitution, conceding the vote to adult white males of "good character," resident six months in a town, who were $7 freeholders or militiamen or state taxpayers, was considered by many a successful effort to purge the suffrage of undesirable and overly democratic elements. Indeed, the *Connecticut Herald* denied on September 28, 1818, that the constitution rested upon universal manhood suffrage, saying that the illegal practices which had prevailed before had "approached far nearer to universal suffrage than the . . . suffrage article of the Constitution."

Nevertheless, the provision of the constitution and the act of 1821, which removed the theoretical distinction between the freeman qualification and the qualification for non-freemen for voting in town affairs, brought the law into conformity with the practice in towns at various times, i.e., voting by males who were resident taxpayers. If the growth of parties caused a more stringent enforcement of the laws than previously, it is a distinct possibility that in actual practice the suffrage was less "democratic" after 1818 than it had been in the eighteenth century. At all events, the numbers voting in elections declined rather than increased after the reform was instituted. Moreover, the requirement that voters be citizens indicated an increase in legal precision and a suspicion of foreigners. Oliver Wolcott, for one, shared the growing bias of his generation against immigrants. During 1803 he had written Fisher Ames that the landowners of Pennsylvania had unwisely stimulated the rapid settlement of their colony by offering citizenship on easy terms "till at length the powers of Government, have been transformed to a Class of People, too heterogeneous . . . & too violent and ignorant to use with moderation."

The citizenship requirement came just one year after Chief Justice Marshall, in the case of *Chirac* v. *Chirac*, had laid down the dictum that naturalization lay exclusively in the sphere of federal competence. Henceforth, states which inserted citizenship clauses had reference to citizenship gained under federal statutes rather than those which some states had inherited from colonial times. Another indication that the convention was more prejudiced about race than about class was its confinement of the suffrage to persons who were white.

For a number of reasons, therefore, the constitution in its suffrage and other clauses was a moderate document for which even Federalists could vote. Indeed, their aid was almost indispensable in achieving the adoption of a constitution which aroused criticism because it did not meet demands for universal suffrage or for a redistricting of seats in the legislature. The adoption of the constitution, however, caused a slump in reform interest as indicated by the decline in voting. "In Connecticut," said the *National Advocate* of New York, "they disarmed the poorer classes by taking them into the body politic." A taxpaying qualification in Connecticut, as in many other states, was almost manhood suffrage, so long as males of voting age were almost all polled.

The success of Connecticut reform helped to generate elsewhere in the northeast a questioning of the effectiveness, utility, and justice of state constitutions which had existed since the close of the Revolution without much modification. In Massachusetts, for example, the press kept the public informed of developments in Connecticut. However, when Massachusetts decided on constitutional revision and reform, the immediate occasion was the decision of the people of the District of Maine to set up their own state. In 1819 the separation was formalized. Maine drafted a constitution which conceded universal manhood suffrage in state elections and a taxpaying qualification in town meetings, thus writing into law an approximation of the prevailing practice in Massachusetts, as Vermont had legalized the loose practices prevailing in her parent state, Connecticut, before the Revolution.

One year later Maine became a separate state, a notable convention met in Boston. The suffrage was an important subject of its debate, particularly during the exchange of views between old John Adams, the chairman of the convention, and the young Daniel Webster. The last Federalist President of the United States could not abandon his adherence to the Blackstonian school. He had declared himself against a taxpaying qualification in 1811 and, as late as 1816, he was shocked by the venality of British elections. He knew, moreover, that Massachusetts was changing, and in his opinion not always for the better. Another prominent citizen, Josiah Quincy, was alarmed by the increase in paupers, writing Oliver Wolcott that "the poor come in shoals from Nova Scotia & Ireland; and we must find some means to reduce the number or we shall all be candidates for the alms house." A Boston paper averred that pauperism was increasing more rapidly in Massachusetts than in Britain and that the increase was due to alcoholism, early and improvident marriages, and an irrational system of outdoor poor relief like that against which liberal British economists railed. Manufacturing was aggravating rather than ameliorating the situation. The parallel between old and New England seemed too marked to ignore. Massachusetts seemed just a step or two behind Britain.

For these reasons, John Adams was convinced more stubbornly than ever that the future happiness and welfare of the American people rested not only upon a system of checks and balances but also upon sound suffrage principle and practice. It is therefore understandable that he abandoned his impartial role as chairman of the convention long enough to make known his views, now reactionary even for Federalism. The French Revolution, he said sarcastically, was a "perfect and complete" example of the "utility and excellence of universal suffrage." Its British advocates, he exclaimed, were "ruining themselves."

In one of the more notable addresses of the convention, Daniel Webster answered the old gentleman obliquely. He spoke as a man greatly influenced by the seventeenth-century English theorist, James Harrington, whose most famous assertion was that dominion follows property, and also by ideas bearing a Jeffersonian stamp. Acknowledging that, where there were great extremes between the propertied and the non-propertied, universal suffrage would indeed be dangerous, Webster went on to say that in this country "the people possess the property more emphatically than it could be said of the people of any country," and that the real task of statesmen was to see that property was distributed in such a way as to give the "great majority of society an interest in defending it." Only where great inequalities in property existed would universal suffrage be a menace to property, liberty and order.

The majority of the members of the convention were in agreement with Webster, and for this reason the suffrage debate was not so important as the issue of representation. Webster was an advocate of representation, not on the basis of population exclusively but on the basis of taxation as well, particularly in the senate. He was not fearful of a liberal suffrage in the future as much as he was concerned about a more equitable representation for commercial and manufacturing interests and a better balance between the various interests in the state. New York's *National Advocate* of July 21, 1821, published a brilliant analysis of Webster's role at the convention. Claiming that celebrated men were more "attentive to local interests than to great principles of free government," it said that no one at the convention had displayed more ingenuity than Webster, "for while he was apparently advocating the Agrarian, or rather, freehold plan of government, and seemed disposed to lodge the power with the agriculturalists he was actually laboring to secure to the commercial portion of the commonwealth the power in the senate. This complexion," the paper exclaimed, "was probably thrown over his reflections, to obtain the votes of the country members."

Webster failed to secure the adoption of his plan of representation, but he collaborated successfully in the plan for suffrage by which taxpayers could vote if qualified by age, residence, and citizenship. He maintained that no one who did not contribute to the support of government should be allowed to vote, a principle very different from that underlying universal suffrage and a logical position for one who advocated representation based upon taxation for the senate.

When the convention composed an address to the people, it supported the suffrage clause with the observation that it would "relieve Selectmen from much perplexity, and will enable them easily to distinguish between those who have a right to vote and those who do not." Newspaper discussion of the suffrage clause was so slight as to indicate that the general torpor of opinion about constitutional matters in general extended to suffrage matters. Only one newspaper hailed it as a triumph for the rights of man and as of "more importance in principle than all the others put together." On November 1, 1820, the *Essex Register* of Salem approved the clause, declaring that a property qualification was an encouragement to fraud in times of political excitement, "and these are the only times when any qualifications are necessary, for it is only at such times that they are attended to. If there was any way by which no one but those who would exercise their judgment freely, and without influence or corruption should be admitted to the vote, we would most gladly subscribe to it. But we are satisfied no such way exists—we therefore must, most certainly open the door of universal suffrage." Because adult males without property were liable to a poll tax and, if overlooked by the tax assessors, had the right to demand that they be taxed, suffrage without reference to property had been effected without being expressly recognized by law. In the light of the suffrage history of Massachusetts, it may be said that the document altered, but not essentially, the old qualification.

Response to the qualification was not wholly favorable, however. In answer to the comments of some who were disappointed that unmarried women who owned property or paid taxes could not vote, "Gracchus" replied that they had disobeyed God's injunction to multiply and subdue the earth. Aristotle's authority was invoked because he had written that women were less fit to govern than men. The provision of the constitution which allowed minors enrolled in the militia to vote in militia elections was attacked on the grounds that some masters would be obliged to train under their apprentices, "to the great detriment of the principle of subordination established from the beginning of the world." These criticisms had little effect. The suffrage clause was ratified by a vote of 18,702 to 10,150.

In the same year, the Boston town-meeting form of government was finally abandoned in favor of a city form of government, the suffrage being extended to all taxpayers. Two years later, the last propertied distinction between voters in town affairs and state voters was abolished. The simplification of the suffrage thus achieved did not increase popular participation in government, unless the electorate received an unusual political stimulus. For example, votes for governor declined from 53,297 in 1820 to 49,086 in 1821, shot up to 73,051 in 1824, then dropped to 40,338 in 1826. Lack of interest, for whatever reason, rather than lack of enfranchisement has been the vital fact in Massachusetts electoral history. It is doubtful if the right to vote in Massachusetts just before the Civil War was any more widely shared than it had been before the American Revolution, despite the "democratization" of the suffrage. Only one person in six of the total population was a legal voter in 1857.

A quite different pattern of enfranchisement, or unenfranchisement, prevailed in New York, where, in 1821, a convention distinguished by the presence of many notable Americans was the seat of one of the great suffrage debates in American history. The desire, long dormant, to revise or to scrap the Revolutionary constitution was stimulated by the efforts of British reformers to liberalize the franchise in Britain. New York and Albany papers reported mass meetings addressed by Orator Hunt and others in Manchester, Smithfield, and Leeds. William Cobbett's *Political Register* was quoted. Finally, accounts in the press of the Connecticut and Massachusetts conventions also encouraged criticism of New York's political institutions. Many persons favorably impressed by what was happening in nearby eastern states met in conventions to demand reform in Washington County in 1817 and in Montgomery County in 1820. The members of the latter convention were said to be watching the outcome of the Massachusetts deliberations "with anxious solicitude."

Some New Yorkers were critical of revisionism wherever it might occur and happy to learn that it had not been as extreme as feared. Rufus King, for example, was pleased that Massachusetts had rejected universal suffrage. The *New York Evening Post* declared that scenes of "mobocratic gallantry" which had occurred recently in some British cities were an inevitable result of the demagoguery of men like Burdett and Hunt. The *Albany Daily Advertiser* expressed the hope on May 3, 1817, that the morals of Connecticut would not be destroyed "in the whirlpool of democratic liberty and Jacobin frenzy."

A major impulse for revision of New York's constitution came from the great changes taking place in the character of the population of the state. Not only did Yankee merchants move into the port of New York early in the nineteenth century to engage in trade, but Yankees also came over the barrier of the Berkshires and the Green Mountains to settle upstate New York. Whereas in 1777 two-thirds of the population of New York lived south of Albany, in 1820 the figure was only one-third. Furthermore, the nature of this population was changing the state and its political outlook because Yankees, coming from states which had not since the Revolution known a balanced form of government or, with the exception of Rhode Island, a freehold qualification for voting, or even much enforcement of the suffrage laws, found New York's constitution undemocratic. Of the 107 members of the constitutional convention which met in Albany in 1821, 31 had been born in Connecticut and 7 in Massachusetts. Contemporaries realized the significance of these facts. Rufus King, Federalist turned Republican, wrote Christopher Gore that the population of the state was "nearly divided between the old and the new Inhabitants—the latter are out of New England where laws, customs, and usages differ from those of N York." James Wadsworth, a major landowner of the Genesee, declared flatly in 1821 that "whatever abstract opinions old Inhabitants on the Hudson may entertain on the subject of civil government," it should not be overlooked that "we are a Republic surrounded by sister republics, whose Constitutions are more liberal than our own—and the common people of those republics have acquired a general intelligence & a sense of moral obligation which guaranty to their governments a stability & a fidelity . . . which ours does not possess. You cannot retard, you cannot stay, the progress of these liberal provisions for the improvement of the people of this state."

In New York, suffrage became a much more important issue than it had been in either Connecticut or Massachusetts, and for good reason. The existence of a balanced form of government resting upon a dual electorate, composed of 20-pound freeholders and 40-shilling renters for the assembly, and 100-pound freeholders for the senate and for governor, was threatened. By 1821, the total electorate of both classes comprised 14.76 per-cent of the total population, or approximately 78 per-cent of adult males. Only 38.7 per-cent of all electors could vote legally, however, for governor and the senate. In New York City, about 62 per-cent of the total male population could vote legally while only 24 per-cent could vote for senators and governor. Critics found it impossible to understand why the New York founding fathers, in a convention elected by the mass of the people, created such complex and undemocratic suffrage qualifications. One observer declared that it was due to the colonial aristocracy of New York whose allegiance to the Revolution would have been jeopardized if an overly democratic government had been established. Also, it was said that, without residence and property tests, Tories, Hessians, and other undesirables would have made more difficult the election of safe and sound Whigs. The *National Advocate* had another explanation: the founding fathers knew the rights of man in theory but they had yet to learn them by practice. "Whatever the cause for the suffrage clauses of the constitution, they must go," said the newspaper. "We are not a government of the people while such disabilities exist. . . ." Arguments based on natural rights, now platitudinous, were used here as elsewhere by reformers, and at various meetings held on July 4, 1820, to advocate suffrage reform there were demands to extend the franchise to militia men and taxpayers.

Practical no less than theoretical considerations figured in the burden of arguments against the existing suffrage laws. "Republican Young Men," comprising a group which could least easily meet the qualifications, held a meeting at Saratoga on January 22, 1821, and criticized the constitution for limiting the suffrage and not placing more local offices at the disposal of the electorate. As fundamental was the argument that the suffrage laws meant different things in different parts of the state. Evidence was presented that in some places all adult male residents on tax lists were being permitted to vote, that the distinction between the voters for the assembly and for the senate and governor broke down under the impact of party ambition, that fagot voting was widespread, and that with no sure method of determining who could or could not qualify, many persons, when tendered the elector's oath, perjured themselves, unwittingly or not. One observer commented that to extend the franchise "would leave us just where we are now; since every man who can be trusted with a deed, is made a freeholder long enough to vote in elections worth the expense of such a contest."

An added complication arose from the difficulty of determining what kinds of leases should be considered freeholds. By statute, only leases for an indefinite number of years had been declared freeholds. A contemporary analysis showed, however, that different rules obtained in different parts of the state, probably all different from the law, and that in most cases long-term leaseholds were considered freeholds. The confusion in those parts of New York where the manor system survived, until swept away in the aftermath of the Anti-Rent War of the 1840's, was comparable to the situation in the extreme western part of the state, where the Holland Land Company and other great absentee landowning interests disposed of lands by a peculiar method. The company refused to give title deeds to lands until the purchaser had paid for them in full. Not having deeds to their lands, the early settlers were unable to qualify as voters for governor and senate, or serve legally on juries or fulfill other important duties in local government. The agent of the company, Joseph Ellicott, was faced with an ugly situation when, in the election of 1807, Federalists challenged the right of settlers from Vermont, accustomed to universal manhood suffrage, to vote on the grounds that they were not freeholders. Some of these, exasperated at having come as far as twenty miles to vote, employed their fists, as a contemporary account said, and voted.

This problem was met in various ways. Election officials might ignore the qualification, a deed might be given for that part of the land which had been improved, or payments under contract might be interpreted as creating an equity in the freehold sufficient to enable the purchaser to vote. Elsewhere, it was said, those persons buying land in installments were not voting. One can appreciate the comment of a contemporary that the requirements for qualification of the freehold voter, being so much "matters of law, fact, and opinion, frequently render the right so questionable, as to excite an opposition which can only be removed by the oath of the party." Disputes over assembly voters were much less numerous, because it was relatively easy to determine who was a renter and a taxpayer. The outmoded character of the freehold qualification is indicated further by the fact that a man who owned ten feet of ground worth 100 pounds voted, while a middle-class man worth a million, an honest mechanic, or prosperous merchant could not vote.

At all events, one critic branded the freehold qualification as the product of Norman lawyers. "In this enlightened age, and in this republican country," he said, the rights of free men "should not be tested by the refinements and subtleties of Norman jurisprudence." Furthermore, the distinction between assembly and other voters did not serve any useful purpose in a country where property was so diffused, where for a long time the freeholders would be in the ascendancy, and where the poor of today were the rich of the morrow. Even bicameralism, as a feature of balanced government, he argued, could be abandoned if its worth were disproved.

The leading politicians of the two major opposing factions in New York, the Clintonians and the Bucktails, understood the issue of democracy at stake but understood also the partisan issues and interests involved. Van Buren and other Bucktails hoped that associating themselves with reform would enable them to persuade the electors to turn DeWitt Clinton out of office and vote the Bucktails in. Clinton, on his part, was said to be in a dilemma because he relied greatly on freehold votes but at the same time wanted reform, to the extent at least of eliminating the Council of Appointment and consolidating power over patronage matters in the hands of the governor. Clinton knew that the Bucktails had felt their defeat at the polls, as a friend wrote him in May of 1820, "to the pith of their bones and to the core of their hearts but are recovering from their dismay and hope to revolutionize everything. . . ." So far as suffrage was concerned, only Van Buren's mouthpiece, the *Albany Argus*, advocated universal suffrage. Nevertheless, all factions accused each other of harboring elements opposed to suffrage reform in a way which determined that it would not be a clearcut party issue.

When the bill to submit the question of a convention was

drafted, the effort of its sponsor to use the Massachusetts plan of 1780, allowing universal white manhood suffrage, was turned down in favor of a freehold, taxpaying, or militia qualification, thus breaching only in a cautious way the constitutional requirement of 1777. The resulting election was the most openly democratic since the stirring elections just before the Revolution. *The Columbian* was correct in stating that for the first time all young men, twenty-one to thirty years of age, had the privilege of voting; it urged them to use it well. The *Argus* exhorted the "brave and generous youth of Albany" to go to the polls with the same alacrity with which they reached for their muskets. Whereas only 93,437 votes had been cast for governor in the election of 1820, 144,247 were cast on the question of having a convention in 1821, of whom only 34,891 voted in opposition. Whether or not this increase was due in any considerable degree to the enfranchisement of 30,000 young men, otherwise unqualified by property tests to vote, has not been determined.

Suffice it to say that the election of 1821 breached the suffrage barriers of 1777. The sequel showed that Van Buren had been substantially correct when, during the convention, he opposed universal suffrage, partly on Blackstonian and Jeffersonian grounds and partly on the grounds that the experiment, once tried, would be irrevocable. A qualification allowing adult white male citizens to vote, if taxpayers or militia men, was actually the qualification written into the constitution of 1821. Chief Justice Spencer's efforts, with quotations from Jefferson about the virtues of the cultivators of the earth, to preserve the freehold qualification for the senate were vitiated by the retort that Jefferson had changed his mind on the suffrage issue. James Kent, upholder of Blackstonian and even Jeffersonian principles, found that agrarianism was criticized by a defender of the working classes. Daniel D. Tomkins asserted that there was more honesty and integrity to be found in them than in the higher classes, and paid his respects to the emphasis of the classical economists upon the crucial role of labor in the creation of capital. Disavowing an intention to enfranchise the poor, Samuel Young, American Ricardian, said that he favored the enfranchisement of "the intermediate class," and that the time when America would have to wrestle with the problems of an urban proletariat in the grip of Malthusian laws was far distant. "Chill penury," he declared, in a quotation from Oliver Goldsmith's *Deserted Village*, was not a characteristic of the country. So long as there was an abundance of land and a relative absence of land speculation, it never would be.

The New York City delegation was particularly sensitive to Kent's dicta. If we can believe Rufus King, only two members of the New York delegation, Nathan Sanford and Jacob Radcliff, favored a more democratic suffrage than that which was adopted. The others were opposed to a broader franchise not only because they were sincerely convinced that Kent had the correct vision of the American future, but because they found their city suffering from the tribulations of early nineteenth-century urbanism. The cry that pauperism was on the increase was often raised in the city's conservative press. Moreover, property owners in the city were alarmed at the mounting municipal tax burden which they associated with the modest rent-paying qualification for voting in the city since 1804, and which they said that Tammany Hall exploited. On February 2, 1821, the *New York Evening Post* declared that the doctrine that all men are created free and equal had created enormous mischief, pointing in particular to the fact that the poor performance of the Corporation of New York was the result of applying to government the principle of no taxation without representation, without proper safeguards. It suggested that a special governing board composed exclusively of freeholders be established, to be elected by persons qualified to vote in city affairs. Another proposal was to create a chamber of landowners in which only landowners could sit or vote.

A proposal more friendly and more sympathetic to the problems of workers in city factories was made several years later, one indicating an indebtedness to Robert Owen's schemes for a social democracy within the framework of the institution of private property. Declaring that a new kind of feudalism had emerged in which wealthy manufacturers were in a position to control hundreds of votes, the proposal envisaged as necessary the planning of the growth of manufacturing, itself eminently desirable, in such a way as to prevent society's suffering from its disadvantages. This could be achieved by creating a joint stock company of small capitalists, each one of whom would have a part of the factory under his general supervision, each part being managed directly by men elected by the "free suffrage of all." Universal suffrage in factories would prevent the workers from being subjected to degradation, as they were in England, and provide them with a political education equal to that of the agricultural classes.

Despite their concern as to what the future might hold, sensible men regardless of political ties accepted suffrage reform as inevitable, if for no other reason. Rufus King probably expressed majority opinion when he advocated acceptance of the new constitution on the grounds that it would make for repose and stability. Its rejection, he thought, would shake the very foundations of society. It was impossible to prevent the lowering of the voting qualification, he said, and added, "One of the things last learned is the Duty of every Government to concur in & approve measures which they could not if they would hinder—in this way things are stopped from going to Extremes. . . ."

The belief of many New Yorkers that they were at a historic turning point is not justified by the immediate consequences of the suffrage reform of 1821. The proportion of electors for assemblymen among the adult male population increased only from about 78 per cent to 90 per cent. This was not, in Carlyle's phrase, "shooting Niagara." Those who had agreed to a taxpaying or a militia qualification for voting had hoped that it closed the suffrage debate indefinitely. Nevertheless, that universal suffrage which almost all New York reformers had disavowed was conceded in the form of an amendment to the constitution in 1826. In contrast to Maryland, where there was an uproar over the suffrage in 1800, New York was not aroused to any extent over the issue.

The transition from taxpaying to universal suffrage was achieved without even much comment in the press. The reasons lay in the mundane problems to which a simplified, but still complex qualification had given rise. In the first place, a taxpaying qualification encouraged numerous frauds at the polls. In the Sixth Ward of New York, for example, a voter was challenged on the ground that he was not a taxpayer. The collector of taxes consulted his books and asserted that he was. When the books were examined closely after election, it was determined that he was not a voter and that the collector had lied. Whether or not renters who paid taxes on the property they occupied should be deemed taxpayers, in the meaning of the constitution, was determined only by a law passed in 1823. As late as 1825, the senate was wrestling with the problem of clarifying the taxpaying qualification of lessees and lessors. Where tenants paid the taxes, a landlord might lose his vote. Where the landlord paid them, the tenant, who was often a laborer or mechanic, might lose his, unless he were otherwise qualified by the constitution. The *Argus* claimed that 500 men had lost the franchise in 1823 because they had been exempted from militia duties, having served with the volunteer fire department. Governor Joseph C. Yates had, therefore, ample reason for declaring, in his message of January 1823, that difficulties had arisen at the polls over the proper interpretation of the suffrage clauses of the new constitution, implying that something should be done.

Suffrage extension, on the grounds of preventing fraud and injustice, as much as on the grounds that it was a necessary step toward suffrage democracy, became a political issue in the gubernatorial campaign of 1824. The Republicans chose to capitalize on the roles which Samuel Young and Erastus Root had played as suffrage reformers in the convention by selecting them as their candidates for governor and lieutenant-governor to run against DeWitt Clinton and his running mate. During the campaign, opponents of Clinton attacked him for his opposition to the calling of the convention, and the candidate for lieutenant-governor for his conservative views on suffrage in the past. The Clintonians were quick to repudiate their past equivocations, but no more so than the Republicans. To such an extent did both factions stand for further simplification and purification of the suffrage that there was little real choice on the matter in the election.

As the victor in the campaign, Clinton honored his commitments to the electorate and his own convictions, privately expressed before election, that the suffrage needed to be "more carefully defined and more liberally extended." He recommended in January 1825 that because the existing qualification did not include all citizens it should be revised. He indicated that perhaps universal suffrage would be necessary because the state tax, which had recently been reduced from 2 mills to ½ mill on the dollar, might soon be eliminated completely. If it were, the taxpaying qualification would be a major disfranchiser and would virtually restrict the electorate to those who served in the militia, a palpable absurdity. For this reason, as well as others, Clinton advocated a qualification based solely on citizenship, age, and residence. His common-sense approach appealed to New Yorkers. Amid cries that Republicans, rather than Clintonians, had been the first to advocate suffrage reform, the amendment eliminating the taxpaying qualification became a part of the constitution in 1826. With remarkable swiftness, the minority opinion of 1821 had become the majority conviction by 1826. The spectacular lack of resistance to further reform in 1826 is reasonable when it is borne in mind that the proportion of the population qualified to vote increased only 1 per cent.

The suffrage reforms in Connecticut, Massachusetts, and New York brought to an end an often harsh and strident debate on the suffrage. The contribution which these reforms made to the practice of a democratic suffrage has been exaggerated, but not their contribution to that conception essential to American nationalism that this country was very different from Europe, and that the suffrage conservatism of Europe, from Aristotle forward, had little meaning in the United States. In this country, there would be no repetition of European developments, no matter what else might take place. The *National Advocate* illustrated the divorce of American suffrage thought from Europe when it criticized Daniel Webster for not having declared his independence from James Harrington. "In forming our government," it said, "we may borrow some of Mr. Harrington's notions here and reject them there. . . . A free people will adopt that form of government which please the majority, without regard to what might have pleased nations in other times and in other conditions."

The New Politics and Political Innovation

Changing Concepts of Party in the United States: New York 1815–1828

by Michael Wallace

In the first quarter of the nineteenth century, the form and style of American politics underwent important changes. By the late 1820's popular participation had become a leading factor in American politics. Not only did more men exercise their right to vote, but the symbolic importance of the campaigns against property qualifications for the franchise and for officeholding contributed significantly to the replacement of the old elitist political order by a more egalitarian one.

The new order rested on modern forms of political organization and voter stimulation. Not only did strong national parties begin to appear, ending the Republican one-party reign, but such practices as the nominating convention became common and useful to the politicos organizing the emerging parties. The convention device could be used for the dual purpose of strengthening the party apparatus, while simultaneously providing the illusion of greater popular participation in the nominating process. The older caucus nominating system—either in state legislatures or in Congress—had been successfully denounced as aristocratic, and whatever its practical uses, had to be abandoned. The convention proved an ideal substitute, one that party managers quickly utilized to strengthen their machines.

But an even more fundamental change took place in the minds of Americans—the acceptance of the idea *of parties. Following adoption of the Federal Constitution which created a national political arena, Americans organized the first modern parties. Yet they refused to recognize the legitimacy of their own offspring, attacking the very idea of party on the ground that in a good society, community of interest should take precedence over personal interest, or the political interest of one group. Parties, scored as "factions," were supposedly lethal to republicanism, since they were vehicles by which selfish groups advanced their interests at public expense. By the 1820's, however, a new generation of American politicians began to see the problem more realistically and to square their professions with their actions. Political machines sprang up in several states, machines which not only operated on a different doctrine but whose spokesmen openly defended the necessity and morality of party organization. They rejected the charge that parties were no more than expanded cliques, arguing instead that parties were popular, democratically run bodies, and a distinctively American innovation.*

The new politicians clearly exaggerated the democratic aspect of parties, but egalitarian policies required the mobilization of popular support, an end that party organization served efficiently. Michael Wallace's analysis shows how the best-run of these political machines, New York's Albany Regency, fought a long and successful war for domination of that state's politics, and how acceptance of the idea of party became a cohesive factor that kept together the Regency leaders and their followers.

During the first thirty years of its existence the United States developed, quite unintentionally, a party system. Organized popular parties regularly contested for power; Federalists and Republicans fought passionately and acrimoniously in Congress and cabinet, in town squares and county courthouses throughout the nation. The

From *The American Historical Review,* LXXIV (December 1968), 453, 456–60, 468–71, 476–77, 479–91. Reprinted by permission of the author; most footnotes omitted.

evidences of party spirit alarmed many Americans, for the existence of parties and their constant contention violated powerful and ancient traditions of proper political behavior. According to cannons inherited from British and colonial thought and practice, parties were evil: they were associations of factious men bent on self-aggrandizement. Political competition was evil: the ideal society was one where unity and consensus prevailed, where the national interest was peacefully determined by national leaders. Because partisan behavior violated normal ethical standards, many men, politicians among them, saw in the rise of parties a sign of moral decline. Not until a new generation of politicians emerged—men who had been raised in parties and had grown to maturity in a world that included party competition as a fixture of political life—were Americans able to re-evaluate the ancient traditions and establish new ones that justified their political activities.

Much of this re-evaluation and development of new ideals took place in New York State in the 1820's. There a group of professional politicians, leaders of the Republican party known as the Albany Regency, developed the modern concept of a political party and declared party associations to be eminently desirable. They adhered to a set of values that insisted on preserving, not destroying, political parties. They denounced and derided the consensus ideal and praised permanent political competition as being beneficial to society. . . .

In New York, after the War of 1812, a new conception of party emerged, modeled more closely on reality; in turn, the new definition of what a party ought to be legitimated existing structures. This re-evaluation developed out of what at first seemed just one more intraparty feud among New York Republicans, but that rapidly took a new and significant turn. The focus of the struggle was De Witt Clinton, in 1817 the leader of the party. Clinton held to the old view of party: he was a patrician politician who considered the party his personal property. This attitude is not surprising, given the nature of his career. Clinton assumed his position of leadership effortlessly, inheriting control of the faction that had been led by his uncle, George Clinton, New York's Revolutionary War governor. Despite the fact that the organization he headed in 1817 was quite different from what it had been when he entered politics in the 1790's, his style of leadership remained characteristic of the earlier period. Snobbish, spiteful, and supercilious, he was forbiddingly aristocratic. He craved flattery, he rejected advice from subordinates that conflicted with his own political judgments, and he directed the party largely as he saw fit. Above all, he dispensed the rewards of the party—political patronage and party nominations—as he pleased, often to personal friends, often to Federalists at the expense of deserving Republicans.

This type of leadership became increasingly unacceptable to a group of younger politicians in the party. As the party had become richer, more powerful, more obviously a vital route to a successful career in public life, many men whose allegiance lay not to any person or family but to the party itself had joined the organization. Inevitably such men would resent the idiosyncratic and unpredictable quality of party life, particularly the capricious dispensation of party rewards. Beginning about 1817, a group of these younger politicians known as the Bucktails began a quiet campaign to oust Clinton from the leadership. They were not interested merely in substituting one set of leaders for another. Rather their position may be likened to that of a group of young executives in a family firm who think that the business is being misrun because familial, not managerial, standards govern its operation.

By 1819 the Bucktails, who included such able men as Martin Van Buren, Benjamin Franklin Butler, Silas Wright, William Learned Marcy, and Azariah Cutting Flagg, felt ready to challenge Clinton openly. At first they attacked him personally, charging that he put his own interests above those of the organization. "De Witt Clinton, has acted incompatibly with his situation as the head of the republican party of this state, and in direct hostility to its best interest and prosperity. . . ." "Personal aggrandizement," they declared, "has been his personal maxim, even at the sacrifice of the republican party." As one Bucktail wrote in the Albany *Argus,* the organ of the insurgents, "notwithstanding his capacity, his manners are too repulsive, his temper too capricious and imperious, his deportment too dictatorial and tyrannical to acquire the affections or retain the confidence of any party."

The Bucktails wanted to go beyond indicting Clinton's personal style and to get at the anachronistic system of personal politics that he represented. Yet it was difficult to criticize Clinton's kind of leadership within the traditional framework of ideas about parties, for he was acting in accord with centuries-old standards of behavior. They were thus forced to proclaim a new definition of party and new standards of proper behavior for party politicians that would discredit both Clinton and his style of politics. They accomplished this task by adopting the rhetoric of democracy and egalitarianism and applying it to intraparty organization. Parties, they declared, should be democratic associations, run by the majority of the membership. It was a simple assertion, but it immediately put them in a position of strength. The ideal was virtually unassailable; to undermine the Bucktail position, critics would have to denounce republicanism itself—in the 1820's a political impossibility. Republican ideals became the Bucktails' weapons, and they were weapons that Clinton could not counter.

The Bucktails asserted that a party organized about an individual or patrician family was unacceptable as it was not republican. Personal parties were not parties at all, but factions, aristocratic remnants from the deferential days of colonial politics. Clinton was denounced as "raising up not only an aristocracy, but what has more hideous features, a species of monarchy." He was "the chieftain and head of an aristocracy"; his followers, "governed by no principle or party discipline," were "servile dependents . . . solely devoted to his views"; they were a "dangerous faction, bearing the badge of his family name," and solely concerned with "ministering to personal ambition." His patronage policy was denounced, not simply as unfair, but as producing undemocratic concentrations of power: "Devotion to the person of a chief becomes a passport to public distinction, and servility to men in power is rewarded . . . by honors and emoluments." In sum, Clinton's whole vision of politics, "characterized by personal attachments on the one hand and by personal antipathies on the other," was "highly prejudicial to the interests of the people, and if successful [would] have a tendency to subvert our republican form of government."

The proper form of political organization in a democratic state, the Bucktails argued, was not a personal faction but a political party. A true party was not the property of a man or a family, but transcended any of its members. Like a corporation it outlived its officers and did not, as had been the rule, expire when its leaders died or were removed from office. The proper party was "bound to the fortunes of no aspiring chief." A political party, moreover, was responsible to the mass of its members: it was a democratic organization. The "cardinal maxim with the great republican party [should be] . . . always to seek for, and when ascertained, always to follow the will of the majority." Politicians like Clinton, who felt themselves to be above the majority, could no longer be tolerated. "Those who refuse to 'abide by the fairly expressed will of the majority' . . . forfeit all claims to the character of republicans, and become recreant to the principles of that party." This did not mean an end to leadership: "Republicans know full well that . . . some must bear the brunt of the battle, and that to some hands must be consigned the interest and honor of the party; the system, the management, the labor and the anxiety." But leaders were expected to consider themselves the instruments or agents of an organization, not its owners. He "whose talents and zeal have benefitted the republican party will be supported as long as he consults the interests and ascendancy of that party, and no longer." The proper criteria for advancement were faithful dedication to the party and long service in its support, not pedigree or property.

By these standards, Van Buren was a model party leader. He proclaimed his obligation to the organization: "There are few men in the state," he told a gathering of the faithful, "more indebted to the favor of the Republican Party than myself and none more willing to acknowledge it." He rose to power in the prescribed fashion: "We speak of him with pride," declared a mass meeting of Albany Republicans in 1820, "because without the influence of fortune, or the factitious aid of a family name, he has, by his entire devotion to the republican cause, raised himself to the first grade as a statesman and a patriot."

By 1820 the Bucktail revolt had succeeded. Largely because they were able to convince many of the party that they were more faithful to the organization and the will of its majority than was Clinton, they managed to oust Clinton and his adherents; they then appropriated the apparatus and symbols of the Republican party entirely for themselves. Despite vigorous protests at being read out of the party because they failed to measure up to the new criteria, the Clintonians were relegated to the status of a distinct personal party. Van Buren and his fellow Republicans entrenched themselves in the legislature and all of the executive branch but the governorship and came to be characterized, by Clintonian and Federalist opponents, as the Albany Regency.

The Bucktails thus succeeded in distinguishing between party and faction in both the theory and actuality of New York politics. A party (such as their own) was a democratically structured, permanent organization; a faction (such as the Clintonians) was a transient, aristocratic, personal clique. "On one side is arrayed the old republican party, and on the other the followers of a man." Personal factions were bad: they were aristocratic and concerned only with enriching their leader. But parties were good: they allowed all members an equal voice; gave all members an equal chance to rise to positions of leadership and to receive party nominations for important elective positions; and provided all members an equal chance at receiving patronage, now no longer dispensed at the whim of an arbitrary leader. The degree to which the newer politicians rejected the antiparty tradition and the personal basis of politics can be seen in their extraordinary degree of attachment to their organization. They went far beyond merely justifying the existence of their party in ideological and practical terms and developed a system of political discipline that enjoined every politician, at whatever cost to himself, to preserve and perpetuate the party. It is to the development of their doctrines of party loyalty and party discipline that we now turn. . . .

The unity and thus the continuity of the party were to be achieved by party discipline, the willingness of members to set aside personal considerations for the greater good.[1] But there is a final point to be made about this code of political ethics, one that takes us to the core of the regency mind. As we have noted, the Bucktails distinguished a true party as one responsive to the majority of its members. Party discipline and such practices as the caucus were the devices that enabled the majority to rule; they ensured, moreover, that it would rule. They were thus the guarantees of intraparty democracy. They were also believed to be bulwarks of democracy in a larger arena. Party unity allowed the common people (most of whom, of course, were assumed to be Republicans) to deal as equals with aristocratic opponents like the Federalists; the power and influence of family and fortune could be offset by banding together and presenting a united front

1. The reasons for this mass acceptance of party loyalty were many and complex. One point is that the caucus system, to regency followers, did not connote a locked room full of political bosses hacking out nominations. Rather it betokened an elaborate network of ward, city, village, county, and district conventions (a term virtually synonymous with caucus on levels below the legislature) that laced the state into a pyramidal party structure open to the public through most of its tiers. At the top, the caucus of the state legislature was free from direct public influence, though after 1817 it was broadened to include some elected party delegates. Local nominations, however, were the prerogative of the local caucuses, composed of all local Republicans (and often opponents as well, for there were no clear criteria of party membership). While these bodies were often manipulated by local leaders, and while the party as a whole was, like most other mass organizations, subject to Michels's "iron law of oligarchy," the caucus system (broadly conceived) did allow for much participation by the party rank and file. Another reason for mass support of the doctrine of regularity involves the psychological function of party loyalty and the role that inherited affiliation to an organization plays in allowing individuals to cope with a complex political world.

at the polls. Again, party discipline was an agent of democracy.[2]

In the 1820's a subtle but important shift occurred: party discipline, from being essential to democracy, became the essence of democracy. What had been the practices became the principles of the party. Noah put the matter precisely.

> *Regular nominations . . . are not so much the engines as they are the principles of a party,* because any system which tends to unite the people, to give them their rights, to promote harmony and unanimity, to effect reconciliation and a submission to the will of the majority, and a relinquishment of private attachments, such a system we call a cardinal principle in the administration of a representative government [italics mine].

The practices that tended to preserve the party became the real "principles" of the party, for the ultimate "principle" was self-preservation. The fact that republicans "were cordially disposed to respect and sustain the regular nominations of the party" was deemed "a principle of essential importance," indeed "a criterion of political orthodoxy." The system of discipline "which enjoins upon its members, the obligation of submitting to nominations fairly and regularly made" was declared to be "a great PRINCIPLE," and "adherence to regular nominations" was pronounced "a sacred and inviolable principle. . . ."

Because their goal was the preservation of the party, the politicians lost interest in other, more ideological objectives. This is evident from their election appeals and campaign rhetoric. There

2. Thus, "the caucus . . . was highly instrumental in enabling [the party] to wrest the power of this state . . . from the hands of its aristocratic opponents." Only the caucus doctrine, by clearly affixing a well-known party label to a man, could coalesce the needed support behind candidates otherwise unknown (members of the middle or lower classes) and thus neutralize the aristocracy's greatest asset, the familiarity of their family names. Van Buren said that, conversely, whenever the Republican party was "wise enough to employ the caucus or convention system, and to use in good faith the influence it is capable of imparting to the popular cause," it was successful.

were virtually no substantive planks in regency platforms—no programs of internal improvements, no plans for expanded education or agricultural improvements, no demands for expansion of the franchise, virtually no demands at all. There were many declarations that Republicans were the party of democracy, and their opponents the standard-bearers of aristocracy, but these were either vague statements asserting differences in temperament and style or, when made specific, differences in the structure of their organizations. Their basic campaign appeal was aimed at those who already identified with them, and it was simple enough: now is the time for all good men to come to the aid of their party. Most of their political advertisements were in fact apolitical; they were calls to the colors, exhortations to keep the organizational faith. Classic in its simplicity was this broadside: "Republicans, will you abandon that party which has done so much for your country? Remember the dying words of the brave Lawrence and 'DON'T GIVE UP THE SHIP!!' " Republicans were reminded of their party's glorious history. "Let scenes gone by, and blessings enjoyed, arouse every republican to a sense of his duty. Remember that republicans saved the nation from anarchy; that republicans stood firm in the 'trying times' of '98; . . . O Ye patriots of '76! Ye preservers of Democracy in '98; ye defenders of our rights in '12, '13, '14; come forth. . . ." The most popular issues in regency campaigns were those that had been safely dead for twenty years. Republicans were enjoined to ignore objections to particular regency policies, as they were simply threats to the safety of the organization; complaints about the defeat of the electoral bill, while seemingly legitimate, masked an insidious design. "It is not a question about the electoral law . . . that is now pending. It is whether the republican party shall stand or fall."

Such ideological urges as Republicans had were satisfied by their association in a democratic political party. Unlike the party's founders, they felt no need to use the party to achieve certain goals, for the perpetuation of a democratic organization was goal enough. The second-generation politicians were operational democrats.[3]

The "defense" of party association outlined in the preceding pages was relatively simple. Except for harnessing the legitimizing force of majoritarianism, the Republicans had merely recognized and ratified actual changes in the structure and function of parties. The more serious traditional rejection of party had always been closely associated with the rejection of political competition; to justify party fully, it was necessary to justify competition. . . .

The primary goal of regency politicians was to preserve their party. This is of utmost importance for understanding their attitudes toward their opponents in New York politics. Their goal was not to destroy, overwhelm, or eliminate their opponents; they were not ideologues bent on the destruction of evildoers. They were able, therefore, to realize that the continued existence of an opposition was necessary, from the perspective of perpetuating their own party; opposition was highly useful, a constant spur to their own party's discipline. While the party might, it was argued, "suffer temporary defeats" in the interparty struggle, "it is certain to acquire additional strength . . . by the attacks of adverse parties." Indeed, the party was "most in jeopardy when an opposition is not sufficiently defined." As another writer noted, "there is such a thing as a party being too strong; a small and firm majority is more to be relied upon than an overwhelming and loose one." The politicians were aware that during "the contest between the great rival parties . . . each found in the strength of the other a powerful motive of union and vigor."

3. Not only were what were called "abstract" principles increasingly ignored because of the overriding concern with organizational support, but, in the rush of politics, they were increasingly betrayed. Edwin Croswell, editor of the Albany *Argus*, reflected on the problems the incontrovertibly democratic electoral bill raised for the party: "Admit the general correctness of it & yet is this the proper time for its introduction? Ought the question of expediency to be entirely disregarded; or ought it with Republicans, to be one of the first consideration?" Expediency triumphed increasingly. The notion that legislators should vote as their constituents wished also became a hindrance to men like Marcy, who wanted legislators to vote as their party directed.

This need for opposition led to a fertile paradox. The Federalists and their latter-day avatars, the Clintonians, were, of course, guilty of heinous political sins: they were aristocrats, personalists, factionalists, no-party heretics. Yet they were also the opposition. As a consequence, the Federalist party (a label Republicans attached to their major opponents of the moment), while condemned, was simultaneously praised; it was the strong, flourishing, and virtuous organization to which Republicans would accede should it obtain the support of the state's majority. From the need for a sustained opposition came verbal bouquets like the following:

> From the first organization of the government . . . this country has been divided into two great parties. . . . Neither party has yielded to the other in the zeal with which it has sought to procure concert among its members, or to give ascendancy to its principles, and although we may lament the occasional inconsistencies and the dangerous excesses into which both have unavoidably been betrayed, . . . we cannot for a minute admit that the majority of either have been actuated by any other than the purest, the most patriotic, and the most disinterested motives.

The *Argus* declared that "we wish not to be understood as having the slightest objection to the maintenance of the old federal party, broadly and with the spirit of other times." The two competing parties, the paper observed, "have existed among us almost from the formation of our constitution, and we are content with their present organization."

The regency, then, had no desire to eliminate its opponents. Rather it hoped for a "tranquil though determined opposition." It is significant that during the 1820's the word "opposition" itself gained popularity in Republican circles. They noted things in "the conduct of the Opposition which afford both amusement and instruction"; rejoiced in frustrating "the hopes and expectations of the Opposition"; and discussed in their papers "the views and opinions of what may now be termed the Opposition to the Democratic Party. . . ."

These were the attitudes regency politicians developed toward their opponents amid daily political struggles. Their lack of ideological fervor and their emphasis on preserving their institution contributed to a lowering of the political temperature. In the cooler atmosphere of the 1820's the politicians perceived that an opposition was necessary, and they came to think in terms of the continued existence of two parties, each sincere, legitimate, and capable of administering the government. Within this framework of attitudes a re-evaluation of the consensus ideal could easily emerge. But ideas seldom spring forth without some encouragement, no matter how conducive the times. A stimulus was needed, some reason to force the regency men to think about their political universe and to make them articulate their attitudes toward political parties. The stimulus came in the mid-twenties with a barrage of antiparty criticism from their New York opponents. Only confronted with a severe challenge to their habits and practices would they formulate a rebuttal. A brief look at the position of the New York antiparty spokesmen may help us understand what provoked the regency response.

The New York opponents of the Albany Regency, drawing on the antiparty spirit of the national leaders, reasserted the old consensus ideal. Clinton, for example, declared that the clash of parties has "rent us asunder, degraded our character, and impared our ability for doing good." He too felt there was no need for a division:

> I hardly understand the nomenclature of parties. They are all republicans, and yet a portion of the people assume the title of republican, as an exclusive right. . . . It is easy to see that the difference is nominal —that the whole controversy is about office, and that the country is constantly assailed by ambitious demagogues for the purpose of gratifying their cupidity.

Many New Yorkers shared Clinton's attitude. They correctly observed that no deep differences of principle divided the parties:

"We ask [the regency] to lay down what it considers to be the republican creed, and then to designate any considerable body of men in this country whom it would not embrace." But they went on to conclude that no matters of controversy remained that required opposing political organizations. "What does the great mass of the people . . . care for party? Why should the people be divided into a thousand different interests without knowing for what, and made hostile to each other, when their true and only interest is to be united?" Many assumed that the politicians, with their vested interest in discord, were perpetuating artificial divisions among a happy and passive people. Regency leaders like Erastus Root were charged with engaging in a "mean and contemptible effort to revive party names, and to excite prejudices by cant phrases."

The solution was obvious: eliminate parties. If one could "knock aside all artificial arrangements and the whole machinery of party," it would prevent the "citizens of the state having their sentiments perverted by intrigue and corruption." If parties could not be exorcised, they could at least be merged and amalgamated, particularly as there existed no difference between them. The critics proclaimed an end of parties. The Federalists, "having no longer any ground of principle to stand on, [have] necessarily ceased to exist as a party." Again "[both parties] have manifested a willingness to drop old animosities and obsolete names, and to unite with their former political opponents." And again, "the barriers of party are completely broken down and the lines of political demarcation cannot be again drawn."

When it became apparent that the Republicans had no intention of merging with their opponents, much less of dissolving, the antiparty men moved beyond rhetoric. They organized. They formed, of all things, a party, an antiparty party, a party to end parties. The People's party, formed in 1823 by Clintonians, Federalists, and dissident Republicans, appealed to the electorate "not in the spirit of *party* warfare, for this is emphatically the cause of the People. . . ." They offered their party as a means whereby members of all groups could unite, but it was highly unlikely that many regency Republicans would be lured into support of the fledgling party in light of the candidate it chose to support in 1824 —De Witt Clinton. Yet here a theoretical assault on party was linked to a potentially powerful organization and a popular candidate. If the antiparty message appealed to many in the electorate, the regency was in trouble. The emergence of the People's party threatened regency hegemony and forced its members to defend the party system that had evolved in New York. This they consciously set about to do. . . .[4]

The regency defense against the amalgamation attack took five forms. Their first, most parochial, and probably most effective position was that the philosophy of amalgamation, for all its seeming disinterestedness, was actually an opposition trick, the purpose of which was not to unite the country but to destroy the Republican party. Secondly, on a more theoretical level, regency Republicans denied that parties had dissolved, but rather that they continued in undiminished strength, a result traceable to powerful ideological and historical forces perpetuating them, which the Good Feeling men had ignored. Thirdly, they rejected the entire vision of a society based on consensus; the proper political universe was characterized by constant contention; the truly moral man was not one who put himself above party, but was a committed partisan. Fourthly, echoing the English justification of opposition, they declared that parties had to exist in a free state, that the elimination of parties occurred only under despotism. Fifthly, and most broadly, they declared that, for several reasons, competition be-

4. There was another, equally conscious conflict on the national level, waged primarily against Monroe. Van Buren reminisced about the "degree of odium" brought upon him by his staunch resistance to amalgamation doctrines "within the precincts of the White House and in most of the circles, political and social, of Washington." "The noisy revels," he recalled, "of bacchanalians in the Inner Sanctuary could not be more unwelcome sounds to devout worshippers than was this peal of the party tocsin in the ears of those who glorified the 'Era of Good Feeling.' "

tween parties benefited the state. We must examine each of these arguments in detail.

Republicans declared that advocacy of Good Feeling was a Federalist plot. By persuading Republicans that parties no longer existed, or by convincing them that they no longer should exist, the Federalists would loosen the bands of party discipline so vital to the party, and it would dissolve; then the Federalists would step in and recapture the government. . . .

At the heart of the appeal of Good Feeling was the assertion that no differences in principle divided the country; therefore, no legitimate basis for party competition existed. This proved a difficult argument to answer, for it contained much truth, but regency men responded in two ways. One was an exercise in exaggeration, the other an observation of great shrewdness. Their first answer was to assert that a great division did exist in the country, based upon differing constructions of the Constitution and disagreements over the value of republicanism. Van Buren's formulation of this Republican equivalent of a Whig history is among the more concise:

> The origin of the two great political parties which have divided the country, from the adoption of the Constitution to the present day . . . has . . . been attributed to causes which had either become obsolete, or been compromised by mutual concession. . . . [In reality] they arose from other and very different causes. They are, in truth . . . mainly to be ascribed to the struggle between the two opposing principles that have been in active operation in this country from the closing scenes of the revolutionary war to the present day—the one seeking to absorb, as far as practicable, all power from its legitimate sources, and to condense it in a single head. The other, an antagonist principle, laboring as assiduously to resist the encroachments and limit the extent of executive authority. . . . The former is essentially the monarchical, the latter the democratical spirit, of society.

There was, of course, some truth at the core of the argument: there had been important distinctions in ideology and style between the two parties in the [preceding] generation. But this portrait of politics had much less relevance to the state of parties in New York in the 1820's; the attribution of a monarchical spirit to the Federalists was clearly overdrawn. . . . But regency men simply pointed to past party performance and declared that no real change had occurred. "The whole Federal party cannot so suddenly have altered their opinions nor abandoned their distinctive principles. As well might the Ethiopian change his skin or the leopard his spots." And they insisted that differences in principle remained so striking that it was impossible "to destroy the old landmarks of party," impossible to "draw men into a political union who were never united before, and who, from the utter dissimilarity of their views and notions, never could act cordially together."

The regency's second, more muted response to the amalgamationists was also more radical. Parties, they declared, were not simply ideologically coherent organizations, at odds over fundamental issues. They were social institutions in their own right, largely independent of their earlier ideological stances. The men who advocated Good Feeling had confused competition between parties with the bickering of factions. . . . New issues did not require new parties; rather the two traditional organizations remained to act as vehicles for opposing positions. The parties maintained themselves not so much by love of "principle" as by the attachment of the members to the organization itself. . . .

Association with a political party, therefore, was not simply the result of a conscious decision; parties were not to be dissolved after certain issues were resolved. Rather, party affiliation and thus party divisions were handed down, like heirlooms, from generation to generation. Once again, amalgamation was precluded.

The Republicans' third rejection of amalgamation was perhaps their most radical, for it condemned the consensus ideal itself, declaring that it led to politically immoral behavior. The regency conception of what comprised political honesty and morality was not an avoidance of party, but a consistent adherence to party. Amalgamationists insisted that party men of opposite faiths should come together; with Republicans it was an article of political morality for them to remain apart. The Republicans did not respect the man who, following the consensus tradition, put himself above party. They were partisans and respected only other partisans. . . .

Men who abandoned one party for another were thoroughly denounced. They were condemned, with almost ecclesiastical fervor, as "apostates." [5] But even worse than apostasy was vacillation. The politician who drifted from party to party was condemned as "inconsistent"; Butler lucidly outlined the immorality of this attitude. Writing to Van Buren, Butler declared that "*political consistency* [is] as indispensable as any other *moral qualification.* For say what you will it is a *moral* qualification." This was so because the "man who is dishonest and unstable in his politics" is "equally dishonest and unstable in the relations of his private life. . . ." This partisan spirit proved the deadliest foe of the consensus mentality. It governed relations between party organizations, not just party members, and thus barred amalgamation. Partisans did not switch, and parties did not mix: organizations as well as individuals were consistent.

The terminology of morality, not tactics, was used when discussing interparty relations. Alliances, temporary joining of party forces, were frowned upon. . . .

The fourth argument advanced by the Republicans concerned the inevitability of parties in a free state; their absence or amalgamation was evidence of repression. Republicans assumed that in any society there would be more than one conception of the national interest. In order to express these differences, men form parties: those whose "general interests are the same" will always combine to promulgate their ideas, for "all experience has shown, that efforts to be powerful, must be concentrated." It followed that society normally contained parties contending with one another. . . .

Yet they might not exist, if repressed: parties developed only in

5. It must be admitted that the regency could more readily stomach apostates if they were arriving rather than departing. In 1820, for example, a portion of the old Federalist party known as "the high-minded" moved into the Republican ranks.

societies that tolerated organized dissent. The very existence of parties was, therefore, an indication that freedom of expression existed. Parties "will prevail where there is the least degree of liberty of action on the part of the public agents, or their constituents; . . . they are . . . inseparable from a free government." The association of parties and freedom was a basic theme of the regency defense. "Parties," they declared, "will ever exist, in a free state." The maintenance of parties, they asserted, was "necessary to the just exercise of the powers of free governments." Because this was such an obvious equation, they hinted darkly that their Good Feeling opponents, in calling for an end to parties, were contemplating an end of freedom. It was much commented on that military men like Jackson were fervent advocates of eliminating parties, and they contrasted such behavior with their own: "Fortunately for our country, and its institutions, there is another class of politicians, whom we delight to honor, who believe, that when party distinctions are no longer known and recognized, our freedom will be in jeopardy, as the 'calm of despotism' will then be visible." Party competition was the hallmark of a free society.[6]

The fifth ground for rejecting the consensus ideal derived from the belief that permanent competition between political parties was a positive benefit to the state. This was their broadest argument, most likely to appeal to nonpoliticians. "We are party men, attached to party systems," they declared, but added, "we think them necessary to the general safety. . . ." And again, "for the safety of the republic & the good of the people" it was imperative to "keep up and adhere to old party distinctions." How did they justify this position? For one thing, party competition provided a check upon the government; it was an extraconstitutional aid to

6. When Van Buren decided to support Jackson for the presidency in 1828, he had a difficult time convincing his party to do the same. Most regency politicians considered Jackson a no-party heretic. Even someone as high in party circles as Marcy proved recalcitrant: "I am somewhat thick skulled about making distinctions," he wrote Van Buren acidly. "I do not very clearly see how I can prefer with a strong preference an anti-caucus—amalgamation—no party candidate to another who has held the same heretical doctrines."

the people. "The spirit of party," they declared, was "the vigilant watchman over the conduct of those in power." The parties were "among the firmest bulwarks of civil liberty," and politicians insisted that they were "necessary to keep alive the vigilance of the people, and to compel their servants to act up to principle." But exactly how did they do this? One of their major functions was to inform the people.

> [Parties] on either side of the question, become the counsel who argue the cause before the people. . . . The solicitude and interest of political rivalship, will sufficiently expose the crimes, and even the failings, of competitors for the people's confidence. Competitors of this description *force* into notice facts, . . . which the people at large could never have derived from the ordinary commerce of thought.

The people are thus presented with expert watchdogs: "leading men, on both sides of the question check one another," and the people, presented with informed alternatives, "know when to support and when to oppose." Governor Enos Throop asserted that the party system allowed the people to participate intelligently in government.

> Those party divisions which are based upon conflicting opinions in regard to the constitution of the government, or the measures of the administration of it, interest every citizen, and tend, inevitably, in the spirit of emulation and proselytism, to reduce the many shades of opinion into two opposing parties. . . . [The] organized parties watch and scan each other's doings, the public mind is instructed by ample discussions of public measures, and acts of violence are restrained by the convictions of the people, that the prevailing measures are the results of enlightened reason.

Party competition had another value: it agitated the public and kept the mass of people interested in the operation of the government. It produced discord, and discord, despite the attitudes of the men who advocated Good Feeling, was of utmost value to republics. For, in the eyes of the Bucktails, the real danger to republics was not division, as in consensus cosmology, but apathy. And the surest cure for apathy was party competition. This idea is most closely associated with Van Buren. From the beginning of his political life he had appreciated the value of conflict. In 1814, for example, amidst the bitter animosities of the war, he said that

> on the various operations of government with which the public welfare are connected, and honest difference of opinion may exist—[and] when those differences are discussed and the principles of contending parties are supported with candor, fairness, and moderation, the very discord which is thus produced, may in a government like ours, be conducive to the public good.

Then, paradoxically, party competition bound the country together. Here was one of the shrewdest observations that the politicians made. While only in its formative stages in the 1820's, the idea would quickly enter the main current of antebellum thought. Van Buren and his colleagues realized that contrary to antiparty mythology, the really divisive threat to the nation was not party, but section. Party associations that cut across sectional lines were, in fact, an antidote to interregional stress. The Good Feeling men, by calling for the elimination of parties, were exacerbating sectionalism. Republicans accused them of wanting "to ABROGATE THE OLD PARTY DISTINCTIONS" in order to "organize new ones founded in the territorial prejudices of the people." The consequence of abolishing the old political distinctions would be "to array republicans against each other under such new and artificial distinctions . . . as geographical locations, such as North and South, East and West." Van Buren rested much of his case for the maintenance of the old parties on this ground: "We must always have party distinctions, and the old ones are the best. . . . If the old ones are suppressed, geographical differences founded on local instincts or what is worse, prejudices between free & slave holding states will inevitably take their place."

Finally, contests between political parties benefited society by eliminating the fierce contentions of personal parties. . . . It was now obvious, as Throop noted, that it was "one of the peculiar benefits of a well-regulated party spirit in a commonwealth, that it employs the passions actively in a milder mood, and thus shuts the door against faction. . . ."

By the end of the 1820's, the amalgamation attack had been met, the consensus tradition rejected. "Let us be greeted no more," demanded the Albany *Argus*, "by the cant and whining about the extinction of party feelings and the impropriety of endeavoring to keep them alive." "Parties of some sort must exist. 'Tis in the nature and genius of our government."

4

Jacksonian Politics in Action, 1824–1848

Nationalizing the Presidential Vote

New Perspectives on Jacksonian Politics

by Richard P. McCormick

The extension of the suffrage and the growing acceptance of party organization eventually reshaped presidential politics. The founding fathers had by design kept election of the President far from the people, and the presidential electors were supposed to exercise judgments free from popular pressures. But the course of American political practices ruled otherwise. Although the electoral college continued in existence, the electors lost their independence and became subject to party discipline. The congressional nominating caucus, by which the first parties nominated presidential candidates, also gave way to the national convention as the nominating device. Politicians once again fought openly over the presidency and the resulting competition sharpened voter interest in the outcome.

The renewed interest in national affairs rested on a firm and well-established foundation: state politics. In the following article, Richard P. McCormick *probes beneath the surface of the fact that in* 1828, *Andrew Jackson won the presidency with a vote considerably larger than the entire presidential vote for all candidates four years before, and he shows that although Jackson's election held great significance, it did not signify a "popular revolution" in voting as described by several generations of historians. Mc-*

Cormick tabulated the percentage of eligible voters who participated in presidential elections (1824–44), a much more meaningful figure than the raw vote alone.

This article upset many previously held notions about the Jacksonian "explosion at the polls"; nevertheless, the student should not lose sight of an equally important and positive fact. As clearly demonstrated in McCormick's data, the Jackson campaign of 1828, while no revolution, did begin to nationalize *American voting by bringing the percentage of eligible voters participating in a presidential election up to the levels of previous participation in state elections. In 1828 the presidential election began to lose its "clubby" aspect, and it started to assume its modern shape, as a two-way and highly organized contest for political preferment.*

The historical phenomenon that we have come to call Jacksonian Democracy has long engaged the attention of American political historians, and never more insistently than in the past decade. From the time of Parton and Bancroft to the present day, scholars have recognized that a profoundly significant change took place in the climate of politics simultaneously with the appearance of Andrew Jackson on the presidential scene. They have sensed that a full understanding of the nature of that change might enable them to dissolve some of the mysteries that envelop the operation of the American democratic process. With such a challenging goal before them, they have pursued their investigations with uncommon intensity and with a keen awareness of the contemporary relevance of their findings.

A cursory view of the vast body of historical writing on this subject suggests that scholars in the field have been largely preoccupied with attempts to define the content of Jacksonian Democracy and identify the influences that shaped it. What did Jacksonian Democracy represent, and what groups, classes, or sections gave it its distinctive character? The answers that have been given to these central questions have been—to put it succinctly—bewil-

From *The American Historical Review*, LXV (January 1960), 288–301. Reprinted by permission of the author; most footnotes omitted.

dering in their variety. The discriminating student, seeking the essential core of Jacksonianism, may make a choice among urban workingmen, southern planters, venturous conservatives, farm-bred *nouveaux riches,* western frontiersmen, frustrated entrepreneurs, or yeoman farmers. Various as are these interpretations of the motivating elements that constituted the true Jacksonians, the characterizations of the programmatic features of Jacksonian Democracy are correspondingly diverse. Probably the reasonable observer will content himself with the conclusion that many influences were at work and that latitudinarianism prevailed among the Jacksonian faithful.

In contrast with the controversy that persists over these aspects of Jacksonian Democracy, there has been little dissent from the judgment that "the 1830's saw the triumph in American politics of that democracy which has remained pre-eminently the distinguishing feature of our society." The consensus would seem to be that with the emergence of Jackson, the political pulse of the nation quickened. The electorate, long dormant or excluded from the polls by suffrage barriers, now became fired with unprecedented political excitement. The result was a bursting forth of democratic energies, evidenced by a marked upward surge in voting. Beard in his colorful fashion gave expression to the common viewpoint when he asserted that "the roaring flood of the new democracy was . . . [by 1824] foaming perilously near the crest. . . ." Schlesinger, with his allusion to the "immense popular vote" received by Jackson in 1824, creates a similar image. The Old Hero's victory in 1828 has been hailed as the consequence of a "mighty democratic uprising."

That a "new democracy, ignorant, impulsive, irrational" entered the arena of politics in the Jackson era has become one of the few unchallenged "facts" in an otherwise controversial field. Differences of opinion occur only when attempts are made to account for the remarkable increase in the size of the active electorate. The commonest explanations have emphasized the assertion by the common man of his newly won political privileges, the democratic influences that arose out of the western frontier, or the magnetic attractiveness of Jackson as a candidate capable of appealing with singular effectiveness to the backwoods hunter, the plain farmer, the urban workingman, and the southern planter.

Probably because the image of a "mighty democratic uprising" has been so universally agreed upon, there has been virtually no effort made to describe precisely the dimensions of the "uprising." Inquiry into this aspect of Jacksonian Democracy has been discouraged by a common misconception regarding voter behavior before 1824. As the authors of one of our most recent and best textbooks put it: "In the years from the beginning of the government to 1824, a period for which we have no reliable election statistics, only small numbers of citizens seemed to have bothered to go to the polls." Actually, abundant data on pre-1824 elections is available, and it indicates a far higher rate of voting than has been realized. Only by taking this data into consideration can voting behavior after 1824 be placed in proper perspective.

The question of whether there was indeed a "mighty democratic uprising" during the Jackson era is certainly crucial in any analysis of the political character of Jacksonian Democracy. More broadly, however, we need to know the degree to which potential voters participated in elections before, during, and after the period of Jackson's presidency as well as the conditions that apparently influenced the rate of voting. Only when such factors have been analyzed can we arrive at firm conclusions with respect to the dimensions of the political changes that we associate with Jacksonian Democracy. Obviously in studying voter participation we are dealing with but one aspect of a large problem, and the limitations imposed by such a restrictive focus should be apparent.

In measuring the magnitude of the vote in the Jackson elections it is hardly significant to use the total popular vote cast throughout the nation. A comparison of the total vote cast in 1812, for example, when in eight of the seventeen states electors were chosen by the legislature, with the vote in 1832, when every state except South Carolina chose its electors by popular vote, has limited meaning. Neither is it revealing to compare the total vote in 1824 with that in 1832 without taking into consideration the population increase during the interval. The shift from the legislative choice of electors to their election by popular vote, together with the steady population growth, obviously swelled the presidential vote. But the problem to be investigated is whether the Jackson elections brought voters to the polls in such enlarged or unprecedented proportions as to indicate that a "new democracy" had burst upon the political scene.

The most practicable method for measuring the degree to which voters participated in elections over a period of time is to relate the number of votes cast to the number of potential voters. Although there is no way of calculating precisely how many eligible voters there were in any state at a given time, the evidence at hand demonstrates that with the exception of Rhode Island, Virginia, and Louisiana the potential electorate after 1824 was roughly equivalent to the adult white male population.[1] A meaningful way of expressing the rate of voter participation, then, is to state it in terms of the percentage of the adult white males actually voting. This index can be employed to measure the variations that occurred in voter participation over a period of time and in both national and state elections. Consequently a basis is provided for comparing the rate of voting in the Jackson elections with other presidential elections before and after his regime as well as with state elections.[2]

Using this approach it is possible, first of all, to ascertain whether or not voter participation rose markedly in the three presidential elections in which Jackson was a candidate. Did voter participation

1. The only states in which property qualifications were a factor in restricting voting in presidential elections after 1824 were Virginia and Rhode Island. New York did not completely abolish property qualifications until 1826, but the reform of 1821 had resulted in virtually free suffrage. In Louisiana, where voters were required to be taxpayers, the nature of the system of taxation operated to confine the suffrage to perhaps half of the adult white males. See Joseph G. Tregle, "Louisiana in the Age of Jackson: A Study in Ego Politics," doctoral dissertation, University of Pennsylvania, 1954, 105–108. To be perfectly accurate, estimates of the size of the potential electorate would have to take into account such factors as citizenship and residence requirements and, in certain states, the eligibility of Negro voters.

2. After 1840 when the proportion of aliens in the population increased markedly and citizenship became an important requirement for voting, the

in these elections so far exceed the peak participation in the pre-1824 elections as to suggest that a mighty democratic uprising was taking place? The accompanying data (Table 1) provides an answer to this basic question.[3]

In the 1824 election not a single one of the eighteen states in which the electors were chosen by popular vote attained the percentage of voter participation that had been reached before 1824. Prior to that critical election, fifteen of those eighteen states had recorded votes in excess of 50 per cent of their adult white male population, but in 1824 only two states—Maryland and Alabama exceeded this modest mark. The average rate of voter participation in the election was 26.5 per cent. This hardly fits the image of the "roaring flood of the new democracy . . . foaming perilously near the crest. . . ."

adult-white-male index becomes less reliable. In order to calculate accurately the number of qualified voters in 1850, the alien adult white males would have to be deducted in those states where citizenship was a qualification for voting. Unfortunately, federal census data on aliens is not obtainable prior to 1890, except for the censuses of 1820 and 1830. In the latter year there were only 107,832 aliens out of a total population of nearly thirteen millions, a fraction so small as to be insignificant. But by 1850, according to one calculation, adult male aliens may have amounted to one-twelfth of the total voting population. J. D. B. De Bow, *Statistical View of the United States* (Washingtion, D.C., 1854), 50. In certain eastern states the proportion of aliens was higher than the national average. In New York, for example, 18.5 per cent of the total population in 1855 were aliens; the proportion in 1835 had been only 3.79 per cent. Franklin B. Hough, *Census of the State of New York for 1855* (Albany, 1857), xiv, xliii.

3. The figures on voter participation have been computed from a compilation I have made of returns of state-wide elections covering twenty-five states over the period from 1800 to 1860. For the post-1836 years the returns may be consulted in the *Whig Almanacs* and *Tribune Almanacs* issued by Horace Greeley and, for presidential elections, in W. Dean Burnham's *Presidential Ballots, 1836–1892* (Baltimore, Md., 1955). For the period prior to 1836 the best general sources are the official manuals of certain states, the legislative journals, and the contemporary newspapers. For several states, among them Massachusetts, Connecticut, New Jersey, Maryland, Virginia, North Carolina, and Georgia, it is necessary to use the manuscript sources. The estimate of the adult white male population was computed for each decennial year from the federal census, and the figure for the particular election year was obtained by interpolation. I have computed for each gubernatorial and presidential election in the twenty-five states admitted to the Union by 1836 (exclusive of South Carolina) the percentage of adult white males voting.

Table 1

Percentages of Adult White Males Voting in Elections

State	Highest Known % AWM Voting before 1824: Year	Highest Known % AWM Voting before 1824: % AWM	Presidential Elections: 1824	1828	1832	1836	1840	1844
Maine	1812[g]	62.0	18.9	42.7	66.2 *	37.4	82.2	67.5
New Hampshire	1814[g]	80.8	16.8	76.5	74.2	38.2	86.4 *	65.6
Vermont	1812[g]	79.9	—	55.8	50.0	52.5	74.0	65.7
Massachusetts	1812[g]	67.4	29.1	25.7	39.3	45.1	66.4	59.3
Rhode Island	1812[g]	49.4	12.4	18.0	22.4	24.1	33.2	39.8
Connecticut	1819[l]	54.4	14.9	27.1	45.9	52.3	75.7 *	76.1
New York	1810[g]	41.5	—	70.4 *	72.1	60.2	77.7	73.6
New Jersey	1808[p]	71.8	31.1	70.9	69.0	69.3	80.4 *	81.6
Pennsylvania	1808[g]	71.5	19.6	56.6	52.7	53.1	77.4 *	75.5
Delaware	1804[g]	81.9	—	—	67.0	69.4	82.8 *	85.0
Maryland	1820[l]	69.0	53.7	76.2 *	55.6	67.5	84.6	80.3
Virginia	1800[p]	25.9	11.5	27.6 *	30.8	35.1	54.6	54.5
North Carolina	1823[c]	70.0 †	42.2	56.8	31.7	52.9	83.1 *	79.1
Georgia	1812[c]	62.3	—	35.9	33.0	64.9 *	88.9	94.0
Kentucky	1820[g]	74.4	25.3	70.7	73.9	61.1	74.3	80.3 *
Tennessee	1817[g]	80.0	26.8	49.8	28.8	55.2	89.6 *	89.6
Louisiana	1812[g]	34.2	—	36.3 *	24.4	19.2	39.4	44.7
Alabama	1819[g]	96.7	52.1	53.6	33.3	65.0	89.8	82.7
Mississippi	1823[g]	79.8	41.6	56.6	32.8	62.8	88.2 *	89.7
Ohio	1822[g]	46.5	34.8	75.8 *	73.8	75.5	84.5	83.6
Indiana	1822[g]	52.4	37.5	68.3 *	61.8	70.1	86.0	84.9
Illinois	1822[g]	55.8	24.2	51.9	45.6	43.7	85.9 *	76.3
Missouri	1820[g]	71.9	20.1	54.3	40.8	35.6	74.0 *	74.7
Arkansas		—	—	—	—	35.0	86.4	68.8
Michigan		—	—	—	—	35.7	84.9	79.3
National Average			26.5	56.3	54.9	55.2	78.0	74.9

* *Exceeded pre-1824 high*
[g] *Gubernatorial election*
[p] *Presidential election*
† *Estimate based on incomplete returns*
[c] *Congressional election*
[l] *Election of legislature*

There would seem to be persuasive evidence that in 1828 the common man flocked to the polls in unprecedented numbers, for the proportion of adult white males voting soared to 56.3 per cent, more than double the 1824 figure. But this outpouring shrinks in magnitude when we observe that in only six of the twenty-two states involved were new highs in voter participation established. In three of these—Maryland, Virginia, and Louisiana—the recorded gain was inconsiderable, and in a fourth—New York—the bulk of the increase might be attributed to changes that had been made in suffrage qualifications as recently as 1821 and 1826. Six states went over the 70 per cent mark, whereas ten had bettered that performance before 1824. Instead of a "mighty democratic uprising" there was in 1828 a voter turnout that approached—but in only a few instances matched or exceeded—the maximum levels that had been attained before the Jackson era.

The advance that was registered in 1828 did not carry forward to 1832. Despite the fact that Jackson was probably at the peak of his personal popularity, that he was engaged in a campaign that was presumably to decide issues of great magnitude, and that in the opinion of some authorities a "well-developed two party system on a national scale" had been established, there was a slight decline in voter participation. The average for the twenty-three states participating in the presidential contest was 54.9 per cent. In fifteen states a smaller percentage of the adult white males went to the polls in 1832 than in 1828. Only five states bettered their pre-1824 highs. Again the conclusion would be that it was essentially the pre-1824 electorate—diminished in most states and augmented in a few—that voted in 1832. Thus, after three Jackson elections, sixteen states had not achieved the proportions of voter participation that they had reached before 1824. The "new democracy" had not yet made its appearance.[4]

4. It may be suggested that it is invalid to compare voter participation in each state in the presidential contests of 1824, 1828, and 1832 with the highs, rather than the average participation in each state prior to 1824. The object of the comparison is to ascertain whether the Jackson elections brought voters

A comparison of the Jackson elections with earlier presidential contests is of some interest. Such comparisons have little validity before 1808 because few states chose electors by popular vote, and for certain of those states the complete returns are not available. In 1816 and 1820 there was so little opposition to Monroe that the voter interest was negligible. The most relevant elections, therefore, are those of 1808 and 1812. The accompanying table (Table 2) gives the percentages of adult white males voting in 1808

Table 2

Percentages of Adult White Males Voting in Presidential Elections

State	*1808*	*1812*	*1824*	*1828*
Maine	Legis.	50.0	18.9	42.7
New Hampshire	62.1	75.4	16.8	76.5
Massachusetts	Legis.	51.4	29.1	25.7
Rhode Island	37.4	37.7	12.4	18.0
New Jersey	71.8	Legis.	31.1	70.9
Pennsylvania	34.7	45.5	19.6	56.6
Maryland	48.4	56.5	53.7	76.2
Virginia	17.7	17.8	11.5	27.6
Ohio	12.8	20.0	34.8	75.8

Note: No complete returns of the popular vote cast for electors in Kentucky or Tennessee in 1808 and 1812 and in North Carolina in 1808 could be located.

and 1812 in those states for which full returns could be found, together with the comparable percentages for the elections of 1824 and 1828. In 1824 only one state—Ohio—surpassed the highs established in either 1808 or 1812. Four more joined this list in 1828

to the polls in unprecedented numbers, as has so often been asserted. Moreover, it is hardly feasible to compare average participation in elections before and after 1824 in many states because of the changes that were made in the methods of electing governors and presidential electors or—in certain instances—because the state had only recently entered the Union. However, among those states in which average voter participation was obviously higher before 1824 than it was in the three Jackson elections were Alabama, Connecticut, Georgia, Massachusetts, Mississippi, New Hampshire (1809–1817), Pennsylvania, Rhode Island, Tennessee, and Vermont (1807–1815).

—Virginia, Maryland, Pennsylvania, and New Hampshire—although the margin in the last case was so small as to be inconsequential. The most significant conclusion to be drawn from this admittedly limited and unrepresentative data is that in those states where there was a vigorous two-party contest in 1808 and 1812 the vote was relatively high. Conversely, where there was little or no contest in 1824 or 1828, the vote was low.

When an examination is made of voting in other than presidential elections prior to 1824, the inaccuracy of the impression that "only small numbers of citizens" went to the polls becomes apparent. Because of the almost automatic succession of the members of the "Virginia dynasty" and the early deterioration of the national two-party system that had seemed to be developing around 1800, presidential elections did not arouse voter interest as much as did those for governor, state legislators, or even members of Congress. In such elections at the state level the "common man" was stimulated by local factors to cast his vote, and he frequently responded in higher proportions than he did to the later stimulus provided by Jackson.

The average voter participation for all the states in 1828 was 56.3 per cent. Before 1824 fifteen of the twenty-two states had surpassed that percentage. Among other things, this means that the 1828 election failed to bring to the polls the proportion of the electorate that had voted on occasion in previous elections. There was, in other words, a high potential vote that was frequently realized in state elections but which did not materialize in presidential elections. The unsupported assumption that the common man was either apathetic or debarred from voting by suffrage barriers before 1824 is untenable in the light of this evidence.

In state after state (see Table 1) gubernatorial elections attracted 70 per cent or more of the adult white males to the polls. Among the notable highs recorded were Delaware with 81.9 per cent in 1804, New Hampshire with 80.8 per cent in 1814, Tennessee with 80.0 per cent in 1817, Vermont with 79.9 per cent in 1812, Mississippi with 79.8 per cent in 1823, and Alabama with a highly improbable 96.7 per cent in its first gubernatorial contest in 1819. There is reason to believe that in some states, at least, the voter participation in the election of state legislators was even higher than in gubernatorial elections. Because of the virtual impossibility of securing county-by-county or district-by-district returns for such elections, this hypothesis is difficult to verify.

Down to this point the voter turnout in the Jackson elections has been compared with that in elections held prior to 1824. Now it becomes appropriate to inquire whether during the period 1824 through 1832 voters turned out in greater proportions for the three presidential contests than they did for the contemporary state elections. If, indeed, this "new democracy" bore some special relationship to Andrew Jackson or to his policies, it might be anticipated that interest in the elections in which he was the central figure would stimulate greater voter participation than gubernatorial contests, in which he was at most a remote factor.

Actually, the election returns show fairly conclusively that throughout the eight-year period the electorate continued to participate more extensively in state elections than in those involving the presidency. Between 1824 and 1832 there were fifty regular gubernatorial elections in the states that chose their electors by popular vote. In only sixteen of these fifty instances did the vote for President surpass the corresponding vote for governor. In Rhode Island, Delaware, Tennessee, Kentucky, Illinois, Mississippi, Missouri, and Georgia the vote for governor consistently exceeded that for President. Only in Connecticut was the reverse true. Viewed from this perspective, too, the remarkable feature of the vote in the Jackson elections is not its immensity, but rather its smallness.

Finally, the Jackson elections may be compared with subsequent presidential elections. Once Jackson had retired to the Hermitage, and figures of less dramatic proportions took up the contest for the presidency, did voter participation rise or fall? This question can be answered by observing the percentage of adult white males who voted in each state in the presidential elections of 1836 through

1844 (Table 1). Voter participation in the 1836 election remained near the level that had been established in 1828 and 1832, with 55.2 per cent of the adult white males voting. Only five states registered percentages in excess of their pre-1824 highs. But in 1840 the "new democracy" made its appearance with explosive suddenness.

In a surge to the polls that has rarely, if ever, been exceeded in any presidential election, four out of five (78.0 per cent) of the adult white males cast their votes for Harrison or Van Buren.[5] This new electorate was greater than that of the Jackson period by more than 40 per cent. In all but five states—Vermont, Massachusetts, Rhode Island, Kentucky, and Alabama—the peaks of voter participation, reached before 1824 were passed. Fourteen of the twenty-five states involved set record highs for voting that were not to be broken throughout the remainder of the antebellum period. Now, at last, the common man—or at least the man who previously had not been sufficiently aroused to vote in presidential elections—cast his weight into the political balance. This "Tippecanoe Democracy," if such a label is permissible, was of a different order of magnitude from the Jacksonian Democracy. The elections in which Jackson figured brought to the polls only those men who were accustomed to voting in state or national elections, except in a very few states. The Tippecanoe canvass witnessed an extraordinary expansion of the size of the presidential electorate far beyond previous dimensions. It was in 1840, then, that the "roaring flood of the new democracy" reached its crest. And it engulfed the Jacksonians.

The flood receded only slightly in 1844, when 74.9 per cent of the estimated potential electorate went to the polls. Indeed, nine

5. It can be calculated that the total of adult white males in the twenty-five states was 3,090,708. The total popular vote was 2,409,682. In the presidential election of 1896 the total vote approximated 80 per cent of the potential electorate. In 1940 and 1952 the comparable figures would be 63 per cent and 65 per cent respectively. These percentages have been calculated on the assumption that the potential electorate in 1896 included all adult male citizens and in 1940 and 1952 all adult citizens.

states attained their record highs for the period. In 1848 and 1852 there was a general downward trend in voter participation, followed by a modest upswing in 1856 and 1860. But the level of voter activity remained well above that of the Jackson elections. The conclusion to be drawn is that the "mighty democratic uprising" came after the period of Jackson's presidency.

Now that the quantitative dimensions of Jacksonian Democracy as a political phenomenon have been delineated and brought into some appropriate perspective, certain questions still remain to be answered. Granted that the Jacksonian electorate—as revealed by the comparisons that have been set forth—was not really very large, how account for the fact that voter participation doubled between the elections of 1824 and 1828? It is true that the total vote soared from around 359,000 to 1,155,400 and that the percentage of voter participation more than doubled. Traditionally, students of the Jackson period have been impressed by this steep increase in voting and by way of explanation have identified the causal factors as the reduction of suffrage qualifications, the democratic influence of the West, or the personal magnetism of Jackson. The validity of each of these hypotheses needs to be re-examined.

In no one of the states in which electors were chosen by popular vote was any significant change made in suffrage qualifications between 1824 and 1828. Subsequently, severe restrictions were maintained in Rhode Island until 1842, when some liberalization was effected, and in Virginia down to 1850. In Louisiana, where the payment of a tax was a requirement, the character of the state tax system apparently operated to restrict the suffrage at least as late as 1845. Thus with the three exceptions noted, the elimination of suffrage barriers was hardly a factor in producing an enlarged electorate during the Jackson and post-Jackson periods. Furthermore, all but a few states had extended the privilege of voting either to all male taxpayers or to all adult male citizens by 1810. After Connecticut eliminated its property qualification in 1818, Massachusetts in 1821, and New York in 1821 and 1826, only Rhode Island, Virginia, and Louisiana were left on the list of "restrictionist" states. Neither Jackson's victory nor the increased vote in 1828 can be attributed to the presence at the polls of a newly enfranchised mass of voters.

Similarly, it does not appear that the western states led the way in voter participation. Prior to 1824, for example, Ohio, Indiana, and Illinois had never brought to the polls as much as 60 per cent of their adult white males. Most of the eastern states had surpassed that level by considerable margins. In the election of 1828 six states registered votes in excess of 70 per cent of their adult white male populations. They were in order of rank: New Hampshire, Maryland, Ohio, New Jersey, Kentucky, and New York. The six leaders in 1832 were: New Hampshire, Kentucky, Ohio, New York, New Jersey, and Delaware. It will be obvious that the West, however that region may be defined, was not leading the "mighty democratic uprising." Western influences, then, do not explain the increased vote in 1828.

There remains to be considered the factor of Jackson's personal popularity. Did Jackson, the popular hero, attract voters to the polls in unprecedented proportions? The comparisons that have already been made between the Jackson elections and other elections—state and national—before, during, and after his presidency would suggest a negative answer to the question. Granted that a majority of the voters in 1828 favored Jackson, it is not evident that his partisans stormed the polls any more enthusiastically than did the Adams men. Of the six highest states in voter participation in 1828, three favored Adams and three were for Jackson, which could be interpreted to mean that the convinced Adams supporters turned out no less zealously for their man than did the ardent Jacksonians. When Van Buren replaced Jackson in 1836, the voting average increased slightly over 1832. And, as has been demonstrated, the real manifestation of the "new democracy" came not in 1828 but in 1840.

The most satisfactory explanation for the increase in voter participation between 1824 and 1828 is a simple and obvious one.

During the long reign of the Virginia dynasty, interest in presidential elections dwindled. In 1816 and 1820 there had been no contest. The somewhat fortuitous termination of the Virginia succession in 1824 and the failure of the congressional caucus to solve the problem of leadership succession threw the choice of a President upon the electorate. But popular interest was dampened by the confusion of choice presented by the multiplicity of candidates, by the disintegration of the old national parties, by the fact that in most states one or another of the candidates was so overwhelmingly popular as to forestall any semblance of a contest, and possibly by the realization that the election would ultimately be decided by the House of Representatives. By 1828 the situation had altered. There were but two candidates in the field, each of whom had substantial sectional backing. A clear-cut contest impended, and the voters became sufficiently aroused to go to the polls in moderate numbers.

One final question remains. Why was the vote in the Jackson elections relatively low when compared with previous and contemporary state elections and with presidential votes after 1840? The answer, in brief, is that in most states either Jackson or his opponent had such a one-sided advantage that the result was a foregone conclusion. Consequently there was little incentive for the voters to go to the polls.

This factor can be evaluated in fairly specific quantitative terms. If the percentage of the total vote secured by each candidate in each state in the election of 1828 is calculated, the difference between the percentages can be used as an index of the closeness, or one-sidedness, of the contest. In Illinois, for example, Jackson received 67 per cent of the total vote and Adams 33; the difference—thirty-four points—represents the margin between the candidates. The average difference between the candidates, taking all the states together, was thirty-six points. Expressed another way this would mean that in the average state the winning candidate received more than twice the vote of the loser. Actually, this was the case

Table 3

Differential between Percentages of Total Vote Obtained by Major Presidential Candidates, 1828–1844

State	*1828*	*1832*	*1836*	*1840*	*1844*
Maine	20	10	20	1	13
New Hampshire	7	13	50	11	19
Vermont	50	10	20	29	18
Massachusetts	66	30	9	16	12
Rhode Island	50	14	6	23	20
Connecticut	50	20	1	11	5
New York	2	4	9	4	1
New Jersey	4	1	1	4	1
Pennsylvania	33	16	4	1	2
Delaware	—	2	6	10	3
Maryland	2	1	7	8	5
Virginia	38	50	13	1	6
North Carolina	47	70	6	15	5
Georgia	94	100	4	12	4
Kentucky	1	9	6	29	8
Tennessee	90	90	16	11	1
Louisiana	6	38	3	19	3
Alabama	80	100	11	9	18
Mississippi	60	77	2	7	13
Ohio	3	3	4	9	2
Indiana	13	34	12	12	2
Illinois	34	37	10	2	12
Missouri	41	32	21	14	17
Arkansas	—	—	28	13	26
Michigan	—	—	9	4	6
Average Differential	36	36	11	11	9

in thirteen of the twenty-two states (see Table 3).[6] Such a wide margin virtually placed these states in the "no contest" category.

A remarkably close correlation existed between the size of the

6. The index figures in the table represent the difference between the percentages of the total popular vote secured by the two major candidates in each state. For the election of 1832, the figures represent only the difference between the votes obtained by Clay and Jackson.

voter turnout and the relative closeness of the contest. The six states previously listed as having the greatest voter participation in 1828 were among the seven states with the smallest margin of difference between the candidates. The exception was Louisiana, where restrictions on the suffrage curtailed the vote. Even in this instance, however, it is significant that voter participation in Louisiana reached a record high. In those states, then, where there was a close balance of political forces the vote was large, and conversely, where the contest was very one sided, the vote was low

Most of the states in 1828 were so strongly partial to one or another of the candidates that they can best be characterized as one-party states. Adams encountered little opposition in New England, except in New Hampshire, and Jackson met with hardly any resistance in the South. It was chiefly in the middle states and the older West that the real battle was waged. With the removal of Adams from the scene after 1828, New England became less of a one-party section, but the South remained extremely one sided. Consequently it is not surprising that voter participation in 1832 failed even to match that of 1828.

Here, certainly, is a factor of crucial importance in explaining the dimensions of the voter turnout in the Jackson elections. National parties were still in a rudimentary condition and were highly unbalanced from state to state. Indeed, a two-party system scarcely could be said to exist in more than half of the states until after 1832. Where opposing parties had been formed to contest the election, the vote was large, but where no parties, or only one, took the field, the vote was low. By 1840, fairly well-balanced parties had been organized in virtually every state. In only three states did the margin between Harrison and Van Buren exceed twenty points, and the average for all the states was only eleven points. The result was generally high voter participation.[7]

7. Careful analysis of the data in Table 3 will suggest that there were three fairly distinct stages in the emergence of a nationally balanced two-party system. Balanced parties appeared first in the middle states between 1824 and 1828. New England remained essentially a one-party section until after

When Jacksonian Democracy is viewed from the perspectives employed in this analysis, its political dimensions in so far as they relate to the behavior of the electorate can be described with some precision. None of the Jackson elections involved a "mighty democratic uprising" in the sense that voters were drawn to the polls in unprecedented proportions. When compared with the peak participation recorded for each state before 1824, or with contemporaneous gubernatorial elections, or most particularly with the vast outpouring of the electorate in 1840, voter participation in the Jackson elections was unimpressive. The key to the relatively low presidential vote would seem to be the extreme political imbalance that existed in most states as between the Jacksonians and their opponents. Associated with this imbalance was the immature development of national political parties. Indeed, it can be highly misleading to think in terms of national parties in connection with the Jackson elections. As balanced, organized parties subsequently made their appearance from state to state, and voters were stimulated by the prospect of a genuine contest, a marked rise in voter participation occurred. Such conditions did not prevail generally across the nation until 1840, and then at last the "mighty democratic uprising" took place.

Adams had passed from the scene; then competing parties appeared. In the South and the newer West, a one-party dominance continued until divisions arose over who should succeed Jackson. Sectional loyalties to favorite sons obviously exerted a determining influence on presidential politics, and consequently on party formation, in the Jackson years.

Rich Men and Politics

Money and Party in Jacksonian America

by Frank Otto Gatell

Jackson's presidency was one of the most controversial in American history. Every political battle became a crisis, a battle between Light and Darkness in the minds of the President and his opponents, fought at peaks of emotional intensity far exceeding the objective importance of even such significant issues as internal improvements, the tariff, or the location of the Federal government's financial accounts. In particular, banking and finance—the money question—set the tone for Democratic politics during the 1830's. By the end of that decade, many wealthy Americans had become frightened, and they blamed the Jacksonians for stimulating anti-business feeling that threatened the rights of property. They labeled that feeling, and whatever else displeased them politically, Loco-Focoism, a scareword connoting wild-eyed radicalism.

The aftermath of the Panic of 1837 intensified conservative fears in a way that paralleled the constant anxieties of Southerners over the possibility of slave revolts. Northern businessmen reacted apprehensively to social protest movements, and to the rising tide of urban violence. A monied man who might well have supported Jackson's vague program in 1828 was far less likely to do so in 1840, when the Democratic party attacked bankers and other businessmen. Neither Jackson nor his chosen successor, Martin Van Buren, were anti-capitalist, but the Bank War and the subsequent alignment of most businessmen in the anti-Jackson or Whig camp injected an obvious class element into the two-party system. During these years a major reshuffling occurred that altered the political structure for a time, and gave the parties after 1837 a greater class orientation than before.

The following study of the political behavior of the wealthiest men in New York between 1828 and 1844 shows the emergence of the class basis of party preference. Frank Otto Gatell found that a clear preference had developed for Whiggery over Jacksonian Democracy, and he contends that many rich men acquired their anti-Jacksonian bias during the 1830's as a fearful response to Democratic banking and financial policies.

In olden times, that is, a generation or more ago, American historians proceeded upon a basic assumption when discussing the Jacksonian period: the Democratic party was the party of the people, and the Whig party was the party of economic privilege. The Democrats included in their ranks the common man, the farmers, the artisans, and the mechanics, the poor but honest sinew of Jacksonian Democracy. Conversely, the Whigs were the rich merchants and the wealthy planters who made up a self-styled "better sort." They were thinly disguised Federalists, vainly striving to stem the populistic tide.

This economic class interpretation of political divisions came under severe attack during the two decades following the Second World War. First the entrepreneurial or "Columbia" school argued that Jacksonians shared the capitalistic ethos of their Whig antagonists, and that they were merely demanding equal time at the feeding trough. A short time later, the writers of the complementary consensus school went beyond the identity of outlook

From the *Political Science Quarterly*, LXXXII (June 1967), 235–52. Reprinted by permission; most footnotes omitted.

that supposedly existed between established Whig capitalists and nascent Jacksonian capitalists, and argued that agreement on fundamental issues has been the hallmark of American politics at all levels. They insisted that meaningful correlations between voting behavior and economic status were hard to come by, if not nonexistent.

In the latter category, the work of Lee Benson stands as an influential example. His study of voting behavior in New York State in 1844, *The Concept of Jacksonian Democracy*,[1] has in the few years since its publication in 1961 gone through several printings, including two paperback editions, and has become one of the most widely discussed volumes on Jacksonianism, even gaining the rare accolade of a session at a historical convention devoted entirely to its appraisal. Benson's book has not swept all before it—the conservatism of the historical profession is guarantee against such sweeping triumphs whatever the new viewpoint may be—but even critics have conceded that it made a breakthrough in methodology, a departure which afforded a fresh approach to the Age of Jackson, and perhaps to American politics in general.

Benson's methodology breathed academic modernity from every pore. He employed the rhetorical and structural paraphernalia of the social sciences. And particularly in those passages which demolished historiographical shibboleths, Benson ardently championed a marriage of historical dilletantism with the virile social sciences —an alliance meant to rescue history from old-maid antiquarianism. Such a union will be solemnized before long, and the historical discipline will profit by it; so say most of the younger practitioners of the historian's craft. Thus Benson placed himself in the vanguard, and his methodological *tour de force* gave almost irresistible impetus to his thesis.

Benson was especially assiduous in attacking the older view that in the Jacksonian era parties divided along class lines. In a section

1. Benson does not write of an America without social conflicts, but he gives primacy to ethnic and religious factors as determinants for group behavior, discarding the haves-versus-the-have-nots basis of liberal historiography.

on party leadership, he attempted to establish a sociological identity among New York State Democrats and Whigs at the top rank, and his analysis extended with similar results into "Middle-Grade Leaders." But in the process, to borrow a figure from the politics of New York in the eighteen-forties, Benson may have turned Barnburner to get rid of a few rats. A closer inspection of a small but important part of the smoldering ashes than has previously been attempted is called for. The comments which follow are not offered as an assessment of Benson's book as a whole. His theory of voting cycles and his call for a multivariate analytical approach to voting behavior are stimulating, and they will doubtless receive careful appraisal and criticism as his hypotheses are tested.

I

"Partial answers," Benson declared at the beginning of his section on party leadership, "frequently give rise to misleading or erroneous conclusions." No one can fault that observation, but in practice Benson himself emerged with answers that were partial, misleading, and erroneous. The questions he posed in that section went beyond the stated initial problem of the social composition of middle grade political leadership. In addition, and much more significantly, he asked: "Did men of wealth strongly tend to give their resources, talents, and prestige to the Whigs rather than to the Democrats? Did a large proportion of the business community —however defined—adhere to the Whig faith?" [2] In arguing for the negative, Benson cited an unnamed Whig orator to the effect that New York's rich men were divided politically and that many Democrats were in fact wealthy. The orator did not contend, however, that the wealthy men were divided *evenly* between the parties. But according to Benson, "by exploiting the clue" provided by the orator's imprecise claim, "historians may be able to clear away

2. Two questions (composition of middle-grade political leadership and voting behavior of wealthy citizens) run through the discussion. I am concerned with the second.

the rhetorical rubbish and reveal the social structure of party leadership during the Age of Egalitarianism." Rhetorical rubbish, or the injection of something resembling class conflict into the Democratic-Whig struggle of the late eighteen-thirties, thus became the impediment. "Who from 1834 to 1844 took the [Democratic] campaign claptrap literally?" Benson asked derisively. A fairer question might be: Who took the campaigning seriously? and the answer would be: A great many people. For, as is the case of twentieth-century advertising, which is also not to be taken literally, the effectiveness of rhetorical claptrap cannot be dismissed.

So much for rhetoric. What about verifiable data? Benson quoted from an editorial in Greeley's *Tribune* which tried to distribute part of the odium attached to the possession of wealth to the Democrats: "The Whigs are by no means all wealthy, nor are the wealthy all Whigs," etc., etc. Some of Greeley's statements were themselves rhetorical claptrap. For example, Greeley "charged" that Democrats chartered most of New York City's banks. Since the Democratic Albany regency had controlled the legislature almost continuously for a generation, the statement was a truism. But Greeley also specified that many New York City Democrats were worth $100,000 or more. Benson explained that "the design of this study does not permit the research necessary to test all the claims" Greeley made, but one assertion (the presence of $100,000-or-over Democrats) could be tested precisely to learn about "party division among economic groups in New York."

Eventually, all discussions of New York City wealth in the eighteen-forties depend upon those exasperating, fascinating, incomplete, and indispensable compendia of the city's economic elite, *Wealth and Biography of the Wealthy Citizens of New York City* . . . , published annually during most of the eighteen-forties and fifties by Moses Y. Beach, editor of the New York *Sun*. Many historians have used them, Robert G. Albion wrote an article about them, and Benson took samples from the sixth edition of 1845.

Beach's list of wealthy citizens for that year included about one thousand names. Benson chose not to analyze the list *in toto*, despite his stated intention to evaluate this specific Greeley claim. Therefore, "some sampling procedure must be devised." He first matched the names of men who were officers of "ratification meetings" held in New York City in 1844 by both major parties with the names on the Wealthy Citizens list, and found that twelve Whig officers (or 34 per cent) qualified, as did thirteen (or 26 per cent) of the Democratic officers. Although Benson dismissed the percentage differential of 8 per cent as "not large enough to be significant in any case," he nevertheless took the trouble to explain it away by the claim of "rank order position." In other words, the importance of Middle Grade Leaders decreased as one read down from the top of the list. Thus if one took the first ten names, both parties supplied six (or 60 per cent) Wealthy Citizens. If one took only the first thirty-five names, the Democrats supplied 34 per cent Wealthy Citizens to the Whigs' 35 per cent. This reduction procedure, although ingenious was questionable to say the least. Benson nowhere established that the men were listed in order of social or political prominence. The Democrats may have been listed that way (although that is doubtful); the Whigs certainly were not. They appeared arranged not in "rank order," but by city wards. The eighth name among the many Whig vice-presidents, for example, was not that of the eighth most important New York City Whig, but that of the Whig sent to the city-wide party convention to represent the Eighth Ward. And it should also be remembered that Benson's "ratification meeting sample" involved but twenty-five men out of the thousand Wealthy Citizens.

Benson's second sampling procedure was simpler but equally unsatisfactory. Taking the list at face value, he scanned Beach's biographical vignettes for political identifications and found information concerning the party affiliations of another twenty-five men, thirteen Democrats (52 per cent) and twelve Whigs (48 per cent). Again, a consensus historian's dream. But the stumbling block here was the inaccuracy of the identifications. Beach, or his compilers, called two of the alleged Jacksonian Democrats, Jonathan Thompson and William W. Todd, "democrats." Both men were in fact National Republicans who supported John Quincy Adams in 1828 and Whig candidates thereafter. Thompson was Adams's collector of the port, whom Jackson removed in 1829. Corrected, the second sample then becomes fourteen Whigs (56 per cent) and eleven Democrats (44 per cent). But the "sample" is not useful in any case. Beach's political identification of his Wealthy Citizens was arbitrary. Some men of political prominence were not identified by party (Benjamin F. Butler, for example), and some were identified incorrectly.

So, on the basis of these forty-five individuals (five were repeaters) out of one thousand (or 4.5 per cent of the total), Benson asked us to believe that his "hypotheses appear potentially verifiable." This is a very tall order for such scanty research to accomplish, however tentative the claims. Obviously, the only constructive way to resolve the problem is to direct attention to the remaining 95 per cent and examine the Wealthy Citizens list in its entirety.

II

As already noted, the principal recommendation for the use of Beach's list is its availability. It contained no explanation of the selection procedure employed, but merely implied that *every* New Yorker of 1845 worth $100,000 or more could be found on the list. Nor was there any assurance of accuracy concerning the estimates of wealth (usually rounded off to the "nearest" $50,000).

Striking omissions were plentiful. Take, for example, William E. Dodge of the important metals firm, Phelps, Dodge & Company. Dodge, aptly termed a "merchant prince" by his biographer, was already a very wealthy citizen at the time of the Beach compilation. Even more perplexing is the fact that Dodge was omitted although the company's senior partner, Anson G. Phelps, was listed at one million dollars, and junior partners Anson G. Phelps Jr., and Daniel James (worth $400,000 each), were both included. Similarly, Edwin D. Morgan, merchant and politician, did not receive a listing; nor did Marshall O. Roberts, a young capitalist worth $250,000 by 1847. Dodge, Morgan, and Roberts were all Whigs, but one can probably produce names of some prominent Democrats of means who did not gain inclusion. Obviously, Moses Beach was as capricious a practitioner of the art of "elite listing" as any of his predecessors or successors.

Theoretically, one might spurn Beach's offering and try to draw up a comprehensive and accurate list of New York City wealth in the eighteen-forties or any other decade of the period. But the task would involve a lifetime of research in the city directories and tax lists, among other sources. The scope of *this* inquiry does not permit such a luxuriance of preliminary investigation. I propose to limit myself to the one thousand individuals found in the Beach list of 1845.

The figure "one thousand" has cropped up several times. It is an approximation, since the precise number of "workable" names is actually 909. The elimination of some names was advisable for several reasons. Female wealthy citizens could not vote or participate politically, whatever their views. Men who died before 1828 (the first year of a meaningful pro- or anti-Jackson alignment) have been eliminated, as have those identified by a last name only. There were also a dozen names repeated on the list.

Among the remaining 909 names, problems of identification arose. In some cases, men shared the same name, sometimes with another man on the list and far more often with another citizen who was not listed. There are two wealthy citizens named David Banks, and two men named George Douglass. In these instances, separate identifications were possible, and each pair split politically. But significantly, perhaps, at least as far as this study is concerned, the two Whigs were wealthier than their namesakes. There was also the problem of identifying the politics of men with common given and family names. For example, many John Wards lived in New York City at the time, but businessmen (who made up the vast majority of those on the list) often signed their firms' names to political pronouncements, such as calls for ratification meetings, or patronage petitions. Thus the presence of "Prime, Ward & King" on a Whig call or petition provided the political stand of John Ward, as well as that of Edward Prime, Samuel Ward, and James G. King, his partners in that well known brokerage firm. Of course, not all the names were that "common." Happily for the investigator, there was only one Aquilla G. Stout in New York City in 1845, and, of course, only one Preserved Fish.

Whatever the deficiencies and difficulties, the list still beckons. An intensive search in both primary and secondary sources, Whig and Democratic, produced the political identification of 642 men, or 70.6 per cent. The extent of political involvement varied widely. Thus, among the Whigs, the men ranged from Moses H. Grinnell, a Whig congressman, and Jonathan Goodhue, president of many an anti-Jackson New York City rally, to merchants such as George T. Trimble and Oliver T. Hewlett, who apparently were not lured into participating in political meetings but who publicly opposed Democratic policies, such as the removal of the deposits and the refusal to charter a new national bank. The Democratic minority showed a similar spread, from ex-cabinet member Benjamin F. Butler to Democratic merchants such as Reuel Smith, who voiced general approval of the Van Buren administration in 1840. In any case, of the 642 men identified politically, the overwhelming majority (541, or 84.3 per cent) were of the Whig persuasion. New York City money in 1845 was decidedly Whig.

Not only was New York City wealth Whiggish to the general extent of 84.3 per cent but big money showed an even more pronounced affinity for the party of "sound principles." If we divide the Wealthy Citizens into groups according to the size of their estates, at the highest levels the incidence of Democratic affiliation shrinks well below the already miniscule over-all average of 15.7 per cent. All four men worth five million dollars or more were anti-Jacksonians. And at the next three levels, the Democrats averaged only 8.4 per cent of those identified. Thus among those worth

$400,000 or more (with one hundred identified out of a total of 129), ninety-two men (92 per cent) were Whigs. Democrats fared better in the categories $300,000 to $399,000 and $250,000 to $299,000, dropping off again sharply in the $200,000 to $249,000 class. But to revert to America's common yardstick for measuring great wealth, of the seventeen millionaires identified out of a total of twenty-two, sixteen (94.1 per cent) were Whigs.[3]

Table 1

Party Affiliation by Amount of Wealth

	Total No.	*Politics Identified* No. (%)	*Whigs* No. (%)	*Democrats* No. (%)
$5,000,000 or more	4	4 (100.0)	4 (100.0)	0 (0.0)
$1,000,000 to $4,999,000	18	13 (72.2)	12 (92.3)	1 (7.7)
$500,000 to $999,000	80	59 (73.8)	54 (91.5)	5 (8.5)
$400,000 to $499,000	27	25 (92.6)	23 (92.0)	2 (8.0)
$300,000 to $399,000	101	67 (66.3)	50 (74.6)	17 (25.4)
$250,000 to $299,000	63	47 (74.6)	37 (78.7)	10 (21.3)
$200,000 to $249,000	162	110 (67.9)	98 (89.1)	12 (10.9)
	455	325 (71.4)	278 (85.5)	47 (14.5)

III

Benson could not have chosen a less suitable point in time than 1844–45 to seek validation for his thesis. In fact, his study of Jacksonian Democracy is curiously unhistorical in its neglect of chronology. True, he provided a summary of New York political history from 1815 to 1844 which set the Fox-Schlesinger accounts topsy-turvy, and he specifically chided political historians for their unhistorical use of isolated election returns, but in essence his study concentrated upon voting behavior in 1844. With regard to a negative correlation between upper-class membership and party, 1828 would have served far better.

3. The only millionaire identified as a Democrat, Jacob Lorillard, died in 1838. Had he lived on into the forties he might well have become one of the many wealthy Democratic defectors to Whiggery.

In 1828, a New York City businessman or professional might as easily have supported Jackson as Adams. Or with equal probability, he might have ignored the organized aspects of politics and done no more than cast his vote. This was no longer the case in 1844. In the intervening sixteen years, businessmen had soured on Jacksonism–Loco-Focoism in a series of revolts which culminated in opposition to Van Buren's subtreasury proposal during the late eighteen-thirties and in the feverish enthusiasm of the election of 1840. The defection process began in New York City as early as 1827, when several Tammany sachems supported Adams instead of Jackson. Then during the Bank Veto campaign of 1832 several Democratic leaders bolted (among them Gulian Verplanck and Moses Grinnell), and a year later the crisis brought on by the removal of federal deposits from the Bank of the United States caused further defections. The Panic of 1837 and the subtreasury proposal, which ostensibly would have cut the ties between the national government and the bank credit system, produced the major party split known as the conservative revolt, and created more recruits for the Whig column. Most conservatives found their way back to the Democratic party in time, but not all.

Among the Wealthy Citizens of 1845, many such defectors from the Democracy can be found. Of the men identified as Whigs by the eighteen-forties, fifty-two (or almost 10 per cent) were former Democrats. The total of men identified as having been Democrats at one time or other was 153 (101 in good standing by 1845, and 52 defectors). Thus fully one-third of the wealthy who had originally been Democrats reacted violently to their party's policies in the eighteen-thirties and joined the enemy. One simply cannot dismiss the "Loco-Focoizing" of the Democratic party in the middle and late eighteen-thirties as rhetorical claptrap; *something* caused a third of the wealthy Democrats to bolt. And there was no corresponding reversal of the process. Not a single individual among the 101 Democrats of 1845 had previously been an anti-Jacksonian.

As important as were the defections, perhaps even more significant was the fact that the Democratic response to the Bank War and Panic of 1837 temporarily solidified the New York City business community into an anti-Democratic force. It may be difficult now to comprehend what terrors the subtreasury scheme would have imposed on the merchants, or to tremble at the Loco-Foco oratory, but the businessmen of that day did not have the balm of historical perspective to soothe them. Many believed that they were standing on the "ragged edge of anarchy," to employ a conservative pronouncement of the latter part of the nineteenth century. In the late eighteen-thirties, New York City businessmen displayed their colors, many of them for the first time. A contemporary observer described a leading merchant financier's reaction:

> With very clear and decided notions on public subjects, Mr. Ward had yet kept himself—as was, indeed, until 1834, the case with very many of the leading and active commercial men in New York—free from party strife. . . . When, however, in 1834, that series of disastrous measures commenced, which, under the auspices of General Jackson and his successor, have caused such accumulated ruin and misery, Mr. Ward . . . entered the political arena.

Merchants supporting the Whig ticket convened a meeting in September 1840 in front of the Merchants Exchange. Over two thousand firms signed the call for the meeting, a list which took up the entire front page of the Whig newspapers. The Whig diarist Philip Hone was both exultant and accurate when he wrote:

> The great meeting of Whig merchants took place to-day. . . . The appearance of the mass of people was perfectly sublime. It was a field of heads, occupying a space about six times as large as the area of Washington hall, from which I calculated the number at fifteen thousand; all respectable and orderly merchants and traders. . . .

The Democratic merchants also held a meeting. Its call, again in the form of company names tabulated in small print, consumed one-tenth the space in newspaper columns that the Whig call had used. As Democrat Joseph A. Scoville (the "Old Merchant") put it, colorfully but not exultantly: "Very few merchants of the first class have been Democrats. . . . The Democratic merchants could have easily been stowed in a large Eighth avenue railroad car."

Table 2 illuminates the intensification of political activity on the part of New York City businessmen following the initiation of the Bank War. In the period 1828–31 slightly less than 10 per cent of the Wealthy Citizens could be identified politically and, of them, nearly half were Democrats. But in the next four-year period, 1832–35, a span which coincided with the Bank Veto and the Removal of Deposits, the number of Wealthy Citizens taking a political stand more than quadrupled, and the proportion of Democrats fell to 23.2 per cent. The Democratic percentages continued to dip in the late eighteen-thirties and early forties. By the mid-forties the incidence of political identification declined as the fires of the Bank and currency questions died down, but by then the bond between the business community and the Whig party had been established. Of course, these figures are not a mirror of the political loyalties of all the Wealthy Citizens from 1828 to 1851, but they do reflect the willingness of the elite economic groups to make public their political preferences at certain times. We can reasonably assume that nearly all of the Wealthy Citizens voted in 1828, but the fact that only 10 per cent were part of the visible political superstructure indicates a lack of mercantile hostility toward the Jacksonians before the coming of the Bank Wars.

Table 2

Party Affiliation by Time Period

	*Total No.**	*Politics Identified No. %*	*Whigs No. %*	*Democrats No. %*
1828–31	909	90 (9.9)	48 (53.4)	42 (46.6)
1832–35	909	379 (41.9)	291 (76.8)	88 (23.2)
1836–39	905	298 (32.9)	244 (81.9)	54 (18.1)
1840–43	900	324 (36.0)	270 (83.4)	54 (16.6)
1844–47	892	190 (21.3)	156 (82.2)	34 (17.8)
1848–51	880	134 (15.2)	106 (79.2)	28 (20.8)

* *Twenty-nine Wealthy Citizens died between 1828 and 1847.*

IV

It is abundantly clear that by 1845 New York City wealth was allied to Whiggery, and that the process had taken place progressively during the preceding fifteen years. Were there other factors which might have produced this pattern of political allegiance? Religious and ethno-cultural variables as determinants of political behavior are being investigated more and more, and I shall follow the trend.

Not surprisingly, the denomination with by far the largest representation among the Wealthy Citizens was the Episcopalian. Presbyterians followed next, and then Quakers and Dutch Reformed. The striking thing about the political breakdown for these four dominant denominations is that the percentages of Whig affiliation ran close to the over-all Whig average of 84 per cent. Thus 84 per cent of the Episcopalians were Whig; 88 per cent of the Presbyterians; 84 per cent of the Dutch Reformed; and 92 per cent of the Quakers. Benson observed that Protestant denominationalism was of little use in pinpointing political alignment, and this seems to be true for the wealthy. What we can observe is such a well known phenomenon as denominational social climbing. Of twenty-three men who switched religions, twelve became Episcopalians and joined, if not the established church, then the church of the establishment.

The number of Wealthy Citizens in the remaining denominations was too small for generalizations. Unitarians were Democratic by 66 per cent, but only two men were involved. Congregationalists and Jews were 100 per cent Whig—all four Congregationalists and all seven Jews. There were only eight Catholics, including a mathematician from Columbia College who converted as an adult, and the Delmonico brothers, the Italian-Swiss restauranteurs, but only one man from Ireland (a Democrat).

On the ethnocultural front, I have followed the native-immigrant division (and sub-categorization) employed by Benson. He also provided rough estimates of political affiliation among the groups—native Dutch, for example, he estimated to have been 60 per cent Democratic. Although the estimates are expressed in percentages, Benson requested that the figures not be taken "literally." Their precision cannot be verified, but precise or not, there is a pronounced dissimilarity between Benson's ethnocultural estimates for the New York electorate as a whole, and the ethnocultural breakdown of wealthy New Yorkers.

Table 3

Religious Affiliation

		Politics Known		*Whigs*		*Demo-crats*	
	No.	No.	%	No.	%	No.	%
Baptists	8	7	(87.5)	5 [1] *	(71.4)	2	(28.6)
Catholics	8	4	(50.0)	2	(50.0)	2	(50.0)
Congregationalists	6	4	(66.7)	4	(100.0)	0	(0.0)
Dutch Reformed	33	25	(75.8)	21 [2]	(84.0)	4	(16.0)
Episcopalians	204	157	(78.0)	132 [13]	(84.0)	25	(16.0)
Jews	8	7	(87.5)	7	(100.0)	0	(0.0)
Methodists	9	8	(89.0)	7	(87.5)	1	(12.5)
Moravians	2	2	(100.0)	2	(100.0)	0	(0.0)
Presbyterians	118	99	(83.9)	87 [4]	(87.8)	12	(12.2)
Quakers	45	36	(80.0)	33 [1]	(91.7)	3	(8.3)
Unitarians	3	3	(100.0)	1	(33.3)	2	(66.7)
Fundamentalists	1	0	(0.0)	0	(0.0)	0	(0.0)
No Religion	2	1	(50.0)	1	(100.0)	0	(0.0)
	447	353	(79.0)	302 [21]	(85.5)	51	(14.5)

* *Numbers in brackets indicate Democrats who defected.*

Among the natives, Benson estimated that the Old British and Dutch were both 60 per cent Democratic; but among the wealthy, the Old British were 80 per cent Whig, and the Dutch were 83 per cent Whig. These two categories were large, but the largest single native category was the "Yankees," or as Albion put it "the swarm of New Englanders who were seeking their fortunes in New York City, just as it was clinching its leadership over the rival

American ports." Benson estimated that New York Yankees as a whole voted Whig by 55 per cent; wealthy New Englanders in New York City voted Whig by 92 per cent. Two other native groups identified as Democratic by Benson, Germans (60 per cent) and Penn-Jerseyites (55 per cent), were also Whig by 75 per cent and 72 per cent respectively. There were a dozen native Southerners. Though they came from Jackson's banner region, they were 83 per cent Whig.

Table 4

Ethnocultural Background

	Total	*Politics Identified*	*Whigs*		*Benson's Estimates for Whigs*	*Demo-crats*
Natives	No.	No. %	No.	%	%	No. %
British	146	106 (72.6)	85 [10] *	(80.2)	40	21 (19.8)
Dutch	102	77 (75.5)	64 [7]	(83.1)	40	13 (16.9)
German	11	8 (72.8)	6	(75.0)	40	2 (25.0)
Huguenot	7	3 (42.8)	2	(66.7)	75	1 (33.3)
Penn.–Jersey	26	21 (80.8)	15 [3]	(71.5)	45	6 (28.5)
Southern	13	12 (92.3)	10	(83.3)	—	2 (16.7)
Yankee	147	122 (83.0)	112 [3]	(91.8)	55	10 (8.2)
Sub-totals	452	349 (78.0)	294 [23]	(84.2)		55 (15.8)
Immigrants						
Dutch	4	4 (100.0)	4 [1]	(100.0)	—	0 (0.0)
English	32	14 (43.7)	14	(100.0)	75	0 (0.0)
French	12	7 (58.4)	6 [1]	(85.7)	10	1 (14.3)
German	15	13 (86.6)	7 [1]	(53.8)	20	6 (46.2)
Cath.-Irish	1	1 (100.0)	0	(0.0)	5	1 (100.0)
Prot.-Irish	17	14 (82.4)	10 [3]	(71.4)	90	4 (28.6)
Scottish	31	29 (93.6)	27 [2]	(93.1)	90	2 (6.9)
Swiss	5	0 (0.0)	0	(0.0)	—	0 (0.0)
West Indian	1	1 (100.0)	1	(100.0)	—	0 (0.0)
Polish	1	0 (0.0)	0	(0.0)	—	0 (0.0)
Sub-totals	119	83 (69.7)	69 [8]	(83.2)		14 (16.8)
Totals	571	432 (75.7)	363 [31]	(84.0)		69 (16.0)

* *Numbers in brackets indicate Democrats who defected.*

The immigrant categories reveal the same patterns. All but one group represented among the wealthy were Whig. There was only one Irish Catholic, no French Canadians, no Welsh, and no Negroes on the Wealthy Citizens list. Immigrant French, supposedly 90 per cent Democratic, were 86 per cent Whig (but that includes only seven men). The immigrant English, estimated at 75 per cent Whig, were 100 per cent Whig (fourteen of fourteen). The Scots, estimated at 90 per cent Whig, were 93 per cent Whig. The lowest Whig percentage among immigrant groups (excluding the one Irish Catholic), was the German (54 per cent), a group estimated at 80 per cent Democratic. Although the German percentage involves but a dozen men, it seems to demonstrate the tug of various factors operating on a man's political decision-making process. One can accept, almost axiomatically, the proposition that religious and ethnocultural background will influence his response to politics, but surely one need not have to argue excessively for considering the possession of great wealth as an important factor, perhaps the preponderant factor, in analyzing the American wealthy as political men.

V

What do these data prove about the political alignment of America's wealthy classes in cities other than New York? Nothing. To what extent New York, City or State, represents the country at large, or to what extent it can usefully be called a "test case," remains to be determined, especially among non-commercial, rural elites. Several additional studies using other "Wealthy Citizens" lists (they exist for Boston and Philadelphia, for example) would be feasible and profitable. Even the absence of such lists does not close the door to counting the heads of the elite. There are directories for all major cities in the Jackson period, and in some cases they go beyond a mere alphabetical listing of heads of households to include classified business and professional directories. From these one might "do" the politics of, say, the importing merchants of Providence, or the lawyers of Pittsburgh, or the physicians of Charleston.

But it is important to begin with men of a non-political grouping and then proceed to their political identification. To start with vice-presidents of ratification meetings or with members of Congress from Tennessee in the antebellum period is to beg the question, since a sociological identity, or near-identity, is almost predictable in those instances. In the case of ratification-meeting vice-presidents we can expect that both parties, whatever their rhetoric, produced lists of solid men—that is, men of material substance—even though one party might have had a much smaller reservoir of "vice-presidential types" to draw upon.[4] It was not likely that the New York City Democracy, whatever its Loco-Foco professions, would put a score of illiterate and inarticulate hod carriers on the Tammany Hall platform. In the second case cited, it was no surprise that the Tennessee congressmen were usually middle-aged lawyers of similar social background. The nature of the group chosen for investigation predetermined that result. But what of the Tennessee professional and commercial classes, the upper crust of the state (and other states as well), taken as solid blocs? Only after such groups have been isolated and examined can we begin to speak with certainty about upper class and party in Jacksonian America.

Much of the previous debate has floundered upon the semantic difficulty of whether Whigs were wealthy. Once again, the terms are in reverse order; the question should read: Were wealthy Americans Whigs? If by "Whigs" we mean all who voted for that party, or even the party functionaries at all levels, it is obvious that the possession of great wealth was not a prerequisite to association with Whiggery. The party had to appeal to a mass electorate in an age of ballot-box egalitarianism. By definition, a man

4. Yet even among the vice-presidents of ratification meetings who were Wealthy Citizens there was considerably more Whig money than Democratic. The thirteen Democrats were worth, collectively, 2.5 million dollars; the twelve Whigs were worth 13.4 million.

of wealth was one who owned more than the majority of his neighbors, and there were simply not enough of the "wealthy" available to achieve election-day victories without the creation of an exclusive, high-level electorate. One Democratic editor described the situation in 1840 in simple terms: "There was a meeting of Whig merchants in Wall Street, and a meeting of the people in the Park, both of which were very large, but the latter much the larger, for the very simple reason that there are more people,—more mechanics and laborers,—than there are merchants." If we begin with the parties, and especially with the entire electorate, it is indeed difficult to find "any evidence that the party situation reflected basic economic or social cleavages in the population," as has recently been remarked of New Jersey. But perhaps the judgment would be altered if one plotted the location of economic status groups in the New Jersey political spectrum, especially for the eighteen-forties.

In a viable two-party system, operating within the context of universal white manhood suffrage, the class nature of political alignment must be sought in areas other than a pristine partisan division of rich versus poor. The validity of projecting the New York City experience to points beyond has yet to be established, but I suspect that the monied men of New York City in the eighteen-forties were not out of step with their peers elsewhere in thinking that the Whig party of that decade better served their interests and better calmed their fears than did the Democracy.

The Southerner as American

Who Were the Southern Whigs?

by Charles Grier Sellers, Jr.

During much of the Jacksonian period the Whig party of the South was a nationally oriented group, aligned with the capitalistic-commercial interests elsewhere in the entire country, a theme developed by Charles Sellers in the following article. By the late 1830's, the Jackson party of 1828 had evolved into the Democratic party, and opposition had crystallized into the Whig party. The nation then enjoyed the short-lived luxury of two major national parties that were strong in all sections.

A Southern Whig in 1840, the year of the first Whig presidential victory, had more in common with his partisan counterpart in the North and Northwest than he had with the "dangerous Loco-Focos," or Democrats, of his Southern state. Such issues as banking, internal improvements, and the tariff created national economic interests that brought together in one party like-minded interests from all parts of the country. The traditional view of the South before the Civil War as a united section marching directly toward secession and war while chanting the ideological catch-phrases of its greatest political philosopher, John C. Calhoun, obscures the reality of internal sectional divisions. Yet in the decades before secession a real struggle took place in the South over principles and tactics. Sellers demonstrates that although Calhoun and his followers prepared the way for the growth of Southern nationalism, most of the South, still convinced that their vital interests could be served within the Union, rejected extremist formulas during the Jacksonian period.

But almost as soon as this national, two-party system had been established, it began to break down under the weight of sectional conflict in the late 1840's and the 1850's. The end of the system signaled the end of the Jacksonian coalition and ultimately the end of an era. The second American party system survived as long as men observed the unwritten law of that era's politics: that contention over slavery be kept out of national politics. When politicians abandoned that formula, they unleashed forces beyond their control.

Students of the Old South have spent much of their time in recent years dispelling myths about that fabled land of moonlight and magnolias. Our understanding of the social, intellectual, and economic life of the antebellum South has been considerably revised and immeasurably widened by the work of a large number of able scholars.

Political history, however, has been unfashionable, and one of the results has been the survival of a series of myths about the political life of the South in the 1830's and 1840's. The key myth may be called the myth of a monolithic South: a section unified as early as the 1820's in its devotion to states' rights doctrines and its hostility to the nationalistic, antislavery, capitalistic North. The result of approaching antebellum history by way of Fort Sumter and Appomattox, this point of view found its classic statements in the apologias of Jefferson Davis and Alexander H. Stephens, but it was made respectable in the first generation of professional scholarship by such historians as Herman Von Holst and John W. Burgess. It colored such early monographs as U. B. Phillips's

From *The American Historical Review*, LIX (January 1954), 335–46. Reprinted by permission of the author; most footnotes omitted.

"Georgia and State Rights" and H. M. Wagstaff's *States Rights and Political Parties in North Carolina, 1776–1861,* and is to be seen in most of the more recent works on the pre–Civil War South.[1] It has also given rise to the corollary myths that Calhoun was the representative spokesman and political leader of the South after about 1830, and that the Whig party in the South mainly reflected the state's rights proclivities of the great planters.

These myths have been strengthened by Frederick Jackson Turner's sectional analysis of our early national history. Turner's approach has been extremely fruitful, but its sweeping application has tended to exaggerate differing sectional tendencies into absolute sectional differences. The application of geographic sectionalism to individual states, moreover, has fostered the further myth that political strife within the Old South was confined largely to struggles over intrastate sectional issues between upcountry and low country, hill country and "black belt."

All of these myths have some basis in fact. They are, however, the product of a misplaced emphasis which has permeated nearly all the studies of pre–Civil War southern politics. Sectionalism and states' rights have been made the central themes of southern political history for almost the entire antebellum period. Southern opposition to nationalistic legislation by Congress has been over-

1. Charles S. Sydnor, in what is, in many respects, the finest work on the antebellum South, presents a persuasive restatement of the traditional sectional–states' rights interpretation. His chapter headings on politics from the Panic of 1819 to nullification describe a developing sectionalism: "From Economic Nationalism to Political Sectionalism," "End of the Virginia Dynasty," "The Lower South Adopts State Rights," and "Bold Acts and Bolder Thoughts." The 1830's and 1840's, however, present a paradox. Professor Sydnor finds a growing "Regionalism in Mind and Spirit," but a "decline of sectionalism in politics." This he explains as a result of the fact that "major Southern hopes and fears found no champion in either party," so that "party conflict south of the Potomac . . . had the hollow sound of a stage duel with tin swords." "The agrarian South felt little interest," writes Professor Sydnor, in that conflict between the "wealthier and more conservative segments of society" and the liberal, democratic elements "which formed a major issue between the Democratic and Whig parties" in the nation as a whole. *The Development of Southern Sectionalism, 1819–1848* (Baton Rouge, 1948), especially p. 316.

emphasized. And the social, economic, and ideological lines of political cleavage within the slave states have been obscured. The early history of the Whig party below Mason and Dixon's line shows the character of these distortions.

It is too often forgotten that in the antebellum period the South had a vigorous two-party system, an asset it has never since enjoyed. Until at least the later 1840's, the voting southerner was much more interested in the success of his own party and its policies than in banding together with southerners of the opposite party to defend the Constitution and southern rights against invasion by the North. The parties were evenly matched, and elections were bitterly contested. It was rare for any southern state to be regarded as absolutely safe for either party. Of the 425,629 votes cast in the slave states at the election of 1836, the Whigs had a majority of only 243 popular votes. In this and the three succeeding presidential elections, a total of 2,745,171 votes were cast, but the over-all margin, again in favor of the Whigs, was only 66,295, or 2.4 per cent of the total votes. In these four elections the Whigs carried a total of twenty-seven southern states and the Democrats twenty-six.

An equally close rivalry is evident in congressional representation. In the five congressional elections between 1832 and 1842, southern Democrats won an aggregate total of 234 seats, while their opponents captured 263. Whigs predominated among southern representatives in three of these five Congresses, and Democrats in two. In three of them the margin between the southern wings of the parties was five or less. We have then a picture of keen political competition, with a vigorous Whig party maintaining a slight ascendancy.

What did this Whig party stand for? The pioneer account of the southern Whigs was the essay by U. B. Phillips which, significantly, appeared in the *Festschrift* to Frederick Jackson Turner. This study shows Phillips's characteristic tendency to generalize about the entire South on the basis of conditions in his native Georgia. "The great central body of southern Whigs," he declares, "were the cotton producers, who were first state-rights men pure and simple and joined the Whigs from a sense of outrage at Jackson's threat of coercing South Carolina."

Two years after Phillips's essay appeared, Arthur C. Cole published his exhaustive monograph on *The Whig Party in the South.* Less than a third of the Cole volume is concerned with the period before 1844, when Whiggery was of greatest importance in the South, and he generally follows the Phillips interpretation of its origins. His account of the birth of the party devotes three pages to early National Republicanism in the South, twenty to the anti-Jackson sentiment aroused during the nullification crisis, and only four and a half to the fight over the national bank and financial policy. "Various interests," he says, "linked in political alliance with the few southerners whose interests and inclinations led to the support of latitudinarian principles, a still larger faction made up of those who supported constitutional doctrines on the opposite extreme and whose logical interests seemed to point against such an affiliation."

An analysis, however, of the record of the Twenty-second Congress (1831–1833) leads to somewhat different conclusions. It was this Congress which dealt with the tariff, nullification, and national bank questions, and it was during this Congress that the groundwork for the Whig party was laid. Of the ninety southerners in the House of Representatives, sixty-nine had been elected as supporters of Andrew Jackson, while twenty-one, nearly a fourth, were National Republicans. Of the sixty-nine Democrats, twenty-five were subsequently active in the Whig party. Eighteen of the latter were state rights Whigs, while seven were not identified with the state rights wing of the opposition. These twenty-five men then, together with the twenty-one National Republicans, may be regarded as representative of the groups which formed the Whig party in the South.

These incipient Whigs voted twenty-four to twenty-one in favor of the tariff of 1832, a measure denounced by state rights men and nullified by South Carolina. They also voted twenty-four to nineteen for the Force Bill, which was designed to throttle the nullifiers. This backing of administration measures was hardly a portent of an opposition state rights party. The real harbinger of Whiggery was the vote on the national bank bill, which this group supported twenty-seven to seventeen.

The Whig party actually took shape during the Twenty-third Congress (1833–1835), in which it gained the allegiance of fifty-two of the ninety-nine southern members of the House. They voted twenty-nine to sixteen in favor of rechartering the national bank and unanimously in favor of restoring the government deposits to Biddle's institution. By a closer vote of twenty-two to twenty they supported repairing and extending the Cumberland Road. In the Twenty-fourth Congress (1835–1837) the forty-eight Whig Representatives from the South divided thirty-eight to three in favor of Clay's bill to distribute the proceeds from sales of public lands to the states. Other votes showing similar tendencies might be cited, but enough has been said to suggest that, even in the beginning, a majority of southern anti-Jackson men were far from being state rights doctrinaires.

In the light of this record it is not so surprising that only a handful of southern Whigs followed Calhoun when he marched his supporters back into the Democratic household during Van Buren's administration. The record also prepares one for the increasing manifestations of nationalism among southern Whigs which Phillips and Cole found so difficult to explain. The southern wing of the party backed Clay almost unanimously for the presidential nomination in 1840. Tyler's nomination for Vice President was more a sop to the disappointed Clay men, of whom Tyler was one, than a concession to the state rights proclivities of southern Whiggery, the reason usually given for his choice.

The nature of southern Whiggery had its real test when Tyler challenged Clay for leadership of the party. Of the fifty-five southern Whigs in the lower house of the Twenty-seventh Congress (1841–1843), only three stuck by the Virginia president and his state rights principles, whereas Mangum of North Carolina pre-sided over the caucus which read Tyler out of the party, and southern Whig editors joined in castigating him unmercifully. Southern Whigs supported Clay's legislative program—repeal of the Subtreasury, a national bank, distribution, and tariff—by large majorities. Even the Georgians, Berrien, Toombs, and Stephens, defended the protective features of the tariff of 1842.

Having said so much to the point that the Whig party in the South did not begin as and did not become a state rights party, it is necessary to add that neither was it consciously nationalistic. State rights versus nationalism simply was not the main issue in southern politics in this period. It is readily apparent from the newspapers and correspondence of the time that, except for Calhoun and his single-minded little band, politicians in the South were fighting over the same questions that were agitating the North—mainly questions of banking and financial policy.

It is hard to exaggerate the importance of the banking question. State and federal governments, by their policy in this sphere, could cause inflation or deflation, make capital easy or difficult to obtain, and facilitate or hinder the marketing of staple crops and commercial activity generally. And by chartering or refusing to charter banks, they could afford or deny to the capitalists of the day the most profitable field of activity the economy offered.

The banking issue is the key to an understanding of southern as well as northern Whiggery. Merchants and bankers were most directly concerned in financial policy, but their community of interest generally included the other business and professional men of the towns, especially the lawyers, who got most of their fees from merchants, and the newspaper editors, who were dependent on the merchants for advertising revenues. The crucial point for southern politics, however, is that the large staple producers were also closely identified economically with the urban commercial groups. These were the principal elements which went into the Whig party.

The Whigs generally defended the national bank until its doom was sealed, then advocated a liberal chartering of commercial banks by the states, and finally, after the Panic of 1837, demanded a new national bank. The Democrats fought Biddle's institution and either favored state-operated banks to provide small loans for farmers, as distinguished from commercial banks, or tried to regulate banking strictly or abolish it altogether.

Much of the misunderstanding about the Whig party in the South may be traced to the technique of plotting election returns on maps. Such maps tell us much, but they may also mislead. They show, for example, that the "black belts" of the lower South were the great centers of Whig strength. This has led scholars to reason: (1) that the Whig party was a planters' party *par excellence,* (2) that planters were necessarily rigid state rights men, and (3) that the Whig party was, therefore, a state rights party. *Q. E. D.!*

What the maps do not illustrate, however, is the dynamics of the political situation—the elements of leadership, impetus, financing, and propaganda, which are the real sinews of a political organization. In the case of the Whig party, these elements were furnished mainly by the commercial groups of the cities and towns, with their allied lawyers and editors. Lawyers were the practicing politicians for both parties, but the greater incidence of lawyers among the Whigs is an indication of the commercial affiliations of the party. Seventy-four per cent of the southern Whigs who sat in Congress from 1833 to 1843 are identified as practicing attorneys, as compared with 55 per cent of the Democrats. In the lower house of the Tennessee legislature of 1839, farmers predominated, but a fourth of the Whigs were lawyers, as compared with only a tenth of the Democratic membership.

The size and importance of the urban middle class in the Old South has yet to be fully appreciated. As early as 1831, Nashville, for example, contained twenty-two wholesale houses and seventy-seven retail stores, not to mention numerous other businesses, such as the sixty taverns and tippling houses. Even the little county seat town of Gallatin, Tennessee, boasted in 1840 ten mercantile firms, a grocer, a merchant tailor, three hotels, five lawyers, five doctors, a paper and grist mill, and eighteen artisans' establishments of one kind or another.

Businessmen dominated the towns socially, economically, and politically, and the towns dominated the countryside. This was particularly true of the "black belts" of the lower South, since the great cotton capitalists of this region were especially dependent on commercial and credit facilities for financing and carrying on their extensive planting operations. In recogition of the urban influence on politics, congressional districts were commonly known by the names of the principal towns in each—as, for example, the Huntsville, Florence, Tuscaloosa, Montgomery, and Mobile districts in Alabama.

Other evidence points in the same direction. A large majority of the stockholders in Virginia banks in 1837 lived in the areas of heaviest Whig voting. The principal commercial towns of the state—Richmond, Petersburg, and Norfolk—gave unbroken Whig majorities throughout the period 1834–1840. In North Carolina twenty of the twenty-one directors of the two principal banks in 1840 were Whigs. The first Whig governor of North Carolina was a railroad president; the second was a lawyer, cotton manufacturer, and railroad president; and the third was one of the wealthiest lawyers in the state.

Similar party leadership obtained elsewhere. In Virginia, younger men of the type of John Minor Botts of Richmond and Alexander H. H. Stuart of Staunton actually directed the party of which Tyler and Tazewell were nominal leaders. Senators George A. Waggaman and Judah P. Benjamin were typical of the New Orleans lawyers who guided Louisiana Whiggery. Poindexter and Prentiss in Mississippi were intimately associated both personally and financially with the bankers and businessmen of Natchez. The Tennessee Whigs were led by John Bell, Nashville lawyer and iron manufacturer, who had married into the state's leading mercantile and banking house; Ephraim H. Foster, bank director and Nashville's most prominent commercial lawyer; and Hugh Lawson White, Knoxville lawyer, judge, and bank president.[2]

This commercial bias of the Whig party did much to pave the way for the industrial development of the South after the Civil War. It was no accident that former Whigs provided a large part of the leadership for the business-minded Conservative-Democratic parties which "redeemed" the South from Republican rule and then proceeded to make the conquered section over in the image of the victorious North, often in the interest of northern capital.

Commercial considerations and the banking question did not, of course, determine political alignments in the Old South by themselves. Pro-tariff sentiment made for Whiggery among the sugar planters of Louisiana, the hemp growers of Kentucky, and the salt and iron manufacturers of western Virginia and Maryland. The more liberal policy of the Whigs toward internal improvements by both the state and federal governments won them support in landlocked interior sections and along the routes of projected transportation projects. And the fact that the Democrats generally championed a broadened suffrage, apportionment of congressional and legislative seats on the basis of white population, and other

2. Lawyers provided much of the leadership for the Democratic party also, but they tended to be from the smaller towns rather than the big commercial centers—as, for example, James K. Polk, Cave Johnson, and Aaron V. Brown, in Tennessee. There were also a goodly number of "Democrats by trade"—men like James K. Polk's merchant-banker-mail contractor brother-in-law, James Walker—who were active in Democratic politics for personal profit. The top Whig leadership, however, contained few men of the decidedly noncommercial backgrounds of such Democrats as Andrew Johnson, the Greenville tailor; Bedford Brown, the upcountry small planter who inherited Nathaniel Macon's mantle in North Carolina; Richard M. Johnson, the ebullient Tecumseh-slayer, who continued to wait on customers in his Great Crossings inn while Vice President of the United States; David Hubbard, the self-educated carpenter who championed the poor whites of northern Alabama; Franklin E. Plummer, the picturesque loco-foco from the piney woods of eastern Mississippi; and General Solomon W. Downs, who led the "Red River Democracy" of northern Louisiana in the fights for suffrage extension and bank reform. Davy Crockett was, of course, the exception among the Whigs that proved the rule.

measures for extending political democracy, inclined propertied and conservative men to rally to the Whig party as a bulwark against mobocracy.

These factors, however, merely reinforced the commercial nature of southern Whiggery. The business orientation of the Whigs and the relative unimportance of their state rights wing become quite apparent if the party is described as it actually developed in the various states, rather than on the basis of general assumptions about southern politics.

A state by state analysis would indicate that, in the four border slave states and Louisiana, Whiggery was simply National Republicanism continued under a new name. The National Republicans were also strong in Virginia, but here they were joined in opposition to the Democrats by a body of state rights men alienated from Jackson by his attitude toward nullification. The National Republican and commercial wing of the party, however, was the dominant one, especially after the business-minded Conservative Democrats joined the Whigs on the Subtreasury question. In North Carolina and Tennessee, the Whig party was formed by the secession of pro-Bank men from the Democratic party, aided in Tennessee by the local popularity of Hugh Lawson White as a presidential candidate in 1835–1836.[3]

3. The difficulty historians have had understanding why the North Carolina planters perversely remained in the Democratic party arises from the initial error of regarding the Whig party as primarily a planter group. The basic explanation is that the Old Republican planters of North Carolina, unlike the agricultural capitalists of the lower South, were antagonistic toward the commercial-financial group, rather than identified with it. With a smaller investment in land and slaves than his Mississippi counterpart, with little chance to make large profits by further investment, and relying less on a single cash crop, the average North Carolina planter was much less dependent on the town merchant and banker. For some years before the Jackson era, the planters had been resisting demands for banks and internal improvements, while simultaneously trying to stem the tide of democratic discontent with planter rule. It was the union of these two anti-planter forces, commercial and democratic, which produced the Whig party in 1833–1835. Businessmen controlled the new party, but they retained popular support by championing constitutional reform and by progressive legislation in the fields of internal improvements and public education. There is no adequate account of the North Carolina Whigs in print. The situation in Virginia was somewhat

The state rights element was more conspicuous in the four remaining states of the lower South. But it was by no means the majority wing of the Whig party in all of them. Both Alabama and Mississippi had an original nucleus of pro-Clay, anti-Jackson men, and in both states the nullification episode caused a substantial defection from the Jackson ranks. In Mississippi, however, a greater defection followed the removal of government deposits from the national bank. The state rights men were clearly a minority of the opposition party, which elected an outspoken foe of nullification to the governorship in 1835 and sent the ardent Clay partisan, Seargent S. Prentiss, to Congress two years later.

The state rights defection seems to have been more important in Alabama, where it was led by the able Dixon H. Lewis. The Lewis faction, however, maintained only a tenuous connection with the regular Whigs, and in 1837 Lewis and his supporters followed Calhoun back into the Democratic party. The significant fact is that in neither Alabama nor Mississippi were the Whigs greatly weakened by the departure of Calhoun's admirers.

Only in South Carolina and Georgia did avowed state rights men make up the bulk of the anti-Jackson party. When the real nature of the new party alignments became apparent, the politicians of Calhoun's state gave proof of their sincerity (and of the presidential aspirations of their chief) by moving back to the Democratic ranks at the first decent opportunity.

The principal Whig leader in Georgia was John M. Berrien, a Savannah lawyer and attorney for the United States Bank who had been forced out of Jackson's cabinet by the Peggy Eaton affair. At the time of the election of 1832, Jackson's Indian policy was so popular in Georgia that Berrien did not dare oppose the

similar, in that a majority of the planters, Phillips and Cole to the contrary notwithstanding, remained Democrats. In the period 1833–1843, the twelve congressional districts of plantation Virginia, lying east of the Blue Ridge and south of the Rappahannock, were represented thirty-eight times by Democrats and twenty-two times by Whigs or Conservatives, with nine of the Whig elections being won in the commercial Norfolk, Richmond, and Fredericksburg districts. The Democratic party of Virginia differed from that of North Carolina, however, in having a much larger popular element.

President openly. Instead, he went about stirring up anti-tariff and state rights sentiment, while secretly trying to prevent anti-Bank resolutions by the legislature. Immediately after Jackson's re-election, however, Berrien and his allies managed to reorganize the old Troup political faction as an openly anti-Jackson state rights party. In view of Berrien's pro-Bank attitude and his subsequent staunch support of Clay's policies, it seems probable that he was merely capitalizing on state rights sentiment to defeat Democratic measures which he opposed on other grounds. At any rate, the Georgia Whigs were soon arrayed against the Jackson financial program, and they held their lines nearly intact in the face of the desertion of state rights Whigs to the Democrats on the Subtreasury issue. By 1840 Berrien had brought his Georgia followers into close harmony with the national party.

This summary sketch of southern Whiggery raises, of course, more questions than it could possibly answer definitively. It has attempted to suggest, however, that preoccupation with the origins and development of southern sectionalism has led to distortions of southern political history in the 1830's and 1840's. Specifically, it is suggested:

That only John C. Calhoun and a small group of allied southern leaders regarded state rights as the most important issue in politics in this period.

That the southern people divided politically in these years over much the same questions as northern voters, particularly questions of banking and financial policy.

That the Whig party in the South was built around a nucleus of National Republicans and state rights men, but received its greatest accession of strength from business-minded Democrats who deserted Jackson on the Bank issue.

That the Whig party in the South was controlled by urban commercial and banking interests, supported by a majority of the planters, who were economically dependent on banking and commercial facilities. And finally,

That this alliance of the propertied, far from being inherently particularistic, rapidly shook off its state rights adherents and by 1841 was almost solidly in support of the nationalistic policies of Henry Clay.

There is a great need for intensive restudy of southern politics in the 1830's and 1840's, and particularly for critical correlation of local and national developments. The story as it comes from the contemporary sources is full of the resounding clash of solid interests and opposing ideologies, hardly having "the hollow sound of a stage duel with tin swords" which one historian seems to detect. And recent events should make the student wary of state rights banners, especially when raised by conservative men against national administrations not conspicuously devoted to the interests of the propertied.

5

The Politics of Slavery, 1820–1860

Slavery and the Jacksonian Coalition

The Missouri Crisis, Slavery, and the Politics of Jacksonianism

by Richard H. Brown

Before the Civil War slavery always played an important though sometimes hidden role in the development of American politics. Even before the rise of abolitionism and antislavery politics, a Southern political interest, originating largely out of the existence of plantation slavery, made itself felt. James Madison believed that the major division of interests at the Constitutional Convention of 1787 was between the slave and free states, and during the Federalist and Jeffersonian eras Southerners were quick to sense (and often to imagine) threats or potential threats to slavery and the Southern way of life.

The debates over the admission of Missouri into the Union that took place between 1819 and 1821 provided a significant occasion for Southern apprehension—and for sectional political accommodation. Although the formula for resolving this crisis now seems beautifully simple (the admission of Missouri as a slave state and Maine as a free state), the exchanges in Congress went beyond the immediate issues to explore the subject that the South always considered non-negotiable: the status and future of slavery. Nearly every polemical point made during the prolonged sectional crisis of the 1850's can be found thirty years earlier in the Missouri debates.

Richard H. Brown argues that the Missouri crisis fundamentally affected Southern politics for decades to come, and that in the 1820's Andrew Jackson's rise to power was to a large extent the result of a movement by Southerners to defend their sectional interests. They found allies among Northerners who believed that their own advancement could best be served by preserving the stability of Southern institutions and the Union. Martin Van Buren played a key role in reforging the Jeffersonian alliance between New York and Virginia. He sought to revive the Republican (soon to become the Democratic) party by putting Jackson in the White House. Brown contends that Southern politics and interests played a crucial role in making this alliance. In support of this view, one might note that the Missouri debates added the term "doughface" (a Northerner willing to "appease" the South) to the vocabulary of American political invective. Yet by concentrating on his major interpretative point, Brown has necessarily slighted divisions within the South and other groups in other parts of the nation which rallied to the Democratic party for reasons other than the slavery question.

From the inauguration of Washington until the Civil War the South was in the saddle of national politics. This is the central fact in American political history to 1860. To it there are no exceptions, not even in that period when the "common man" stormed the ramparts of government under the banner of Andrew Jackson. In Jackson's day the chief agent of Southern power was a Northern man with Southern principles, Martin Van Buren of New York. It was he who put together the party coalition which Andrew Jackson led to power. That coalition had its wellsprings in the dramatic crisis over slavery in Missouri, the first great public airing of the slavery question in antebellum America.

From *The South Atlantic Quarterly*, LXV (Winter 1966), 55–72. Reprinted by permission.

I

More than anything else, what made Southern dominance in national politics possible was a basic homogeneity in the Southern electorate. In the early nineteenth century, to be sure, the South was far from monolithic. In terms of economic interest and social classes it was scarcely more homogeneous than the North. But under the diversity of interests which characterized Southern life in most respects there ran one single compelling idea which virtually united all Southerners, and which governed their participation in national affairs. This was that the institution of slavery should not be dealt with from outside the South. Whatever the merits of the institution—and Southerners violently disagreed about this, never more than in the 1820's—the presence of the slave was a fact too critical, too sensitive, too perilous for all of Southern society to be dealt with by those not directly affected. Slavery must remain a Southern question. In the antebellum period a Southern politician of whatever party forgot this at his peril. A Northern politician might perceive it to his profit. There had been, Martin Van Buren noted with satisfaction late in life, a "remarkable consistency in the political positions" of Southern public men. With characteristic insouciance the Little Magician attributed this consistency to the natural superiority of republican principles which led them to win out in a region relatively untainted by the monied interest. But his partisan friend Rufus King, Van Buren admitted, ascribed it to the "black strap" of Southern slavery.

The insistence that slavery was uniquely a Southern concern, not to be touched by outsiders, had been from the outset a *sine qua non* for Southern participation in national politics. It underlay the Constitution and its creation of a government of limited powers, without which Southern participation would have been unthinkable. And when in the 1790's Jefferson and Madison perceived that a constitution was only the first step in guaranteeing

Southern security, because a constitution meant what those who governed under it said it meant, it led to the creation of the first national political party to protect that Constitution against change by interpretation. The party which they constructed converted a Southern minority into a national majority through alliance with congenial interests outside the South. Organically, it represented an alliance between New York and Virginia, pulling between them Pennsylvania, and after them North Carolina, Georgia, and (at first) Kentucky and Tennessee, all states strongly subject to Virginia's influence. At bottom it rested on the support of people who lived on that rich belt of fertile farmland which stretched from the Great Lakes across upstate New York and Pennsylvania, southward through the Southern piedmont into Georgia, entirely oblivious of the Mason-Dixon line. North as well as South it was an area of prosperous, well-settled small farms. More farmers than capitalists, its residents wanted little from government but to be let alone. Resting his party on them, Jefferson had found a formula for national politics which at the same time was a formula for Southern pre-eminence. It would hold good to the Civil War.

So long as the Federalists remained an effective opposition, Jefferson's party worked as a party should. It maintained its identity in relation to the opposition by a moderate and pragmatic advocacy of strict construction of the Constitution. Because it had competition, it could maintain discipline. It responded to its constituent elements because it depended on them for support. But eventually its very success was its undoing. After 1815, stirred by the nationalism of the postwar era, and with the Federalists in decline, the Republicans took up Federalist positions on a number of the great public issues of the day, sweeping all before them as they did. The Federalists gave up the ghost. In the Era of Good Feeling which followed, everybody began to call himself a Republican, and a new theory of party amalgamation preached the doctrine that party division was bad and that a one-party system best served the national interest. Only gradually did it become apparent that in victory the Republican party had lost its identity—

and its usefulness. As the party of the whole nation it ceased to be responsive to any particular elements in its constituency. It ceased to be responsive to the South.

When it did, and because it did, it invited the Missouri crisis of 1819–1820, and that crisis in turn revealed the basis for a possible configuration of national parties which eventually would divide the nation free against slave. As John Quincy Adams put it, the crisis had revealed "the basis for a new organization of parties . . . here was a new party ready formed, . . . terrible to the whole Union, but portentously terrible to the South—threatening in its progress the emancipation of all their slaves, threatening in its immediate effect that Southern domination which has swayed the Union for the last twenty years." Because it did so, Jefferson, in an equally famous phrase, "considered it at once as the knell of the Union."

Adams and Jefferson were not alone in perceiving the significance of what had happened. Scarcely a contemporary missed the point. Historians quote them by the dozens as prophets—but usually *only* as prophets. In fact the Missouri crisis gave rise not to prophecy alone, but to action. It led to an urgent and finally successful attempt to revive the old Jeffersonian party and with it the Jeffersonian formula for Southern pre-eminence. The resuscitation of that party would be the most important story in American politics in the decades which followed.

II

In Jefferson's day the tie between slavery, strict construction of the Constitution, and the Republican party was implicit, not explicit. After Missouri it was explicit, and commented upon time and again in both public and private discussion. Perceptive Southerners saw (1) that unless effective means were taken to quiet discussion of the question, slavery might be used at any time in the future to force the South into a permanent minority in the Union, endangering all its interests; and (2) that if the loose constitutional construction of the day were allowed to prevail, the time might come when the government would be held to have the power to deal with slavery. Vital to preventing both of these—to keeping the slavery question quiet and to gaining a reassertion of strict construction principles—was the re-establishment of conditions which would make the party in power responsive once again to the South.

Not only did the Missouri crisis make these matters clear, but it shaped the conditions which would govern what followed. In the South it gave marked impetus to a reaction against the nationalism and amalgamationism of postwar Republicanism and handed the offensive to a hardy band of Old Republican politicians who had been crying in the wilderness since 1816. In the early 1820's the struggle between Old Republicans and New would be the stuff of Southern politics, and on the strength of the new imperatives to which the Missouri conflict gave rise the Old Republicans would carry off the victory in state after Southern state, providing thereby a base of power on which a new strict construction party could be reared.

For precisely the same reason that it gave the offensive to the Old Republicans of the South—because it portrayed the tie between slavery and party in starkest form—the Missouri crisis put Northern Old Republicans on the defense. Doing so, it handed the keys to national party success thereafter to whatever Northern leader could surmount charges of being pro-Southern and command the necessary Northern votes to bring the party to power. For that reason Thomas Jefferson's formula for national politics would become, when resurrected, Martin Van Buren's formula for national politics. What has long been recognized as happening to the Democratic party in the forties and fifties happened in fact in 1820. After Missouri and down to the Civil War the revised formula for Southern pre-eminence would involve the elevation to the presidency of Southerners who were predominantly Westerners in the public eye, or of Northern men with Southern principles.

Because they shaped the context of what was to come, the

reactions to the Missouri crisis in the two citadels of Old Republican power, Richmond and Albany, were significant. Each cast its light ahead. As the donnybrook mounted in Congress in the winter of 1820, the Virginia capital was reported to be as "agitated as if affected by all the Volcanic Eruptions of Vesuvius." At the heart of the clamor were the Old Republicans of the Richmond Junto, particularly Thomas Ritchie's famous *Enquirer*, which spoke for the Junto and had been for years the most influential newspaper in the South. Associates of Jefferson, architects of Southern power, the Old Republicans were not long in perceiving the political implications of the crisis. Conviction grew in their minds that the point of Northern agitation was not Missouri at all but to use slavery as an anvil on which to forge a new party which would carry either Rufus King or DeWitt Clinton of New York to the presidency and force the South from power forever. But what excited them even more was the enormity of the price of peace which alone seemed likely to avert the disaster. This was the so-called Thomas Proviso, amending the Missouri bill to draw the ill-fated 36° 30′ line across the Louisiana Purchase, prohibiting slavery in the territory to the north, giving up the lion's share to freedom.

No sooner had the proviso been introduced in Congress than the temper of the Old Republicans boiled over, and with prescient glances to the future they leapt to the attack. Ritchie challenged the constitutionality of the proviso at once in the *Enquirer*, a quarter century before Calhoun would work out the subtle dialectic of a Southern legal position. Nathaniel Macon agreed. "To compromise is to acknowledge the right of Congress to interfere and to legislate on the subject," he wrote; "this would be acknowledging too much." Equally important was the fact that, by prohibiting slavery in most of the West, the proviso forecast a course of national development ultimately intolerable to the South because, as Spencer Roane put it to Monroe, Southerners could not consent to be "dammed up in a land of Slaves." As the debates thundered to their climax, Ritchie in two separate editorials predicted that if the proviso passed, the South must in due time have

Texas. "If we are cooped up on the north," he wrote with grim prophecy, "we must have elbow room to the west."

When finally the Southern Old Republicans tacitly consented to the Missouri Compromise, it was therefore not so much a measure of illusion about what the South had given up, as of how desperately necessary they felt peace to be. They had yielded not so much in the spirit of a bargain as in the spirit of a man caught in a holdup, who yields his fortune rather than risk his life in the hope that he may live to see a better day and perhaps even to get his fortune back. As Ritchie summed it up when news of the settlement reached Richmond, "Instead of joy, we scarcely ever recollect to have tasted of a bitterer cup." That they tasted it at all was because of the manipulative genius of Henry Clay, who managed to bring up the separate parts of the compromise separately in the House, enabling the Old Republicans to provide him his margin of victory on the closely contested Missouri bill while they saved their pride by voting to the end against the Thomas Proviso. They had not bound themselves by their votes to the proviso, as Ritchie warned they should not. If it was cold comfort for the moment, it was potent with significance for the future.

In fact, the vote on the proviso illuminated an important division in Southern sentiment. Thirty-seven slave state congressmen opposed it, while thirty-nine voted for it. On the surface the line of division ran along the Appalachian crest and the Potomac, pointing out seemingly a distinction in interest between the South Atlantic states on the one hand and those in the Southwest and mid-Atlantic regions on the other—between those states most characteristically Southern and those which in 1820 were essentially more Western or Northern in outlook. More fundamental, within each section it divided Southerners between those who were more sensitive to the relationship of slavery to politics and those who were less so; between those who thought the party formula for Southern pre-eminence and defense important and those who thought parties outmoded; between particularists and postwar Republican nationalists; between the proponents of an old Republican polity and the proponents of a new one as defined in the years of postwar exuberance; between those closest to Jefferson, such as the Richmond Junto and Macon, and those closest to Monroe, such as Calhoun. It was a division which prefigured Southern political struggles of the twenties. When two years later 70 per cent of those congressmen from the South Atlantic states who had opposed the Thomas Proviso returned to the next Congress, compared to 39 per cent of those who had supported it, it was a measure of the resurgence of Old Republicanism. Two years after that, in the chaotic presidential election of 1824, the Southerners who had opposed the proviso were the Southerners who sought to sustain the party caucus as a method of nominating in a vain attempt to restore old party discipline. Four years after that they marched back to power at last under the banner of Andrew Jackson, restoring to effectiveness in so doing a political system intended to make future Missouri crises impossible, and committed in due time to rectify the Thomas Proviso.

Equally important to the reaction in Richmond was what went on in Albany. There command of the state's Old Republicans was in the hands of the Bucktails, a group of which State Senator Martin Van Buren, at thirty-eight, was already master spirit. Opposed to the Bucktails was Governor DeWitt Clinton, an erstwhile Republican who drew a good deal of his support from former Federalists. With the Bucktails committed to the old Virginia–New York alliance, the Missouri question offered Clinton a heaven-sent opportunity; indeed there were those who suspected the ambitious governor of playing God himself and helping to precipitate the crisis. Whether or not this was true, Clinton tried desperately while the storm was raging in Washington to get a commitment from the Bucktails which would stamp them as proslavery, but the Bucktails acted cautiously. When a large meeting was called in Albany to indorse the prohibition of slavery in Missouri, Van Buren found it convenient to be off on circuit. When the Clintonians whipped a resolution indorsing the restriction through the legislature, not a Bucktail raised a voice in dissent.

But for all their caution against public commitment it was generally understood both in Washington and New York that the Bucktails were anxious for peace, and that they supported the corporal's guard of Northern Republicans in congress who, retreating finally from the Missouri prohibition made peace possible. Several of the Bucktail newspapers said as much, and despite the lack of public commitment on the part of party leaders, more than one Clintonian newspaper would brand them the "Slave Ticket" in the legislative elections which followed.

In private, Van Buren left no doubt where he stood, or where he meant to go once the storm had passed. No sooner had the compromise been adopted in Washington than the Little Magician got off a letter to his friendly rival Rufus King, promising at "some future day" to give that veteran Federalist his own views on the expediency of making slavery a party question, and remarking meanwhile that notwithstanding the strong public interest in the Missouri question, "the excitement which exists in regard to it, or which is likely to arise from it, is not so great as you suppose." It was a singularly important assessment of Northern public opinion for a politician who had fallen heir to a tattered Southern alliance, and in it King apprehensively saw the panorama of forty years of national politics stretching before him:

> The inveteracy of party feelings in the Eastern States [he wrote a friend], the hopes of influence and distinction by taking part in favor of the slave States, which call themselves, and are spoken of by others as the truly republican States and the peculiar friends of liberty, will keep alive & sustain a body considerably numerous, and who will have sufficient influence, to preserve to the slave States their disproportionate, I might say exclusive, dominance over the Union.

Twenty months after that, in the late fall of 1821, Van Buren set off for Washington as a newly elected United States senator. With his party having taken the measure of Clinton in the meantime, he carried with him into the lion's den of presidential politics effective command of the thirty-six uncommitted electoral votes of New York. If he would be the most disinterested statesman in all the land, he could not avoid for long the responsibility that went with that power. It was an opportunity to be used for large purposes or small, as a man might choose, and the Little Magician lost no time in indicating his intended course. Within weeks of his arrival he was pulling the strings of the New York delegation in the House to bring about return of the speakership to the slave states, from whom it had been wrested by a straight sectional vote upon Clay's retirement the year before. The new speaker was P. P. Barbour of Virginia, a leader of the Old Republican reaction in the South. Three months after that Van Buren was on his way to Richmond to plan the resurrection of the Old Republican Party.

That he should do so was partly for reasons of personal ambition, partly because the Bucktails after years of frustrating struggle with Clinton had their own clear reasons for wanting to redraw party lines. Beyond this there would appear to be the simple fact that Van Buren believed implicitly in the whole system of republican polity as Thomas Jefferson had staked it out. Committed to the principle of the least possible government, the Republican party was the defender of that republican liberty which was the sole political concern of the disinterested agrarian constituency for which, through life, Van Buren saw himself as a spokesman, and which constituted the majority of Americans. That majority was strongest where it was purest, least subject to the corrupting power of money. That was in the South. Slavery was a lesser issue than republicanism. Nor was it by any means clear in 1820 that agitation was the best way to deal with it. For while some who were nominally Old Republicans, such as Senator William Smith of South Carolina, were beginning to argue that slavery was a positive good, it was generally true that no men in America were more honestly committed to the notion that the institution was wrong than those men of Jeffersonian conscience who were the Old Republicans of the South. Eleven years later, in 1831, some of them would mount in the Virginia legislature the last great effort south of the Mason-Dixon line to abolish slavery. It required no very extended rationalization to argue in 1820 that the whole perplexing question would be best left in their hands, even if in fact the North had the right to take it up. Particularly was this true when, as Van Buren put it, the motives of those in the North who sought to take it up were "rather [more] political than philanthropical." Because he believed as he did, Van Buren's efforts to revive party distinctions and restore the Old Republican Party were to be more than a mere matter of machinations with politicians, looking toward the making of the Democratic party. He looked to Southern power, and he would quiet the slavery question if he could. He was dealing with the root principle of the whole structure of antebellum politics.

III

In the long history of the American presidency no election appears quite so formless as that of 1824. With no competing party to force unity on the Republicans, candidates who could not command the party nomination were free to defy it. They did so, charging that "King Caucus" was undemocratic. Eventually no fewer than four candidates competed down to the wire, each a Republican, every man for himself. Because they divided the electoral votes between them, none came close to a majority, and the election went to the House of Representatives. There, with the help of Henry Clay, John Quincy Adams outpolled the popular Andrew Jackson and the caucus nominee, William H. Crawford of Georgia, and carried off the prize.

Historians, viewing that election, look at King Caucus too much through the eyes of its opponents, who stated that the caucus represented an in-group of political officeholders attached to Crawford and anxious to preserve their own political power. In fact it was the Old Republicans who organized the caucus, not so much to sustain Crawford and preserve power as to revive the Virginia–New York party and regain power. They took up Crawford unenthusiastically because he came closest to the Old Republican pattern, and because he alone of all the candidates could hope to carry Virginia. They took up the caucus at the behest of Van Buren after two years of searching for a method of nominating which would command the support of all, because four years after Missouri the only hope of winning New York for a Southern candidate was to present him, however unpopularly, as the official party nominee.

Hidden in the currents and crosscurrents of that campaign was the reiterated issue of party versus amalgamation. Behind it, in turn, were repeated pleas by Old Republican presses, North and South alike, that unless genuine Republicans agreed on a method of choosing a candidate the division must be along sectional lines, in which case a Federalist or proto-Federalist might sneak into the White House. Behind it too was the repeated warning that party organization alone would make democracy work. Without it, the Old Republicans correctly prophesied, the election would end up in the House of Representatives, subject to the worst kind of political intrigue, and with the votes of the smallest states the equals of those of populous Virginia and New York.

When the caucus failed it was because amalgamation had destroyed the levers which made party discipline possible. Exhortation could not restore them. Meantime the issue of democracy had been turned against the advocates of party, because in key states like New York and North Carolina they tried to use the power of the party organizations for Crawford, bucking more popular candidates such as Jackson and Adams. It was a bogus issue. The real issue was whether a party was necessary to make democracy work, and because they were more nearly right than their opponents about this, and the election in the House shortly proved it, the Old Republicans would recover quickly after 1824, after Crawford and the caucus issue were politically dead. Let circumstances limit the number of candidates, and tie up party and democracy on the same side, and the results would be different another time.

In the campaign of 1824 and the years immediately following, the slavery issue was never far below the surface. The Denmark Vesey conspiracy for an insurrection in Charleston (now a subject of controversy among historians) was to contemporaries a grim reminder of the Missouri debates, and it was attributed publicly to Rufus King's speeches on the Missouri question. In 1823–1824 some Southerners suspected that an attempt by Secretary of State Adams to conclude a slave trade convention with Great Britain was an attempt to reap the benefit of Northern antislavery sentiment; and some, notably Representative John Floyd of Virginia, sought to turn the tables on Adams by attacking him for allegedly ceding Texas to Spain in the Florida treaty, thus ceding what Floyd called "two slaveholding states" and costing "the Southern interest" four Senators.

Old Republicans made no bones about their concern over the issue, or their fear that it might be turned against them. In the summer of 1823 an illuminating editorial debate broke out between the New York *American*, which spoke the thoughts of the old Federalists in New York, and the Richmond *Enquirer*. So vehemently had the *American* picked up a report of a plan to revise the Illinois constitution to admit slavery that Ritchie charged its editors with reviving the slave question to put New York into the lap of the "Universal Yankee Nation" and to put the South under the "ban of the Empire." "Call it the Missouri question, the Illinois question, what you please; it was the *Slave question*," Ritchie shrilled, which the *American* was seeking to get up for political purposes. Shortly, the Albany *Argus* got into the argument. The *Argus*, which got its signals from Van Buren and spoke the thoughts of New York's Old Republicans, charged the *American* with trying to revive the slave question to "abrogate the old party distinctions" and "organize new ones, founded in the territorial prejudices of the people." "The more general question of the North and South," the *Argus* warned, "will be urged to the uttermost, by those who can never triumph when they meet the democracy of the country, openly, and with the hostility they bear towards it." Over and over the debate rang out the argument that the attempt to revive party distinctions was an attempt to allay sectional prejudices, and by the time the debate was over only the most obtuse citizen could have missed the point.

Nor was the election of Adams destined to calm Southern fears on issues having to do with slavery. A series of incidents early in 1825 suggested that the New Englander's election had made antislavery advocates more bold, and Southern tempers grew shorter in the summer of 1825 than they had been at any time since Missouri. One of the incidents was a reported argument before the Supreme Court in the case of the South Carolina Negro Seaman's Act by Attorney General William Wirt, stating that slavery was "inconsistent with the laws of God and nature." A second was a resolution offered in the Senate a scant nine days after Adams's election by Rufus King, proposing to turn the proceeds from the sale of western lands to the emancipation and export of slaves through the agency of the American Colonization Society. In the same week the New Jersey legislature proposed a system of foreign colonization which "would, in due time, effect the entire emancipation of the slaves in our country." John Floyd enclosed a copy of the New Jersey resolution to Claiborne Gooch, Ritchie's silent partner on the *Enquirer*, was salient warning:

> Long before this manifestation I have believed, connected with the Missouri question, would come up the general question of slavery, upon the principles avowed by Rufus King in the Senate. . . .
>
> If this indication is well received, who can tell, after the elevation of Mr. A. to the presidency—that he, of Missouri effort, or DeWitt C. or some such aspirant, may not, for the sake of that office, fan this flame—to array the non-slaveholding States against the Slaveholding states, and finally quiet our clamor or opposition, by the application of the slaves knife to our throats. Think of this much, and often.

Meantime, the New York *Commercial Advertiser* expressed publicly the hope that Adams' administration would introduce "a new era, when the northern, eastern, and non-slaveholding states, will assume an attitude in the Union, proportionate to their moral and physical power." Ritchie responded hotly in an editorial asking what the designs of such a combination would be against the "southern and *slave-holding* states." Soon in Georgia the Old Republican Governor George M. Troup, at the instigation of Senator John M. Berrien, put before the legislature a request for resolutions stating slavery to be exclusively within the control of the states and asking that the federal government "abstain from intermeddling." In May there was another violent editorial exchange between the New York *American* and the *Enquirer*, growing out of an *American* editorial which attacked the "slave press" and taunted the South with the comment that "the sceptre has departed from Judah, and those who have long ruled must be content to obey." Ritchie picked up the taunt as a challenge to the South, admitting that slavery was evil but insisting pointedly that the South had "too much at stake" to allow decisions on the matter by men ignorant of Southern "habits, manners, and forms of society." Ultimately, the Virginian concluded belligerently, Southern defense would be found in the traditional mechanisms of national politics: "Mr. John Adams the 2d is now upon his trial, [and] his friends consult as little his own interest as the public good, by conjuring up these prejudices against the *Slave people*. Should they persevere in their misguided policy, it will require no prophet to foretell that the son will share the fate of his father."

With the slavery issue thus drawn taut, the Old Republicans recovered quickly from the setback of 1824. Calhoun's inveterate foe William Smith was returned to the Senate from South Carolina, completing for the moment an Old Republican sweep of the South Atlantic states begun in 1821, a sweep which put Calhoun's political career in jeopardy and forced the Carolinian, now vice president, to break with Adams. For the Old Republicans, moreover, Adams made an infinitely better target than Monroe. The hightoned nationalism of the New Englander, combined with popular revulsion to the alleged bargain which secured his election, put the kiss of death on amalgamation as a political theory. The stage was set, under more favorable circumstances, for the Old Republicans to try again.

IV

For all the illuminating insights into Jacksonianism to which Americans have been treated in recent years, Jacksonian politics are still interpreted in Victorian terms, along classic lines descended from an early biographer of Jackson, James Parton, who recorded them one hundred years ago. To the Victorians, it is perhaps not too much to say, most of history could be ultimately attributed either to whores or to the unbridled pursuit of ambition. It was a simple view of history, and the Jacksonians got both barrels, one through the beguiling story of Peggy Eaton, the other through the notion of a sterile and essentially meaningless struggle for the succession between Van Buren and Calhoun. As Parton quaintly put it, "the political history of the United States, for the last thirty years, dates from the moment when the soft hand of Mr. Van Buren touched Mrs. Eaton's knocker."

When finally it rode to power, the Jacksonian party was made up of two clearly discernible and distinct wings. One comprised the original Jacksonians, those who had supported him in 1824 when he ran on his own, bereft, like all the rest, of party, and nearly of allies. As measured in that election this strength was predominantly in the West. It spilled over into a few states east of the mountains, most notably Pennsylvania, where the chaos of the existing political structure enabled Jackson as military hero to ride roughshod over all the rest. But this was all. The Western vote, especially when shared with Clay, amounted in electoral terms to little. Even with the votes of the Carolinas, thrown to him gratuitously by Calhoun and counting one-quarter of his total, he was far short of an electoral majority. To get even this much he had been formally before the public for two years, and all his considerable natural appeal as a Westerner and a hero had gone into the bargain.

After 1824 Jackson found himself the candidate of a combined opposition. The concrete measure of difference between defeat in 1824 and victory in 1828 was the Old Republican strength of the

South Atlantic states and New York, brought to the Jackson camp carefully tended and carefully drilled by Van Buren. Nearly equal in size to the original Jackson following, they constituted a political faction far older, far more permanent, far more purposeful, far better led, and in the long run far more important. Their purposes were set forth by Van Buren in a notable letter to Ritchie in January, 1827, proposing support of the old hero. Such support, as the New Yorker put it, would be "the best and probably the only practicable mode of concentrating the entire vote of the opposition & of effecting what is of still greater importance, the substantial reorganization of the Old Republican Party." It would "restore a better state of things, by combining Genl Jackson's personal popularity with the portion of old party feeling yet remaining." It would aid Republicans of the North and middle states "by substituting *party principle* for *personal preference* as one of the leading points in the contest. . . . Instead of the question being between a northern and Southern man, it would be whether or not the ties, which have hitherto bound together a great political party should be severed." Most important, its effects would be highly salutary for the South:

We must always have party distinctions and the old ones are the best of which the nature of the case admits. Political combinations between the inhabitants of the different states are unavoidable & the most natural & beneficial to the country is that between the planters of the South and the plain Republicans of the north. The country has once flourished under a party thus constituted & may again. It would take longer than our lives (even if it were practicable) to create new party feelings to keep those masses together. If the old ones are suppressed, geographical divisions founded on local interests or, what is worse prejudices between free and slave holding states will inevitably take their place. Party attachment in former times furnished a complete antidote for sectional prejudices by producing counteracting feelings. It was not until that defence had been broken down that the clamour agt. Southern Influence and African Slavery could be made effectual in the North. . . . Formerly, attacks upon Southern Republicans were regarded by those of the north as assaults upon their political brethren & resented accordingly. This all powerful sympathy has been much weakened, if not, destroyed by the amalgamating policy. . . . it can & ought to be revived.

Lastly, Van Buren noted, a Jackson administration brought to power by the "concerted effort of a political party, holding in the main, to certain tenets & opposed to certain prevailing principles" would be a far different thing from one brought to power by the popularity of a military hero alone. An administration brought to power by Old Republican votes would be governed by Old Republican principles. Van Buren would make himself the guarantor of that.

Because the Jacksonian party was what it was, Jacksonian policy was what it was, and Jacksonian politics as well. Because the administration rested on an Old Republican alliance which bridged the Mason-Dixon line and linked New York with the Old South, the two most important steps in the development of Jacksonian policy were the veto of the Maysville Road bill and the veto of the bill to recharter the Bank of the United States. Whatever the social and economic consequences of each, they were in their origins political measures, designed to solidify and hold together the Old Republican party; and they were predicated, each of them, on a strict construction of the Constitution. And, too, because its political base was what it was, the one great question of public policy which nearly brought the administration to disaster, one with which it could not deal and never did, was the tariff.

No less important, it was the structure of the Jackson party which gave meaning to—and dictated the course of—that struggle between Van Buren and Calhoun which bulks so large in the politics of the Jackson years. It was far more than an empty struggle for the succession. Its essence was competition between two conflicting ideas as to how best to protect Southern security in the Union, and thus, inferentially, how to preserve the Union itself. One of those ideas was the old Jeffersonian idea, resuscitated by Van Buren, sustained by the Jackson party and by the Democratic party until the Civil War. It was that Southern security rested ultimately on the maintenance in national office of a political party which would be responsive to the South because dependent on it for election. A political answer, not a doctrinaire one, it was product of the practical, pragmatic, and thoroughly political minds of Thomas Jefferson and Martin Van Buren. It depended for its success on the winning of national elections by a party which would maintain its identity in relation to the opposition as a states' rights–strict construction party, but which would at the same time be moderate, flexible, pragmatic in tone, able to win support in the North as well as the South if it would serve its purpose.

Counter to this was the proposition developed by John C. Calhoun. Last of the Southern nationalists, Calhoun had held to his position through 1824, long after the Old Republicans had routed Southern nationalism in every state but his own. In the mid-twenties, with his own political strength at rock bottom, his hold slipping even in South Carolina, Calhoun made his portentous switch from Nationalist to Sectionalist, squaring the two in his own mind with the development of a counter theory to that of the Jeffersonians. This was that Southern security was dependent in the last analysis on the maintenance of an effective Southern power to veto anything it didn't like—thus nullification—and that failing, on the right to secede. In contrast to the political and moderate remedy of the Old Republicans, this was a constitutional remedy, product of the brilliant legal, doctrinaire, and essentially non-political mind of the great Carolinian.

That Van Buren won out over Calhoun in the Jackson years had nothing to do fundamentally with Mrs. Eaton or with a long chronicle of personal intrigue. It had everything to do with the fact that the Old Republican moderates controlled the South, all but South Carolina, almost that, in the twenties. While Calhoun brought only South Carolina and some personal support in Congress to the Jackson fold, Van Buren brought all the rest of the South, and New York as well. The fact was not lost on Jackson or his Tennessee friends, either before his election or after. Van Buren's triumph over Calhoun was won not on Washington backstairs after 1829 but on the Southern hustings in the early twenties. Two years before it came to power the Jackson party was already, in fact, a Jackson–Van Buren party.

V

There were postscripts, too, which harked back to the structure of the Jackson party, to the Missouri question, and to the political prophecies of Thomas Ritchie, woven into the very fabric of the party by the skilled political weaver from New York. First of these was that the Jackson party, the issue once raised, was committed to Texas. When in 1844 a new drumfire of antislavery sentiment in the North made it impossible for Van Buren to honor that commitment, Ritchie and Van Buren, after nearly a quarter-century of fruitful political teamwork, would part company, and Van Buren would give up leadership of the party he had created. After 1844 the party of the Jeffersonian formula sustained itself in the face of the rising slavery issue by giving vent to its expansionist tendencies; and the Northern man with Southern principles who replaced Van Buren was in fact a Northwestern man with Southern principles, Stephen A. Douglas of Illinois. It was to be Douglas, governed by the irresistible logic of the party structure, who carried through Congress finally, in 1854, the repeal of the Missouri Compromise. And when three years after that the Supreme Court in the Dred Scott decision held the Thomas Proviso of the Missouri Compromise unconstitutional, as Ritchie and Nathaniel Macon had said it was thirty-seven years before, who were the judges who comprised the majority? Of six, one had been appointed in 1846 by "Young Hickory" James K. Polk, a second in 1853 by the next successful Democrat, Franklin Pierce. The four others were James M. Wayne of Georgia, coadjutor of Van Buren's Georgia lieutenant John Forsyth, appointed to the court by Jackson in 1835; Roger B.

Taney of Maryland, appointed by Jackson in 1836; John Catron, Van Buren campaign manager in Tennessee, appointed by Jackson in 1837; and Peter V. Daniel of Virginia, long-time member of the Richmond Junto, confidant of Thomas Ritchie, appointed in 1841 by Van Buren.

The Politics of Compromise

Democratic Senate Leadership and the Compromise of 1850

by Holman Hamilton

The building of a successful Jacksonian coalition made the Democrats the majority party in America. They lost the White House only twice in the thirty-two years between the election of Jackson in 1828 and the election of Lincoln in 1860. When, after the Mexican War (1846–48), sectionalism and slavery re-emerged as dominant issues which threatened to bring the machinery of national politics to a halt, leading politicians rushed to head off this disaster. The Democrats proved especially receptive to compromise moves, since they had the most to lose if the political system broke down.

To them—and to compromise-minded Whigs, too—the alternatives were limited to either accommodation or confrontation. They chose accommodation in preference to the dissolution of the Union and the bloodshed that was sure to follow. This attitude produced the Compromise of 1850, a catch-all phrase for the half-dozen measures designed to cool political passions, ease sectional conflict, and, hopefully, bring Americans peace in their time. Getting the bills through Congress required complex political bargaining and legwork, and as Holman Hamilton here makes clear, once the "big guns" of the United States Senate, John C. Cal-

houn, Henry Clay, and Daniel Webster, had had their say—the first against compromise, the latter two in favor—others took charge of the serious legislative business. Stephen A. Douglas and other Senate Democrats first took the compromise "omnibus" apart, and then reassembled it after separate passage of each measure.

Douglas seemingly accomplished the impossible: he put Humpty-Dumpty together again. The nation had accepted the Compromise and rejected extremism. Democrats would continue to rule throughout the 1850's, and they would continue to call themselves the party of compromise and popular sovereignty. Yet Douglas's efforts did not end in his politcal advancement. Instead, his party made presidents out of nonentities, Franklin Pierce (1852) and James Buchanan (1856), and when Douglas made his most serious bid for the presidency in 1860, the Democratic coalition shattered.

In approaching the Compromise of 1850, the modern historian is likely to find himself on ground previously and even repeatedly traversed. The last appearance of Clay, Calhoun, and Webster in the Senate spotlight, the shadow of the second Fugitive Slave Law, the growing prominence of William H. Seward and Salmon P. Chase—these and similar landmarks make the usual roads to the Compromise familiar terrain.

Yet one wonders whether the old historical highways can lead to a successful reappraisal of an oft-accepted story, which the eloquent triumvirate of "America's silver age" has all but monopolized. A number of facts project reasonable doubt. Despite the repeated emphasis which writers have placed on Daniel Webster's "Seventh of March Speech," only one northern Whig senator, James Cooper of Pennsylvania, supported Webster as long as President Zachary Taylor lived. Owing to Henry Clay's prominence in the debates, readers are disposed to assume that Whigs

From *The Mississippi Valley Historical Review*, XLI (December 1954), 403–18. Reprinted by permission; footnotes omitted.

provided most of the votes for Clay's "Omnibus Bill." Actually, it was a Whig, James A. Pearce of Maryland, who spiked Clay's efforts on July 31, 1850; nearly all the Whigs then deserted Clay, and the bulk of the backing given first to Clay and later to Stephen A. Douglas stemmed from Democratic ranks. It is known, of course, that John C. Calhoun died when the "Great Debate" was barely under way. But the role of another southern senator, Henry S. Foote of Mississippi, from the mild winter days of early 1850 through the steamy Washington summer, has been obscured —perhaps by Calhoun's reputation and death.

Although such truths as these have been touched upon by a number of writers, there has been no documented synthesis of the detached parts of the picture puzzle. Some of the fragmentary parts have but recently been discovered. Others, large and small, remain missing today. Still, the major outlines of the picture can be re-created through a point-by-point analysis of aims, methods, votes, and contributions of Senate Whig and Democratic leaders. Such an analysis provides a key or clue to precisely what was going on behind the spectacular façade of rhetoric and drama.

Albert Bushnell Hart, Albert J. Beveridge, and Charles A. and Mary R. Beard are only a few of the numerous authors who have magnified Clay's and Webster's influence far beyond the limits of the facts. According to Hart, in early 1850 "the Compromise was already decided, since the agreement of Clay and Webster meant the effective coalition of Southern Whigs and Northern 'Cotton Whigs.'" Also, said Hart, Webster's Seventh of March Speech "was virtually an announcement that the Senate would vote for the Compromise." Actually, President Taylor's death in July and Millard Fillmore's accession—together with the switch from Clay's methods to Douglas's methods—provided the deciding factors, and none of these things could have been foreseen in March.

Beveridge went into considerable detail to do justice to the remarks of Jefferson Davis, Seward, Douglas, and Chase. For this he deserves commendation. But, in the pages of his second volume on Abraham Lincoln, his lucid discussion suddenly breaks down.

The importance of Taylor's death is slighted. Beveridge seems satisfied to say: "So opposition disintegrated and, one after another, the measures suggested by Clay were enacted." A poorly informed reader of Beveridge's book is at a loss to know how and why the Compromise finally survived.

Charles A. and Mary R. Beard, in *The Rise of American Civilization*, have no doubt influenced students by the tens of thousands. Yet the Beards declared: "Once more, as in 1820 and 1833, Clay was to prevail. But he won this time only through the aid of Webster." Still another facet of the same fallacy was later presented by Burton J. Hendrick, who wrote that Howell Cobb "deserted his Democratic party in 1850 and joined forces with the antislavery Whigs in upholding the Compromise measures of that year." In other words, we are asked to believe that the Democratic party opposed the Compromise; that the antislavery Whigs were outstanding in its support; that Clay pushed through the Compromise, but only with the aid of Webster; and that an effective coalition of northern and southern Whigs spelled success for the Compromise as early as March. With each and all of the allegations, the facts themselves take issue.

Lest it be objected that most of these scholars belonged to a past generation, it may be instructive to look into Allan Nevins's *Ordeal of the Union*. Published as recently as 1947, the *Ordeal* contains much that the specialist should value. Nevins does not fall into Edward Channing's error in terming the pro-Compromise position of Cobb a "marked overturn" in the Georgian's sentiments. Nor does he say with James Ford Rhodes that "Webster's influence was of the greatest weight in the passage of the compromise measures," or that "Clay's adroit parliamentary management was necessary to carry them through the various and tedious steps of legislation." But the *Ordeal* does describe Clay's influence as "unrivalled," and the Seventh of March Speech as 1850's "great turning point."

The record shows that the speech of March 7 was not nearly as great a "turning point" as President Taylor's death or the subsequent adoption of the Douglas strategy. The votes demonstrate that Clay's influence was not only rivaled but surpassed by that of the Douglas–Cass Democrats. An equally pertinent criticism lies in the area of Nevins' emphasis. He mentions aspects of the Compromise tangle to which the Beards, Beveridge, and the others appeared oblivious. The irony is that, time and again, he relegates significant material to mere footnote status and neglects to integrate it with his text and conclusions.

In one footnote, Nevins cites Orlando Brown's reference to Lewis Cass's broaching a compromise on January 11, nearly three weeks before Clay's first compromise proposal. In a second footnote, he quotes Robert C. Winthrop's luminous prediction that "any other course" than Taylor's "will kill Whiggery at our end of the Union." In a third footnote, he gives a little space to the contribution of Foote and Thomas Ritchie in forming the Committee of Thirteen. These happen to be a few of the vital links in the chain, but the chain as a whole remains to be forged.

Among the papers of William M. Meredith is a letter written on June 1, 1850, by Whig Senator John H. Clarke of Rhode Island. Clarke was anti-Compromise, as was Secretary of the Treasury Meredith. Reporting to the secretary, Clarke expressed his belief that "from the North & West we can safely depend upon" Senators John Davis, Samuel S. Phelps, William Upham, Albert C. Greene, Truman Smith, Roger S. Baldwin, William H. Seward, William L. Dayton, Jacob W. Miller, Thomas Corwin, and Clarke (Whigs); Hannibal Hamlin, James W. Bradbury, Alpheus Felch, Isaac P. Walker, and Henry Dodge (Democrats), plus John P. Hale and Salmon P. Chase (Free Soilers). When Clarke wrote "we," he referred to the anti-Compromise people who followed President Taylor and Senator Thomas H. Benton. Of the Delaware senators, John Wales was a pro-Taylor and anti-Compromise Whig; Presley Spruance wavered, but Clarke expected him to vote against Clay's Omnibus Bill.

Clarke's summation is echoed, in almost every detail, in a revealing document written by Senator Lewis Cass twelve days later, and addressed to his son-in-law, Henry Ledyard. Cass was pro-Compromise and anti-Taylor, which lends special credence to his assertion that his own Michigan colleague, Felch, was deserting him and lining up with Taylor and Benton.

A third manuscript, until recently in private hands, was sent by Illinois Senator Douglas to the two Democratic journalists responsible for his paper in Springfield. Dated August 3, 1850, the Douglas communication disclosed some of the reasons for the failure of Clay's attempt to pass the Compromise in what was known as the "omnibus" form, even after the death of Taylor. From the first, Douglas and Clay had seen eye to eye respecting the Compromise end-product in which each was interested. The "Little Giant," however, wanted component parts of compromise legislation voted on separately, one at a time. Clay, on the other hand, was determined to rush the program through Congress at one swoop. Realizing that he could not bring Clay around to the methods he himself preferred, the younger man gave way to the elderly Kentuckian in the late winter and spring (when Taylor was living), and even as late as the end of July (when Fillmore occupied the White House). Douglas did this although, as chairman of the Senate committee on territories, he had at least as good a claim to the authorship of the Compromise as anyone else.

The certainty that Clay's "Omnibus Bill" would have failed with Zachary Taylor in the Executive Mansion is indicated by its recorded failure when the favorably disposed Fillmore resided there, with the patronage power ranged on Clay's side. After Clay saw his measure vanquished, the exhausted old Whig beat a retreat to Newport's beaches, while Douglas captained Compromise forces and succeeded where he had failed. Douglas did exactly what he had thought he could do at the outset, masterfully promoting piecemeal, instead of combined, legislation. Douglas's letter of August 3 to Charles H. Lanphier and George Walker accurately prophesied that what did happen would happen.

The ultimate passage of the Compromise, under Douglas's guidance, raises the question as to the nature of the strength behind it. It also leads to inquiry concerning the origin of the parts of the compromise arrangement, which from 1850 to 1854 was thought to have settled the sectional controversy.

An analysis of the Senate votes on the integral portions of the Douglas-sponsored Compromise, between August 9 and September 16, shows only four senators supporting all five bills. These were Augustus C. Dodge, Democrat of Iowa; Sam Houston, Democrat of Texas; Daniel Sturgeon, Democrat of Pennsylvania; and John Wales, Whig of Delaware. Eight other senators voted "yea" on four occasions and abstained from casting ballots on a fifth. With the exceptions of Dodge, Houston, Sturgeon, and Wales, these men came closest to giving the Compromise their complete backing in August and September. The eight were Jesse D. Bright, Democrat of Indiana; Lewis Cass, Democrat of Michigan; Stephen A. Douglas, Democrat of Illinois; Alpheus Felch, Democrat of Michigan; Moses Norris, Democrat of New Hampshire; James Shields, Democrat of Illinois; Presley Spruance, Whig of Delaware; and James Whitcomb, Democrat of Indiana. Of the twelve senators who lent the Compromise the greatest strength under Douglas's sponsorship, ten were Democrats and two were Whigs.

For the individual bills, Democrats likewise provided the greatest share of needed support. On August 9, sixteen Democrats and fourteen Whigs approved the Texas boundary measure. On August 13, seventeen Democrats joined fourteen Whigs and two Free Soilers in voting statehood to California. Two days later, nineteen Democrats and only eight Whigs supplied the winning total for New Mexico's territorial legislation. The *Congressional Globe* does not contribute a yea-and-nay breakdown on the fugitive slave bill, but August 23 found eighteen Democrats and nine Whigs assenting to its engrossment for a third reading—virtually tantamount to passage. Finally, on September 16, the abolition of the slave trade in the District of Columbia was due to eighteen Democrats, thirteen Whigs, and two Free Soilers. In every one of the five tests, the Democratic part of the pro-Compromise majority was larger than the Whig part. For the fugitive slave and New Mexico measures, the ratio was at least two to one.

By the same token, when three sections of Clay's Omnibus Bill had been defeated on July 31, only five of the Kentuckian's fellow-Whigs sustained him on the New Mexico question while sixteen Democrats followed his "lead." On the Texas boundary, Clay and ten other Whigs went down with seventeen Democrats in an extremely close vote. And on the California statehood issue, Clay had only six Whigs in his camp together with sixteen Democrats and two Free Soilers. Senators siding with Clay on all three tests were Daniel S. Dickinson of New York, George W. Jones of Iowa, Bright, Cass, Augustus C. Dodge, Norris, Spruance, Sturgeon, and Whitcomb. Eight of the nine were Democrats. In defeat as in subsequent victory, under Clay's aegis as well as Douglas's, Democrats stood for the Compromise more consistently and faithfully than Whigs.

It will be observed that there were shifts of sentiment on the part of some members of the Senate between the dates of Clarke's and Cass's letters and the critical votes of July 31, August, and September. Most of these changes involved Whigs. Spruance, whose position had been uncertain in June, was pro-Compromise in July and August. Wales had been correctly considered an anti-Compromise man by Clarke; and even Clay characterized him as such. Yet in August, Wales took new ground. Clarke himself and his fellow Rhode Islander, Albert C. Greene, supported Douglas's Texas boundary bill; Clarke did not vote on three of the August trials, and Greene voted "nay" on two of them. But the approval given the Texas boundary on August 9 by Clarke, Greene, John Davis, Phelps, Smith, Spruance, and Wales (together with the absence of Dayton and Miller) made the difference between defeat and victory.

A case might be made that Whig deviations from anti-Compromise to pro-Compromise positions were of transcendent importance in the reckoning. Admittedly, last-minute additions to the

Compromise forces transformed disaster into triumph for the compromisers. These additions also demonstrated the effect of Taylor's death and Fillmore's succession on Whig late-comers whose votes were sorely needed by the Douglas high command. There also is no gainsaying the fact that, even as some Whigs favored the Compromise first under Clay and then under Douglas, not a few Democrats were ranged in opposition before and during Clay's seashore vacation. But both the hard core and the greater number of Compromise votes in the dramatic and decisive contests were Democratic in origin. This fact is fundamental in gaining a clear comprehension of the story as a whole.

It is equally imperative, in clarifying political attitudes and votes of senators, to determine the connection between legislative instructions and the Compromise of 1850. Over fifty years ago, William E. Dodd observed that in the second quarter of the nineteenth century the principle of state legislatures instructing United States senators was "accepted fully by one party and partially by the other." Although Dodd and other scholars have stressed the importance of the practice during the Jackson–Van Buren period, no comparable studies of the 1850 scene have been printed. From 1846 to 1850, fourteen northern legislatures sent resolutions to Washington, and southern capitols lagged but little. All this was done on the theory that since the state legislators elected the senators they had a right to tell them what to do. Whereas Whigs had been the chief victims of instructions from 1834 to 1840, now Democrats were impaled on their own precedents; this was especially true of Northwesterners. No one resigned from the Senate on account of instructions in 1850, but Cass threatened to do so unless Michigan withdrew its instructions—whereupon Lansing at once complied. Douglas was embarrassed by instructions, while John P. Hale made light of the instructions idea. Generally, instructions showed that politicians at home were less inclined to compromise than were a majority of the men they had elected to the Senate.

Ever since the annexation of Texas and the onset of the Mexican War, extremist and moderate arguments and plans of settlement had been advanced and presented in Washington. The ill-starred Clayton Compromise of 1848, which Clay stated he had never read, proved no model two years later. Extension of the Missouri compromise line to the Pacific, advocated by such Southerners as Jefferson Davis and Hopkins L. Turney, held no attraction for Clay or the Douglas Democrats. The new fugitive slave bill was primarily sponsored by James M. Mason of Virginia, a Calhoun–Davis Democrat; in its final form, it contained harsher provisions (in northern eyes) than the ones Daniel Webster desired. California statehood had been promoted in the Thirtieth Congress by the Democrat Douglas and the Whig William B. Preston. Yet the boundaries of the California state envisioned by Douglas and Preston were far from those defined in the Compromise of 1850, and the California picture had been altered economically and politically by the discovery of gold. The Texas boundary solution of 1850 was premised on ideas backed by successive Texas governors. Abolition of the slave trade in the District of Columbia, frequently broached in the past, commanded the assent of many northern Whigs and Democrats.

If California statehood and ending the slave trade in the District were predominantly northern measures in 1850, and if the fugitive slave and Texas boundary bills derived most of their support from Southerners, two other parts of the Compromise had a different appeal. Designed to dispose of the New Mexico and Utah problems, they gave territorial governments to those western regions, with a proviso that states formed from them would be admitted with or without slavery as their constitutions should provide.

The New Mexico territorial bill was the issue which wrecked Clay's omnibus plan, and perhaps it ought to be remembered that about three-fourths of the Senate Whigs contributed to its fate. When Douglas took control, he did not promote the New Mexico bill until after the Texas boundary and California statehood measures had been passed. With a considerable show of skill he then directed the adoption of the New Mexico measure.

In achieving his New Mexico aim, Douglas was aided directly by eighteen Democrats and eight Whigs, and indirectly by twenty-three absentees. Only three Democrats—Hamlin, Walker, and Henry Dodge—spoiled the Democratic record. When one realizes that these three were also the only Senate Democrats out of thirty-three to oppose the Utah bill of July 31, it is evident that Democrats had the key role with regard to both New Mexico and Utah.

This was no accident. For upwards of two years, the majority or national element of the Democratic party had initiated and repeated the "non-intervention" or "popular sovereignty" doctrine embodied in this territorial plan. As far back as December 14, 1847, Dickinson, the New York Democrat, had introduced resolutions specifying that territorial legislatures should decide all questions of domestic policy within the territories. Ten days later, Lewis Cass addressed his famous "Nicholson Letter" to Alfred O. P. Nicholson of Tennessee. Cass's position, comparable to Dickinson's, was summarized by the injunction: "Leave to the people who will be affected" by the slavery issue "to adjust it upon their own responsibility and in their own manner." The Nicholson letter became Cass's personal platform in his campaign for the 1848 Democratic presidential nomination. Dickinson, who publicly enunciated the idea before Cass did, served as the Michigan Democrat's lieutenant both in that contest (which Cass won handily) and in the post-convention canvass. The Democratic national platform was vague, but was capable of being interpreted along the lines of the Dickinson resolutions and the Nicholson letter. In fact, it was thus interpreted by Jefferson Davis and by the host of northern Democrats loyal to Cass in his presidential quest.

Historians have commented on the antipodal contrast between what Cass and Dickinson seemed to mean by non-intervention and what John C. Calhoun certainly did mean. Before Cass said a word on the subject, Calhoun had employed the same label to mark a radically different doctrine. Calhoun's non-intervention was designed to permit Southerners to take their slaves into the western territories, without interference by the federal government or by the territories themselves. During the Taylor–Cass–Van Buren struggle of 1848, most southern Democrats said that Cass's non-intervention was the same as Calhoun's. Davis suspected that this was not the case at all. Cass himself in 1850, becoming more candid than in 1847 or 1848, verified the Davis suspicion. According to Cass's remarks in the "Great Debate," territorial legislatures could sanction or prohibit slavery as they preferred.

Regardless of whether Cass's 1850 contention was justified or consistent, not a few of the southern Democratic senators went along with the New Mexico and Utah arrangement in the Compromise of 1850, just as most northern Democratic senators did. At various stages, Foote, Houston, William R. King of Alabama, and others joined Northerners along the non-intervention route. A single phrase in the bills, "consistent with the Constitution," made it possible for Southerners to put their own gloss on the Compromise keystone. Anomalous or hazy as the territorial provisions were, they were Democratic provisions. Created by Democrats and supported by Democrats from both the sections, they were championed late and secondarily by Henry Clay and Daniel Webster.

Whether Webster would assent to what tradition has termed "Clay's plan" remained in doubt until March 7, 1850. How late Clay was can best be illustrated by an exchange of views between Foote and Clay on February 14. Foote had first presented a plan closely resembling what came to be the Compromise. He had called for a select committee of fifteen, to pass upon the sectional problems and united most or all of them in a single bill. Foote said he made this move on the assumption that Clay favored just such strategy in his remarks of February 5 and 6, supporting his own resolutions of January 29. Clay, however, denied that this was his aim. In fact, the Kentucky Whig disparaged the Democrat's "omnibus speech, in which he introduced all sorts of things and every sort of passenger, and myself among the number."

"My desire," Clay explained, "was that the Senate should express its sense upon each of the resolutions in succession, beginning with the first and ending with the eighth. If they should be affirmatively adopted, my purpose was to propose the reference of them to appropriate [standing] committees. There are some of the subjects which may be perhaps advantageously combined. . . . But never did I contemplate embracing in the entire scheme of accommodation and harmony . . . all these distracting questions, and bringing them all into one measure." Foote, on the contrary, "certainly thought that all or most of these matters could be embraced in one bill, at least so far as positive legislative action was concerned. I think so yet; and, acting upon this opinion, I have actually embraced them in the bill introduced by me." The Mississippian went on to charge Clay with "playing the game of political power with our neighbors of the North in a manner decidedly unskillful. He is throwing into the hands of his adversaries all the *trump cards* in the pack."

Whoever may have held the trump cards in 1850, evidently by 1852 it was the Democratic party that benefited from the Compromise. Although its platform was scarcely less ambiguous than in 1848, Franklin Pierce rode confidently to the White House on the magic carpet of the most important letter of his life, in which he pronounced himself a Compromise Democrat. In 1854, another twist of the popular sovereignty doctrine resulted in the Kansas–Nebraska Act. In 1856, James Buchanan's banner proclaimed a variety of non-intervention, and the 1850's saw Douglas making popular sovereignty his political steed. Thus what was done on Capitol Hill in August and September, 1850, was in line with Democrats' policies—enunciated in 1847, 1848, and 1852, and often echoed by leading Democrats in the post-Compromise decade.

Both the Democratic and the Whig spokesmen and leaders most intimately identified with the Compromise of 1850 then and thereafter gave proof of this interpretation. Just as the Democrats produced most votes, such Democratic stalwarts as Douglas, Cass, Foote, Houston, Dickinson, and King were on Clay's side in successive tests. Were they siding with him? Or was he siding with them? Here another question of emphasis confronts the historian.

Douglas asserted in the Senate, without Whig denials, that nearly all the omnibus measures advanced by Clay's Committee of Thirteen had previously been considered and approved by the territorial committee, which had a Democratic majority and of which Douglas was chairman. What Clay did was to connect old bills, change some of them slightly, and cause the enactment of one to depend on the enactment of all. This was a procedure Clay lifted from Foote, and one Douglas's committee had decided against. Clay was less the originator and more the improviser. Incorporated in his recommendations, indeed the epitome of them, was the non-intervention theory of Dickinson and Cass.

Several persons claimed the role of originator of the compromise settlement. One, on the Senate floor, was Foote, who said "without egotism" (his own words) that "the report of the Committee on Territories was based upon bills introduced by myself." Jefferson Davis' response to this sally was a relaxed "Oh, yes, I am willing to give you all the credit for that." Referring to the Compromise itself, however, Davis added: "If any man has a right to be proud of the success of these measures, it is the Senator from Illinois." Years afterward, Foote traced popular sovereignty's inception back past his own contribution and Cass's Nicholson letter to Dickinson's resolutions. Without subtracting an inch from the Little Giant's stature, credit must also be given to Cass, Foote, and Dickinson—Democrats all—as well as to Douglas.

The Whigs' point of view, and especially that of Webster and Clay, should be borne in mind. Daniel Webster was in a tiny minority where opinion of Senate Whigs from the North was concerned as long as President Taylor lived. Webster hoped to obtain the presidential nomination in 1852. But the Whig delegates rebuffed Webster and Fillmore, bestowing the worthless palm on Winfield Scott. Webster died on October 24, 1852. His biographer, Claude M. Fuess, has written: "If Webster had lived and had been able to go to the polls, he would undoubtedly have cast his ballot for Franklin Pierce."

Clay, who died on June 29, 1852, had favored Fillmore, in

opposition to Scott and Webster, for the Whig nomination. Because of his death at that particular time, no one can say with precision what he would have done on November 2. Possibly he might have taken the road which Webster had begun to follow. Clay's statement in Frankfort, Kentucky, in the autumn of 1850, strongly suggests that he could not have voted for the Whig ticket two years later—with Scott running under the aegis of William H. Seward and Thurlow Weed. Earlier in 1850, Clay insisted that he was not the least interested in parties, party maneuvers, or party statutes; and in 1851, he was brought forward as a Democratic or Union presidential possibility, with Cass for vice-president. Throughout the 1850 controversy, Clay's speeches emphasized the placing of national interests ahead of party interests. This has been interpreted as a sure proof of statesmanship. Yet could it not as logically mean abandonment of allegiance to the majority element within the Whig party, and adherence to the non-intervention program of the Democrats?

Dickinson's resolutions of 1847, Cass's Nicholson letter of 1847, the territorial aspect of Cass's candidacy in 1848, and Foote's proposals of late 1849 were Democratic contributions. The majority of Douglas's committee on territories was Democratic, as were most of the Compromise leaders on the floor. If Douglas the Democrat guided the Compromise through to success, if Democrats supplied most of the votes, and if Democrats were far more consistent than Whigs in underwriting component parts, small wonder that in 1852 the Democrats ran a pro-Compromise nominee—and that the Whigs went down to party defeat and party death.

Two other matters merit mention. One is the likelihood that the Whig party was hopelessly split on the sectional question, in 1850 and even before. Unable to elect one of their seasoned statesmen to the presidency, the Whigs had to rally their faltering forces and appeal to independents behind the glamor of military heroism; this mirrored intrinsic weaknesses. During Taylor's lifetime, the bulk of the Whig senators stoutly opposed the Compromise.

After his death, Clay's "omnibus" was halted despite the push Democrats gave it. Even under Fillmore, and with Douglas in command in the Senate, the piecemeal measures could not have passed if many Whigs had not absented themselves when the yea-and-nay roll was called. Thus opposition, followed by negation, should be highlighted in accounts of the Compromise and integrated with the decline of Whiggery.

The second vital corollary is related to the first. Why the underscored prominence of Clay and Webster in virtually every version of the debates? Why the exaggerated emphasis on what they are presumed to have contributed? True, Clay returned to the Senate from retirement and for months did take charge of the Compromise efforts in the public gaze. Webster delivered one of the most brilliant speeches in American annals under circumstances loaded with drama. Such facets certainly deserve to be taken into account. Yet on the basis of many another fact developed here, from the standpoint of strength, of votes, of practical influence, the Clay–Webster contribution was merely secondary and supplemental alongside the major and primary Democratic backing of the Compromise.

Democratic senators and representatives, Democratic newspapers, Democratic party chieftains did much to play up Clay's and Webster's co-operation with them. It was not unlike what we have seen in our own era, in connection with Democratic foreign policy —to which such Republicans as the late Arthur H. Vandenberg, the present Henry Cabot Lodge, and other senators gave allegiance. Who loomed largest during the 1940's in the internationalist phase of Senate foreign policy? Was it Alben W. Barkley of Kentucky, James E. Murray of Montana, Brien McMahon of Connecticut, Elbert D. Thomas of Utah, or one of the numerous other Democrats who were steadfast in this regard? Or was it Vandenberg of Michigan? The popular interpretation appears to favor Vandenberg. There is something so sensational about a man who bucks the majority element within his minority party, to join the majority party on a fundamental issue, that this seems to ensure a certain kind of immortality.

According plenty of credit to Clay and Webster, as also we give it to Vandenberg and Lodge, should not historians take a closer look at what the protagonists represented? Are men who deliver two or eight votes more significant than those who speak for twenty? By what strange alchemy was Douglas long relegated to a really negligible part in the Compromise achievement? Did the relationship of Daniel Pomeroy Rhodes to the Douglas estate have anything to do with James Ford Rhodes's assigning Douglas to the limbo in 1850? Is the prominence of Republicans among historical writers from 1865 to 1920 to be equated with Clay–Webster Whig emphasis? These questions are packed with possibilities, warranting thorough investigation.

Nearly forty years ago, in the *Mississippi Valley Historical Review*, St. George L. Sioussat emphasized the need of re-exploring the Compromise of 1850. Not all that Sioussat found wanting has yet been supplied. The evidence is never all in. But benefiting from the discovery of old manuscripts penned by Senators Cass, Clarke, and Douglas, and from a rereading and perhaps a more extensive reading of the *Congressional Globe* and kindred sources, it is possible to come closer now to the realities of 1850, and to view the true structure behind the façade.

Paranoia and American Politics

Some Themes of Counter-Subversion: An Analysis of Anti-Masonic, Anti-Catholic, and Anti-Mormon Literature

by David Brion Davis

Periodically, politics registers the anxieties of Americans gripped by paranoid fears of conspiracies that supposedly threaten their way of life. In the 1760's the colonists perceived a British conspiracy against their liberty; in the 1790's, Federalists and Jeffersonians viewed each other as subversive plotters, in the one case with designs to restore monarchy and in the other to replace American republicanism with French Jacobinism; in the 1890's hard-pressed Midwestern and Southern farmers spoke of a plot by Big Business to crush them, and well-heeled conservatives mistook Populism for the opening wedge of socialism and, paradoxically, anarchism. In recent times, despite the chronic weakness of the American Communist party, millions of Americans were terrified by an alleged internal *Communist conspiracy said to have reached into the highest places in government.*

Political paranoia, whenever it gains sway in America, reveals a common etiology. The relatively fluid and open nature of the society makes Americans especially susceptible to this sort of paranoia. Millions of Americans are insecure in their status, and the resulting status anxieties, rooted in social mobility (upward or downward), are intensified by the diversity of the American social order. American political history has been, among other things, a struggle for recognition between those who have arrived and those aspiring to arrive, conflicts pitting Northerners against Southerners, farmers against city folk, Protestants against Catholics, immigrants against the native-born. Added to the strains arising from social mobility and diversity are the strains deriving from rapid social change. Many Americans have failed to cope rationally with these pressures. Convinced that America is, or should be, the "Happy-ending Country" where prosperity is the natural order of things, many have fallen prey to paranoid when confronted with adversity.

The conspiratorial mentality flourished with particular vigor between 1825 and 1855. America has always been a nation of men on the move and a nation of immigrants, but during the second quarter of the nineteenth century, internal mobility within the United States and foreign immigration to it accelerated at tremendous rates. First, after the War of 1812, came large-scale population movements from the farm areas of eastern seaboard states to new lands in western New York and across the Appalachians. And although immigration subsided early in the period between 1825 and 1855, by the 1840's it picked up again; by the end of that decade it became an avalanche, with Irish Catholics comprising the bulk of the newcomers.

Both forces worked to weaken the social structure of traditional America, and both let loose or stimulated negative reactions among those frightened by social change and apprehensive over the existence of alleged perils to American institutions. David Brion Davis here examines three such organizational forms—anti-Masonry, nativism, and anti-Mormonism—and attempts to show what was common to all three.

During the second quarter of the nineteenth century, when danger of foreign invasion appeared increasingly remote, Americans were told by various respected leaders that Freemasons had

From *The Mississippi Valley Historical Review*, XLVII (September 1960), 205–24. Reprinted by permission; most footnotes omitted.

infiltrated the government and had seized control of the courts, that Mormons were undermining political and economic freedom in the West, and that Roman Catholic priests, receiving instructions from Rome, had made frightening progress in a plot to subject the nation to popish despotism. This fear of internal subversion was channeled into a number of powerful counter movements which attracted wide public support. The literature produced by these movements evoked images of a great American enemy that closely resembled traditional European stereotypes of conspiracy and subversion. In Europe, however, the idea of subversion implied a threat to the established order—to the king, the church, or the ruling aristocracy—rather than to ideals or a way of life. If free Americans borrowed their images of subversion from frightened kings and uneasy aristocrats, these images had to be shaped and blended to fit American conditions. The movements would have to come from the people, and the themes of counter-subversion would be likely to reflect their fears, prejudices, hopes, and perhaps even unconscious desires.

There are obvious dangers in treating such reactions against imagined subversion as part of a single tendency or spirit of an age. Anti-Catholicism was nourished by ethnic conflict and uneasiness over immigration in the expanding cities of the Northeast; anti-Mormonism arose largely from a contest for economic and political power between western settlers and a group that voluntarily withdrew from society and claimed the undivided allegiance of its members. Anti-Masonry, on the other hand, was directed against a group thoroughly integrated in American society and did not reflect a clear division of economic, religious, or political interests. Moreover, anti-Masonry gained power in the late 1820's and soon spent its energies as it became absorbed in national politics; anti-Catholicism reached its maximum force in national politics a full generation later; anti-Mormonism, though increasing in intensity in the 1850's, became an important national issue only after the Civil War. These movements seem even more widely separated when we note that Freemasonry was traditionally associated with anti-Catholicism and that Mormonism itself absorbed considerable anti-Masonic and anti-Catholic sentiment.

Despite such obvious differences, there were certain similarities in these campaigns against subversion. All three gained widespread support in the northeastern states within the space of a generation; anti-Masonry and anti-Catholicism resulted in the sudden emergence of separate political parties; and in 1856 the new Republican party explicitly condemned the Mormons' most controversial institution. The movements of counter-subversion differed markedly in historical origin, but as the image of un-American conspiracy took form in the nativist press, in sensational exposés, in the countless fantasies of treason and mysterious criminality, the lines separating Mason, Catholic, and Mormon became almost indistinguishable.

The similar pattern of Masonic, Catholic, and Mormon subversion was frequently noticed by alarmist writers. The *Anti-Masonic Review* informed its readers in 1829 that whether one looked at Jesuitism or Freemasonry, "the organization, the power, and the secret operation, are the same; except that Freemasonry is much the more secret and complicated of the two." William Hogan, an ex-priest and vitriolic anti-Catholic, compared the menace of Catholicism with that of Mormonism. And many later anti-Mormon writers agreed with Josiah Strong that Brigham Young "out-popes the Roman" and described the Mormon hierarchy as being similar to the Catholic. It was probably not accidental that Samuel F. B. Morse analyzed the Catholic conspiracy in essentially the same terms his father had used in exposing the Society of the Illuminati, supposedly a radical branch of Freemasonry, or that writers of sensational fiction in the 1840's and 1850's depicted an atheistic and unprincipled Catholic Church obviously modeled on Charles Brockden Brown's earlier fictional version of the Illuminati.

If Masons, Catholics, and Mormons bore little resemblance to one another in actuality, as imagined enemies they merged into a nearly common stereotype. Behind specious professions of philanthropy or religious sentiment, nativists[1] discerned a group of unscrupulous leaders plotting to subvert the American social order. Though rank-and-file members were not individually evil, they were blinded and corrupted by a persuasive ideology that justified treason and gross immorality in the interest of the subversive group. Trapped in the meshes of a machine-like organization, deluded by a false sense of loyalty and moral obligation, these dupes followed orders like professional soldiers and labored unknowingly to abolish free society, to enslave their fellow men, and to overthrow divine principles of law and justice. Should an occasional member free himself from bondage to superstition and fraudulent authority, he could still be disciplined by the threat of death or dreadful tortures. There were no limits to the ambitious designs of leaders equipped with such organizations. According to nativist prophets, they chose to subvert American society because control of America meant control of the world's destiny.

Some of these beliefs were common in earlier and later European interpretations of conspiracy. American images of Masonic, Catholic, and Mormon subversion were no doubt a compound of traditional myths concerning Jacobite agents, scheming Jesuits, and fanatical heretics, and of dark legends involving the Holy Vehm and Rosicrucians. What distinguished the stereotypes of Mason, Catholic, and Mormon was the way in which they were seen to embody those traits that were precise antitheses of American ideals. The subversive group was essentially an inverted image of Jacksonian Democracy and the cult of the common man; as such it not only challenged the dominant values but stimulated those suppressed needs and yearnings that are fulfilled in a mobile, rootless, and individualistic society. It was therefore both frightening and fascinating.

It is well known that expansion and material progress in the

1. Though the term "nativist" is usually limited to opponents of immigration, it is used here to include anti-Masons and anti-Mormons. This seems justified in view of the fact that these alarmists saw themselves as defenders of native traditions and identified Masonry and Mormonism with forces alien to American life.

Jacksonian era evoked a fervid optimism and that nationalists became intoxicated with visions of America's millennial glory. The simultaneous growth of prosperity and social democracy seemed to prove that Providence would bless a nation that allowed her citizens maximum liberty. When each individual was left free to pursue happiness in his own way, unhampered by the tyranny of custom or special privilege, justice and well-being would inevitably emerge. But if a doctrine of laissez-faire individualism seemed to promise material expansion and prosperity, it also raised disturbing problems. As one early anti-Mormon writer expressed it: What was to prevent liberty and popular sovereignty from sweeping away "the old landmarks of Christendom, and the glorious old common law of our fathers"? How was the individual to preserve a sense of continuity with the past, or identify himself with a given cause or tradition? What, indeed, was to ensure a common loyalty and a fundamental unity among the people?

Such questions acquired a special urgency as economic growth intensified mobility, destroyed old ways of life, and transformed traditional symbols of status and prestige. Though most Americans took pride in their material progress, they also expressed a yearning for reassurance and security, for unity in some cause transcending individual self-interest. This need for meaningful group activity was filled in part by religious revivals, reform movements, and a proliferation of fraternal orders and associations. In politics Americans tended to assume the posture of what Marvin Meyers has termed "venturesome conservatives," mitigating their acquisitive impulses by an appeal for unity against extraneous forces that allegedly threatened a noble heritage of republican ideals. Without abandoning a belief in progress through laissez-faire individualism, the Jacksonians achieved a sense of unity and righteousness by styling themselves as restorers of tradition. Perhaps no theme is so evident in the Jacksonian era as the strained attempt to provide America with a glorious heritage and a noble destiny. With only a loose and often ephemeral attachment to places and institutions, many Americans felt a compelling need to articulate their loyalties, to prove their faith, and to demonstrate their allegiance to certain ideals and institutions. By so doing they acquired a sense of self-identity and personal direction in an otherwise rootless and shifting environment.

But was abstract nationalism sufficient to reassure a nation strained by sectional conflict, divided by an increasing number of sects and associations, and perplexed by the unexpected consequences of rapid growth? One might desire to protect the Republic against her enemies, to preserve the glorious traditions of the Founders, and to help insure continued expansion and prosperity, but first it was necessary to discover an enemy by distinguishing subversion from simple diversity. If Freemasons seemed to predominate in the economic and political life of a given area, was one's joining them shrewd business judgment or a betrayal of republican tradition? Should Maryland citizens heed the warnings of anti-Masonic itinerants, or conclude that anti-Masonry was itself a conspiracy hatched by scheming Yankees? Were Roman Catholics plotting to destroy public schools and a free press, the twin guardians of American democracy, or were they exercising democratic rights of self-expression and self-protection? Did equality of opportunity and equality before the law mean that Americans should accept the land claims of Mormons or tolerate as jurors men who "swear that they have wrought miracles and supernatural cures"? Or should one agree with the Reverend Finis Ewing that "the 'Mormons' are the common enemies of mankind and ought to be destroyed"?

Few men questioned traditional beliefs in freedom of conscience and the right of association. Yet what was to prevent "all the errors and worn out theories of the Old World, of schisms in the early Church, the monkish age and the rationalistic period," from flourishing in such salubrious air? Nativists often praised the work of benevolent societies, but they were disturbed by the thought that monstrous conspiracies might also "show kindness and patriotism, when it is necessary for their better concealment; and oftentimes do much good for the sole purpose of getting a better opportunity to do evil." When confronted by so many sects and associations, how was the patriot to distinguish the loyal from the disloyal? It was clear that mere disagreement over theology or economic policy was invalid as a test, since honest men disputed over the significance of baptism or the wisdom of protective tariffs. But neither could one rely on expressions of allegiance to common democratic principles, since subversives would cunningly profess to believe in freedom and toleration of dissent as long as they remained a powerless minority.

As nativists studied this troubling question, they discovered that most groups and denominations claimed only a partial loyalty from their members, freely subordinating themselves to the higher and more abstract demands of the Constitution, Christianity, and American public opinion. Moreover, they openly exposed their objects and activities to public scrutiny and exercised little discrimination in enlisting members. Some groups, however, dominated a larger portion of their members' lives, demanded unlimited allegiance as a condition of membership, and excluded certain activities from the gaze of a curious public.

Of all governments, said Richard Rush, ours was the one with most to fear from secret societies, since popular sovereignty by its very nature required perfect freedom of public inquiry and judgment. In a virtuous republic why should anyone fear publicity or desire to conceal activities, unless those activities were somehow contrary to the public interest? When no one could be quite sure what the public interest was, and when no one could take for granted a secure and well-defined place in the social order, it was most difficult to acknowledge legitimate spheres of privacy. Most Americans of the Jacksonian era appeared willing to tolerate diversity and even eccentricity, but when they saw themselves excluded and even barred from witnessing certain proceedings, they imagined a "mystic power" conspiring to enslave them.

Readers might be amused by the first exposures of Masonic ritual, since they learned that pompous and dignified citizens, who had once impressed non-Masons with allusions to high degrees and elaborate ceremonies, had in actuality been forced to stand blindfolded and clad in ridiculous garb, with a long rope noosed around their necks. But genuine anti-Masons were not content with simple ridicule. Since intelligent and distinguished men had been members of the fraternity, "it must have in its interior something more than the usual revelations of its mysteries declare." Surely leading citizens would not meet at night and undergo degrading and humiliating initiations just for the sake of novelty. The alleged murder of William Morgan raised an astonishing public furor because it supposedly revealed the inner secret of Freemasonry. Perverted by a false ideology, Masons had renounced all obligations to the general public, to the laws of the land, and even to the command of God. Hence they threatened not a particular party's program or a denomination's creed, but stood opposed to all justice, democracy, and religion.

The distinguishing mark of Masonic, Catholic, and Mormon conspiracies was a secrecy that cloaked the members' unconditional loyalty to an autonomous body. Since the organizations had corrupted the private moral judgment of their members, Americans could not rely on the ordinary forces of progress to spread truth and enlightenment among their ranks. Yet the affairs of such organizations were not outside the jurisdiction of democratic government, for no body politic could be asked to tolerate a power that was designed to destroy it. Once the true nature of subversive groups was thoroughly understood, the alternatives were as clear as life and death. How could democracy and Catholicism coexist when, as Edward Beecher warned, "The systems are diametrically opposed: one must and will exterminate the other"? Because Freemasons had so deeply penetrated state and national governments, only drastic remedies could restore the nation to its democratic purity. And later, Americans faced an "irrepressible conflict" with Mormonism, for it was said that either free institutions or Mormon despotism must ultimately annihilate the other.

We may well ask why nativists magnified the division between unpopular minorities and the American public, so that Masons,

Catholics, and Mormons seemed so menacing that they could not be accorded the usual rights and privileges of a free society. Obviously the literature of counter-subversion reflected concrete rivalries and conflicts of interest between competing groups, but it is important to note that the subversive bore no racial or ethnic stigma and was not even accused of inherent depravity.[2] Since group membership was a matter of intellectual and emotional loyalty, no *physical* barrier prevented a Mason, Catholic, or Mormon from apostatizing and joining the dominant in-group, providing always that he escaped assassination from his previous masters. This suggests that counter-subversion was more than a rationale for group rivalry and was related to the general problem of ideological unity and diversity in a free society. When a "system of delusion" insulated members of a group from the unifying and disciplining force of public opinion, there was no authority to command an allegiance to common principles. This was why oaths of loyalty assumed great importance for nativists. Though the ex-Catholic William Hogan stated repeatedly that Jesuit spies respected no oaths except those to the Church, he inconsistently told Masons and Odd Fellows that they could prevent infiltration by requiring new members to swear they were not Catholics. It was precisely the absence of distinguishing outward traits that made the enemy so dangerous, and true loyalty so difficult to prove.

When the images of different enemies conform to a similar pattern, it is highly probable that this pattern reflects important tensions within a given culture. The themes of nativist literature suggest that its authors simplified problems of personal insecurity

2. It is true that anti-Catholics sometimes stressed the inferiority of lower-class immigrants and that anti-Mormons occasionally claimed that Mormon converts were made among the most degraded and ignorant classes of Europe. This theme increased in importance toward the end of the century, but it seldom implied that Catholics and Mormons were physically incapable of being liberated and joined to the dominant group. Racism was not an original or an essential part of the counter-subversive's ideology. Even when Mormons were attacked for coarseness, credulity, and vulgarity, these traits were usually thought to be the product of their beliefs and institutions.

and adjustment to bewildering social change by trying to unite Americans of diverse political, religious, and economic interests against a common enemy. Just as revivalists sought to stimulate Christian fellowship by awakening men to the horrors of sin, so nativists used apocalyptic images to ignite human passions, destroy selfish indifference, and join patriots in a cohesive brotherhood. Such themes were only faintly secularized. When God saw his "lov'd Columbia" imperiled by the hideous monster of Freemasonry, He realized that only a martyr's blood could rouse the hearts of the people and save them from bondage to the Prince of Darkness. By having God will Morgan's death, this anti-Mason showed he was more concerned with national virtue and unity than with Freemasonry, which was only a providential instrument for testing republican strength.

Similarly, for the anti-Catholic "this brilliant new world" was once "young and beautiful; it abounded in all the luxuries of nature; it promised all that was desirable to man." But the Roman Church, seeing "these irresistible temptations, thirsting with avarice and yearning for the reestablishment of her falling greatness, soon commenced pouring in among its unsuspecting people hoardes of Jesuits and other friars." If Americans were to continue their narrow pursuit of self-interest, oblivious to the "Popish colleges, and nunneries, and monastic institutions," indifferent to manifold signs of corruption and decay, how could the nation expect "that the moral breezes of heaven should breathe upon her, and restore to her again that strong and healthy constitution, which her ancestors have left to her sons"? The theme of an Adamic fall from paradise was horrifying, but it was used to inspire determined action and thus unity. If Methodists were "criminally indifferent" to the Mormon question, and if "avaricious merchants, soulless corporations, and a subsidized press" ignored Mormon iniquities, there was all the more reason that the "*will of the people* must prevail."

Without explicitly rejecting the philosophy of laissez-faire individualism, with its toleration of dissent and innovation, nativist literature conveyed a sense of common dedication to a noble cause and sacred tradition. Though the nation had begun with the blessings of God and with the noblest institutions known to man, the people had somehow become selfish and complacent, divided by petty disputes, and insensitive to signs of danger. In his sermons attacking such self-interest, such indifference to public concerns, and such a lack of devotion to common ideals and sentiments, the nativist revealed the true source of his anguish. Indeed, he seemed at times to recognize an almost beneficent side to subversive organizations, since they joined the nation in a glorious crusade and thus kept it from moral and social disintegration.

The exposure of subversion was a means of promoting unity, but it also served to clarify national values and provide the individual ego with a sense of high moral sanction and imputed righteousness. Nativists identified themselves repeatedly with a strangely incoherent tradition in which images of Pilgrims, Minute Men, Founding Fathers, and true Christians appeared in a confusing montage. Opposed to this heritage of stability and perfect integrity, to this society founded on the highest principles of divine and natural law, were organizations formed by the grossest frauds and impostures, and based on the wickedest impulses of human nature. Bitterly refuting Masonic claims to ancient tradition and Christian sanction, anti-Masons charged that the Order was of recent origin, that it was shaped by Jews, Jesuits, and French atheists as an engine for spreading infidelity, and that it was employed by kings and aristocrats to undermine republican institutions. If the illustrious Franklin and Washington had been duped by Masonry, this only proved how treacherous was its appeal and how subtly persuasive were its pretensions. Though the Catholic Church had an undeniable claim to tradition, nativists argued that it had originated in stupendous frauds and forgeries "in comparison with which the forgeries of Mormonism are completely thrown into the shade." Yet anti-Mormons saw an even more sinister conspiracy based on the "shrewd cunning" of Joseph Smith, who convinced gullible souls that he conversed with angels and received direct revelations from the Lord.

By emphasizing the fraudulent character of their opponents' claims, nativists sought to establish the legitimacy and just authority of American institutions. Masonic rituals, Roman Catholic sacraments, and Mormon revelations were preposterous hoaxes used to delude naïve or superstitious minds; but public schools, a free press, and jury trials were eternally valid prerequisites for a free and virtuous society.

Moreover, the finest values of an enlightened nation stood out in bold relief when contrasted with the corrupting tendencies of subversive groups. Perversion of the sexual instinct seemed inevitably to accompany religious error. Deprived of the tender affections of normal married love, shut off from the elevating sentiments of fatherhood, Catholic priests looked on women only as insensitive objects for the gratification of their frustrated desires. In similar fashion polygamy struck at the heart of a morality based on the inspiring influence of woman's affections: "It renders man coarse, tyrannical, brutal, and heartless. It deals death to all sentiments of true manhood. It enslaves and ruins woman. It crucifies every God-given feeling of her nature." Some anti-Mormons concluded that plural marriage could only have been established among foreigners who had never learned to respect women. But the more common explanation was that the false ideology of Mormonism had deadened the moral sense and liberated man's wild sexual impulse from the normal restraints of civilization. Such degradation of women and corruption of man served to highlight the importance of democratic marriage, a respect for women, and careful cultivation of the finer sensibilities.

But if nativist literature was a medium for articulating common values and exhorting individuals to transcend self-interest and join in a dedicated union against evil, it also performed a more subtle function. Why, we may ask, did nativist literature dwell so persistently on themes of brutal sadism and sexual immorality? Why did its authors describe sin in such minute details, endowing even the worst offenses of their enemies with a certain fascinating appeal?

Freemasons, it was said, could commit any crime and indulge any passion when "upon the square," and Catholics and Mormons were even less inhibited by internal moral restraints. Nativists expressed horror over this freedom from conscience and conventional morality, but they could not conceal a throbbing note of envy. What was it like to be a member of a cohesive brotherhood that casually abrogated the laws of God and man, enforcing unity and obedience with dark and mysterious powers? As nativists speculated on this question, they projected their own fears and desires into a fantasy of licentious orgies and fearful punishments.

Such a projection of forbidden desires can be seen in the exaggeration of the stereotyped enemy's powers, which made him appear at times as a virtual superman. Catholic and Mormon leaders, never hindered by conscience or respect for traditional morality, were curiously superior to ordinary Americans in cunning, in exercising power over others, and especially in captivating gullible women. It was an ancient theme of anti-Catholic literature that friars and priests were somehow more potent and sexually attractive than married laymen, and were thus astonishingly successful at seducing supposedly virtuous wives. Americans were cautioned repeatedly that no priest recognized Protestant marriages as valid, and might consider any wife legitimate prey. Furthermore, priests had access to the pornographic teachings of Dens and Liguori, sinister names that aroused the curiosity of anti-Catholics, and hence learned subtle techniques of seduction perfected over the centuries. Speaking with the authority of an ex-priest, William Hogan described the shocking result: "I have seen husbands unsuspiciously and hospitably entertaining the very priest who seduced their wives in the confessional, and was the parent of some of the children who sat at the same table with them, each of the wives unconscious of the other's guilt, and the husbands of both, not even suspecting them." Such blatant immorality was horrifying, but everyone was apparently happy in this domestic scene, and we may suspect that the image was not entirely repugnant to husbands who, despite their respect for the Lord's Commandments, occasionally coveted their neighbors' wives.

The literature of counter-subversion could also embody the somewhat different projective fantasies of women. Ann Eliza Young dramatized her seduction by the Prophet Brigham, whose almost superhuman powers enchanted her and paralyzed her will. Though she submitted finally only because her parents were in danger of being ruined by the Church, she clearly indicated that it was an exciting privilege to be pursued by a Great Man. When Anti-Mormons claimed that Joseph Smith and other prominent Saints knew the mysteries of Animal Magnetism, or were endowed with the highest degree of "amativeness" in their phrenological makeup, this did not detract from their covert appeal. In a ridiculous fantasy written by Maria Ward, such alluring qualities were extended even to Mormon women. Many bold-hearted girls could doubtless identify themselves with Anna Bradish, a fearless Amazon of a creature, who rode like a man, killed without compunction, and had no pity for weak women who failed to look out for themselves. Tall, elegant, and "intellectual," Anna was attractive enough to arouse the insatiable desires of Brigham Young, though she ultimately rejected him and renounced Mormonism.

While nativists affirmed their faith in Protestant monogamy, they obviously took pleasure in imagining the variety of sexual experience supposedly available to their enemies. By picturing themselves exposed to similar temptations, they assumed they could know how priests and Mormons actually sinned. Imagine, said innumerable anti-Catholic writers, a beautiful young woman kneeling before an ardent young priest in a deserted room. As she confesses, he leans over, looking into her eyes, until their heads are nearly touching. Day after day she reveals to him her innermost secrets, secrets she would not think of unveiling to her parents, her dearest friends, or even her suitor. By skillful questioning the priest fills her mind with immodest and even sensual ideas, "until this wretch has worked up her passions to a tension almost snapping, and then becomes his easy prey." How could any man resist such provocative temptations, and how could any girl's virtue withstand such a test?

We should recall that this literature was written in a period of increasing anxiety and uncertainty over sexual values and the proper role of woman. As ministers and journalists pointed with alarm at the spread of prostitution, the incidence of divorce, and the lax and hypocritical morality of the growing cities, a discussion of licentious subversives offered a convenient means for the projection of guilt as well as desire. The sins of individuals, or of the nation as a whole, could be pushed off upon the shoulders of the enemy and there punished in righteous anger.

Specific instances of such projection are not difficult to find. John C. Bennett, whom the Mormons expelled from the Church as a result of his flagrant sexual immorality, invented the fantasy of "The Mormon Seraglio" which persisted in later anti-Mormon writings. According to Bennett, the Mormons maintained secret orders of beautiful prostitutes who were mostly reserved for various officials of the Church. He claimed, moreover, that any wife refusing to accept polygamy might be forced to join the lowest order and thus become available to any Mormon who desired her.

Another example of projection can be seen in the letters of a young lieutenant who stopped in Utah in 1854 on his way to Cailfornia. Convinced that Mormon women could be easily seduced, the lieutenant wrote frankly of his amorous adventures with a married woman. "Everybody has got one," he wrote with obvious pride, "except the Colonel and Major. The Doctor has got three—mother and two daughters. The mother cooks for him and the daughters sleep with him." But though he described Utah as "a great country," the lieutenant waxed indignant over polygamy, which he condemned as self-righteously as any anti-Mormon minister: "To see one man openly parading half a dozen or more women to church . . . is the devil according to my ideas of morality virtue and decency."

If the consciences of many Americans were troubled by the growth of red light districts in major cities, they could divert their attention to the "legalized brothels" called nunneries, for which no one was responsible but lecherous Catholic priests. If others were disturbed by the moral implications of divorce, they could point in horror at the Mormon elder who took his quota of wives all at once. The literature of counter-subversion could thus serve the double purpose of vicariously fulfilling repressed desires, and of releasing the tension and guilt arising from rapid social change and conflicting values.

Though the enemy's sexual freedom might at first seem enticing, it was always made repugnant in the end by associations with perversion or brutal cruelty. Both Catholics and Mormons were accused of practicing nearly every form of incest. The persistent emphasis on this theme might indicate deep-rooted feelings of fear and guilt, but it also helped demonstrate, on a more objective level, the loathsome consequences of unrestrained lust. Sheer brutality and a delight in human suffering were supposed to be the even more horrible results of sexual depravity. Masons disemboweled or slit the throats of their victims; Catholics cut unborn infants from their mothers' wombs and threw them to the dogs before their parents' eyes; Mormons raped and lashed recalcitrant women, or seared their mouths with red-hot irons. This obsession with details of sadism, which reached pathological proportions in much of the literature, showed a furious determination to purge the enemy of every admirable quality. The imagined enemy might serve at first as an outlet for forbidden desires, but nativist authors escaped from guilt by finally making him an agent of unmitigated aggression. In such a role the subversive seemed to deserve both righteous anger and the most terrible punishments.

The nativist escape from guilt was more clearly revealed in the themes of confession and conversion. For most American Protestants the crucial step in anyone's life was a profession of true faith resulting from a genuine religious experience. Only when a man becomes conscious of his inner guilt, when he struggled against the temptations of Satan, could he prepare his soul for the infusion of the regenerative spirit. Those most deeply involved in sin often made the most dramatic conversions. It is not surprising that conversion to nativism followed the same pattern, since nativists sought unity and moral certainty in the regenerative spirit of nationalism. Men who had been associated in some way with un-American conspiracies were not only capable of spectacular confessions of guilt, but were best equipped to expose the insidious work of supposedly harmless organizations. Even those who lacked such an exciting history of corruption usually made some confession of guilt, though it might involve only a previous indifference to subversive groups. Like ardent Christians, nativists searched in their own experiences for the meanings of sin, delusion, awakening to truth, and liberation from spiritual bondage. These personal confessions proved that one had recognized and conquered evil, and also served as ritual cleansings preparatory to full acceptance in a group of dedicated patriots.

Anti-Masons were perhaps the ones most given to confessions of guilt and most alert to subtle distinctions of loyalty and disloyalty. Many leaders of this movement, expressing guilt over their own "shameful experience and knowledge" of Masonry, felt a compelling obligation to exhort their former associates to "come out, and be separate from masonic abominations." Even when an anti-Mason could say with John Quincy Adams that "I am not, never was, and never shall be a Freemason," he would often admit that he had once admired the Order, or had even considered applying for admission.

Since a willingness to sacrifice oneself was an unmistakable sign of loyalty and virtue, ex-Masons gloried in exaggerating the dangers they faced and the harm that their revelations supposedly inflicted on the enemy. In contrast to hardened Freemasons, who refused to answer questions in court concerning their fraternal associations, the seceders claimed to reveal the inmost secrets of the Order, and by so doing to risk property, reputation, and life. Once the ex-Mason had dared to speak the truth, his character would surely be maligned, his motives impugned, and his life threatened. But, he declared, even if he shared the fate of the illustrious Morgan, he would die knowing that he had done his duty.

Such self-dramatization reached extravagant heights in the ranting confessions of many apostate Catholics and Mormons. Maria Monk and her various imitators told of shocking encounters with sin in its most sensational forms, of bondage to vice and superstition, and of melodramatic escapes from popish despotism. A host of "ex-Mormon wives" described their gradual recognition of Mormon frauds and iniquities, the anguish and misery of plural marriage, and their breath-taking flights over deserts or mountains. The female apostate was especially vulnerable to vengeful retaliation, since she could easily be kidnapped by crafty priests and nuns, or dreadfully punished by Brigham Young's Destroying Angels. At the very least, her reputation could be smirched by foul lies and insinuations. But her willingness to risk honor and life for the sake of her country and for the dignity of all womankind was eloquent proof of her redemption. What man could be assured of so noble a role?

The apostate's pose sometimes assumed paranoid dimensions. William Hogan warned that only the former priest could properly gauge the Catholic threat to American liberties and saw himself as providentially appointed to save his Protestant countrymen. "For twenty years," he wrote, "I have warned them of approaching danger, but their politicians were deaf, and their Protestant theologians remained religiously coiled up in fancied security, overrating their own powers and undervaluing that of Papists." Pursued by vengeful Jesuits, denounced and calumniated for alleged crimes, Hogan pictured himself single-handedly defending

American freedom: "No one, before me, dared to encounter their scurrilous abuse. I resolved to silence them; and I have done so. The very mention of my name is a terror to them now." After surviving the worst of Catholic persecution, Hogan claimed to have at last aroused his countrymen and to have reduced the hierarchy to abject terror.

As the nativist searched for participation in a noble cause, for unity in a group sanctioned by tradition and authority, he professed a belief in democracy and equal rights. Yet in his very zeal for freedom he curiously assumed many of the characteristics of the imagined enemy. By condemning the subversive's fanatical allegiance to an ideology, he affirmed a similarly uncritical acceptance of a different ideology; by attacking the subversive's intolerance of dissent, he worked to eliminate dissent and diversity of opinion; by censuring the subversive for alleged licentiousness, he engaged in sensual fantasies; by criticizing the subversive's loyalty to an organization, he sought to prove his unconditional loyalty to the established order. The nativist moved even farther in the direction of his enemies when he formed tightly-knit societies and parties which were often secret and which subordinated the individual to the single purpose of the group. Though the nativists generally agreed that the worst evil of subversives was their subordination of means to ends, they themselves recommended the most radical means to purge the nation of troublesome groups and to enforce unquestioned loyalty to the state.

In his image of an evil group conspiring against the nation's welfare, and in his vision of a glorious millennium that was to dawn after the enemy's defeat, the nativist found satisfaction for many desires. His own interests became legitimate and dignified by fusion with the national interest, and various opponents became loosely associated with the un-American conspiracy. Thus Freemasonry in New York State was linked in the nativist mind with economic and political interests that were thought to discriminate against certain groups and regions; southerners imagined a union of abolitionists and Catholics to promote unrest and rebellion among slaves; gentile businessmen in Utah merged anti-Mormonism with plans for exploiting mines and lands.

Then too the nativist could style himself as a restorer of the past, as a defender of a stable order against disturbing changes, and at the same time proclaim his faith in future progress. By focusing his attention on the imaginary threat of a secret conspiracy, he found an outlet for many irrational impulses, yet professed his loyalty to the ideals of equal rights and government by law. He paid lip service to the doctrine of laissez-faire individualism, but preached selfless dedication to a transcendent cause. The imposing threat of subversion justified a group loyalty and subordination of the individual that would otherwise have been unacceptable. In a rootless environment shaken by bewildering social change the nativist found unity and meaning by conspiring against imaginary conspiracies.

Nativism and the Political Vacuum

The Power of Political Frenzy

by Michael Fitzgibbon Holt

The anti-Catholic paranoia, rising in intensity with the arrival of hundreds of thousands of "papist" immigrants (1846–56), was bound to have serious political repercussions. With the Whig party fast disintegrating, and with the Democrats badly shaken by the introduction of Douglas's Kansas–Nebraska bill, a period of extreme political instability began. Frustration with traditional political leadership and fear of foreigners gave rise to the short-lived Native American, or Know-Nothing, party. This anti-Catholic and anti-immigrant movement blended honest conviction and concern with the worst forms of xenophobia and ignorant prejudice. And for a few years it challenged slavery as the principal surface issue in American politics, jeopardizing the growth of the fledgling Republican party.

Nativism offered cynical politicians the possibility of rebuilding national unity—never the sturdiest edifice under the best of circumstances, and now shuddering under the sectional conflict—on foundations of bigotry. Nativism first bloomed in the 1830's, and during the next decade it scored modest political successes, electing a mayor in New York City and several congressmen elsewhere. A heavy rise in immigration in the late 1840's caused nativism to undergo a mushroom-like growth, and by 1854 the anti-immigrant "110% American" party had acquired considerable political clout. Native-born Americans who believed that Catholics had no use for either political democracy or the separation of Church and State became alarmed as the number of Irish and German Catholics continued to mount. Sporadic violence broke out between foreign-born Catholics and native-born Protestants, especially in the ethnically mixed cities.

Party politics played an important role in the rise of nativism. In the eastern cities the Irish and Germans both participated in politics soon after arrival because of easy voting requirements. Democratic politicians had marshalled these immigrant votes effectively, making Whigs and ex-Whigs receptive to nativist ideas and organization. Several secret societies of nativists, usually formed by Whigs, sprang up to oppose the Catholic role in politics. In 1853 they merged into the Order of the Star Spangled Banner, which became known popularly as the Know-Nothing party.

The party enjoyed its greatest success in the ethnically diverse Eastern states, capturing 6 governorships and electing 75 congressmen between 1854 and 1856. Republicans played a cagey game with the nativists, sensing that when the Know-Nothing's ephemeral game had run its course, they, the Republicans, would pick up the election-day marbles. In the following selection, Michael F. Holt describes the chaotic nature of parties within the Pittsburgh microcosm in those years, and the significantly parasitic relationship between Know-Nothing decline and Republican rise.

Between 1853 and 1856 party alignments fluctuated rapidly throughout the Northern states. The Whig party, weakened after 1852, disappeared, and old politicians frantically tried to mold new coalitions. Because of the habit of shaping the history of the 1850's into a pattern of events leading to the Civil War, historians

From *Forging a Majority: The Formation of the Republican Party in Pittsburgh, 1848–1860* (New Haven: Yale University Press, 1969), pp. 123–25, 133–43, 154–58, 167–74. most footnotes omitted.

have traditionally stressed these years as the period in which the reaction to Stephen A. Douglas's Kansas–Nebraska Bill destroyed the Whig party, shattered the Democratic organization in the North, and prompted the formation of anti-Nebraska coalitions of Whigs, Free-Soilers, and those Democrats who opposed the further extension of slavery into Kansas. Channeling the aroused antislavery sentiment of the North, these new parties swept the Democrats out of office in the fall elections of 1854. Only transitory bodies, they then evolved into Republican parties by 1856.

However accurately this pattern describes events in some Northern states, it does not completely explain developments in Pittsburgh during this period. Not the Kansas–Nebraska Act alone, but a combination of factors coincided to split the Democratic party and precipitate political realignments there. Nor did a Republican party grow up quickly, for by the beginning of 1856 no viable Republican organization yet existed in Pittsburgh. As the Whig party was disintegrating nationally and Whigs in Pittsburgh were looking for a new vehicle, they were offered two choices—an anti-Nebraska coalition and the nativist Know-Nothing party. In contrast to western states where an anti-Nebraska Republican party emerged rapidly, in Pennsylvania and many other eastern states the Know-Nothing order grew more substantially in the years 1854 and 1855. Indeed, it enjoyed phenomenal, if ephemeral, success.

An analysis of the causes of the rise of the Know-Nothing order and its real nature explains much about how the Pittsburgh Whig party divided in these years. Moreover, this investigation of the social bases of political developments in these years casts light on the rivalry between Democrats and their foes during the whole period from 1848 to 1860. The ethnic and religious tensions reflected in the rise of the Know-Nothings influenced political behavior both before and after their appearance. Because of the enduring importance of these factors, any monistic interpretation of the politics of the pre-Civil War decade based on the hardening of sectionalism and antislavery sentiment seems unreliable for Pittsburgh and probably for the other areas where the Know-Nothings were strong. . . .

In the early 1850's several specific blunders by the Catholic Church crystallized the fears of a papal conspiracy and intensified the Protestants' hatred of Catholics. Archbishop Hughes, the recognized head of the Catholic Church in America, reopened the demand for ownership of church property by the clergy rather than by laymen, a system which would increase the economic power of priests. Nativists quickly denounced the undemocratic character of such ecclesiastical ownership. A more serious mistake was the mission of a papal envoy, Gaetano Bedini, to the United States. Nativist newspapers represented Bedini, who actually came to clear up some disputes about church ownership in Buffalo and Philadelphia, as an agent of the papal plot to subvert American freedom. This symbolic extension of papal authority into the United States greatly angered American and German Protestants, and when Bedini came to Pittsburgh on a tour of the country in December 1853, a mob jostled him roughly.

By far the most catastrophic policy of the Catholic Church in Pittsburgh, however, was the ill-conceived attack on the public school system. Archbishop Hughes and Bishop O'Connor had first complained that Catholic children were being corrupted and driven from their parents' faith in public schools because of Bible reading and other practices. Bishop O'Connor then protested that it was unfair to tax Catholics to support such schools, and he demanded a separate school fund for Catholics to support an independent system of parochial schools. In early 1854, Jonas R. McClintock, the Democratic state senator from Allegheny County elected in 1853, acted for the Catholic Church and introduced a bill into the legislature calling for such a division of the public school fund. Anti-Catholic editors charged that this war on the school system originated in Rome and was part of the papal conspiracy to destroy the freedom of thought and love of liberty in America. Only by perpetuating ignorance and depriving Catholic children of a good open education, they chided, could the Catholic church survive.

The strong bias against Catholics complemented the anti-Nebraska sentiment. In one of his early editorials trying to agitate protests against the Kansas–Nebraska Bill, [William A.] White argued that if American Protestants cried out against Catholicism "and its ancient cruelties," they must logically denounce slavery and try to save Nebraska from it. Thus White pointed out the connection between the anti-Catholic and antislavery aspects of Protestant zeal which Democrats had long since noted in their efforts to woo the Catholic vote. Moreover, naturalized Germans seemed to hate the Pope as much as they did slavery. The mass meeting of Germans which denounced the Kansas–Nebraska Bill also passed an even longer set of resolutions against recent Catholic aggressions. The Germans protested against the Bedini mission, against the use of the religious power of the Catholic priests in politics, against "the attempt of the Catholic Hierarchy to destroy our common schools," against the efforts of the Pope, "a worldly tyrant," to extend his power throughout the world, and against the Catholic press in the United States for trying to "uproot the love of liberty and self-government." White applauded the Germans' attack on the "two greatest evils of the day"—slavery and the papal conspiracy.

In the first few months of 1854 the Whigs expressed as much anti-Catholic sentiment as they did antislavery feeling. The resolutions of the Whig county convention in early February which only included a line against the Nebraska Bill also declared:

> That we are in favor of a *liberal system of education*, and to effect the promotion of civil and religious liberty, we pledge ourselves to support, with unfeigned effort, the *Common School System*, as the great bulwark of our Institutions.

In other words, they would brook no division of the public school fund. The Whig state platform declared that universal education and religious liberty should be goals of all state legislation, and the address of the Whig state central committee charged that Governor Bigler favored a division of the school fund.

In the first part of 1854, the Whig press also blatantly identified the Whig party with Protestantism and the Democrats with Catholicism. White boasted, "The Whig party always was and is, the standard bearer of Protestantism and Free Soilism, whilst the Democratic party represents the opposite principles." Later he insisted "that the great mass of Catholic voters in this county are members of the Democratic party" and "that the papers and leaders of that party have always been ready to yield to the wishes and demands of Popery as far as they could venture without driving away their Protestant supporters." Earlier White had denounced Franklin Pierce's appointment of James Campbell as Postmaster General as a blatant appeal to Catholic support and warned that he would live to regret the favoritism of that denomination. During the campaign he commented that major reasons for opposition to Bigler were his connection with Campbell, whom he had appointed State Attorney General, and the widespread disgust with the political power of Catholics. Combining the issues, White insisted that the gubernatorial canvass would turn on the Nebraska Bill and opposition to popery.

After the passage of the Nebraska Act in May, however, the Whigs ceased to agitate the anti-Catholic issue and concentrated solely on slavery expansion in order to form an anti-Nebraska coalition. As early as March the *Gazette* called for a fusion of all Northern opponents of slavery extension into a sectional party. Magnanimously White declared on several occasions, "We are willing to make any reasonable sacrifice of party ties to a great and undying principle"—"resistance to all future encroachments of slavery." The second Whig county convention in June tried to transform the Whig party into an anti-Nebraska party by luring Free-Soil Democrats while maintaining the Whig name. Dropping now all talk of issues, such as the tariff, internal improvements, and the school fund, found in the February resolutions, this later convention dealt exclusively with the Nebraska Act. Adopting virtually the Free-Soil position on slavery, the Whigs condemned the effort "to propagate, confirm, and diffuse that national sin and shame" of slavery and vowed to oppose its further extension, the admission of any more slave states, and additional compromises with the South. Defiantly the Whigs warned that "for the future the South must take care of itself—take care of its peculiar property; supply its own bloodhounds and doughfaces; the freemen of the North design to and will crush out the breeds." In a final gesture to win over the Free-Soilers, they added: "That in view of the dangers of the crisis—a crisis overriding all former party distinctions—we hereby pledge ourselves in the camp of Freedom—we inscribe Free Men to Free Labor and Free Lands upon our banner, and enlist for the whole war." In addition to adopting this familiar pledge which the Free-Soil Democrats had reaffirmed at a state convention a few days earlier, the Whigs placed on their ticket for state assembly William E. Stevenson, a Free-Soiler whom the *Post* called a "well-known abolitionist." White lauded this nomination as proof that the Whigs would make concessions to draw Free-Soil support and reiterated that political antecedents would not matter in the new anti-Nebraska party. When the address of the Whig state central committee in July dropped other issues, denounced the Nebraska Act, and called for an assertion of Northern rights against the South, White called it a "platform broad enough to secure the cooperation of every Anti-Slavery man in the State." By the time of the election the Free-Soil party agreed to support both the local and state Whig tickets, and in effect, an anti-Nebraska party had been formed under the Whig name.

But when the Whigs dropped their anti-Catholic appeal, another movement emerged which stressed it. It is not exactly certain when the Know-Nothing order, a secret organization dedicated to the proscription of foreigners and Catholics from public office, was first formed in Pittsburgh, but newspapers first referred to its existence around the beginning of July. Although the order had political goals, it was organized initially in fraternal lodges whose membership was drawn from all the old political parties. Gradually, however, the order evolved into a political organization as its members were sworn by oath to support the candidates selected by the lodges. It must be emphasized at this point that the new Know-Nothing order was a separate and distinct entity from the Native American party which had existed since the late 1840's, had far fewer supporters than the Know-Nothings, and was open in its organization. Throughout the 1850's this Native American party maintained its open existence and held open conventions, while the larger Know-Nothing order chose its candidates secretly. For a variety of reasons this new political order rivaled the Whig party for the anti-Democratic vote.

For one thing, many native-born citizens who had voted Whig were genuinely outraged at Catholics and immigrants. Not only Catholic aggressions but certain evils attributed to immigrants aroused native-born Protestants in these years. Immigrants filled the poorhouse, huckstered illegally in the city's marketplace, drank on Sundays, and increased the crime rate, cried editors in Pittsburgh. To escape the seemingly pernicious impact of aliens, the wealthy native-born citizens who could afford to moved away from their old strongholds, the first, second, and fourth wards, and were replaced by Germans. Newspapers commented that because of the much improved means of transportation offered by the plank roads and passenger railroads the men of means moved to country homes to escape the crowded city.

Because the actual increase in the numbers of immigrants in Pittsburgh between 1850 and 1860 was so small, the virulent nativism which appeared in 1853 and 1854 probably resulted from anger at the increasing political participation by the foreign-born and Catholics. Forbidden to vote until the five-year naturalization period expired, many Germans and Irishmen who had come over in the late 1840's were beginning to vote in the early and mid-1850's. J. Heron Foster, an admitted Know-Nothing, later declared that resentment of the political power of foreigners and Catholics, and especially of the courting of the foreign-born vote by both old parties, had been a primary motive for starting the movement. Because the Know-Nothings were dedicated to the proscription of

Catholics and immigrants from political office and demanded a total repeal of naturalization laws or the extension of the period to twenty-one years, they seemed a more likely vehicle than the Whigs to redress the grievances of native-born Americans.

Another reason why men joined the Know-Nothings was to clean up politics. Not only bloc voting by immigrants but the corruption of the ward primary meetings and of the county nominating conventions by party bosses angered many citizens. Foster wrote in 1855:

> One great reason the American orders swelled so rapidly in numbers was the profound disgust every right-thinking man entertained for the corrupt manner in which the machinery of the party had been perverted to suit the base purpose of party wireworkers—an evil they honestly believed the orders would remedy.

A correspondent wrote Simon Cameron that the Democrat J. K. Moorhead defected to the Know-Nothings because of disgust "with the trickery and rascality of the old parties." In brief, many complained that ward primary meetings were infiltrated by outsiders and that county conventions were dominated by professional politicians who often chose candidates distasteful to the party's voters.

Through secrecy and a direct primary system the Know-Nothings hoped to correct these faults. They kept a tight discipline on party membership through oaths and then had direct primaries in the wards in which every member of the order handed in a ballot with his choices for all the nominations on the county ticket. An executive committee then named as the ticket the men who had received the most votes for the respective offices.

In 1854 the movement was new, and it secretly selected its slate of candidates from the tickets of the three existing parties—Whig, Democratic, and Native American. Secrecy was so tight that the *Gazette*, which knew of the arrangement, was far wide of the mark in its predictions of the number of Democrats and

Native Americans the Know-Nothings would support. In 1855 the party held secret primaries before the mayoral and county elections, but announced the tickets publicly before the elections.

The very newness of the Know-Nothings combined with their expression of nativist hostilities and desire for political reform to make the party an attractive alternative for Whigs and Democrats. Many Whigs who opposed slavery may have preferred the American party to their altered organization because the Whigs were clearly dead as a national party while the Know-Nothings appeared on the rise. This growing strength became especially apparent after the Know-Nothing victories in 1854 in Massachusetts, Pennsylvania, and New York. Moreover, to many Whigs, Know-Nothingism probably seemed a better way to rally antislavery sentiment against the Democrats than the Whig anti-Nebraska coalition. By joining the Know-Nothings, native-born citizens could express simultaneously their nativist antipathies, their desire for political reform, and their free-soil hostility to the South. The new Whig party was less attractive because it campaigned after June on the slavery issue alone. To Democrats who wanted to leave their party for any reason, the Know-Nothings as a new and amorphous party were more appealing than an anti-Nebraska coalition controlled by their old foes—the Whigs.

White of the *Gazette* recognized the appeal of this new order to native Americans who had previously voted Whig, and he considered it a great threat to the incipient anti-Nebraska coalition he had struggled for. An old Antimason who could not tolerate secret organizations of any kind, he repeatedly denounced the stealthy methods of Know-Nothings as "unwise, dangerous, and Anti-American," so akin to the tyranny of popery that American Protestants should resist the movement. He complained that by exploiting the nativist issue, the Know-Nothings were preventing the anti-Nebraska sentiment of the North from uniting behind one party. In October, immediately before the election, he begged Whigs not to go along with Know-Nothing schemes which might send pro-Nebraska, proslavery Democrats to the state legislature. White greatly exaggerated the number of Democrats with Know-Nothing backing, but two of the three Democrats whom the Know-Nothings did support in October had endorsed the Nebraska Act. . . .

The vast bulk of Know-Nothing voters by 1855 were probably former Whigs, since most native-born Protestants had voted for that party. A former Democrat in the order complained to Simon Cameron, who joined the Know-Nothings in 1854,

> It requires the most indomitable energy to overcome the deeprooted Whig *prejudices* that still exist in this county *notwithstanding* the change which has occurred through the influence of the new organization. There are nearly 8000 order men in this *county*, but the bloated visage of Whiggery still peers from under the cloak of Americanism.

An examination of the Know-Nothing leadership confirms this Whig predominance and casts light on the type of men who joined the movement. Identifying Know-Nothings is difficult since membership was secret, but from published lists of candidates in 1855 and 1856 and of delegates to the open conventions of the American party, most of whom belonged to the secret order as well, and from letters to Cameron, a list of 143 Know-Nothing leaders could be constructed. The former political affiliation of 64 of these was determined; 39 (61%) were former Whigs, while 20 (31%) had been Democrats, four were members of the old Native American party, and one had been a Free-Soiler. In order not to appear a mere continuation of the Whig party and frighten off Democrats, however, the Know-Nothings chose their slates of candidates equally from the old parties. The Know-Nothing county ticket in 1855, for example, was evenly divided between seven Whigs and six Democrats, with one Free-Soiler holding the balance. Of the men whose ages were determined, over half were younger than thirty-five in 1855. Sixty per cent owned property valued at less than $5,000.[1] Thus Know-Nothing leaders were young men who generally came from the middle or lower classes. Like the Whig voters who joined the order, Know-Nothing chieftains who had been Whigs were not as wealthy as the old patrician Whig elite. To be sure, there were eight Know-Nothing leaders who owned property worth more than $25,000, but five of these had been Democrats; the former Whigs were unusually poor for political leaders.

Nor had the leaders often been in positions of control in their former parties. Opposition newspapers characterized the American leaders as "broken-down politicians and persistent office-hunters." This name-calling is perhaps too hostile, but the outs of both the Whigs and the Democrats who desired to improve their lot did turn to the Know-Nothings, not to the anti-Nebraska coalition. C. O. Loomis, once called the leader of the Young Whig faction, joined the movement. Both of the Native Americans elected to the state assembly by the Know-Nothings in 1854 and nominated to the American ticket again in 1855, C. S. Eyster and D. L. Smith, were former Whigs who had tried unsuccessfully for nominations in their party in 1853 and 1854. The nomi-

1. The figures on age, occupation, and property holdings of these men were taken from the manuscript censuses of both 1850 and 1860. The distribution among categories of age, occupation, and property holdings were:

Age in 1855		*Wealth*		*Occupation*	
21–25	2 (3.5%)	$25,000+	8 (15%)	Iron & Glass Manufacturers	5 (7%)
26–30	9 (16 %)	$10,000–24,999	5 (10%)	Other Manufacturers	8 (11%)
31–35	19 (33 %)				
36–40	7 (12 %)	$5,000–9,999	8 (15%)	Merchants	6 (9%)
41–45	2 (3.5%)	$1,000–4,999	16 (30%)	Brokers & Gentlemen	3 (4%)
46–50	10 (18 %)	$100–999	7 (13%)	Professional	15 (21%)
51–55	6 (10.5%)	$1–99	1	Clerks & Shopkeepers	17 (24%)
56–60	1	None	8 (15%)	Artisans	16 (23%)
60 plus	1			Unskilled Laborers	1

nee for state senator on the 1855 American ticket, Francis C. Flanegin, had been an office-seeker and former officeholder in the Whig party, and Ephraim Jones, the Know-Nothing candidate for sheriff, had sought that nomination in the Whig party for nine years.

The Democrats who bolted also had grievances against their party. Simon Cameron, the unsuccessful foe of James Buchanan for control of the Democratic state organization, sprang into the Know-Nothing ranks when he realized that his chances for high office were negligible in the Pennsylvania Democracy, and when his correspondents told him that everyone connected with Douglas's act would fall. James K. Moorhead and William M. Edgar, prominent anti-Buchanan Democrats in Pittsburgh, joined the new movement shortly after the fall elections of 1854. Other Pittsburgh Democrats among Know-Nothing candidates for the state assembly or the city councils such as John M. Kirkpatrick, Samuel Morrow, William Ward, and George L. McCook had also clashed unsuccessfully with the dominant Buchanan–Bigler wing of the party.

Whether they fled the Democratic party because of anti-Nebraska fervor, disgust with the influence of Catholics within the party, dissatisfaction with Bigler's patronage policies, or impatience with the power and exclusiveness of the "in" Bigler–Buchanan clique, these dissenters went into the Know-Nothing party. New and leaderless, it was more attractive to old Democrats than an antislavery party already headed by the established Whig leadership. Once in it, they could adopt the Whig principles of the majority of Know-Nothings. Early in 1855, the new Assemblyman Kirkpatrick addressed ten questions to Simon Cameron, the leading candidate for the United States Senator to be chosen that year, in order to learn his position on various issues. The first six dealt with opposition to slavery extension and the Fugitive Slave Act. Three others concerned a protective tariff and rivers and harbors improvements; only the last took up a repeal or extension of the naturalization laws. That the former Democrat Kirkpatrick tried to get Cameron's endorsement of these essentially Whig positions on slavery and economic issues is very significant. One of the major functions of the Know-Nothing party in Pittsburgh was to allow Democratic politicians, long saddled with the unpopular stands of their party on national issues, to swing over to the more popular Whig positions once they had bolted the Democratic ranks. Because it also offered a chance for Democratic politicians to lead, the Know-Nothing party, not the anti-Nebraska coalition, was the halfway house through which Democrats passed on their journey into the Republican party. . . .

The Democrats tried desperately to hold together the anti-Know-Nothing coalition of January, and, as they had done in 1854, they concentrated on winning the votes of those groups most alienated by the order. After the formal attempt to prolong the Fusion party failed, the Democratic county executive committee adopted a resolution pledging that its members were not and never had been members of secret political societies, although some on that committee complained that it would proscribe foreigners who had been Muscovies or had belonged to the Protestant Association. The Democratic state platform denounced the Know-Nothing party by name and insisted that citizens should not be discriminated against because of place of birth or religion. Obviously these planks were aimed at immigrants and Catholics. Less clearly, but equally important, by establishing their anti-Know-Nothing pedigree, the Democrats, like the Republicans, courted the Antimasonic Whigs. Because of the secrecy and ineffectiveness of the Know-Nothings in the legislature, boasted the *Post,* staunch old-line Whigs as well as Democrats, old and young, were out campaigning to rid the city of the Know-Nothing plague.

The election results bore out the editor's confidence. The Democrats carried their entire ticket over the Know-Nothings, and the hapless Republicans, despite White's calls to Armageddon to battle against the advance of slavery in Kansas, received only a small fraction of the vote. If one assumes that the separate Native American vote came from men who voted Know-Nothing in January, then about 330 Know-Nothings joined the Republicans, and about 300 antislavery Whigs left the Fusion ranks for the new party. Many who voted Republican were evidently Antimasonic Whigs who could not accept coalition with either Democrats or Know-Nothings. In any case, the failure of the Republicans to draw enough votes away from the Know-Nothings brought their defeat.

Explanations for the Know-Nothing loss varied, but all agreed that the result revealed a disgust with the Americans rather than any particular preference for Democratic principles. Both the *Gazette* and the *Post* maintained that many Whigs joined the Democrats to overthrow the Know-Nothings. If one assumes that three hundred former Whigs left the Fusion party between January and October, about six hundred former Whigs and foreign-born Protestants remained with the Democrats. An anti-Know-Nothing coalition had been continued in fact, if not in name. Contrary to predictions, the antislavery sentiment could not keep Whigs and Democrats from acting together when a local issue, the presence of the Know-Nothings, seemed more vital and relevant to them than the crisis in Kansas.

Indeed, the voting followed the same patterns as in January when there had been an open effort to demolish the order. Native-born Protestants again tended to vote for the Know-Nothings while Germans and Irishmen, indeed, most immigrants, apparently voted against them. Even though the Know-Nothings adopted Whig economic positions, they failed to win the unified support of the wealthy businessmen who formerly voted for the Whigs. On the other hand, the other native Americans in the community who lacked the wealth to give them social status superior to the immigrant Catholics continued to vote Know-Nothing.[2] The *Post* pointed out that while many Know-Nothings

2. It seems reasonable to conclude that the poorer a native American was, the more likely he was to vote Know-Nothing to express his resentment against the economic and social competition of Catholic immigrants. On the other hand, it is difficult to believe that Irish and German Catholics among the

were more antislavery than nativist, many others, while opposing slavery extension, had "joined the new party for other purposes" and would not join an "abolitionist Republican party" which did not aim at those purposes—i.e. proscription of Catholics and immigrants. In short, the Americans continued to win a nativist, anti-Catholic vote which the single-purpose Republican party could not capture.

Thus the voting in 1855 turned on one's opinion of the Know-Nothings. Commenting on the election a year later, a Democrat testified that German and Irish Protestants voted with their Catholic countrymen against the nativist order. Right after the election, another Democrat wrote Bigler that "the result here is mainly owing to the strong foreign vote, to the Catholic vote, to the liquor movement, and to the fact that a Republican ticket was in the field. It needed all these elements to break down the power of the opposition in this country." Devoted to opposing slavery alone and hostile to the secrecy of the Know-Nothings, the Republican party was swamped in an election for canal commissioner and local offices where slavery was an irrelevant issue. To note this fact is not to say that many in the ranks of all parties were not opposed to the extension of slavery, but to argue that because other issues were important to people at this time in this election, a party based on that issue alone could not succeed. Once again, local issues and differences prevented the re-establishment of the old nativist and anti-Southern Whig majority of 1848 and 1852.

The Americans, however, were not destroyed, and they captured the mayor's office in the election of 1856. The anti-Know-Nothing coalition split when many Democrats refused to support Volz again and supported a separate Democrat. The anti-Know-Nothings, though, had majorities in both councils. Significantly, the Republican party, aborted after the defeat of 1855, did not even enter a candidate. Russell Errett, the other editor

poorest group voted for the Know-Nothings. This paradox is explained in part by the fact that the group owning $100–$999 tended to be immigrant while the poorest group tended to be native American.

of the *Gazette,* dismally reported to Salmon P. Chase after that defeat about Republican chances: "The short and long of the matter is that, as things are now, I have no hope of Pennsylvania. I cannot see how all parties can cooperate here without a sacrifice of principle or loss of votes sufficient to insure defeat." At the beginning of 1856, the Pennsylvania Republicans had not found a formula for successful organization. The Know-Nothings had undermined the initial attempts to form an anti-Nebraska Republican party just as they had ruined the last efforts to rally the Whig party on that issue in 1854.

Before 1853 the Whigs in Pittsburgh had flourished on a combination of nativism and an antislavery, anti-Southern sentiment which was strengthened by the Antimasonic tradition. When the local Whig party began to collapse at the time of the passage of the Kansas-Nebraska Act, new parties appeared which drove apart the elements that had joined in the Whig party. At first it appeared that the Whigs would be rejuvenated as an anti-Nebraska party. Then the secret Know-Nothing order arose in response to a very real hostility to Catholics and immigrants. To many Whigs who were convinced their old party was dead, this nativist order seemed the best way to oppose the Democracy and to achieve political reform. It also attracted those native-born and, at first, foreign-born Protestants whose hatred of Catholics determined how they voted. For many former Antimasons among the Whigs, however, the methods of the Know-Nothings were obnoxious. At first, they remained in the transformed Whig party; then they joined a Fusion party with the Democrats solely in order to defeat the Americans. In the fall of 1855 they followed divided counsels. Many sincere antislavery men joined the new Republican party which tried to preserve Antimasonic principles by condemning secret political action. Others, however, remained with the Democrats in an anti-Know-Nothing coalition, for to them the menace of secret proscriptive orders seemed more real than the threat of slavery expansion in Kansas. If any one factor destroyed the Whig party in Pittsburgh, it was not the Kansas–Nebraska Act, which actually strengthened Whigs there. It was the strength and form of organized anti-Catholic sentiment.

While the Whig party was shattering, a combination of grievances coincided with the Kansas–Nebraska Act to destroy party loyalty among Democrats. Party regulars disliked Bigler's patronage policies or the influence of Catholics within the party. Moreover, out politicians had reached the limit of their patience with the control of the in Buchanan–Bigler faction. Just at the moment when public wrath boiled over at the Nebraska Act, these disgruntled elements bolted from the party. Particularly important in their decision to switch allegiance was the availability of the American party, into which most of them went. It provided a much greater opportunity for advancement than did the anti-Nebraska coalition, led by old Whig chiefs.

By the beginning of 1856 political alignments remained confused. The Democrats had gained strength from Whigs and foreign Protestants who detested Know-Nothings. The Know-Nothings had won a large part of the Whig coalition, but their methods alienated a vital portion of it, and they could not muster a majority. The incipient Republican party had failed to rally all the anti-Nebraska voters, for it defied rather than wooed Know-Nothings and did not attract the poorer and middle-class Protestant native-born Americans who wanted to express their hostility to immigrant Catholics emphatically when they voted. As a Pittsburgh Know-Nothing wrote to Simon Cameron, the way to succeed in Pennsylvania was to drop secrecy and "step on two planks of a new platform and carry the state with a rush—viz. Americanism and antislavery." [3] In January 1856 no party had yet followed this advice.

3. I disagree with Ray Billington's contention. (*The Protestant Crusade*, p. 262) that Americans sublimated their hatred of Catholics and foreigners in the latter part of 1854 to sectional stands on the slavery issue. Not only did the Know-Nothing party continue through 1855 and into 1856 in Pittsburgh, but the religious and ethnic tensions reflected in its rise continued to influence voting behavior long after the party merged with the Republicans. The Republican party in 1856 was just as much a vehicle for anti-Catholic sentiment as it was for antislavery sentiment.

The Labor of Free Men

Free Labor, Slavery, and the Republican Ideology

by Eric Foner

A specter had been haunting the American Republic ever since its inception, the specter of sectional politics. The successes of the first two American party systems—limited and short-lived though they were—depended in large measure on the suppression of the sectional irritant and its most obvious manifestation: the debate over slavery. When this proved impossible, and the North grew in population and developed its resources at rates far exceeding the Southern experience, it was but a matter of time before an assertive Northern party would appear to compete for national political power. The rise of the Republican party fulfilled that prophecy. The new grouping, unlike its national predecessors, was a sectional party, its strength confined exclusively to the North. And the Democratic party, though it survived in the North, became a political captive of Southern demands.

Southern nationalists and Northern antislavery men agreed that fundamental sectional differences existed. Republicans tended to look upon the South in some ways as a foreign country, whose institutions and attitudes clashed with those they regarded as truly American. The South, Republicans charged, was an undemocratic, hierarchical society dominated by a coterie of near-

sighted planters; a society based on slavery which must remain hopelessly inefficient and economically backward, a drag on the nation as a whole. In contrast, the free North accepted Europe's restless millions, attracted by unmatched opportunity for self-improvement. Northerners honored free labor and rewarded it, whereas Southerners associated physical toil with slavery and degradation.

Northern fear that Southern expansion would force white labor to compete with slave labor, and that the spread of slavery in the West would deprive white Americans of their birthright, gave Republicans a powerful issue that appealed to millions who would never have joined a purely antislavery movement. Nonetheless, dynamic leadership for the party also came from such radical Republicans as Senator Charles Sumner of Massachusetts and Senator Salmon P. Chase of Ohio, men who thought slavery would crumble within the South itself if it were not allowed to expand, and other men who sought full equality for the black men. Nevertheless, many more Republican moderates, like Abraham Lincoln, saw the evil in slavery yet would accept its continuation in the South; moreover, these moderates did not espouse racial equality. Such basic differences laid the foundation for the Republican party's flip-flop course during postwar Reconstruction on the race question.

Republican ideology thus mixed white racism with white idealism, and then joined the two with a commitment to block further expansion of slavery. That commitment remained non-negotiable, however, and gave the party its backbone in the 1850's, as the analysis by Eric Foner clearly demonstrates.

On May 26, 1860, one of the Republican party's leading orators, Carl Schurz of Wisconsin, addressed a Milwaukee audience which had gathered to endorse the nomination of Abraham Lincoln. "The Republicans," Schurz declared, "stand before the country, not only as the antislavery party, but emphatically as the party of free labor." Two weeks later, Richard Yates, the gubernatorial candidate in Illinois, spoke at a similar rally in Springfield. "The great idea and basis of the Republican party, as I understand it," he proclaimed, "is free labor. . . . To make labor honorable is the object and aim of the Republican party." Such statements, which were reiterated countless times by Republican orators in the 1850's, were more than mere election-year appeals for the votes of laboring men. For the concept of "free labor" lay at the heart of the Republican ideology, and expressed a coherent social outlook, a model of the good society. Political antislavery was not merely a negative doctrine, an attack on southern slavery and the society built upon it, it was an affirmation of the superiority of the social system of the North—a dynamic, expanding capitalist society, whose achievements and destiny were almost wholly the result of the dignity and opportunities which it offered the average laboring man.

The dignity of labor was a constant theme of ante-bellum northern culture and politics. Tocqueville noted that in America, "not only work itself, but work specifically to gain money," was considered honorable, and twenty years later, the New York editor Horace Greeley took note of "the usual Fourth-of-July declamation in behalf of the dignity of labor, the nobleness of labor." It was a common idea in both economic treatises and political pronouncements that labor was the source of all value. Lincoln declared in 1859 that "Labor is prior to, and independent of capital . . . in fact, capital is the fruit of labor," and the New York *Tribune* observed that "nothing is more common" than this "style of assertion." Republican orators insisted that labor could take the credit for the North's rapid economic development. Said William Evarts in 1856, "Labor, gentlemen, we of the free States acknowledge to be the source of all our wealth, of all our progress, of all our dignity and value." In a party which saw divisions on political and economic matters between radicals and conservatives, between former Whigs and former Democrats, the glorification of labor provided a much-needed theme of unity. Representatives of all these segments included paeans to free labor in their speeches; even the crusty old conservative Tom Corwin delivered "a eulogy on labor and laboring men" in an 1858 speech.

Belief in the dignity of labor was not, of course, confined to the Republican party or to the antebellum years; it has been part of American culture from the very beginning. In large part, it can be traced to the fact that most Americans came from a Protestant background, in which the nobility of labor was an article of faith. One does not need to accept in its entirety Max Weber's association of the "Protestant ethic" with the rise of capitalism in Europe to believe that there is much validity in Weber's insight that the concept of "calling" provided the psychological underpinning for capitalist values. Weber pointed out that in Calvinist theology each man had an occupation or calling to which he was divinely appointed. To achieve success in this calling would serve the glory of God, and also provide visible evidence that an individual was among the few predestined to enter heaven. The pursuit of wealth thus became a way of serving God on earth, and labor, which had been imposed on fallen man as a curse, was transmuted into a religious value, a Christian duty. And the moral qualities which would ensure success in one's calling—honesty, frugality, diligence, punctuality, and sobriety—became religious obligations. Weber described the Protestant outlook on life as "worldly asceticism," since idleness, waste of time, and conspicuous display or expenditure for personal enjoyment were incompatible with its basic values.

There was more to the Republican idea of free labor, however, than the essentials of the Protestant ethic, to which, presumably, the South had also been exposed, for the relation of that ethic to the idea of social mobility was highly ambiguous. On the one hand, the drive to work zealously in one's calling, the capital accumulation which resulted from frugality, and the stress on economic success as a sign of divine approval, all implied that men would work for an achievement of wealth and advancement in their chosen professions. But if one's calling were divinely ordained, the implication might be that a man should be content with the same occupation for his entire life, although he should strive to grow rich in it. In a static economy, therefore, the concept of "a calling" may be associated with the idea of an hierarchical social order, with more or less fixed classes. But Republicans rejected this image of society. Their outlook was grounded in the Protestant ethic, but in its emphasis on social mobility and economic growth, it reflected an adaptation of that ethic to the dynamic, expansive, capitalist society of the antebellum North.

Contemporaries and historians agree that the average American of the antebellum years was driven by an inordinate desire to improve his condition in life, and by boundless confidence that he could do so. Economic success was the standard by which men judged their social importance, and many observers were struck by the concentration on work, with the aim of material advancement, which characterized Americans. Tocqueville made the following observation during Jackson's presidency: "The first thing that strikes one in the United States is the innumerable crowd of those striving to escape from their original social condition." On the eve of the Civil War, the Cincinnati *Gazette* reported that things had not changed. "Of all the multitude of young men engaged in various employments of this city," it declared, "there is probably not one who does not desire, and even confidently expect, to become rich, and that at an early day." The universal desire for social advancement gave American life an aspect of almost frenetic motion and activity, as men moved from place to place, and occupation to occupation in search of wealth. Even ministers, reported the Cincinnati *Gazette*, "resign the most interesting fields of labor to get higher salaries." The competitive character of northern society was aptly summed up by Lincoln, when he spoke of the "race of life" in the 1850's.

The foremost example of the quest for a better life was the steady stream of settlers who abandoned eastern homes to seek their fortunes in the West. The westward movement reached new heights in the mid-1850's, and it was not primarily the poor who migrated westward, but middle class "business-like farmers," who sold their farms to migrate, or who left the eastern farms of their fathers. "These emigrants," said a leading Republican newspaper of Ohio, "are not needy adventurers, fleeing from the pinchings of penury. They are substantial farmers." Those without means who came to the West were interested in obtaining their own farms as quickly as possible, because to the American of the nineteenth century land was not the bucolic ideal of the pre-capitalist world, but another means for economic advancement. Tocqueville noted that the small farmer of the West was really a landed businessman, an entrepreneur who was prepared to sell his farm and move on, if he could get a good price. What Horace Greeley called "the nomadic tendency" of Americans contributed to the rapid expansion of the western frontier. "The men who are building up the villages of last year's origin on the incipient Railroads of Iowa," said the New York editor, "were last year doing the like in Illinois, and three years since in Ohio." The acquisitive instincts of western settlers were described by Kinsley Bingham, the first Republican governor of Michigan: "Like most new States, ours has been settled by an active, energetic and enterprising class of men, who are desirous of accumulating property rapidly."

The Republican idea of free labor was a product of this expanding, enterprising, competitive society. It is important to recognize that in antebellum America, the word "labor" had a meaning far broader than its modern one. Andrew Jackson, for example, defined as "the producing classes" all those whose work was directly involved in the production of goods—farmers, planters, laborers, mechanics, and small businessmen. Only those who profited from the work of others, or whose occupations were largely financial or promotional, such as speculators, bankers, and lawyers, were excluded from this definition. Daniel Webster took a similarly all-embracing view. In his famous speech of March 7,

1850, Webster asked, "Why, who are the laboring people of the North? They are the whole North. They are the people who till their own farms with their own hands; freeholders, educated men, independent men." And the Republican definition, as it emerged in the 1850's, proved equally broad. Some Republicans did exclude commercial enterprise from their idea of labor—the Springfield *Republican*, for example, suggested that three-quarters of the traders in the country should go into some field of "productive labor." In general, however, Republicans would agree with Horace Greeley that labor included "useful doing in any capacity or vocation." They thus drew no distinction between a "laboring class" and what we could call the middle class. With Webster, they considered the farmer, the small businessman, and the independent craftsmen, all as "laborers."

If the Republicans saw "labor" as substantially different from the modern-day notion of the "working class," it was partly because the line between capitalist and worker was to a large extent blurred in the antebellum northern economy, which centered on the independent farm and small shop. Moreover, for the Republicans, social mobility was an essential part of northern society. The antebellum Republicans praised the virtues of the enterprising life, and viewed social mobility as the glory of northern society. "Our paupers to-day, thanks to free labor, are our yeomen and merchants of tomorrow," said the New York *Times*. Lincoln asserted in 1859 that "advancement, improvement in condition—is the order of things in a society of equals," and he denounced southern insinuations that northern wage earners were "fatally fixed in that condition for life." The opportunity for social advancement, in the Republican view, was what set Americans apart from their European forebears. As one Iowa Republican put it:

> What is it that makes the great mass of American citizens so much more enterprising and intelligent than the laboring classes in Europe? It is the stimulant held out to them by the character of our institutions.

The door is thrown open to all, and even the poorest and humblest in the land, may, by industry and application, attain a position which will entitle him to the respect and confidence of his fellow-men.

Many Republican leaders bore witness in their own careers to how far men could rise from humble beginnings. Lincoln's own experience, of course, was the classic example, and during the 1860 campaign Republican orators repeatedly referred to him as "the child of labor," who had proved how "honest industry and toil" were rewarded in the North. Other Republican leaders like the former indentured servant Henry Wilson, the "bobbin boy" Nathaniel P. Banks, and the ex-laborer Hannibal Hamlin also made much of their modest beginnings in campaign speeches.

In the free labor outlook, the objective of social mobility was not great wealth, but the middle-class goal of economic independence. For Republicans, "free labor" meant labor with economic choices, with the opportunity to quit the wage earning class. A man who remained all his life dependent on wages for his livelihood appeared almost as unfree as the southern slave. There was nothing wrong, of course, with working for wages for a time, if the aim were to acquire enough money to start one's own farm or business. Zachariah Chandler described in the Senate the cycle of labor which he felt characterized northern society: "A young man goes out to service—to labor, if you please to call it so—for compensation until he acquires money enough to buy a farm . . . and soon he becomes himself the employer of labor." Similarly, a correspondent of the New York *Tribune* wrote in 1854, "Do you say to me, hire some of the thousands and thousands of emigrants coming to the West. Sir, I cannot do it. They come West to labor for themselves, not for me; and instead of laboring for others, they want others to labor for them." The aspirations of the free labor ideology were thus thoroughly middle-class, for the successful laborer was one who achieved self-employment, and owned his own capital—a business, farm, or shop.

The key figure in the Republicans' social outlook was thus the small independent entrepreneur. "Under every form of government having the benefits of civilization," said Congressman Timothy Jenkins of New York, "there is a middle class, neither rich nor poor, in which is concentrated the chief enterprise of the country." Charles Francis Adams agreed that the "middling class . . . equally far removed from the temptations of great wealth and of extreme destitution," provided the surest defense of democratic principles. In a nation as heavily agricultural as the antebellum United States, it is not surprising that the yeoman received the greatest praise. "The middling classes who own the soil, and work it with their own hands," declared Thaddeus Stevens, "are the main support of every free government." But the exponents of the development of manufactures also looked to the small capitalist, not the very wealthy, as the agents of economic progress. "The manufacturing industry of this country," said Representative Samuel Blair of Pennsylvania, "must look to men of moderate means for its development—the men of enterprise being, as a class, in such circumstances." In their glorification of the middle class and of economic independence, the Republicans were accurately reflecting the aspirations of northern society. As Carl Schurz later recalled of his first impressions of the United States, "I saw what I might call the middle-class culture in process of formation. . . ."

"Of the American Civil War," James Ford Rhodes wrote over a half a century ago, "it may safely be asserted that there was a single cause, slavery." In this opinion, Rhodes was merely echoing a view which seemed self-evident to Abraham Lincoln and many other participants in the sectional conflict. Their interpretation implicitly assumes that the antebellum Republican party was primarily a vehicle for antislavery sentiment. Yet partly because historians are skeptical of explanations made by participants of their own behavior, Rhodes's view quickly fell under attack. Even bebefore Rhodes wrote, John R. Commons had characterized the Republicans as primarily a homestead party, and Charles and Mary Beard later added the tariff as one of its fundamental concerns. More recently, historians have stressed aversion to the presence of blacks—free or slave—in the western territories as the Republicans' motive for opposing the extension of slavery. Because the Republicans disavowed the intention of attacking slavery in states where it already existed by direct federal action, their antislavery declarations have been dismissed by some historians as hypocritical. And recently, a political analyst, not a professional historian, revealed how commonplace a cynical attitude toward the early Republican party has become when he wrote: "The Republican Party succeeded by soft-pedalling the issue of slavery altogether and concentrating on economic issues which would attract Northern businessmen and Western farmers."

Controversy over the proper place of antislavery in the Republican ideology is hardly new. During the 1850's, considerable debate occurred within abolitionist circles on the proper attitude toward Republicanism. In part, this was simply an extension of the traditional schism between political and non-political abolitionists, and it is not surprising that William Lloyd Garrison and his followers should have wasted little enthusiasm on the Republicans. Yet many abolitionists who had no objection on principle to political involvements considered the antislavery commitment of the Republican party insufficient to merit their support. Gerrit Smith and William Goodell, for example, who had been instrumental in organizing the Liberty party in New York State, declared that they could not support a party which recognized the constitutionality of slavery anywhere in the Union. The Republican party, Smith charged, "refuses to oppose slavery where it is, and opposes it only where it is not," and he continuously urged radicals like Chase and Giddings to take an abolitionist stance. Theodore Parker made the same criticism. When Chase declared in the Senate that the federal government would not interfere with slavery in the states, Parker wrote that while he did not object to attacking slavery one step at a time, he "would not promise *not to take other steps.*"

Yet it is important to remember that despite their criticisms of the Republican party, leading abolitionists maintained close personal relations with Republican leaders, particularly the radicals. The flow of letters between Chase and Smith, cordial even while each criticized the attitude of the other, is one example of this. Similarly, Parker kept up a correspondence with Henry Wilson, Charles Sumner, and William Seward as well as Chase. And he and Wendell Phillips, both experts at the art of political agitation, recognized the complex interrelationship between abolitionist attempts to create a public sentiment hostile to slavery, and the political antislavery espoused by Republicans. "Our agitation, you know, helps keep yours alive in the rank and file," was the way Wendell Phillips expressed it to Sumner. And Seward agreed that the abolitionists played a vital role in awakening the public conscience—"open[ing] the way where the masses can follow." For their part, abolitionists like Theodore Parker were happy to borrow statistics and arguments from the antislavery speeches of politicians.

The evidence strongly suggests that outside of Garrison's immediate circle, most abolitionists voted with the Republican party despite their wish that the party adopt a more aggressive antislavery position. Indeed, abolitionist societies experienced financial difficulties in the late 1850's, as former contributors began giving their money to the Republicans. Even Gerrit Smith, who insisted he could "never vote for any person who recognizes a law for slavery," contributed five hundred dollars to the Frémont campaign. The attitude of many abolitionists was summed up by Elizur Wright, a proponent of Smith and Goodell's brand of political antislavery who nonetheless voted for Lincoln in 1860. While Wright criticized the Republicans for their shortcomings on slavery, he acknowledged that "the greatest recommendation of the Republican Party is, that its enemies do not quite believe its disclaimers, while they do believe that [it is] sincerely opposed to slavery as far as it goes." Prophetically, he added: "Woe to the slave power under a Republican President if it strikes the first blow."

The fact that so many abolitionists, not to mention radical Republicans, supported the Republican party, is an indication that antislavery formed no small part of the Republican ideology. Recent historians have concluded, moreover, that writers like Beard greatly overestimated the importance of economic issues in the elections of 1856, 1858, and 1860. We have already seen how tentative was the Republican commitment to the tariff. As for the homestead issue, Don E. Fehrenbacher has pointed out that the Republicans carried most of the Northwest in 1856 when free land was not a political issue, and that in 1860, Douglas Democrats supported the measure as ardently as Republicans. More important, it would have been suicidal for the Republicans to have put their emphasis on economic policies, particularly the neo-Whiggism described by Beard. If one thing is evident after analyzing the various elements which made up the party, it is that antislavery was one of the few policies which united all Republican factions. For political reasons, if for no other, the Republicans were virtually obliged to make antislavery the main focus of their political appeal. Such questions as the tariff, nativism, and race were too divisive to be stressed, while the homestead issue could be advanced precisely because it was so non-controversial in the North.

Conservative Republicans and radicals, ex-Democrats and former Whigs, all agreed that slavery was the major issue of the 1850's. It was not surprising that Giddings should insist that "there is but one real issue between the Republican party and those factions that stand opposed to it. That is the question of slavery," or that Salmon P. Chase should declare that the election of 1860 had not turned on "subordinate questions of local and temporary character," but had vindicated the principle of "the restriction of slavery within State limits." But Orville H. Browning, as conservative as Giddings and Chase were radical, appraised the politics of 1860 in much the same way. "It is manifest to all," he declared, "that there is an unusual degree of political interest pervading the country—that the people, everywhere, are excited, . . . and yet, from one extremity of the Republic to the other, scarcely any other subject is mentioned, or any other question discussed . . . save the question of negro slavery. . . ." Ex-Democrats in the Republican party fully agreed. Both Francis Spinner and Preston King rejected suggestions that Democratic economic policies be engrafted onto the Republican platform, on the ground that these must await settlement until the slavery issue had been decided. As Spinner tersely put it, "Statesmen cannot make issues for the people. As live men we must take the issues as they present themselves." The potency of the slavery issue, and the way in which it subordinated or absorbed all other political questions, was noted by the anti-Lecompton Democrat from New York, Horace Clark, on the eve of the 1860 campaign:

> It is not to be controverted that the slavery agitation is not at rest. It has absorbed and destroyed our national politics. It has overrun State politics. It has even invaded our municipalities; and now, in some form or other, everywhere controls the elections of the people.

In a recent study of Civil War historiography, Roy F. Nichols observed that we still do not know whether either section had reached its own consensus on major issues by 1861. Some historians have interpreted the strong showing of Stephen A. Douglas in the free states as proof that a substantial portion of the electorate rejected the Republican brand of antislavery. Though there is some truth in this view, it is important to remember that by 1860 the Douglas Democrats shared a good many of the Republicans' attitudes toward the South. One of the most striking aspects of the Democratic debate over the Lecompton constitution was the way in which the Douglasites echoed so many of the anti-southern views which anti-Nebraska Democrats had expressed only a few years earlier. There is a supreme irony in the fact that the same methods which Douglas had used against dissident Democrats in 1854 were now turned against him and his supporters. Buchanan applied the patronage whip ruthlessly, and anti-Lecompton Democrats complained that a new, proslavery test had suddenly been imposed upon the party. And like the anti-Nebraska Democrats, who were now members of the Republican party, the Douglasites insisted that they commanded the support of most northern Democrats. Historians have tended to agree with them. Roy Nichols suggests that the enthusiasm Douglas's anti-southern stand aroused among rank and file Democrats was one reason why he refused to accept the compromise English bill to settle the Lecompton controversy, and recent students of Pennsylvania and Indiana politics agree that the vast majority of the Democracy in those states favored Douglas against the administration.

The bitterness of Douglas Democrats against the South did not abate between 1858 and 1860. They believed that the South had embarked upon a crusade to force slavery into all the territories, and protested that endorsement of such a goal would destroy the northern Democracy. "We have confided in their honor, their love of justice, their detestation of what is wrong," Henry Payne, a prominent Ohio Democrat, said of his southern colleagues in 1858, "*but we can do it no more.*" And many Republicans believed that, even if Douglas made his peace with the Democratic organization, many of his followers had acquired "a feeling against Slavery and its arrogant demands which *if cherished* will prevent their going back. . . ." A few Democrats did defect to the Republican party in 1858, 1859, and 1860, including a former chairman of the Iowa Democracy, several anti-Lecompton Congressmen, and F. P. Stanton, the former Democratic governor of Kansas. That there were not more defections largely reflected the continuation into 1860 of Douglas's contest with the administration, which increasingly took on what one historian calls "a semi-free-soil" tone. And when the 1860 Democratic national convention broke up over the South's insistence on a platform guaranteeing slavery in the territories, the bitterness of the Douglasites knew no bounds. The reporter Murat Halstead observed that he had "never heard Abolitionists talk more rancorously of the people of the South than the Douglas men here." For their part, southerners insisted they would not accept popular sovereignty since this would be as effective as the Wilmot Proviso in barring slavery from the territories.

There were, of course, many important differences between the Douglasites and Republicans. Douglas still insisted in 1860 that the slavery question was not important enough to risk the disruption of the Union, he was much more inclined to use racism as a political weapon, and, as one Republican newspaper put it, in words echoed by several recent scholars, Douglas "does not recognize the moral element in politics. . . ." Yet in their devotion to the Union and their bitter opposition to southern domination of the government, Republicans and Douglasites stood close together in 1860. There was much truth in the observation of one Republican that "the rupture between the northern and southern wing of the democracy, is permanent with the masses . . . ," and the experiences of the Douglas Democrats in the years preceding the Civil War go a long way toward explaining the unanimity of the North's response to the attack on Fort Sumter.

The attitude of the Douglasites toward the South on the eve of the Civil War partially reflected their assessment of northern opinion regarding slavery. Politicians of all parties agreed that northerners opposed slavery as an abstract principle, although they disagreed on the intensity of this sentiment. John C. Calhoun had estimated in 1847 that while only 5 per cent of northerners supported the abolitionists, more than 66 per cent viewed slavery as an evil, and were willing to oppose its extension constitutionally. Similarly, a conservative Republican declared in 1858, "There is no man [in the North] who is an advocate of slavery. There is no man from that section of the country who will go before his constituents and advocate the extension of slavery." Northern Democrats had the same perception of northern sentiments. Even the Hunkers of New York, who consistently opposed the Wilmot Proviso, refused to say "that they are not opposed to slavery." For as William L. Marcy declared in 1849, "In truth we all are."

Antislavery as an abstract feeling had long existed in the North. It had not, however, prevented abolitionists from being mobbed, nor antislavery parties from going down to defeat. Democrats and Whigs had long been able to appeal to devotion to the Union, racism, and economic issues, to neutralize antislavery as a political force. "The antislavery sentiment," Hamilton Fish explained in 1854, "is inborn, and almost universal at the North . . . but it is only as a *sentiment* that it generally pervades; it has not and cannot be inspired with the activity that even a very slight interest excites." But Fish failed to foresee the fundamental achievement of the Republican party before the Civil War: the creation and articulation of an ideology which blended personal and sectional interest with morality so perfectly that it became the most potent political force in the nation. The free labor assault upon slavery and southern society, coupled with the idea that an aggressive Slave Power was threatening the most fundamental values and interests of the free states, hammered the slavery issue home to the northern public more emphatically than an appeal to morality alone could ever have done.

To agree with Rhodes that slavery was ultimately the cause of the Civil War, therefore, is not to accept the corollary that the basis of the Republican opposition to slavery was simple moral fervor. In a speech to the Senate in 1848, John M. Niles listed a dozen different reasons for his support of the Wilmot Proviso—but only once did he mention his belief that slavery was morally repugnant. And thirteen years later, George William Curtis observed that "there is very little moral mixture in the 'Anti-Slavery' feeling of this country. A great deal is abstract philanthropy; part is hatred of slaveholders; a great part is jealousy for white labor, very little is consciousness of wrong done and the wish to right it." The Republican ideology included all these elements, and much more. Rhodes argued that northerners wished to preserve the Union as a first step toward abolition. A more accurate formulation would reverse the equation and say that many Republicans were antislavery from the conviction that slavery threatened the Union. Aside from some radicals, who occasionally flirted with disunion, most Republicans were united by the twin principles of free soil and Unionism. Cassius M. Clay even suggested that the Free-Soilers in 1851 adopt the name "Liberty and Union" party, in order to impress their essential goals upon the electorate. The New York *Times* emphasized this aspect of Republican thought in 1857: "The barbaric institution of slavery will become more and more odious to the northern people because it will become more and more plain . . . that the States which cling to Slavery thrust back the American idea, and reject the influences of the Union."

Still, Unionism, despite its importance to the mass of northerners, and obviously crucial to any explanation of the Republicans' decision to resist secession, was only one aspect of the Republican ideology. It would have been just as logical to compromise on the slavery question if the preservation of the Union were the paramount goal of Republican politics. Nor should Republicanism be seen merely as the expression of the northern drive toward political power. We have seen, to be sure, that resentment of southern power played its part, that many Democratic-Republicans had watched with growing jealousy the South's domination of the Democratic party and the national government, and that many former Whigs were convinced that the South was blocking economic programs essential for national economic development. But there is more to the coming of the Civil War than the rivalry of sections for political power. (New England, after all, could accept its own decline in political power without secession.)

In short, none of these elements can stand separately; they dissolve into one another, and the total product emerges as ideology. Resentment of southern political power, devotion to the Union, antislavery based upon the free labor argument, moral revulsion to the peculiar institution, racial prejudice, a commitment to the northern social order and its development and expansion—all these elements were intertwined in the Republican world-view. What they added up to was the conviction that North and South represented two social systems whose values, interests, and future prospects were in sharp, perhaps mortal, conflict with one another. The sense of difference, of estrangement, and of growing hostility with which Republicans viewed the South, cannot be overemphasized. Theodore Sedgwick of New York perhaps expressed it best when he declared during the secession crisis: "The policy and aims of slavery, its institutions and civilization, and the character of its people, are all at variance with the policy, aims, institutions, education, and character of the North. There is an irreconcilable difference in our interests, institutions, and pursuits; in our sentiments and feelings." Greeley's *Tribune* said the same thing more succinctly: "We are not one people. We are two peoples. We are a people for Freedom and a people for Slavery. Between the two, conflict is inevitable." An attack not simply on the institution of slavery, but upon southern society itself, was thus at the heart of the Republican mentality. Of all historians, I think Avery Craven caught this feature best: "By 1860, slavery had become the symbol and carrier of *all* sectional differences and conflicts." Here and elsewhere, Craven describes the symbolic nature of the slavery controversy, reflected as it was in the widespread acceptance among Republicans of the Slave Power idea—a metaphor for all the fears and resentments they harbored toward the South. But Craven did leave out something crucial. Slavery was not only the symbol, but also the real basis of sectional conflict, for it was the foundation of the South's economy, social structure, aspirations, and ideology.

"Why do we Meddle with Slavery?" the New York *Times* asked in an 1857 editorial. The answer gives us a penetrating insight into the Republican mind on the eve of Civil War:

> The great States of the North are not peopled exclusively by quidnuncs and agitators. . . . Nevertheless, we do give ourselves great and increasing concern about the existence of Slavery in States over whose internal economy we have no right and no wish to exercise any control whatever. Nevertheless, we do feel, and the feeling is growing deeper in the northern heart with every passing year, that our char-

acter, our prosperity, and our destiny are most seriously involved in the question of the perpetuation or extinction of slavery in those States.

What is striking about this statement is a concern directed not only against the extension of slavery, but against its very existence. Lincoln put the same concern even more succinctly to a Chicago audience in 1859, "Never forget," he said, "that we have before us this whole matter of the right or wrong of slavery in this Union, though the immediate question is as to its spreading out into new Territories and States."

Lincoln and the editors of the *Times* thus made explicit that there was more to the contest over the extension of slavery than whether the institution should spread to the West. As Don E. Fehrenbacher puts it, the territorial question was the "skirmish line of a more extensive struggle." Only by a comprehension of this total conflict between North and South, between Republican and southern ideologies, can the meaning of the territorial issue be fully grasped. Its importance went even beyond the belief shared widely in both sections that slavery required expansion to survive, and that confinement to the states where it already existed would kill it. For in each ideology was the conviction that its own social system must expand, not only to ensure its own survival but to prevent the expansion of all the evils the other represented. We have already seen how Republicans believed that free society, with its promise of social mobility for the laborer, required territorial expansion, and how this was combined with a messianic desire to spread the benefits of free society to other areas and peoples. Southerners had their own grandiose design. "They had a magnificent dream of empire," a Republican recalled after the war, and such recent writers as C. Stanley Urban and Eugene Genovese have emphasized how essential expansionism was in the southern ideology. The struggle for the West represented a contest between two expansive societies, only one of whose aspirations could prevail. The conflict was epitomized by two statements which appeared in the Philadelphia *North Amer-*

ican in 1856. Slavery, the *North American* argued, could not be allowed to expand, because it would bring upon the West "a blight whose fatal influence will be felt for centuries." Two weeks later the same paper quoted a southern journal, which, in urging slavery expansionism, used precisely this logic in reverse. Such expansion, the southern paper argued, would "forbid the extension of the evils of free society to new people and coming generations."

Here then was a basic reason why the South could not accept the verdict of 1860. In 1848, Martin Van Buren had said that the South opposed the principle of free soil because "the prohibition carries with it a reproach to the slaveholding states, and . . . submission to it would degrade them." Eight years later, the Richmond *Enquirer* explained that for the South to abandon the idea of extending slavery while accepting Republican assurances of non-interference in the states would be "pregnant with the admission that slavery is wrong, and but for the constitution should be abolished." To agree to the containment of slavery, the South would have had to abandon its whole ideology, which had come to view the institution as a positive good, the basis of an enlightened form of social organization.

Although it has not been the purpose of this study to examine in any detailed way the southern mind in 1860, what has been said about the Republican ideology does help to explain the rationale for secession. The political wars of the 1850's, centering on the issue of slavery extension, had done much to erode whatever good feeling existed between the sections. The abolitionist Elihu Burrit suggested in 1857 that a foreigner observing American politics would probably conclude "that the North and South were wholly occupied in gloating upon each others' faults and failings." During the 1856 campaign, Burrit went on, sectional antagonisms had been brought "to a pitch of rancor, never reached before" in American politics. This was precisely the reason that Union-loving conservatives like Hamilton Fish dreaded the mounting agitation. "I cannot close my eyes to the fact which all history shows," Fish wrote Thurlow Weed in 1855, "that every physical revolution (of governments) is preceded by a moral revolution. [Slavery agitation] leads to estrangement first, and next to hostility and hatred which end inevitably in separation." By the time of the secession crisis another former Whig could observe that "the people of the North and of the South have come to hate each other worse than the hatred between any two nations in the world. In a word the moral basis on which the government is founded is all destroyed."

It is thus no mystery that southerners could not seriously entertain Republican assurances that they would not attack slavery in the states. For one thing, in opposing its extension, Republicans had been logically forced to attack the institution itself. This, indeed, was one of the reasons why radicals accepted the emphasis on non-extension. "We are disposed to select this single point," Sumner explained to Chase, "because it has a peculiar practical issue at the present moment, while its discussion would, of course, raise the whole question of slavery." Frederick Douglass agreed that agitation for the Wilmot Proviso served "to keep the subject before the people—to deepen their hatred of the system—and to break up the harmony between the Northern white people and the Southern slaveholders. . . ." As we have seen, many Republicans, both radicals and moderates, explicitly stated that non-extension was simply the first step, that there would come a day when slavery would cease to exist.

As southerners viewed the Republican party's rise to power in one northern state after another, and witnessed the increasingly anti-southern tone of the northern Democrats, they could hardly be blamed for feeling apprehensive about the future. Late in 1859, after a long talk with the moderate Unionist Senator from Virginia, R. M. T. Hunter, Senator James Dixon of Connecticut reported that the Virginian was deeply worried. "What seems to alarm Hunter is the *growth* of the Anti-slavery feeling at the North." Southerners did not believe that this antislavery sentiment would be satisfied with the prohibition of slavery in the territories, although even that would be bad enough. They also feared that a Republican administration would adopt the radicals' program of indirect action against slavery. This is why continued Democratic control of Congress was not very reassuring, for executive action could implement much of the radicals' program. Slavery was notoriously weak in the states of Missouri, Maryland, and Delaware. With federal patronage, a successful emancipation movement there might well be organized. And what was more dangerous, Lincoln might successfully arouse the poor whites in other states against the slaveholders. "Cohorts of Federal officeholders, Abolitionists, may be sent into [our] midst," a southern Senator warned in January 1861; ". . . Postmasters . . . controlling the mails, and loading them down with incendiary documents," would be appointed in every town. One southern newspaper declared that "the great lever by which the abolitionists hope to extirpate slavery in the states, is the aid of the non-slaveholding citizens of the South." The reply of Republicans to these warnings was hardly reassuring. Commenting on one southern editorial, the Cincinnati *Commercial* declared that the spread of antislavery sentiment among southern poor whites was "an eventuality against which no precautions can avail." And by December 1860, Republican Congressmen were already receiving applications for office from within the slave states.

For many reasons, therefore, southerners believed that slavery would not be permanently safe under a Republican administration. Had not William H. Seward announced in 1858, "I know, and you know, that a revolution has begun. I know, and all the world knows, that revolutions never go backward." Did not Republican Congressmen openly express their conviction that "slavery must die"? The Republican policy of preventing the spread of slavery, one southerner wrote to William T. Sherman, "was but the entering wedge to overthrow it in the States."

The delegates to South Carolina's secession convention, in their address to the people of the state, explained why they had dissolved the state's connection with the Union:

> If it is right to preclude or abolish slavery in a Territory, why should it be allowed to remain in the States? . . . In spite of all disclaimers and professions, there can be but one end by the submission of the South to the rule of a sectional anti-slavery government at Washington; and that end, directly or indirectly, must be—the emancipation of the slaves of the South.

Emancipation might come in a decade, it might take fifty years. But North and South alike knew that the election of 1860 had marked a turning point in the history of slavery in the United States. To remain in the Union, the South would have had to accept the verdict of "ultimate extinction" which Lincoln and the Republicans had passed on the peculiar institution.

The decision for civil war in 1860–61 can be resolved into two questions—why did the South secede, and why did the North refuse to let the South secede? As I have indicated, I believe secession should be viewed as a total and logical response by the South to the situation which confronted it in the election of Lincoln—logical in the sense that it was the only action consistent with its ideology. In the same way, the Republicans' decision to maintain the Union was inherent in their ideology. For the integrity of the Union, important as an end in itself, was also a prerequisite to the national greatness Republicans felt the United States was destined to achieve. With his faith in progress, material growth, and the spread of both democratic institutions and American influence throughout the world, William Seward brought the Republican ideology to a kind of culmination. Although few Republicans held as coherent and far-reaching a world view as he, most accepted Lincoln's more modest view that the American nation had a special place in the world, and a responsibility to prove that democratic institutions were self-sustaining. Much of the messianic zeal which characterized political antislavery derived from this faith in the superiority of the political, social, and economic institutions of the North, and a desire to spread these to their ultimate limits.

When a leading historian says, therefore, that the Republican party in 1860 was bound together "by a common enmity rather than a common loyalty," he is, I believe, only half right. For the Republicans' enmity toward the South was intimately bound up with their loyalty to the society of small-scale capitalism which they perceived in the North. It was its identification with the aspirations of the farmers, small entrepreneurs, and craftsmen of northern society which gave the Republican ideology much of its dynamic, progressive, and optimistic quality. Yet paradoxically, at the time of its greatest success, the seeds of the later failure of that ideology were already present. Fundamental changes were at work in the social and economic structure of the North, transforming and undermining many of its free-labor assumptions. And the flawed attitude of the Republicans toward race, and the limitations of the free labor outlook in regard to the Negro, foreshadowed the mistakes and failures of the post-emancipation years.

6

Division and Forced Reunion, 1860–1877

The Southerner's Nation

The Historian's Use of Nationalism and Vice Versa

by David M. Potter

Sectional loyality (or myopia, depending on who calls the tune) was no Southern monopoly. Residents of the various sections always nourished feelings of regional consciousness and pride in their differences that dated back to colonial times. In the nineteenth century, the South became acutely aware of its sectional identity and most determined to maintain its own interests by checking the growth of national power. Despite the region's economic advances in the early nineteenth century, the South could not keep pace with the rest of the Union. In 1790 it had been the most populous region, and four of the first five Presidents came from below the Mason-Dixon line. But by 1860, Southerners felt themselves a beleaguered minority, and they were unwilling to accept the outcome of a free election in which the victorious candidate won without a single Southern electoral vote.

Southern insecurity and Southern boastfulness went hand in hand. Sensing their moral isolation, Southerners compensated by developing an elaborate myth of regional superiority. They claimed that slavery was "the greatest good of all the great blessings which a kind Providence bestowed upon our glorious region." They boasted, too, that their slave society had produced a superior breed of men—namely, themselves. Noble blood flowed in Southern veins, for Southerners claimed descent from English aristocrats, whereas Yankees allegedly came from peasant stock. Southerners *had a keen sense of moral responsibility, whereas Yankees were devoted exclusively to self and pelf. In short, the true Southerner was a gentleman, the Yankee a moneygrubber.*

Southerners created a closed and increasingly separate society, especially as they confronted attacks from antislavery elements in the North. Even religious denominations split along sectional lines (the Baptists in 1843 started the process), and in this way the South cultivated its own brand of Christianity, one which posed no immediate danger to the white man's conscience. Southerners also established their own educational institutions to resist assimilation by Northern customs and values. Many planters stopped sending their sons to New England colleges. Southern nationalism grew on the literary front as well; the Southern Quarterly Review *actively and truculently sought to foster esteem for all things Southern. Sectional pride mounted in the South in equal proportion to criticism of all things in the North.*

Most of the elements for nationalism—including the essential willingness to risk one's life for his country—were there by the late 1850's. In the selection below, David M. Potter examines first some of the historiographical and methodological problems of delving into the history of nationalism, and then he sets out to show how American historians, particularly Northerners, have been sometimes less than acute or rigorously analytical in their accounts of the birth of the Southern nation.

It is one of the basic characteristics of history that the historian is concerned with human beings but that he does not deal with them primarily as individuals, as does the psychologist or the biographer or the novelist. Instead he deals with them in groups—in religious groups, in cultural groups, in ideological groups, in interest groups, in occupational groups, or in social groups. But

From *The American Historical Review,* LXVII (July 1962), 924–50. Reprinted by permission; footnotes omitted.

most often the historian deals with people in national groups. These national groups usually coincide with a political state, but it would be too restrictive to say that the national group is simply a political group, for very often the historian is not concerned with the political aspects of the history of the group.

Just as the rise of nationalism has been the major political development of modern times, so attention to the national group, rather than to these other groupings, has become correspondingly, perhaps, the major focus of modern historians. Accordingly, the identity of people in terms of their nationality has grown to transcend all other identities, so that we speak and think constantly in terms of the American people, the Japanese people, the Russian people, and others. Our attribution of distinctive traits and attitudes, reactions and values, to these groups shows that we do not conceive of them merely in political terms as bodies who happen to be subject to a common political jurisdiction, but rather as aggregations whose common nationality imparts or reflects an integral identity. The idea that the 2,500,000,000 people of the world fall naturally into a series of national groups is one of the dominating presuppositions of our time.

Because of the constant, pervasive use of this criterion of nationality as the basis for organizing much of modern history, the concept of nationality has become a crucial one in historical thought, with many far-reaching implications. It is the purpose of this essay, therefore, to explore some of the ideas embodied in the historian's concept of nationalism, some of the unrecognized side effects which the concept, with its attendant ideas, has had, and something of the way in which it has affected the treatment of history.

Perhaps the most crucial fact in shaping the historian's use of the idea of nationalism is that he employs it in two quite distinct ways for two different purposes. On the one hand, he uses it in answering a question as to the degree of cohesiveness or group unity that has developed in a given aggregate of people. Here the question is primarily descriptive or observational, and it can be answered in qualified or relative terms, or in terms of degree, with fine distinctions and gradations. Such a question can be dealt with in terms of the psychological attitudes of the group; in fact, the prevailing theory of nationalism today emphasizes its psychological character. Thus, for example, Hans Kohn affirms that "Nationalism is first and foremost a state of mind, an act of consciousness," and, though he points out that one must also explain the surrounding conditions which produce the state of mind, he accepts as valid, though limited, the statement that a nation is "a group of individuals that feels itself one [and] is ready within limits to sacrifice the individual for the group advantage." Proponents of this psychological view recognize, of course, that a subjective group feeling, as a psychological phenomenon, is not likely to develop unless there are objective conditions which give rise to it. These conditions include such factors as the sharing of a common language, the occupation of a territorial area that constitutes a natural unit (an island, a river valley, or a mountain-girt basin), the adherence to a common religion, and a heritage of common mores and traditions. But these factors in themselves are not regarded as components of nationality. They are rather prerequisites or raw materials, conducive to the development of the psychological manifestation.

The psychological character of this approach to nationalism deserves emphasis because it carries with it certain important implications. To begin with, it would follow that since nationalism as a form of group loyalty, it is not generically different from other forms of group loyalty. From this it would follow further that nationality is not an absolute condition, but a relative one, for loyalty evolves gradually by imperceptible degrees, both in the individual and in the group; it ebbs and flows; and it is modified by contingencies. If nationalism is a relative manifestation, this fact would also imply that various national groups must vary in the degree of completeness or intensity of their nationality, and further that various elements of the population within the nationality group must vary in the extent to which they share the sense of group identity and the commitment to the group purpose. This, in turn, would mean that loyalty to the nation must exist in the individual not as a unique or exclusive allegiance, but as an attachment concurrent with older forms of group loyalty to family, to church, to school, and to the individual's native region.

All of these corollaries are accepted, explicitly, or implicitly, by most writers on nationalism. They are consonant with the theory which writers have found most tenable, and when historians are directly engaged in the specific study of the growth of nationalism, their analysis usually gives due weight to the variable, impalpable, evolutionary, and sometimes partially developed nature of the manifestations of nationalism. In this kind of context, the historian seldom loses sight of the fact that nationalism is a tendency, an impulse, an attitude of mind, rather than an objective, determinate thing.

If the historian had only to deal with the question of the extent to which a group has become national, he would probably never treat it in other terms than these, which are so consistent with his theory and so much in line with his general disposition to take a functional rather than a formalistic view of all historical phenomena.

But in a second aspect, the historian uses the concept of nationalism in answering another question that frequently arises in history, as to the validity of a given group's exercising autonomous powers. In human affairs, society has long since agreed to the proposition that when a multiplicity of individuals stand in a certain relationship to one another, or to put it more concretely, when they form a community, they incur certain obligations toward one another which they would not have if they were not a community, and that the community has a "right," or enjoys a sanction to enforce these obligations and to defend itself as a community, if necessary by the use of coercion and violence—which would otherwise be taboo. But the sanction to exercise these powers and the determination as to whom they can rightfully be exercised upon—individuals or minority groups depend entirely upon whether the body seeking to exercise them and the individuals upon whom they are to be exercised form a true community. Thus, the nature of the relationship between the individuals involved, rather than the ethical character of the acts performed, becomes the standard for judging the rightfulness of the acts. The nation occupies a particularly crucial role in this relation, for of the many kinds of human communities in which men are associated, the nation is the one to which this power of regulation, control, coercion, punitive action, and so forth, is especially assigned. Consequently, the attribution of nationalism ceases to be a merely descriptive matter and becomes an evaluative matter, for the verdict upon the act performed by the group depends upon the character of the group performing the act. To come to the crux of the matter, this determination cannot be made in terms of psychological analysis, which speaks only in relativistic, qualified, balanced terms, and does not yield yes-or-no, all-or-nothing-at-all answers. Such analysis can tell what measure of nationality a group has attained, for that is a question of degree, but it cannot necessarily tell whether the group has attained the measure of nationality appropriate to the exercise of national powers, for that is a categorical or classificatory question. The categorical nature of the problem the historian is dealing with, therefore, tends to draw him unconsciously away from his theory and to lead him to deal with nationalism in a way different from what his theory would indicate. Where his theory tells him that nationalism is a relative thing, existing in partial form, his practice may impel him to treat it as an absolute thing, existing in full or not at all. Where his theory emphasizes the view that national loyalty is a form of group loyalty, and generically similar to other forms of group loyalty, his practice impels him to treat it as a unique form of devotion potentially antithetical to other forms of loyalty such as regional loyalty. (He even uses a different word —"allegiance"—for this loyalty.) Where his theory recognizes the fact that nationalism is a form of emotion, and that, like other forms of emotion, it will attain varying degrees of intensity in varying segments of the population, his practice prompts him to treat it as a matter of standard, fixed specifications. (The citizen is either "loyal" or he is "disloyal.")

Thus, the shift from a descriptive to a classificatory approach is also a shift, in a sense, from a psychological (or functional) approach. It is a deceptively easy, and, at times almost imperceptible shift to make, because the nation is, of course, in an extremely real and important sense, an institutional thing. The impulse of nationalism fulfills itself in the formation of national institutions, and while a nation is truly a body of people who feel themselves to be one, it is also, quite as truly, the organized body of people who share this feeling, together with the organization that the feeling prompts them to set up.

But though these two concepts flow rather naturally into one another, they are, in many ways, inconsistent with and even antithetical to one another. One treats the nation as an abstraction having no physical reality: only on a political map, which is itself an abstraction, is it possible to see where one nation ends and another begins. But institutionally, the nation assumes all the concreteness which a census of population, an inventory of resources, an army and navy, and all the apparatus of public authority can give to it. In terms of a psychologically centered theory of nationalism, a nation exists only subjectively, as a focus of men's loyalties, and without these loyalties there would be no nation. But once the nation has been institutionalized, men tend to regard the institution itself as a transcendent something to which the loyalties of men ought to be given simply because it does exist. Again, in terms of theory, the nation survives as a unit because people continue to feel a psychological sense of unity. But in operative institutional terms, its survival may depend upon the power of the state to override divisive impulses and to control a collectivity of people as if they were one, even despite a significant degree of reluctance on the part of some of those who are being thus united.

In short, the institutional view does basic violence to the historian's theory, for it pulls him in the direction of treating nationality as objective rather than subjective, absolute rather than relative, and total rather than partial. It also impels him to distinguish it from and place it in antithesis to other forms of group loyalty, instead of keeping in view the fact that the psychological ingredients of nationalism are the same as for other forms of human identification with large groups. Finally, and most important, it leads him to give a valuative, rather than a purely descriptive meaning to his attribution of nationality.

The political state, as we know it today, possesses tremendously powerful devices for making the aspects of nationality which pertain to the institutional concept seem more real and more applicable than the aspects which the psychological concept would suggest. Indeed the operative importance of formalistic features such as citizenship, jurisdiction, territoriality, and so on, tend to convey an image of nationality which is conceived far more in terms of institutional structure than of psychological attitudes. And this concept is, of course, far more categorical, more absolute, more unitary in its implications, for the individual either is or is not a citizen; the public authority either does or does not have jurisdiction; the disputed area lies either inside or outside the national boundary. None of these matters are partial, any more than sovereignty is partial and sovereignty, it used to be said, is like virginity in that it cannot be surrendered in part.

The sheer weight and momentum of modern institutional nationalism make it difficult for the historian to resist the institutional concept, especially when this concept is, in certain respects, entirely valid and realistic. In his theory, he knows that there is great difference between the nation and the political state, but in a world where all the states claim to be nations and all the nations try to be states, it is difficult for him to remember that they are two things.

The impact of the institutionalized nation, therefore, must be heavy and pervasive indeed, but, to offset this weight, the historian has been to some extent placed on guard against mistaking the nation as a people for the nation as a state. Certainly most treaties on nationalism warn him against confusing nationality itself with the forms that the nationalistic impulse has projected. But what he is not on guard against is the subtle shift from describing the nationalistic impulse as a sociopsychological phenomenon to using the attribution of nationalism as a valuative device. For it is a paradox not generally recognized that the historian cannot make a simple descriptive observation about the degree of group cohesion among an aggregate of people without inadvertently registering a valuative judgment as to the validity of the powers that this aggregation may assert for itself. If he were applying a standard of ethics, it would be recognized at once as a valuative standard, but since he seemingly applies only a measure of relationships, it is easy to overlook the valuative implications. Yet the concept of the nature of the group may be more crucial than the concept of right and wrong in determining the validity of acts committed in the name of nationality. For even the Declaration of Independence did not proclaim the right of everyone to resist tyranny, but rather the right of "one people to dissolve the political bonds which have connected them with another." The separability of "one people" and "another" was a necessary prerequisite to the dissolution of the bonds.

Indeed modern democratic thought, by adopting the view that the ultimate authority lies in the people, has brought us to the point where the nature of the grouping which constitutes a people takes on almost as mystical a quality as once pertained to the nature of the anointment which a crowned king received from God. For the major premise of democracy, that the majority shall rule, is predicated upon the assumption that the majority is a part of some larger whole, whose existence as a totality is identifiable enough to give assurance that those persons who are imposing their will on the one hand, and those who are submitting to the imposition on the other, are really part of the same people and are, as one whole, bound by the will of their larger part. Unless the minority really is identified with and part of such a totality, the decisions of the majority lack any democratic sanction. Hence the question whether the controlling group and the dissident group form a real, verifiable totality is vital and decisive.

For instance, if the Magyars under Louis Kossuth were a "people," they were morally justified in their "revolution" against the old Austro-Hungarian Empire; they were "patriots"; and their uprising was a "war of independence." But if not, they were morally censurable for "rebelling"; they were "traitors"; and their uprising was an "insurrection." If the Croats who, in turn, fought against Kossuth's authority were a "people" then Kossuth was a "tyrant," and his measures against them were "acts of oppression." But if not, he was merely a resolute leader defending his "nation" against "disruptive elements" that sought to "subvert" it. There is hardly any historical situation for which semantics are more crucial.

In sum, when the historian attributes nationality to any group, he establishes a presumption in favor of any acts involving an exercise of autonomy that the group may commit; when he denies nationality, he establishes a presumption against any exercise of autonomy. The attribution of nationality therefore involves a sanction—a sanction for the exercise of autonomy or self-determination.

Of all the consequences of the shift toward an institutional concept, this insertion of the valuative or sanctioning implication has had, perhaps, the most pervasive and sweeping consequences. Indeed, the element of sanction is almost the essence of this concept. It carries with it some far-reaching implications, and these implications have had such pervasive effects upon the interpretation of history that it becomes important to examine and recognize them.

To begin with, it is fundamental that once the quality of nationality is conceived to imply rights or powers for the national group, and not merely to describe the degree of cohesiveness within the national group, the historian will begin to be influenced in his reasoning not only by his observations about the degree of cohesion, but also by his beliefs about the justice or the merits of the group's claim to autonomy. Instead of arguing forward, therefore, from the observation that the evidence indicates a high degree of psychological coherence (nationality), and that consequently the group was justified in acting as a nation, he may be tempted to argue backward, from the conviction that since the group was, in his opinion, justified in exercising national powers, it must have had, psychologically, a high degree of cohesiveness. What appears on its face to be a mere observational or descriptive statement about psychological attitudes may be in fact an indirect form of argumentation about the validity of a set of political claims.

To state this in another way, the writer who is trying to make a case, or to rationalize a position, need no longer rationalize it with legal or ethical arguments, which are the normal medium of rationalization. Instead, he is likely to rationalize it in terms of cultural psychological analysis.

Superficially, it appears that the nineteenth-century writer on nations, who used to engage freely in abstract and formalistic argumentation about "compact," "sovereignty," and the like, has been replaced in the twentieth century by a writer who takes a functional approach, tracing the gradual cultural development by which a "people" became self-consciously united, and measuring the extent of governmental power in terms of the degree of social need. But to an astonishing degree, the old formalism and the new functionalism come to the same thing. In the past, the ultimate sanction for a government was the possession of sovereignty; today its ultimate sanction is that it acts for a population which constitutes a "people" in the special sense which entitles them to self-determination. But the effect, in either case, is that a decision about something else is used to determine the justice of the exercise of autonomy.

A second implication of the valuative aspect of nationalism is that it inhibits the historian's recognition of the general similarity between nationalism and other forms of group loyalty. It does this because national loyalty, in its valuative sense, must be singular, if not indeed, exclusive and unique. This inhibition cuts off a number of useful insights. For instance, it prevents the historian from seeing that in situations where nationalism and sectionalism are both at work, they are not necessarily polar or antithetical forces, even though circumstances may cause them to work in opposition to one another. Nationalism, in fact, may be the terminal result of a full development of strong sectional forces, while sectionalism may be an emergent nationalism which has not yet matured.

At a deeper level, this inhibition may blind the historian to the fact that national loyalty, far from being opposed to other loyalties, is in fact strengthened by incorporating others. Harold Guetzkow, in discussing the creation of international loyalties, makes this point clearly: "The behaviorist leads us to believe that strong family, local, and national loyalties are helpful in building international loyalties. The analyst assures us that loyalty is attachable to various objects—an international object as well as a national object. If loyalty is a generalized way of responding, the stronger the loyalty pattern in a given individual—no matter what its object—the easier it will be to build loyalties."

Going a step beyond Guetzkow, Morton Grodzins, in his *The Loyal and the Disloyal*, argues not only that other loyalties are conducive to strong national loyalty, but even that they are indispensable to it. "Other loyalties," he says, "are . . . the most important foundation of democratic national loyalty. . . . Loyalties are to specific groups, specific goals, specific programs of action. Populations are loyal to the nation as a by-product of satisfactions achieved within nonnational groups, because the nation is believed to symbolize and sustain these groups. From this point of view, one is loyal not to nation but to family, business, religion, friends. One fights for the joys of his pinochle club when he is said to fight for his country."

Historians frequently write about national loyalty as if it were exclusive, and inconsistent with other loyalties, which are described as "competing" or "divided," and which are viewed as detracting from the primary loyalty to the nation. Yet it is a self-evident fact that national loyalty flourishes not by challenging and overpowering all other loyalties, but by subsuming them all and keeping them in a reciprocally supportive relationship to one another. The strength of the whole is not enhanced by destroying the parts, but is made up of the sum of the parts. The only citizens who are capable of strong national loyalty are those who are capable of strong group loyalty, and such people are likely to express this capacity in their devotion to their religion, their community, and their families, as well as in their love of country. The nationalism which will utilize this capacity most effectively, therefore, is not the one that overrides and destroys all other objects of loyalty, but the one that draws them all into one transcendent focus. A well-known phrase runs: "For God, for Country, and for Yale"—not "For God, or Country, or for Yale."

A third implication of the evaluative aspect of nationalism is that it sometimes impels the historian to deny nationality to groups of whom he morally disapproves, even though the group may in every sense fulfill his theoretical criteria of nationality. He does this because he can scarcely accord the sanction of nationality to a group without also seeming to accord some degree of sanction to the cause for which the group stands. Most historians, if confronted with the abstract proposition that people who practice wrong cannot be united by deep cultural commonalities, would dismiss it as absurd. Yet the functional implications of the concept of nationalism are such that historians in fact are frequently unwilling to recognize cultural commonalities of this kind in the case of groups whose values they reject.

Still a fourth warping effect which arises from the evaluative aspect of the nationality concept is the tendency to believe that nationality must be based upon peculiarly deep-seated cultural affinities among a people, since only such fundamental ties would justify the kind of power and unique autonomy usually ascribed to the national group. No trivial or unworthy grounds for association could justify a group in claiming the kind of immunity from external control and the power to abuse internal minorities which are accorded to a nation. Therefore, when the historian is faced with manifestations of nationalism, he will, almost by reflex, begin his analysis of these manifestations by searching for profound common elements in the culture of the group involved. Indeed, there is a standard formula, accepted by all the authorities on the subject, which enjoins him to give his attention to "certain objective bonds [which] delimit a social group [such as] common descent, language, territory, political entity, customs and tradition, and religion." Accordingly, students of nationalism have emphasized the growth of the vernacular languages in Western Europe; they have ransacked folklore and the popular culture for any features illustrating a common tradition among the people. Also they have often treated the territorial area that finally eventuated, no matter how fortuitously, from any nationalist movement, as the logical fulfillment of a mystic impulse among the folk to unite a "common territory." The true believer who found it an evidence of Divine providence that all our seaports have harbors evinced no greater faith than the historian who defines all the land within a given national jurisdiction as a "common territory" and then uses the concept that it is a common territory to prove the validity of the national jurisdiction.

This does not mean, of course, that the common cultural factors are not real, and are not, in many cases of immense importance. Indeed, some of the oldest and most famous nations, such as England and Japan, illustrate the historical fact that some populations, when isolated by physical, linguistic, or other barriers, may develop an extremely clear-cut cultural identity, and that such an identity is by far the most enduring and most cohesive basis of nationality.

But the very preoccupation of historians with classic examples such as these has perhaps led them to overemphasize the cultural component as the one master key to nationality, and to assume too simple an equation between nationality and culture. There is, of course, no doubt that commonalities in culture have a primary role in generating the spirit of nationalism, but secondarily there is also a reverse effect, namely that movements for political statehood, which are commonly regarded as nationalist movements, tend to claim commonalities of culture as a sanction for their objectives, and if these cultural elements do not exist in reality, the nationalist movement may fabricate them. It is notorious, for instance, that Gaelic was culturally a dying speech in Ireland, and Welsh a dying speech in Wales, and that both have received a somewhat artificial rejuvenation because of the zeal of Irish and Welsh nationalists.

It seems increasingly evident in the last quarter of a century that many "nationalist" movements have a minimum of common cultural content and that the impulse moving them is primarily a negative political reaction against an existing regime (especially a colonial regime). For instance, some of the new nations of Africa appear to have territories which, instead of coinciding with any unified culture areas of their own, correspond to the administrative divisions laid down for purposes of bureaucratic convenience by their former colonial masters. It is perhaps the final irony of European colonialism that it is likely to fix the patterns and alignments of the nationalism which replaces it and utterly repudiates it. When a new "nation" is being formed in such circumstances, it will behoove the leaders to claim for their country all the attributes that have been regarded as giving a sanction to the older and more organic nations. If that highest of all sanctions—a national culture—is lacking, the spokesmen of the "nationalism" in question will be impelled to fabricate or simulate the necessary cultural factors. Such simulation will, indeed, not be anything new, for the spokesmen of nationalism have always exaggerated the degree of separateness and coherence of the national group, even in the oldest and most fully defined nations, and these nations have always relied upon a certain amount of carefully cultivated mythology to reinforce the unity of their people. Their success in fostering a belief in a common identity has often been an essential part of the process of forging the identity itself, and the belief has operated as a kind of self-fulfilling prophecy.

But if it is to be expected that nationalist leaders will if necessary contrive a synthetic or ersatz culture for their states, it is all the more necessary that the historian should be forever alert to distinguish between a genuine culture generating a genuine nationalism, and a trumped-up nationalism generating the pretense or illusion of a culture.

The historian, then, to repeat, has an extremely strong predisposition to equate nationality and culture. This predisposition is so strong that if other important sources of nationalism should exist, recognition of them would be inhibited under our present rationale of nationalism. A question arises, therefore, whether other important sources of nationalism do exist, and if so, what their nature may be.

There is certainly at least one other important factor besides common culture which may bind an aggregate of individuals together, and this is community of interest, not in the narrow sense of economic advantage only, but the broad sense of welfare and security through membership in society. It is axiomatic that people tend to give their loyalty to institutions which "protect" them—that is, safeguard their interests—and political allegiance throughout history has been regarded as something given reciprocally in return for protection. At the level of theory this is well known, and historians of nationalism have often called attention to it. Thus, when modern nationalism was in its infancy, Voltaire defined the word *patrie* in terms of community of interest. Among modern historians, Hans Kohn affirms that a nationality derives part of its strength from being regarded as "a source of economic well being"; Karl Deutsch states that when he and his collaborators were "studying cases of successful amalgamation" of diverse groups into a single nation, "we found that it was apparently important for each of the participating territories or populations to gain some valued services or opportunities"; Boyd Shafer is particularly explicit in pointing out that for many nationalists "devotion to the national welfare . . . after all was but devotion to their own welfare," that monarch and middle classes at the inception of modern nationalism "found mutual benefit in the joint extension of their mutual interests, which they could also conceive of as *the* national interests," and that these parties were like "stockholders with voting rights in the common enterprise, the nation." One of the clearest affirmations of this idea was made by Harry M. Schulman in a statement to Louis L. Snyder, quoted in Snyder's *The Meaning of Nationalism.* Nationalism, said Schulman, is not a we-sentiment, but "a form of homeostasis, the equilibration of opposed vested interests within a series of specialized interdependent functional systems."

But despite the presence of theoretical statements such as these, when historians turn to the examination of nationalism in specific cases they seem to neglect the factor of common interest and to focus their attention very heavily upon common cultural factors. This neglect, curious in any case, has been all the more strange in view of the fact that an emphasis upon the importance of self-interest would fit in well with certain points that historians customarily stress. One of these points is the idea that modern nationalism has risen concurrently with modern democracy. Kohn, for instance, regards this correlation as so close that he denies the existence of any fully developed nationalism prior to the French Revolution. In this connection it is clear that the rise of democracy represents an admission of the masses to certain civic privileges and expectations of property ownership, that is, to a stake in society. The nation-state, of course, served as the instrument for the protection of this stake, and the people's spirit of loyalty to the nation was partly their response to that which protected their interests. Until democracy gave them an interest to protect, they were incapable of this response—incapable of nationalism.

Another well-recognized aspect of nationalism, into which the factor of self-interest again fits clearly, is the invigorating effect which war has had upon national spirit. Heinrich von Treitschke reduced this relationship to a simple and oft-repeated formula: "again and again, it has been proved that it is war which turns a people into a nation." Frederick Hertz, who deplored the fact as much as Treitschke rejoiced in it, agreed: "War could be called the greatest instrument of national unification, but for the fact that it also fosters the growth of forces which often imply a new menace to national unity."

How does war produce this effect? No doubt it does so, in a variety of ways and by appealing to a variety of impulses, some of which are irrational. But certainly one of the effects of war is to reorient the pattern of conflicts of interest within any national population. In times of peace, the diversity of interests of various kinds tends to divide the people into antagonistic groups—what James Madison called factions, and what we now call pressure groups—and these groups compete for control of public policy. Their relation to each other is primarily one of rivalry. Even in wartime, these rivalries will continue, but they tend to become secondary, for war subjects all interests to a common danger and to more vital danger than they ever incur from one another. In the presence of such danger, all interests tend to work together. In this way, war harnesses the motives of self-interest, which ordinarily pull in various directions, and causes them all to pull in the same direction and thus to reinforce the spirit of nationalism.

To argue that the factor of common interests is an important and somewhat neglected element in nationalism and that it ought to receive substantial attention does not mean that the concept of interest should replace the concept of culture. Of the two, the concept of culture is, no doubt, of greater weight. The point is rather that nationalism rests on two psychological bases instead of one: the feeling of common culture and the feeling of common interests. It is questionable whether either feeling can support a superstructure of nationality without the other. If the historian will recognize this dualism, he will not only have an effective working concept, but will also free himself from his present compulsion to prove a growth of cultural unity every time he observes an intensification of nationalism and to prove the emergence of a new culture every time that a dissident group proclaims its solidarity in nationalistic terms.

Here, then, are a number of propositions about the historian's treatment of nationalism: that the historian conceives abstractly of nationalism in sound theoretical terms, regarding it as a form of group loyalty psychologically similar to other forms of group loyalty, and having the subjective, relativistic, developmental qualities which other forms of group loyalty possess; that the close relationship between nationalism and the political state warps the historian's view and causes him to treat it functionally as a monolithic and unique form of loyalty, in antithesis to other forms of group loyalty, instead of recognizing that it is associated with and even derived from other forms of loyalty; that his use of the concept as a sanction to validate the demands of some groups for autonomy, while denying the similar demands of other groups, leads him into the fallacy of a false correlation between the ethical rightness of a group's policies and the objective separateness of the group's identity; that this valuative use of the concept also impels him to explain the origins of nationalism in terms of deep-seated, long-enduring natural affinities among a people, or, in other words, to rely too heavily upon cultural factors in his explanation, even where they are tenuous; that this cultural emphasis has, in turn, caused him frequently to overlook factors of self-interest, which have been vital in many historic situations in the integration or in the disintegration of national loyalties.

If these general propositions have any validity, it should be possible to test them by applying them to specific historical situations. Any reader of this paper will perhaps test them in terms of the historical treatment of the nationality or national movement with which he is most familiar. For my purposes, they can most readily be applied in the field of American history. The rest of this paper, therefore, is devoted to a consideration of their applicability at that point in American history where the question of nationalism was most important and most complex—namely at the crisis which led to the Civil War.

It is a truism of American history that, because of the vast extent of the United States and its great physiographic variety, major areas within the Union have often found their interests in conflict, and the alignment on public issues has followed geographical lines far more often than would occur in smaller or more homogeneous countries. These geographically aligned differentials have, in fact, been a pervasive factor and have presented themselves in many different forms. At times, such as the period of Jacksonian Democracy or the Populist Revolt, the divisions between East and West have seemed more fundamental than those between North and South, and careful analysis has always shown that these regional differentiations extended beyond a mere dualism of either North and South, or East and West. The West, with its frontier attributes, played a distinctive role even during the period when North–South antagonisms were most acute, and indeed the struggle that came to a crisis in 1861 has been construed by Frederick Jackson Turner as a rivalry between the North and the South to draw the West into their respective orbits. Even in the era when North and South were approaching the climactic rivalry of the Civil War, internal conflicts also made themselves felt at a different level, as issues arose between industrial and agricultural areas within the North, or between plantation belts and backwoods districts within the South.

Historians speak of these areas in which distinctive groups or special interests are localized or concentrated as sections, and they recognize sectionalism as one of the major themes of American history. In most cases where sectional rivalries have developed, the question of nationalism has not been involved, for the people of one sectional area have not called into question the Union that they share with the rival section, and the loyalties that they give to their own area have not impinged directly upon their national loyalty to the Union. Even when sectional bitterness has reached the emotional pitch that it developed in the campaign of 1896, the rivals have sought only to impose their policies upon one another within the Union and have not sought to sever their ties with one another by disrupting the Union.

In the era between 1848 and 1861, however, American geographically aligned rivalries were focused on an intense conflict between the North and the South, and the group loyalties of people in the South were focused on a southern republic in a way which undercut the American nationalism that had previously focused on the Union. In this case, then, southernism, instead of working sectionally within a framework of nationalism, tended to take on the character of nationalism itself and to break down the existing pattern of nationalism. Since the southern movement began in terms of sectional reaction against this existing pattern, historians frequently evaluate the ensuing conflict in terms of sectionalism versus nationalism.

In strict logic the antithesis of sectionalism versus nationalism would not necessarily link one region (the South) with sectionalism, nor the other region (the North) with nationalism. On the contrary, it might be argued that nationalistic forces in both the North and the South which placed the welfare of the Union above all regional values were pitted against sectional forces in both regions which gave primary value to regional objectives, such as, for the South, the protection of slavery in the territories or, for the North, the exclusion of slavery from the territories. Viewed in this way, the conflict might be said to involve the triumph of sectionalism over American nationalism within both regions and an ensuing struggle between northern sectionalism and southern sectionalism. Alternatively, it might also be argued that northern group loyalty of the most fundamental kind found a focus in the union formed in 1787, while southern group loyalty, also of the deepest sort, found a new focus in a separate southern republic. Regarded in this way, the conflict might be construed (as, in fact, many historians do construe it) as a conflict between northern (Union) nationalism and southern (Confederate) nationalism.

Either of these formulations has a certain tenability in theory, but in operative terms, of course, the forces which saved the American Union were centered in the North, and those which sought to disrupt it were centered in the South. Consequently, it seemed natural afterward, in the light of the fact that it was the Union which had survived, to link each of the forces at work with one of the rival regions and to speak of nationalism as northern and sectionalism as southern.

This attribution, however, at once has the effect of bringing the valuative aspect of the concept of nationalism into play. It clearly implies a sanction for the northern position—the sanction that the "people" involved in the crisis were the American people, both North and South, since it was the North which was defending the nation, and that those in the South who "felt themselves to be one" were not one in the ultimate sense, since the impulse which prompted their unity was sectional rather than national. Of course, in so far as hindsight furnishes a legitimate criterion, the conclusion, if not the reason, was valid, for what the North defended has found fulfillment as a nation and what the South defended has not. But the questionable feature of this approach is that it moves completely away from the psychological or functional analysis of nationalism and places the analysis very much upon an institutional basis. This approach has an a priori effect of prejudging the question that purports to be under examination, for it settles by ascription a point that ought to be settled by the evaluation of evidence. Instead of testing the validity of Union and Confederacy as nations by an evaluation of the character of the group loyalties attached to them, this tests the validity of the group loyalties by a prior assumption as to the character of the Union and the Confederacy.

As has been suggested earlier in this paper, the element of

sanction in the institutional concept sometimes makes it difficult for the historian to attribute nationality to movements of which he morally disapproves. For the attribution itself would imply that the movement has a kind of validity. This factor has certainly influenced the treatment of the question whether the Confederacy was a nation, for the issue between the Union and the Confederacy also became an issue between freedom and slavery. To ascribe nationality to the South is to validate the right of a proslavery movement to autonomy and self-determination. Since few historians in the twentieth century have been willing to do this, their moral position has sometimes run counter to their theory of nationality and has impelled them to shirk the consequences of their own belief that group identity is the basis for autonomy. If the finding that a majority of the southern people wanted a nation of their own is inseparable from the conclusion that the institution of slavery enjoyed a democratic sanction, it is always possible to reverse the reasoning and to argue that since slavery could not have enjoyed a democratic sanction, therefore the southern people must not have been a "people" in the sense that would entitle them to want a nation of their own.

The position of the strongly antislavery historian on the question of southern nationality tends to be particularly ironic, for he usually emphasizes more than most writers the depth of the division between the North and the South. No one stresses more than he the profound authoritarian implications of slavery for the entire intellectual and social life of the South, and the sharpness of the contrast between this society, with its system of legalized caste status, and the free, democratic society of the North. Yet, after making this case, the antislavery historian often takes the view that the southern assertion of nationality was not justified. Of course, he might simply follow the logic of his moral position and argue that war is justified if waged by one nation to compel another nation to give up slavery.[1] But since he also

1. In saying this, I do not mean to deny the priority of moral values. It may well be that the abolition of slavery had a higher value to mankind than the

attaches moral value to the right of self-determination, the recognition of southern nationality would place him in a moral dilemma. The only way he can have his crusade against slavery and his right of self-determination too is to deny that the principle of self-determination could have been involved in the case of the crusade against slavery.

The equation of northernism with nationalism and southernism with sectionalism prejudges by definition the question which purports to be under scrutiny, and denies without actual analysis of group feelings, that the southern movement could have been truly national; it also leads to an easy assumption that all northern support for federal authority must have been nationalistic rather than sectional. But this view tends to obscure the fact that in the North as well as in the South there were deep sectional impulses, and support or nonsupport of the Union was sometimes a matter of sectional tactics rather than of national loyalty. For instance, northern support for a sectional tariff or for sectional internal improvements, adopted by sectional majorities in the national government, was no less sectional than southern opposition to them. Northern efforts to put the terminus of a Pacific railroad at Chicago were no less sectional than southern efforts to put it at New Orleans. Northern determination to keep Negroes (rather than just slaves) out of the territories was no less sectional than southern determination to carry them there. Even northern support for Lincoln, who did not run in most of the slave states in 1860, was perhaps just as sectional as southern support for John C. Breckenridge or for John Bell, who did not carry a single free state.

self-determination of peoples, and that coercion of one nation by another is valid in such a case. A war of subjugation may well be justified by the emancipation of 3,950,000 slaves. It may also be true, as Lincoln apparently thought, that the preservation, by the use of force, of the Union formed in 1787 was more important for mankind than the purely voluntary self-determination of peoples. All I mean to argue is that historians ought not to assert the right of self-determination as if it were absolute and then deny that it is involved in cases where they prefer not to apply it.

In the North, sectional forces tended to support a strong Union because it was evident that this Union was becoming one in which the sectional forces of the North would be dominant. Thus the national Union could be made the instrument of these sectional interests. The South, on the other hand, finding itself in a minority position, could not hope to secure national support for sectional objectives, nor even to keep sectional and national interests in coordination with one another, and therefore it was forced to choose between section and nation. If the proslavery elements seemed less nationalistic than the antislavery elements, it was not because one more than the other put peace or national harmony above the question of slavery, for neither of them did, but because the antislavery elements could expect, with their majority status, to employ the national authority for their purposes, while the proslavery forces could not. A northerner could, and many northerners did, support the Union for sectional reasons; no southerner could possibly support it for any other than national reasons.

The historian certainly should make some distinction between the nationalistic motive to support the political state as the embodiment of the "people" as a whole and the tactical motive to use the authority of the state for the promotion of sectional interests. Very often, though, both of these impulses get called by the same name, nationalism.

If the antithesis of northern nationalism versus southern sectionalism conceals the sectional motivation of much that was done through national means for sectional ends in the North, it also obscures another important reality: that a mixture of regional and national loyalties prevailed in both regions. They did not seem ambiguous or inconsistent in the North because they were kept from conflicting there, whereas in the South they did conflict, and because they did, were made to seem an evidence almost of duplicity or double-dealing, as if devotion to the section in itself demonstrated alienation from the nation and as if nationalism could flourish only as regional loyalties withered away.

But in fact, this view is mistaken, and, to take a concrete example, there was no necessary equivocation or indecision of mind on the part of Josiah Quincy of Massachusetts when he declared in 1811 that "the first public love of my heart is the Commonwealth of Massachusetts . . . the love of this Union grows out of this attachment to my native soil." Nor was there ambiguity in Sam Houston of Texas when he asserted that he was a southerner and a Unionist too, with "a Southern heart, large enough, I trust, to embrace the whole Union if not the whole world"; nor in J. D. B. De Bow when he appealed to his fellow citizens, "as Southerners, as *Americans,* as MEN"; nor in Alexander H. Stephens of Georgia, when he said "I have a patriotism that embraces, I trust, all parts of the Union, . . . yet I must confess my feelings of attachment are most ardent toward that with which all my interests and associations are identified. . . . The South is my home, my fatherland."

If the point here were only that the people of the South became trapped in a conflict of loyalties, it would hardly be worth stating; historians have known it as a truism for a long time. The point is rather that the northerner and the southerner were not distinguished from one another by a singularity of loyalty on one side and a multiplicity of loyalties on the other, as if one were monogamous and the other polygamous. They both had multiple loyalties, and what distinguished them was that one, being in a majority, was able to keep all his loyalties coordinated, and therefore undivided, while the other, being in a minority, was not able to keep them coordinated, with the result that they became divided.

It would be extremely misleading, however, to suggest that the valuative implication of the concept of nationalism has warped only the views of writers whose sympathies lie with the Union. For if it has led some of them to deny that the South was entitled to the sanction of nationality, and to make this denial without much reference to the psychological realities, it has also led some writers whose sympathies lie with the South to assert that the southern claim to nationhood was validated by a complete cultural separateness, and to make this assertion without much reference to the cultural realities.

This is not to deny that there was a considerable measure of distinctiveness in the southern culture. All the factors of southern conservatism, southern hierarchy, the cult of chivalry—the unmachined civilization, the folk society, the rural character of the life, the clan values rather than the commercial values, made for *distinctiveness* of a deeply significant kind. But this is not quite the same as *separateness*, and the efforts of historians to buttress their claim that the South had a wholly separate culture, self-consciously asserting itself as separate, as a cultural counterpart of political nationalism, have led, on the whole, to paltry results. Southern writers, like the nationalistic claimants to culture mentioned above, issued periodic manifestoes proclaiming that the South ought to have its own literature, but their efforts to fulfill this goal failed because southern readers just would not support it. Southern educators likewise deplored the infiltration of Yankee ideas in the schools, and when the crisis was most acute, southern students departed with great fanfare from northern colleges. But southern education continued to be American education. In the economic area, a few southern fire-eaters made a conspicuous point of the fact that they were wearing homespun and consistently proclaimed the need for a southern economic self-sufficiency which was never realized. But it is crucial to recognize that the advocates of a southern culture spent much of their time complaining that the South would not support their cultural program. Evidence of this kind provides a tenuous basis indeed for arguing that southern nationalism sprang from a full-bodied southern culture. If historians had not been captives to the idea that nationality equates with culture, and that where there is separate nationalism there must be culture of equivalent separateness, they would probably have been far quicker to recognize how very thin the historical evidences of a separate southern culture really are. They would also have been disposed to give more emphasis to the many important cultural features that southerners shared with other nineteenth-century Americans: the common language which was a transatlantic modification of English, much the same in both the North and the South; the common religion of a people who were overwhelmingly evangelical and Protestant as well as Christian; the common political commitment to democratic institutions; the common system of values which exalted progress, material success, individual self-reliance, and distrust of authority; and the bumptious, eagle-screaming Americanism which scorned the "decadent monarchies" of the Old World.

To appreciate one important reason why historians with southern sympathies have emphasized the separateness of the southern culture, it is perhaps only necessary to look at the difference in the way in which the defense of the South has been argued in the more remote and in the more recent past. From the Civil War until 1900, it was notorious that no southerner seemed capable of writing on any aspect of the Civil War without including a lengthy disquisition on the legal and constitutional right of secession, with copious attention to the exact contractual understandings reached in 1787. But no historian has elaborated such arguments now for more than a generation. Why? Certainly not because the South no longer has defenders. The answer, I think, is that nowadays one does not couch historical defenses in formalistic or legalistic terms. The sanction for what the South did in 1861 is no longer believed to be what it agreed to in 1787. The sanction is instead that southerners in 1861 constituted a people in the sense which entitled them to exercise what we now call autonomy or self-determination, rather than what we used to call sovereignty. But in so far as the same conclusion is reached as to whether the South was justified, and in so far as the reasons "leading" to the conclusion may be in fact derived from the conclusion instead of the conclusion being derived from them, the great transformation since the nineteenth century from formalism to functionalism, has perhaps not increased the realism of our thinking as much as we sometimes fondly imagine.

The central significance of this subtle relation between descriptive statements and their valuative implications is not, however, that it results in a certain amount of specious reasoning from conclusion to premise. It is rather that it tends to cast the whole analysis in the oversimple terms of false, unrealistic antitheses or polarities, whose greatest drawback is not that they are partisan but simply that they are not very helpful for explanatory purposes.

If North and South fought, if one was a "nation" and one was not, if the people of one were "loyal" and the others were "disloyal," or, on the other hand, if they constituted two diverse civilizations, then the investigator is under strong compulsion to reduce the complex forces of the 1850's to simplicity and to come up with antitheses that will fit these dualisms. Hence, we have had a series of sweeping and dramatic contrasts which present North and South in polar terms. Indeed the historiography of the subject is largely a record of how one antithesis would be set up, only to be knocked down and replaced by another.

Thus we were once told that the South was a land of cavaliers, the North an abode of puritans; or that the South stood for states' rights, while the North stood for the federal supremacy. Later historians rejected these formulas as fallacious or superficial, but the old yearning for a sharp, clear-cut antithesis still shaped historical thought, and two other, more formidable dualisms were advanced. One of these, primarily economic in its tenor, was brilliantly set forth by Charles A. Beard, who argued that southern agrarianism and northern industrialism must necessarily clash because of their dissimilarity. The other, more broadly social in its view, held that North and South were, in fact, "diverse civilizations," and as such, incapable of maintaining a union with one another.

The quest for an unqualified antithesis still continues. Current interpretations have turned back to an emphasis, formerly popular in the nineteenth century, upon the basic incompatibility between a slaveholding and a non-slaveholding regime, with all the far-reaching differences in social values and in mode of life which such systems must entail.

These antitheses are in a sense caricatures, perhaps accurate in singling out some distinctive feature, but grossly distorted in the emphasis which they give to it. Because of their vulnerability, revisionist critics have been able to direct damaging criticism at every one of them.

The problem that such antitheses as these present in the interpretation of history arises not from their exaggeration of differences and their oversimplification of complex matters, but from their attribution of a false quality of mutual exclusiveness to phenomena which naturally coexist and overlap as national identity and regional identity do. The false antithesis assumes that nationalism depends on and can be measured in terms of homogeneity and therefore that regional diversity, at least when it appears on a North–South axis, is inconsistent with national unity. Once the mistaken assumption of mutual exclusiveness is accepted, it falsely follows that the extent of distinctiveness in the section becomes the measure of deviation from the nation, just as it is also falsely argued that the intensity of loyalty to the section becomes the index of disloyalty to the Union. Besides mistaking dissimilarity for antagonism, this kind of interpretation has the great disadvantage that, where friction exists, it shifts attention away from the specific disputes at issue between parties and emphasizes the points in which they are unlike one another, as if their conflict could be explained in terms of their mere lack of resemblance to one another.

The habit of equating diversity with dissension, and using the word "difference" to mean both at the same time, has taken such deep root in the historiography of the Civil War that it becomes difficult to dissociate the two, but history abounds in instances where diversity does not lead to antagonism, where regional identity does not detract from national integrity, and where no one expects them to. In Canada, for instance, the French, Catholic, peasant culture of Quebec Province presents sharper contrasts to the English, Protestant, pioneer culture of Ontario than North and South ever presented, and strong elements of antagonism have been involved historically. Yet there was no "irrepressible conflict" in Canada. Within the United States, New Englanders, with their puritan heritage and their Yankee ways, have shown a marked distinctiveness and have habitually manifested a pronounced sectional affection for their "stern and rockbound coast," yet these qualities are regarded as reinforcing, rather than diminishing the Yankee's Americanism. Where the South is involved, historical interpretation of the effect of sectional differentials has been too inconsistent to bear scrutiny. From the ratification of the Constitution until the high noon of the New Deal, and to some extent even to the present, the South has been set apart by its rural society, its staple crop economy, its tradition of leadership or control by the landowning interest, its large proportion of Negro population, and its formalized biracial system of caste in race relationships. In 1787 these differentials were perhaps more pronounced than during the crisis which led to the Civil War, yet historians who assume that such regional dissimilarities made a continuation of peaceful union impossible after 1850 seem completely untroubled by the fact that the very same diversities did not at all prevent the formation of at least a loose union in 1787–1788 or the rapid and triumphant growth of American nationalism for nearly forty years thereafter. Since the Civil War the one-party system of the "Solid" South, the relative poverty of the region, and the heritage of bitterness from Civil War and Reconstruction have made the sectional contrasts, in some respects, sharper than they were during the antebellum period. Yet these strong sectional factors proved not inconsistent with the swift restoration of American nationalism in the South, increasing steadily at least until 1954. The sectional differentials were still there, but in this new context, since they did not lead to war, no one supposed any longer that they must be inherently disruptive. In fact, the readiness with which the South returned to the Union will defy explanation unless it is recognized that southern loyalties to the Union were never really obliterated, but rather were eclipsed by other loyalties which, for a time, conflicted. It was a dim awareness of this fact on the part of the participants in the Civil War that gave to the conflict its peculiarly tragic tone—its pathos as a "brothers' war."

The historian may feel acutely the need for an explanation of the deep alienation which developed between North and South in the middle of the nineteenth century, but he ought not to allow the urgency of this need to blind him to the fact that he also needs an explanation for the growth of American nationalism between 1800 and 1846 and for the smoothness of the "road to reunion" between 1865 and 1900. No explanation of the sectional strife is really much good if it makes these phenomena of harmony and reconciliation appear impossible. Yet the historian's reliance upon the sharpest conceivable antitheses has led him to explain the schism in terms so deep and total that the readiness of southern men in 1898 and 1917 to enlist in the American army and to fight under the American flag would seem quite incredible.

To explain an antagonism that sprang up suddenly, and died down suddenly, the historian does not need and cannot effectively use a factor that has been constant over a long period, as the cultural differential between the North and the South has been. He needs a factor that can cause bitter disagreement even among a people who have much basic homogeneity. No factor, it might be suggested, will meet this need better than the feeling, widespread in the 1850's in the South, that the South's vital interests were being jeopardized and the region was being exposed to the dangers of a slave insurrection, as a result of the hostility of antislavery men in the North. Applied to the sectional crisis, such a view of the sources of friction would make possible the explanation of the Civil War, without making impossible the explanation of the rapid return to union after the war. No cultural explanation will do this.

The cultural factor and the factor of self-interest are, of course, not wholly unrelated, for essentiality of interests is determined partly by cultural values and vice versa. But the fact remains that within an integrated culture acute conflicts of interest may be generated, and between diverse cultures strong community of interests may develop. A body of citizens may exalt the national state as the instrument that unites them with those with whom they have an affinity, but they may also exalt it as the guardian of certain essential interests and social values that they do not necessarily share with the over-all society in a homogeneous sense. Despite the emphasis in historical literature on cultural homogeneity, history itself offers extensive evidence that if a state protects the interests, either real or fancied, of culturally disparate groups in its population, it can command the nationalistic loyalty of such groups without offering them a homogeneous body of fellow citizens. And if it systematically disregards the interests of a group, it alienates the group and makes cultural affinities with the majority seem irrelevant.

In so far as it is sound to give major attention to the equilibrium of interests as a condition necessary to nationalism, it follows that the American Civil War must be interpreted less in terms of the well-known antitheses that point up the dissimilarities between North and South, and more in terms of the prolonged sequence of interest conflicts that crystallized along sectional lines.

Southerners became progressively more alienated as they became more convinced first that the Union was sacrificing their economic welfare through the tariff, later that it was denying them parity in the process of national expansion, and finally that it was condoning the activities of men who would loose a slave insurrection upon them and expose them to possible butchery. To emphasize this view, of course, does not mean that anyone need turn to a simple interpretation of history in terms of self-interest, but that we should recognize that cultural similarities alone will not provide a basis of affinity between groups who regard each others' policies as endangering their own security.

By stressing conflict of interest as a basic factor, it is possible to explain the otherwise stubborn anomaly that the sectional crisis grew in intensity even as the Republic grew in homogeneity. Originally, cultural unity was not deemed necessary to the welfare of the Union under the Constitution, and both the northern and the southern states fully intended to preserve their respective sectional peculiarities, of which they were acutely aware when they ratified the Constitution. Indeed, they did not ratify until shrewd calculation had assured each section either that it might hope to gain preponderant weight, or at least that it would be strong enough to maintain the balance of sectional equilibrium in the new system. If the Republic had remained static, with the area and population of 1790 more or less permanent, it appears that an equilibrium would have been maintained, and the Union might have enjoyed harmony, even without homogeneity. The "house divided," which had in fact been divided from the beginning, might have continued to stand in the future as it had stood so well for seventy years.

But when growth ensued, with uneven rates of advance for the two sections, the equilibrium was upset. The minority section lost its ability to exercise joint control in the federal government, and with this control went the power to keep national objectives coordinated with sectional ones and thus to maintain the image of the federal government as the guardian of the essential interests or values of southern society. The South, therefore, was forced more and more to regard national objectives and sectional objectives as alternatives that must be made the objects of painful choice. Meanwhile, the North did not have to chose between national and sectional objectives because by use of its power it could incorporate sectional goals into the national program. What was good for the North was good for the country, and thus no problem of priority need arise. The potential dilemma of Josiah Quincy's loyalties, which he had verbalized so clearly remained a latent dilemma and never developed beyond the verbal level. But Sam Houston and Alexander Stephens lived to see a situation where bigness of heart was not enough and where the Union was so divided that it became difficult for patriotism to embrace all parts of it.

If the adjustment of conflicting interests rather than the elimination of cultural differentials is in this case the key to the perpetuation of national unity, and if an equilibrium of power is the condition most conducive to the adjustment of conflicting interests, then the historian has an explanation for the seeming paradox that the crisis of American nationalism came not when regional diversity was greatest, but after many common denominators between the sections had developed and had substantially increased the measure of cultural uniformity.

If the pattern of loyalties in America between 1820 and 1860 was more intricate than the stark antithesis of nationalism and sectionalism would imply, and if the ultimate conflict between North and South was in part the consequence of the failure of the Union to solve the problems of chronic conflict of interest, even after it had successfully begun to transcend the presumably more difficult obstacles of cultural dissimilarity, the implication is not that a new single-factor analysis should be applied in place of the old ones—presenting the Civil War in the exclusive terms of a conflict between culturally similar groups which both spelled their version of nationalism with an alphabet of the letters of self-interest. It is rather to suggest that the valuative elements in the concept of nationalism have influenced too many of the findings of the historian, that the concept has warped his analysis as much as it has assisted it, and that the historical process is far too intricate to be handled in terms of the simple dualisms of culture versus culture, nation versus section, interest versus interest, or Americanism versus southernism.

The Uses of Politics

Party Politics and the Union and Confederate War Efforts

by Eric L. McKitrick

"It is a safe bet," observed one historian during the war's centennial celebration, "that the Civil War has spilt more ink than blood." In both cases, the spillage has been tremendous. The conflict produced a million casualties, and its military, diplomatic, and social history have indeed been dealt with in thousands of books written since Appomattox. No other period in American history except the time of the Revolution can claim to have received more exhaustive treatment. Until recently, however, most political studies of the Civil War have focused either on the careers of Union and Confederate generals or political leaders, notably Lincoln and Lee, or on controversial factions such as the Radical Republicans or the Southern fire-eaters. Few scholars paid much attention to the actual functioning of political parties in the North during the war or to how the formation of the Confederacy all but destroyed the South's political life. Even fewer scholars were attracted to the problem of how political behavior in each region influenced the course of the war itself.

Instead, historians concentrated on comparing the relative merits of Lincoln and Jefferson Davis as "statesmen," or on the relationship between Lincoln and Republican groups such as the war governors or the Radicals, and they believed, until recently, that partisan conflicts within the Republican party seriously hampered the Northern war effort. Similarly, scholars had been in the habit of crediting the high degree of Confederate "unity" and endurance through four bloody years partly to the absence of bitterly devisive two-party political contests.

In an essay published in 1960 on "Jefferson Davis and the Political Factors in Confederate Defeat," David M. Potter questioned both these assumptions, suggesting instead that the Southern war effort lost much of its effectiveness because of the absence of adequate channels for organized, partisan, political life. In his view, the North's conduct of the war benefited from the Lincoln administration's effort to continue most normal political processes. Eric L. McKitrick here amplifies that hypothesis, providing the most important summary and reassessment of Civil War politics published in recent years.

The Civil War has always lent itself naturally and logically to the comparative method. Comparing the resources of the Union and the Confederacy in everything conceivable—manpower, brainpower, firepower—has been highly productive in helping us to understand the process whereby the North ultimately overwhelmed the South. But it is in the realm of government, where the process of historical comparison normally begins, that the results are on the whole least conclusive and least satisfying. The two sets of institutions exhibit a series of uncanny similarities. We may think we can detect in the Southern body politic a certain pallor, a lack of muscle tone that is in some contrast to the apparent resiliency of the North. But this is only a suspicion. We have not been very certain about how to get at such a subjective matter as the health of a metaphorical organism.

From William N. Chambers and Walter D. Burnham, *The American Party Systems: Stages of Political Development* (New York: Oxford University Press, 1967), pp. 117–20, 122–23, 128–29, 131–39, 141–51. footnotes omitted.

The Union and Confederate governments, as set down on paper, were almost identical. The Confederacy deliberately adopted the federal Constitution with very few changes, some of which might have been improvements had they been carried fully into effect. Cabinet members might sit in Congress, though few did; the executive had an itemized veto on appropriation bills, though it was a power he did not use; and bills for departmental appropriations had to be initiated with an estimate from the department concerned. The general welfare clause was dropped, but the "necessary and proper" clause—so useful for expanding national power—was kept. The states were "sovereign" but had no power to make treaties, which meant that they were in fact not sovereign. Nothing was said about the right of secession, and it was not as though no one had thought of it. The relations of the states to the central government would, in the course of things, reveal some crucial differences, but it is hard to find much evidence for this in the organic law of the two governments. A trend toward centralized power was perfectly possible within either of the two constitutions, and it could proceed just as far under the one as under the other. The co-ordinate branches of government were constitutionally the same, though in the election and term of office of the executive there were certain differences. As for the judiciary, the Confederacy too was to have had a Supreme Court, though it never actually got around to establishing one. In the Confederacy judicial review (with generous citations from *The Federalist*, as well as from the opinions of Marshall and Story) occurred in the states. How much difference this made may be debated, though historians have not in general made an issue of it. In any case, of the three branches of government on either side, the judiciary seems to have made the least impact on the waging of war. With regard to the two Congresses, the practices and procedures were strikingly similar. It might be said that even their membership overlapped, since a number of men had served in both. . . .

All such comparisons as those just surveyed, enlightening as they are, must be made within certain limits. Attention is always in some way directed to the formal structure of government and to the individuals occupying the formal positions established by that structure. But comparing these formal arrangements, even in the broadest and most extended way, still does not bring us a very clear idea of why the North won and where it drew the necessary energy for sustaining a long drawn out war effort. At this point one normally retreats to the "concrete realities" of military power and material resources, the logic of which has a reassuring finality. Military and economic organization—"in the last analysis," as we say—is what tells.

Still there may be, as I think, much more to be said for the way in which political organization, in and of itself, affected the respective war efforts. And if so, it is most likely to be found by moving to another level altogether: by turning from the formal to the informal functions of politics, from its official to its unofficial apparatus, from the explicit formulations to the implicit understandings. For at least a generation prior to the Civil War, the most salient unofficial structure in American public life was its system of political parties. No formal provision was ever made for such a system. Yet in this system of parties may be found historically the chief agency for mobilizing and sustaining energy in American government. It thus seems reasonable to consider how, as a matter of actual practice, the energies of government may have been affected by the workings of this unofficial system in waging the American Civil War.

In an essay published in 1960, David Potter suggested "the possibility that the Confederacy may have suffered real and direct damage from the fact that its political organization lacked a two-party system." This, with its implications, constitutes in my opinion the most original single idea to emerge from the mass of writing that has been done on the Civil War in many years. It implicitly challenges two of our most formidable and consistently held assumptions regarding political life of the time, assumptions which until recently have gone unquestioned. One is that Lincoln's leadership of the Union war effort was severely and dangerously hampered by political partisanship—that is, by obstructions put in his path by Democrats on the one hand and, on the other, by extremists within his own Republican party. The other assumption is that Davis and the Confederate government, by deliberately setting aside partisanship, avoided this difficulty. There were no parties in the Confederacy, and thus the South, in this respect at least, had the advantage. . . .

The rapid growth of the Republican party in the brief span of five or six years prior to 1860 had generated certain by-products. It had certainly dissipated the malaise of the early 1850's in which the expanding antislavery and free-soil sentiment of the North had been, for a time, without any clear vehicle for political organization. There were, moreover, established public men who had come to be identified with this sentiment, and whose careers could no longer be promoted without stultification amid the dissolution of the Whig party and the conservatism of the regular Democrats. Such men, of whom William H. Seward and Salmon P. Chase were conspicuous examples, now found in the Republican party a welcome field for their talents and leadership. In addition, the very effort required in organizing the new party in state after state brought to the fore hundreds of new men within the same short space of time. The very marching clubs which sprang up everywhere—the so-called "Wide Awakes"—amounted to much more than a freakish social phenomenon. They represented the "progressive" element of the community. That the Republicans by 1860 had elected governors in every Northern state, to say nothing of capturing the national government, is evidence of a vitality going far beyond the ordinary. The period was one of mounting public crisis; what has been less noticed is that precisely at this time public life began to present an expanding field for younger men of talent, ambition, and energy.

By the time the Confederacy was being established, politics was not attracting the South's best men to anywhere near this degree. An obvious immediate reason, of course, was that the war crisis naturally brought many of the Southern elite into the army, and many writers have commented on this. But antecedent factors were more pervasive. The chief mechanism for managing political talent and bringing it forward—party organizations—had in effect disintegrated in the South by the time the war began. . . . Thus the collapse in the South of the existing parties—the Whigs in the early 1850's and the Democrats in 1860—had created a setting in which the only real political issue came down to that of whether a man did or did not support secession. . . .

A further contrast between the Federal and Confederate governments, looking now at their formation from still another viewpoint, might consist in the standards whereby the cabinets as a whole were organized. For Davis, the chief concern was that each state had to be represented. For Lincoln also, geography counted as a strong consideration; but for him, both merit and geography as factors in choice had to operate within the limits of another criterion, which gave the problem a certain focus and required a certain precision. His cabinet had to be primarily a party alliance, which was its true functioning character, and its character as a coalition of state interests was thus quite secondary. He wanted every shade of commitment within the party, from border-state conservative to antislavery radical—and the influence they commanded—represented in his cabinet and, as it were, under his eye. A further nicety was that, owing to the comparative newness of the party, considerations of present and future support required that a man's antecedents also be weighed: there should be some balance between former Whigs and former Democrats. On the other hand, Davis had no choice but to follow the principle of state representation, and had he not done so he would undoubtedly have suffered even more general dissension and public attacks on his cabinet than he did. But judging both from this and from the cabinet's own instability, the political symbolism of a coalition of states, just in itself, as a focus for loyalty was somehow abstract, lacking in sharpness, and not very compelling. . . .

There were relatively few changes in Lincoln's cabinet, and

they were all made under circumstances firmly controlled by Lincoln himself. The historian of Jefferson Davis's cabinet is unable to account satisfactorily for its lack of stability, except to chronicle a long series of resignations, most of them under fire. (There were six secretaries of war, five attorneys-general, and four secretaries of state.) The legislative branch of government has no constitutional right to interfere in the business of the President's cabinet, and in this light Lincoln would have been quite justified in refusing to deal with the senatorial delegation that challenged him on Seward. But constitutional formality was only one of the guidelines. These men confronted him in at least two capacities, as senators and as leaders of the party, and in their latter capacity, is Lincoln well knew, they could not safely be turned away. The resulting adjustment, though exhausting and worrisome, brought rich dividends in the repair of morale. Davis was not required to adjust to any such principle. He too was harassed by informal groups of legislators on similar missions. In February 1865, with the Confederacy rapidly deteriorating, the legislative delegation of Virginia urged him to make certain changes in his cabinet. He thought it proper to declare, as he had on other occasions: "The relations between the President and the Heads of the Executive Departments are . . . of the closest and most intimate character . . . and it is not a Constitutional function of the Legislative Department to interfere with these relations. . . ." Lincoln's cabinet represented an ever-uneasy alliance, which is why it required so much of his attention. But in the very process of managing it he was, in effect, at the same time managing the party and fashioning it into a powerful instrument for waging war. In reference to that cabinet, it is not too much to say that the choice of its members, its stability, its management, and the major changes made in it, are all to be understood largely with reference to a single principle, the exigencies of party politics.

The whole corps of federal officeholders may be understood in much the same light. We have no full study of Jefferson Davis's patronage policies, which is probably symptomatic; there may never be much of a basis for generalizing about them. But there certainly was one striking, self-evident difference between Lincoln's and his, which was clarity of standards. Davis wanted merit, zeal, and loyalty. (As one writer puts it, he "favored civil service reform.") Lincoln also, naturally, wanted merit, zeal, and loyalty. But he also had some very straightforward criteria for determining in a hurry what those qualities actually meant and how they were to be found. The appointee had to be a Republican—which was at least helpful in narrowing a swarming field by roughly half—and the most dependable general standard for assessing loyalty and zeal was services to the party. It was within this category that he made his choices on "merit." The rules of procedure were also quite precise. For example:

> The appointments of postmasters, with salaries less than $1000 per annum, will be made upon the recommendations of the [Republican] members of Congress in the different districts. Applications addressed to them will receive attention earlier than if sent to the Department, and save much delay and trouble.

Lincoln was, moreover, very meticulous about "senatorial courtesy."

Though Davis, as might naturally be supposed, accepted the recommendations of others, he does not seem to have felt bound by any given rule in acting upon them. For example, by insisting on having his own way over the postmastership of Montgomery, Davis deeply alienated both the senators from Alabama. . . .

Patronage is a care and a worry; it is also a cherished prerogative, with gratifications for those who give as well as those who receive. They are all part of the same sensitive network. The responsiveness and *esprit* of such a network thus require that both the giving and the receiving be widely shared, and on some understood basis. We have no way of measuring the energy with which the men who made up these two patronage systems supported their respective administrations and worked to carry out their purposes. But we do know that one administration had an intricate set of standards for appraising energy and rewarding it—in addition always, of course, to standards of patriotism—which was not available to the other.

The field of comparison in which contrasts between the two governments are perhaps most grossly striking is that of state–federal relations. In both cases there was a set of natural fault-lines, inherent in a federal structure, between the state and national governments. In the Confederacy, these cracks opened ever more widely as the war went on. Toward the end, indeed, some states were in a condition of virtual rebellion against the Confederate government. In the North, the very opposite occurred. The states and the federal government came to be bound more and more closely in the course of the four years, such that by the end of that time the profoundest change had been effected in the character of their relations. In the course of things, moreover, the people themselves would come to be more closely bound to their national government. But the mechanisms are by no means self-evident. It cannot be taken for granted that in the nature of things such a process was bound to occur.

For the Confederacy, the great problem in raising and organizing armies was far less a matter of insufficient manpower than it was of divided authority. The various efforts of the Confederate government to get full access to and control over military manpower in the states were successfully obstructed throughout the war by the state governors. The patriotic ardor of the governors for mobilizing troops need not in itself be doubted. The perpetual question was rather how it ought to be managed and how troops were to be used; state resistance to Confederate policy always came down to one of two principles: local defense, or the dangers of a centralized military despotism. . . .

The organization of the army in the spring and summer of 1861 was held up by shortages not of men but of arms, substantial amounts of which were in possession of the state governments. They were held back partly for what were seen as local needs, and partly in pique at the War Department's receiving of volunteers raised without the intermediary of the governor. Efforts of the states to control the appointment of field officers led them either to hold back regiments until they were fully formed—instead of sending them forward by companies—or else by tendering "skeleton regiments" with a full complement of state-commissioned officers and only a few privates. Their insistence on controlling the clothing and supply of their own state troops in Confederate service led to consequences that were almost disastrous. Resources being not only unequal but at the very best limited, the maximum co-ordination of both purchasing and distribution was imperative. Yet as it was, Confederate purchasing agents had to engage everywhere in the most ruinous competition with agents from the states for sources of supply at home and abroad, while at the same time the output of state-controlled factories was kept consistently out of general reach. Governor Zebulon B. Vance of North Carolina actually boasted that, at the time of Robert E. Lee's surrender (of a tattered and starving army), he himself had huge stores of uniforms, blankets, cloth, leather, overcoats, and bacon in his state warehouses.

Conscription was adopted in the Confederacy in April 1862, a full year before the same step was taken in the North. One of the objects was to reorganize the twelve-months' volunteers whose terms were then running out; the other was to get control of the aggregations of militia which had been built up during the previous year and held in the states for local defense. This latter purpose was never properly achieved. State guards were once again built up, the condition of whose discipline and training made them worthless for almost any purpose so long as they were withheld from general service; and conscription itself, especially after the Act of February 1864, was resisted by the governors in a variety of ways. The chief device was that of exemptions, wherein wide categories of persons were sweepingly redefined as "state officers.". . .

In the North, the story of the recruitment and control of the army was, at least by comparison, relatively straightforward. The raising of troops was at the outset fully in the hands of the state governors, and so in a nominal sense it remained throughout. And yet by a series of steps the actual initiative tended to pass increasingly to the national government. By calling for three-year volunteer enlistments during the first month of hostilities and enlarging the regular army without the authority of law before the assembling of Congress, Lincoln took clear control of the national forces. Through most of the first year the recruiting activities of the governors proceeded with the utmost energy. The first major shift in initiative occurred after the failure of the Peninsular Campaign, when patriotic fervor began wearing thin and volunteers became increasingly harder to find. At this point Secretary Seward persuaded all the governors to unite in memorializing the President to call for 150,000 more volunteers, whereupon Lincoln promptly called for twice that many, together with 300,000 nine-months' militia. Both calls were more than met. Under the threat of a militia draft, the governors threw themselves with renewed zeal into a very aggressive campaign of recruiting. After the Emancipation Proclamation, the administration agreed to the enrolling of Negro troops. Aside from the raising of a few independent regiments, this recruiting was done directly by field commanders, entirely outside the control of any state government, and approximately 186,000 men were thus added to the national army. A further step was the adoption of conscription with the National Enrollment Act of March 1863, which gave the President full power to raise and support armies without state assistance. The unpopular Act was not fully exploited, and conscription as such accounted for no more than about 6 per cent of the total Union forces. It was successfully used, however, from 1863 to the end of the war, as a device for filling deficiencies in state volunteer quotas and for encouraging the governors to see that such deficiencies did not occur. In the mobilization of military manpower the state governors on the whole performed their function with exceptional vigor, even while becoming—as one writer somewhat extravagantly puts it—"mere agents" of the national government.

The energy of the Union government may be seen with even greater clarity in its actions against disaffection and disloyalty. Without any special legislation, Lincoln immediately assumed executive authority to suspend the writ of habeas corpus and make summary arrests in areas particularly endangered by disloyal activities; and in handling such cases the government made very little use of the courts. . . . Congress made some effort to define the President's powers in the Habeas Corpus Act of March 3, 1863, but whether the Act intended to grant these powers for the first time or to recognize powers he had exercised all along was not clear, and in any event executive policy and practice proceeded unaltered. . . .

No such freedom or directness of action was ever permitted to Jefferson Davis. He could make no summary moves against practices whose effect was to obstruct the war effort until the badly unsettled conditions of early 1862 finally persuaded the Confederate Congress that something needed to be done. The Act passed on February 27 thereupon permitted the executive to suspend habeas corpus and apply martial law to places threatened by invasion. But though Davis used his power in a very restricted way, the resulting hostility to martial law as imposed on Richmond and certain other places was such that Congress in April felt constrained to put further limits on the executive and to amend the law by giving it a fixed date of expiration. . . . That opposition had, indeed, been so bitter that Confederate law was in many places rendered practically unenforceable. Governor Brown insisted that the people of Georgia had "more to apprehend from military despotism than from subjugation by the enemy," and when Alexander Stephens harangued the Georgia legislature in March 1864 on the government's "despotic" suspension of habeas corpus, Brown had the speech printed and mailed to the company officers of every Georgia regiment and to every county clerk and county sheriff in Confederate territory. The legislature of North Carolina passed an Act making it compulsory for state judges to issue the writ, in effect nullifying Confederate law. A meeting of governors in October 1864 adopted a resolution "virtually condemning" the suspension of habeas corpus.

One result was a serious weakening of the South's military system. State judges in Virginia, Texas, North Carolina, and elsewhere issued writs of habeas corpus indiscriminately to persons accused of desertion or evading military service, and Governor Vance used his militia to enforce them. Robert E. Lee complained to the Secretary of War that the drain on the army thus caused by the use of habeas corpus was "more than it can bear." Moreover, the deterioration of civil government in many areas made a wide field for lawless bands, disloyal secret societies, and trading with the enemy. Persons arrested for such activities were again and again freed by habeas corpus on grounds of insufficient evidence. All this despite Davis's plea that "the suspension of the writ is not simply advisable and expedient, but almost indispensable to the successful conduct of the war."

The chief mechanism that prevented such centrifugal tendencies from developing in the Northern states, as William B. Hesseltine pointed out some years ago, was the Republican party. It was the energy of the Republican party that established the political structure with which the North began the war, and through which the war was prosecuted to the end. More specifically, the governors of every Northern state in 1861 had been put there through the efforts of that party, and these men represented both the state organizations and the national coalition responsible for bringing a Republican administration to Washington. They were politically committed from the very first to positive measures for suppressing disunion. With remarkable unanimity they invited Lincoln at the outset to take steps—indeed, they insisted he take them—which could only draw more and more power into his hands, leaving them with less and less initiative. As with the raising of armies, there was something cumulative about this process; it came to take on a life of its own.

In turn, the various state administrations—especially after the resurgence of the Democratic party with the reverses of 1862—

came more and more, despite their traditions of particularism, to realize their growing dependence on the federal government for political support. . . .

In the broadest sense the dependence of the state and national administrations was mutual, and was mutually acknowledged; but in any case the binding agency and energizing force was the Republican party. And this in turn was maintained—indeed, made possible—through the continued existence of the Democrats.

There is certainly no need here to discuss the beneficial functions of a "loyal opposition." But something might be said about the functions of an opposition which is under constant suspicion of being only partly loyal. The Northern Democratic party during the Civil War stood in precisely this relation to the Union war effort, and its function in this case was of a double nature. On the one hand, its legitimacy as a quasi-formal institution would remain in the last analysis unchallenged, so long as it kept its antiwar wing within some sort of bounds. But by the same token there was the rough and ready principle that "every Democrat may not be a traitor, but every traitor is a Democrat."

Thus, the very existence of the Democratic party provided the authorities (who badly needed some standard) with a ready-made device for making the first rough approximation in the identification of actual disloyalty. It also provided a kind of built-in guarantee against irrevocable personal damage should the guess turn out to be wrong. When in doubt they could always round up local Democrats, as many a time they did, and in case of error there was always a formula for saving face all around: it was "just politics." There was, in short, a kind of middle way, an intermediate standard that had its lighter side and alleviated such extremes in security policy as, on the one hand, the paralysis and frustration of doing nothing, and, on the other, the perversions of power that accompany political blood-baths. . . .

Two state governments, those of New York and New Jersey, actually did fall into Democratic hands for a time during the war.

But despite much talk of states' rights and arbitrary central authority, neither of these administrations did anything that materially hindered the war effort. Both, in fact, did much to promote it, and it was not as though either state was lacking in Democrats ready for almost any measure which might tie up the federal government. But a strong stimulus to the Democratic governors, as well as to the state Democratic organizations, for keeping such elements in check was the existence in each state of a formidable Republican organization which was watching their every move.

Meanwhile Jefferson Davis also had opposition, in his Congress as well as in the states, and it grew ever larger. But it was not "an" opposition in any truly organized sense. It was far more toxic, an undifferentiated bickering resistance, an unspecified something that seeped in from everywhere to soften the very will of the Confederacy. Davis could not move against this; he had no real way of getting at it. He had no way, for example, without either an organized opposition party or an organized administration party, of dealing with a man like Joseph E. Brown. Had there been such organizations, and had Brown himself been at the head of either the one or the other of them in the state of Georgia, the administration forces would have had some sort of check on him. . . . Unlike the Northern governors, Brown had no informal national structure with a clear set of organizational interests, and on which his own power depended, to persuade him otherwise. . . .

A further note on "opposition" might involve the relations of Lincoln with the "Radical" faction of his own party. This question has produced some strong debate among historians, though the principal issues appear by now to have been largely settled. . . .

The . . . point . . . is that these Radicals, whatever may have been their many differences, represented the most articulate, most energetic, most militant wing of the Republican party. The one thing that did unite such men as Trumbull, Wade, Greeley,

Chandler, Fessenden, Julian, and the rest was their implacable insistence that the war be prosecuted with ever more vigor, and that the President use the national power to the utmost in doing it. There is every evidence that in this over-all objective they and the President were at one, inasmuch as the war was, in the end, so prosecuted. Whether Lincoln welcomed his tormentors is doubtful. But whether he or anyone else would have moved as decisively without them is equally doubtful, and what the Union war effort as a whole would have been without the energy they represented is more doubtful still. The tensions and conflicts of the Lincoln administration—such as those having to do with emancipation, the use of Negro troops, and the complexion of the government that was to stand for re-election in 1864—were, as we know, considerable. But without a party apparatus to harness and direct them, they would surely have been unmanageable.

In any event, we might imagine Jefferson Davis as being quite willing to exchange this sort of "opposition" for the one he had. In the Confederate Congress there seem to have been some who pressed for greater vigor than Davis's in fighting the war; a much larger number inclined to measures that would have resulted in less. But perhaps more fundamental was that these men were all mixed in together. There was no recognized way of segregating or defining them, no basis of expectations, no clear principle for predicting what they might do. "There were no political organizations seeking undivided loyalty," as the historian of that Congress puts it, "nor was there consistent pressure from the electorate. Conditions changed, opinions changed, consequently administration sympathies changed." This lack of sharpness seems to have been accompanied by a . . . lack of initiative which is quite noticeable when contrasted with the wartime federal Congress, and it is apparent that lack of party responsibility had much to do with it. . . . Certainly Davis had no counterpart of Lincoln's "Radicals" to spur him on. Could the rabid secessionists of the 1850's, the so-called Southern "fire-eaters," the Robert Barnwell Rhetts, the William Lowndes Yanceys, the Edmund Ruffins, have made such a counterpart? There is little evidence that they could, or would. Such men are quite absent from the roll of the Confederacy's leading statesmen. The most dynamic "fire-eaters" who came into their own in the war years were two obstructionist state governors, already mentioned, Zebulon Vance and Joseph E. Brown.

It has been asserted throughout this essay that the Republican party, in the presence of an organized party of opposition, performed a variety of functions in mobilizing and managing the energies needed for sustaining the Union war effort. These were carried on both inside and outside the formal structure of government, and by men active in party affairs whether they held office or not. The absence of such a system in the Confederacy seems to have had more than a casual bearing on the process whereby Southern energies, over and beyond the course of military events, became diffused and dissipated. National commitments in the North were given form and direction by an additional set of commitments, those of party. This hardly means that the Republican party is to be given sole credit for the success of the war effort, which was in fact supported by overwhelming numbers of Democrats. But it does mean, among other things, that there were political sanctions against the Democrats' *not* supporting it, sanctions which did not exist in the Confederacy. When Democratic leaders were inclined to behave irresponsibly they could not, like Brown and Vance, play the role of state patriots. A hint of Democratic disloyalty anywhere tightened the Republican organization everywhere.

The emphasis hitherto has been upon leadership, upon how the process of politics affected the workings of government, but a final word should be said about how that process affected the body of citizenry. What may have been the function of a party system as a vehicle of communication? What did it do toward making popular elections a mode whereby the people were in effect called upon to define and reaffirm their own commitment to the national cause? In 1862, 1863, and 1864, through a series of elections which made the heaviest psychological demands on the entire country, the North had annually to come to terms with the war effort. The Republicans, with varying degrees of success, everywhere made attempts to broaden their coalition by bringing as many Union Democrats into it as possible, and naturally tried to attract as many Democratic voters to it as they could. The national party even changed its name in 1864, calling itself the "Union" party to dramatize the breadth of its appeal. And yet the result was in no true sense an all-party front or bipartisan coalition; rather it was a highly successful device for detaching Democrats from their regular party loyalties. The distinction is of some importance. The initiative for this effort remained throughout in Republican hands, and the Democrats everywhere maintained their regular organizations. The structure of parties was therefore such that every election became, in a very direct way, a test of loyalty to the national government.

The tests were by no means consistently favorable. In the fall of 1862, the time of the mid-term elections, the Republicans were significantly divided on the President's policy of emancipation, and a heavy majority of Democrats opposed it. This was reflected in the state and congressional election results, which were deeply depressing to the administration. The Democrats elected governors in two states and majorities in the legislatures of several, and substantially increased their numbers in Congress. This had several important consequences. One was that, inasmuch as the Republicans still maintained their control of Congress, the weakened state organizations were brought a step farther in that progress, already described, of growing dependency on the national party and the national administration for leadership and support. Another was that the Republicans were inspired to great exertions in justifying emancipation as an integral feature of the party program and in minimizing the Democrats' claim that the purposes of the war had been altered to make it an abolition crusade. Still a further consequence was that the Democrats were sufficiently emboldened by their successes that in a number of places they overstepped themselves. The "peace" theme in the Democrats' case against the administration emerged with a clarity that had hitherto been muted, making them much more vulnerable than before to the Republicans' "treason" theme, and drawing clear lines for the state elections of 1863. . . .

Once again in 1864, the Democrats, amid the military discouragements of the summer, assisted in clarifying the choices by writing a peace plank into their national platform and nominating a general, George B. McClellan, who had been dismissed for the failure of the operations of 1862 in the Eastern theater. The re-election of Lincoln was accompanied by the restoration of Republican majorities to every legislature and every congressional delegation, and of Republican governors to every state.

The people of the Confederacy, of course, continued to hold elections. Yet we know surprisingly little—indeed, almost nothing—about these elections. No study has ever been made of them, which is some measure of how comparatively little importance was attached to them at the time. The people were asked in November 1861 to choose Davis and Stephens as heads of the "permanent" government. The election "was marked, however, by general apathy." The first elections to Congress, according to Professor Yearns, "went off quietly." There was virtually no campaigning, and "balloting everywhere was light, as is usual when issues are absent." The elections of 1863, from what little glimpse we have of them, seem aggressive only by contrast. The increased activity at that time was principally a product of increased dissatisfaction with Davis's government. Yet even here the opposition was unorganized and unfocused, and candidates "failed to offer any clear substitute for policies they denigrated." "Mixed with rodomontade was the familiar state rights ingredient which gave much criticism a respectable flavor. All of the strong war measures were condemned as evidence of centralized despotism which was abusing the states."

The sluggishness of communication in the Confederacy has

often been commented on, and yet here the contrast with the North is one which the disparity in technology does not quite fully account for. There was no counterpart in the South of the resonance which party elections provided for the Northern cause. The historian of Confederate propaganda asserts that official efforts in this direction were very deficient, which is not surprising when it is recalled how preponderantly such efforts in the North were handled through party agencies. We have a description of how such activities were carried on in Washington with the heartiest co-operation of the national government during the fall of 1864:

> The National Republican Committee have taken full possession of all the Capitol buildings, and the committee rooms of the Senate and House of Representatives are filled with clerks, busy in mailing Lincoln documents all over the loyal States. . . .
>
> The Post Office Department, of course, is attending to the lion's share of this work. Eighty bags of mail matter, all containing Lincoln documents, are daily sent to Sherman's army.

Not long after this time, a measure was timidly offered in the Confederate Congress whereby the government frank might be used for mailing newspapers to soldiers in the field. The Confederate Postmaster-General was distressed. His department was required by law to be self-supporting, and he was very proud of its being the only one to show a surplus, which he had achieved by doing away with all but the bare minimum services. He spoke to the President about this new bill, and the latter solemnly vetoed it as being unconstitutional.

Whether Northern wartime elections served to give refinement and precision to the issues is perhaps less important than that they served to simplify and consolidate them. When the people of Indiana were urged in 1863 to vote for Republicans in their local elections, they were really being asked to do more than elect a few county officers. And by the same token the candidate for such an office accepted, along with his nomination, a whole train of extraordinary responsibilities: Governor Morton, President Lincoln, emancipation, arbitrary arrests, and war to the end. There was no separating them; under the circumstances of war, the voter who took the Republican candidate took them all. And the candidate, if successful in his debates with his Democratic opponent, would have enacted something akin to the principle of the self-fulfilling prophecy. He defined his position, he defended the administration, he persuaded his audience, and in the process he repersuaded and recommitted himself.

It may be quite proper to say that it was, after all, the Union's military success that made political success possible. The fall of Atlanta in September 1864, for example, certainly rescued Lincoln's chances for re-election. But conceivably it was not that simple, and short-term correlations may be deceiving. How was the Northern will sustained for the three and a half years that were needed before it could reap successes of any kind in late 1864? A continual affirmation and reaffirmation of purpose was built into the very currents of political life in the Northern states. It is altogether probable that the North's political energies and its military will were, all along, parts of the same process.

Every election, moreover, was a step in nationalizing the war. The extension of local and state loyalties into national loyalties during this period was something of a revolution, and it did not occur easily. This profound change cannot be taken for granted, nor is it best undertsood simply by examining the formal federal structure through which it began. It is revealed rather through the far less formal political process whereby the national government in the Civil War was able to communicate its purposes, to persuade, and to exercise its will directly upon individuals in state, city, town, and local countryside.

Reconstruction: A National View

Negro Suffrage and Republican Politics

by La Wanda and John H. Cox

The nation emerged from four years of Civil War only to plunge at once into a decade of political conflict for control of the former slave states. Radical Republicans and Johnson Democrats, freedmen and ex-rebels all shared at least one fundamental perception throughout the "Reconstruction Era," namely a common recognition of its uniqueness. The partisan quarrels of the years 1865–1877 were grounded on a dilemma which all politicians faced: the singular absence of precedents to guide political decision-making.

At war's end, there existed an unwieldly governing coalition in the North, the "Union party" composed of Republicans and some "War Democrats" such as President Andrew Johnson. As Johnson and the congressional Radicals struggled for power, both confronted a revolutionary situation for which neither the Constitution nor the ordinary processes of American government had made provision. What political rights, if any, remain for leaders and followers of a defeated secessionist movement? What place in the Republic's political life should a freed Negro population assume—be given, rather? Which branch of the national government, executive or legislative, should dominate postwar policy formation? The confrontation between Andrew Johnson and the Radicals arose out of these unanswered constitutional and moral questions. Not even the takeover of national government by Republican congressional leaders in 1867 provided firm answers either to the legal or political questions involved. In the process, however, Congress assumed responsibility for imposing its own version of Reconstruction upon the South.

*Who were the Radicals and what were their major goals? Historians have argued over these problems almost from the moment Reconstruction ended, often disagreeing vehemently on Republican motives in supporting Negro suffrage through passage of the Reconstruction Acts and the Fourteenth and Fifteenth Amendments. Some have labeled the Radicals either self-serving political opportunists or pro-black zealots, bent upon cynically manipulating a Southern Negro electorate in order to ensure their own continued domination of national politics and to punish former Confederates. Others have seen congressional Radicals as tools of Northern industrialists determined to block the Democrats' return to power and preserve the economic benefits of Republican rule. Still others have pointed to the contradictions between the general opposition of most white Northerners to Negro suffrage in their own states and Radical support for such legislation in the South. Were Republican politicians "sincerely" in favor of federal support for the freedman—*including *his enfranchisement—and, if so, how did their policies triumph temporarily in spite of their constituents' strong anti-Negro bias? In the following article La Wanda and John Cox explore these questions by reviewing the historiography of Negro suffrage and interpreting the complexities of Republican motivation.*

Republican party leadership of the 1860's was responsible for establishing the legal right of Negro citizens to equal suffrage, first in the defeated South by act of Congress and then through-

From *The Journal of Southern History,* XXXIII (August 1967), 303–30. most footnotes omitted.

out the nation by constitutional amendment.[1] Whether historians have condemned or applauded the grant of suffrage to Negroes in the post–Civil War years, they have more often than not viewed the motives behind this party action with considerable cynicism. The purpose of this article is to review their treatment and to raise for re-examination the question of what moved Republicans in Congress to such far-reaching action.

The earliest study of the origins of the Fifteenth Amendment was prepared by a scholarly lawyer from western Virginia, Allen Caperton Braxton, for presentation to the state bar association in 1903. The work is still cited, and a new edition was printed in the 1930's. Braxton held that Negro suffrage was the result of "gratitude, apprehension and politics—these three; but the greatest of these was politics." To Radical leaders of the Republican party, enfranchisement early appeared "a promising means of party aggrandisement"; it soon became "essential to the perpetuation of their power." In the struggle with President Andrew Johnson over Reconstruction, they had alienated "the entire white race of the South" for at least a generation to come. Once the Southern states were restored to the Union and the white vote of the South added to the Democratic vote of the North, the Republican party would face hopeless defeat; the only means of escape lay through the Southern Negro. In the legislation of March 1867 Radicals effected "a *coup d'etat* of the first magnitude," but it was not a stable foundation on which to build future political power. The law might be rescinded by Congress, overturned by judicial decision, or defied by the Southern states after their readmission. Only a constitutional amendment could provide security. It would also mean votes from an increasing Negro pop-

1. The First Reconstruction Act, passed over President Andrew Johnson's veto March 2, 1867, and the Fifteenth Amendment, passed by Congress February 26, 1869, and declared ratified March 30, 1870. In 1860 the only states with equal suffrage for Negroes were Maine, New Hampshire, Vermont, Massachusetts, and Rhode Island. New York permitted Negroes with a $250 freehold estate to vote. By 1869 the following Northern states had been added to the above list: Nebraska, Wisconsin, Minnesota, and Iowa.

ulation in the North as a potential balance of power in close elections. A few footnotes and quotations, notably one from Charles Sumner, appear as illustrative, and there is a flat assertion that debates in Congress on the Fifteenth Amendment "leave no room to doubt" its political inspiration. It is clear, however, that the author felt no need either to scrutinize or to document his interpretation; a primary relationship between Negro suffrage and party expediency appeared to him self-evident.

Braxton did examine in detail a thesis and the historic contradiction that it implied. "One may well question," he wrote in conclusion, "whether the popular will was executed or thwarted when negro suffrage was written into the fundamental law of this nation." No reader would doubt that the author's answer was "thwarted." Despite some overstatement and minor distortions of fact, this thesis is sound history. The national guarantee of an equal vote to the Negro did not reflect a popular consensus, even in the North. Braxton's attempt to explain how an unwanted policy became the fundamental law of the land, though less convincing, raised an important historical problem.

Despite his emphasis upon political expediency as the impelling causal element behind equal suffrage, the Virginia attorney might have considered Republican leaders who had imposed this result upon the nation, at least a few of their number, men sincerely concerned with the Negro's right to vote. References to "fanaticism," "bigotry," and "negrophiles" suggest that he did, though obviously without sympathy. This implication, however, is explicitly disavowed and with specific reference to Senator Sumner. Braxton found "shocking" evidence of insincerity in the fact that men who argued for the inalienable right of the Negro to vote agreed to exclude Indians and Chinese from the franchise. He considered leaders of the party to be distinguished from the rank and file of Northerners neither by principle nor by lack of prejudice. Unlike their constituents, congressmen were removed from personal competition with the Negro, and their national perspective made them aware of the dependence of Republican party power upon Negro enfranchisement. Braxton's indictment of Republican motivation showed charity on just one count. He granted that some leaders were moved neither by "malice toward the South" nor by "heartless political ambition." They had come to equate the life of the Republican party with the life of the nation and honestly feared a Democratic victory as a national disaster.

The second study of the fifteenth Amendment, by John M. Mathews, appeared in 1909 and was to remain the standard historical account for more than half a century. Originally prepared as a paper for a seminar in political science at Johns Hopkins University, it is a most unhistorical history in the sense that its author was more concerned to analyze concepts than men or events. He narrowly delimited the chronology and substance of his "legislative history" and showed special interest in the judicial interpretation of the amendment. Neither the historic problem posed by Braxton's study nor the question of men's motives as individuals or as party leaders presented a challenge to Mathews; he did not even consider it important to identify with particular congressmen or with political parties the four elements in his analysis—the humanitarians, the nationalists, the politicians, and the local autonomists. Indeed, he explicitly stated that "These forces were primarily principles, rather than men or groups of men. They were not always separable except in thought, for the same senator or representative was often influenced by more than one of them at the same time."

Yet the Mathews monograph does carry certain implications in respect to motivation. The statement that "There was little real difference of opinion among the leaders in Congress as to the desirability of enlarging the sphere of political liberty for the negro race" might be read as an assumption of genuine concern for the Negro on the part of the lawmakers. On the other hand, a quite different interpretation could be given to statements that "The politician was the initiator and real engineer of the movement," that he labored for a concrete objective "fraught with definite, practical results," and that he was not altogether satisfied with the final form of the amendment "because it did not directly and specifically guarantee the African's right to vote" and hence might be evaded. In this study so long considered authoritative, there is nothing to confirm Braxton's identification of equal suffrage with partisan advantage, but neither is there anything that would cause its readers to question that assumption.

The writings of William A. Dunning and of James Ford Rhodes, the two most influential scholars with accounts of Reconstruction published during the first decade of the twentieth century, did sound a warning. To Southerners it had been "inconceivable," Dunning pointed out, that "rational men of the North should seriously approve of negro suffrage *per se*"; hence they assumed that the only explanation was "a craving for political power." Dunning was implying a fallacy in their understanding. Yet he himself attributed Republican sponsorship of Negro suffrage in the First Reconstruction Act of 1867 to the "pressure of party necessity and of Sumner's tireless urging." In writing of the Fifteenth Amendment, Dunning assumed that he had established the motivation behind it. He cited an earlier paragraph as support for the statement: "We have already seen the partisan motive which gave the impulse to the passage of the Fifteenth Amendment." Any reader who took the trouble to turn back the pages would find a passage which, far from proving the contention, did not necessarily imply it. Dunning had written that after the presidential election of 1868 in which Democrats gained majorities in Georgia and Louisiana through the use of violence, moderate Republicans had no uncertainty as to "the policy of maintaining what had been achieved in enfranchising the blacks."

Rhodes was more explicit in his warning and more direct in crediting to humanitarian feelings within Republican party ranks an influence in "forcing negro suffrage upon the South." He cautioned readers not to lose sight of the high motives involved "for it would be easy to collect a mass of facts showing that the sole aim of congressional reconstruction was to strengthen the Republican party." Neither the statement quoted nor his account as a whole would stir to skepticism anyone who had assumed with Braxton the predominance of political expediency. He did not analyze or criticize the Braxton assumption but rather supplemented it. In Rhodes's view, there were men with "intelligence and high character" who were "earnest for the immediate enfranchisement of the freedmen," but they were "numerically small." His writing at times carried an unintended innuendo. For example, he stated that the majority of Republicans in Congress when they reassembled after the Christmas holidays of 1866 did not favor the imposition of Negro suffrage upon the South, a policy which they sustained by a two-thirds vote a few weeks later. The explanation lay in "The rejection of the Fourteenth Amendment by the South, the clever use of the 'outrages' argument, the animosity to the President . . . which was increased to virulence by his wholesale removals of Republicans from office," factors that "enabled the partisan tyranny of Stevens and the pertinacity of Sumner to achieve this result."

The ambivalence in Rhodes's treatment arose primarily from his strong conviction that the grant of suffrage to the Negro during Reconstruction was a major mistake in policy. This judgment was evident in a paper which he delivered before the Massachusetts Historical Society while writing his account of Reconstruction and also in the volumes of his *History of the United States* which appeared two years later. Suffrage had been an abysmal failure which "pandered to the ignorant negroes, the knavish white natives and the vulturous adventurers who flocked from the North" and "neutralized the work of honest Republicans. . . ." Experience in the North, in his opinion, also discredited the grant of equal suffrage to the Negro—he had shown little political leadership, rarely identified himself "with any movement on a high plane," such as civil service, tariff reform, honest money, or pure municipal government, and "arrogantly asserts his right to recognition" because he is "greedy for office and emolument." All this had not been the Negro's fault; he had been "started at the top" despite "all the warnings of science and political experience." Rhodes believed that the findings of science were clear and that they had been available to Sumner and his fellow advocates of Negro enfranchisement through the distinguished Harvard scientist Louis Agassiz, who was Sumner's friend. He did not place all blame on Sumner, however, but indicated that the fault lay in our national character. "I think that England or Prussia would have solved the negro problem better"; they would have "studied the negro scientifically"; in the "age of Darwin and Huxley" Americans had made no attempt to do so.

In discussing the problem with fellow historians, Rhodes revealed more sharply than in his writings his personal assessment of motivation: "From a variety of motives, some praiseworthy and others the reverse, we forced negro suffrage upon the South. . . . Party advantage, the desire of worthless men at the North for offices at the South, co-operated with a misguided humanitarianism." The warning which he sounded, and the less explicit one from Dunning as well, reflected a conscientious desire on the part of these distinguished historians to be fair, restrained, and judicious. The assumption that most Republican members of Congress who voted for equal Negro suffrage did so primarily if not solely, for reasons of political expediency, was an assumption they accepted; it apparently did not occur to either man that there was need for any careful scrutiny to establish the validity of this accusation.

For three decades, until the post–World War II years, few historians handled the question of Republican motivation with as much fairness as had Rhodes and Dunning. Ellis P. Oberholtzer, in his multivolume *History of the United States Since the Civil War*, wrote that "Just as the war had not been waged to free the negro from bondage" so the postwar strife "except to a few minds, had little enough to do with the improvement of the lot of the black man." He continued: "The project to make voters out of black men was not so much for their social elevation as for the further punishment of the Southern white people—for the capture of offices for Radical scamps and the intrenchment of the Radical party in power for a long time to come in the South and in the country at large." The small but influential volume in the Yale *Chronicles of America* series written by Dunning's foremost student, Walter L. Fleming, made the indictment specific. The election of 1868, Fleming wrote showed that Democrats could command more white votes than could Republicans "whose total included nearly 700,000 blacks." This prompted the Radicals to frame the Fifteenth Amendment which, as it appeared to them, would not only "make safe the negro majorities in the South" but also add strength from Negroes previously denied the ballot in the North, thus assuring "900,000 negro voters for the Republican party."

During the late 1920's and the 1930's, a period in Reconstruction historiography which saw the "canonization" of Andrew Johnson, little charity was shown to those who had been Johnson's opponents. Claude G. Bowers developed the "conspiracy" approach to Negro suffrage, seeing it as the culmination of a plot hatched by Sumner and a few Radicals and dating back at least to the early days of 1865. He quoted approvingly the Georgian, Benjamin H. Hill, who charged that Negro suffrage was a matter of knaves using fools " 'to keep the Radical Party in power in the approaching presidential election, . . . to retain by force and fraud the power they are losing in the detection of their treason in the North.' " George Fort Milton recognized that "The Radicals had mixed motives in this insistence on negro suffrage," but his lack of sympathy for the "old Abolitionists" led him to gibe at Sumner. From a letter of the Senator, he quoted, " 'We need the votes of all,' " then observed, "Could it be that practical political necessities moved him as well as lofty idealistic views?" Milton did little more than mention the Fifteenth Amendment but could not resist using the opportunity to belittle its Republican sponsors: ". . . one or two Senators shamefacedly admitted that perhaps an intelligent white woman had as much right as an ignorant negro plow-hand to determine the destinies of the nation. But there seemed little political advantage in women suffrage. . . ." James G. Randall, whose substantial volume on the Civil War and Reconstruction served as a standard college textbook from the 1930's to the 1960's, handled the subject of Negro suffrage with restraint; yet in substance he accepted a mild version of Bowers' conspiracy thesis. Randall's variant was that "the importance of the Negro vote to the Republican party North and South caused leading Radicals to keep their eye upon the issue" although Northern sentiment would not support nationwide Negro suffrage. Gradually, as the power of the Radicals increased, they moved toward their goal. "Step by step they were able to enact laws promoting Negro suffrage without an amendment, and finally to carry the suffrage amendment itself in the first year of Grant's administration." This account was allowed to stand without modification when the volume was revised in 1961 by David Donald.

The chronological limits of Howard K. Beale's study of the election of 1866, perhaps the most influential scholarly product of the pro-Johnson historiography, precluded an examination of the Reconstruction Acts of 1867 and the Fifteenth Amendment. However, there is a chapter devoted to Negro suffrage as a general issue. Beale divided its Radical proponents into four groups —old abolitionists, who believed in the principle of equal suffrage; friends of the Negro, who saw the ballot as his only means of defense; men hostile to racial equality, who would use Negro suffrage to humiliate the defeated South; and, lastly, "a more numerous group" to whom "expediency was the motive." Curiously, his classification had the same weakness as Mathews' disembodied analysis; it offered the reader no evidence that any one of the four "groups" was identifiable in terms of specific individuals. In fact, despite a deep personal commitment to Negro equality and intensive manuscript research, Beale added little new except to link the suffrage issue with his general thesis that Radical leaders were motivated by economic as well as political ends.

"If the South could be excluded, or admitted only with negro suffrage," he wrote, "the new industrial order which the Northeast was developing, would be safe."

Yet Beale did not dismiss the suffrage issue as summarily as had the Republicans in the 1866 campaign. His treatment suggests his interest in the subject, and particularly in the claim made during 1865 and after that the Negro would never be safe unless protected by the ballot. Beale considered it "a powerful [argument]" even though he looked with sympathy upon those who mistrusted a grant of unqualified suffrage to naïve and uneducated freedmen. After struggling with the argument for several pages, he concluded that no one could say with certainty whether without the ballot the status of the newly freed slave among white Southerners would have been shaped by "the fair-minded" or "the vicious." Then he added: "Few cared to know. Extreme Radicals wanted negro suffrage; outrages against the negroes, and an exaggeration of cruel codes would reconcile Northerners to it." In other words, the "powerful argument" was essentially a propaganda device; its prevalence in the 1860's would not lighten the charges against the Republican Radical leadership.

Another election study, Charles H. Coleman's analysis of the Grant–Seymour campaign of 1868, was published in the 1930's and at once took its place as the standard, perhaps definitive, account. Coleman's discussion of the Negro suffrage issue in the elections of 1867 and 1868 is exceptionally fair and informative. Without raising the question of motivation or passing judgment, it yet provides considerable material pertinent to the problem. Also, Coleman, like Walter Fleming, was interested in the importance of the Negro vote. He estimated that it had provided Grant with 450,000 of his total, without which the Republicans would not have gained a popular majority. While Coleman believed that a majority of the white voters of the country favored the Democratic party in 1868 and implied that this remained true until 1896, unlike Fleming, he did not point to any connection between the 1868 election results and the movement immediately thereafter for an equal-suffrage amendment. The omission may have been due to his clear recognition that Grant's victory in the electoral college would have been secure without any Negro votes. The Democrats with better leadership, according to Coleman, might have contended with the Republicans on almost equal terms in 1868, but they did not lose the election "through the operation of the reconstruction acts." Despite a generally careful and balanced presentation, in his opening paragraphs Coleman made reference incidentally and uncritically to "Republican ascendancy" as the motive behind the Fifteenth Amendment. He had not given thought to the relationship between his findings and the time-honored charges of Braxton and Fleming.

By the 1950's a new direction was evident in historical writings dealing with the Negro in nineteenth-century America, one that rejected the assumption of racial inferiority and cherished the quest for racial equality. This trend, which reached major proportions in the 1960's, drew stimulus and support both from the contemporary social and intellectual climate and from interior developments within historical research. During the thirties revisionist articles dealing with so-called "Black" Reconstruction in the South had anticipated postwar attitudes toward race relationships and had upset the negative stereotypes of "scalawags," "carpetbaggers," and "Radical" regimes. In the forties the National Archives provided material for new departures in Reconstruction scholarship by making available the manuscript records of the Freedmen's Bureau with a useful checklist. The extremes to which vindication of Andrew Johnson had been carried in the thirties, together with a program to assemble and publish his papers, led to re-examination of his record and that of his opponents. Military confrontation with Hitler stimulated a challenge to the "needless war" interpretation of the American civil conflict, redirecting attention to slavery as a moral issue. Antislavery agitators became the focus of renewed interest and sympathy, the latter reinforced by a growing sophistication in the historian's borrowings from psychology and sociology. Leadership of Negroes in the contemporary struggle for equality found a counterpart in an increased recognition of the role of Negro leadership during the nineteenth century. Through new biographies and analytical articles, a beginning was made in reassessing the record and motives of leading Radicals. Finally, the coincidence of the Civil War centennial with the great public civil rights issues of the 1960's quickened the pace of historical writings concerned with the status of the Negro.

Out of these recent studies has come a new perspective on the post–Civil War grant of suffrage to the Negro, once widely regarded with dismay. The Fifteenth Amendment is now seen as a "momentous enactment." It included Negroes within "the American dream of equality and opportunity," gave the United States distinction as being the first nation committed to the proposition that in a "bi-racial society . . . human beings must have equal rights," and established an essential legal substructure upon which to build the reality of political equality.

There has also emerged an explanation of political Radicalism during Reconstruction, even of Republicanism generally, in terms of ideas and idealism. The case has been subtly argued and dramatically summarized by Kenneth M. Stampp: ". . . radical reconstruction ought to be viewed in part as the last great crusade of the nineteenth-century romantic reformers." If anything, Radicals were less opportunistic and more candid than the average politician. "To the practical motives that the radicals occasionally revealed must be added the moral idealism that they inherited from the abolitionists." The case for Radicalism has also been persuasively presented by the English historian William Ranulf Brock, who has written that the cement binding together the Radicals as a political group was "not interest but a number of propositions about equality, rights, and national power." In fact, Brock does not limit this generous interpretation of motives to the Radicals, but includes moderate Republicans as well. He was gone even further and identified "the great moving power behind Reconstruction" with "the conviction of the average Republican that the objectives of his party were rational and humane." The study by the present authors led to the conclusion that the moderates in Congress broke with the President in 1866 primarily because of their genuine concern for equal civil rights short of suffrage.

With the ferment and new direction of Reconstruction historiography, the old Braxton–Rhodes–Fleming assumption of party expediency as the controlling motive behind support for Negro suffrage by Republican congressmen might reasonably be expected to meet one of three fates: it might be quietly replaced by the opposite assumption that congressional votes reflected in large measure the strain of idealism in Republicanism; it could be dismissed on the ground that there had been a fusion of principle and expediency so intimate and indivisible as to preclude further inquiry; or it could be subjected to an incisive, detailed, and comprehensive examination. At the present writing neither the first nor third alternative appears at all likely. As for the second, the problem of motivation deserves a better resolution, for it is important both to our understanding of the past and to our expectations of the future.

The "practical" view of Republican motivation is too casually accepted in historical writings and too consonant with prevailing attitudes toward politicians and parties to be in danger of just disappearing. Leslie H. Fishel, Jr., Emma Lou Thornbrough, and Leon F. Litwack in their sympathetic pioneering studies of Negroes in the North all assume that Republican politicians had little interest in the Negro except to obtain his vote. In staking out the well-merited abolitionist claim of credit for having championed the cause of Negro equality during the Civil War and Reconstruction, James M. McPherson perpetuates the traditional attitude toward Republicans: the abolitionists provided moral justification, but party policies "were undertaken primarily for military or political reasons." Indeed, McPherson condemns the whole North for a failure of conscience and belittles the public support given to equal rights as "primarily a conversion of expediency rather than one of conviction." David Donald has attempted to bypass the "difficulty of fathoming . . . motives" by disregarding individuals in favor of "objective behavior patterns" and "quantitatively measurable forces." His procedures and logic, however, start with the assumption that politicians wish either re-election or higher office and that this fact is controlling in presidential policy and congressional voting. It is startling to read that Lincoln's policies could have been arrived at by "A rather simple computer installed in the White House, fed the elementary statistical information about election returns and programed to solve the recurrent problem of winning re-election. . . ."

Even Stampp, who restates the old hostile arguments regarding the political motivation of Radicals in order to challenge them, replies directly only with the observation that conservatives as well were thinking how best to keep the Republican party in power—to them Negro suffrage simply appeared an obstacle rather than an instrument of party unity and control. Stampp also strikes a disparaging note evident elsewhere in recent scholarship. This is the charge of "timidity" and "evasion" leveled against Republican politicians on the question of Negro suffrage. There is irony in the shifting basis of attack upon the reputation of Republican politicians. Once berated from the right for plots and maneuvers to thwart the popular will and establish Negro suffrage, these whipping boys of history are now in danger of assault from the left for having lacked the boldness, energy, and conviction needed for an earlier and more secure victory.

There finally appeared in 1965 to supersede the Mathews monograph an intensive, scholarly work by a young historian, William Gillette, on the passage and ratification of the Fifteenth Amendment. Reflecting the modern temper in its rejection of caste and commitment to equality, the new study nevertheless represents a vigorous survival of the Braxton-Fleming tradition. Gillette's thesis transfers to the North the emphasis formerly placed on the South, but political expediency remains the heart of the matter: "The primary object of the Amendment was *to get the*

Negro vote in the North. . . ." As revealed by the election results of 1868, "prospects for both northern and southern Republicans were not bright" and, according to Gillette, "Republicans had to do something." They were pessimistic about reliance upon the Negro vote in the South but alert to its potential in the North. This prospect motivated the framing of the amendment and accounted for ratification in the face of widespread opposition since it "made political sense to shrewd politicians. . . ." In effect, Gillette accepts as his thesis the judgment pronounced in 1870 by the Democratic party-line newspaper, the New York *World*, that Republican leaders " 'calculated that the Negro vote in the doubtful Northern states would be sufficient to maintain the Republican ascendancy in those states and, through them, in the politics of the country. It was with this in view that they judged the Fifteenth Amendment essential to the success of their party.' "

In challenge to the dominant pattern of interpretation from Braxton through Gillette, we should like to suggest that Republican party leadership played a crucial role in committing this nation to equal suffrage for the Negro not because of political expediency but *despite* political risk. An incontestable fact of Reconstruction history suggests this view. Race prejudice was so strong in the North that the issue of equal Negro suffrage constituted a clear and present danger to Republicans. White backlash may be a recently coined phrase, but it was a virulent political phenomenon in the 1860's. The exploitation of prejudice by the Democratic opposition was blatant and unashamed.

The power base of the Republican party lay in the North. However much party leaders desired to break through sectional boundaries to create a national image or to gain some measure of security from Southern votes, victory or defeat in the presidential elections of the nineteenth century lay in the Northern states. With the exception of the contested election of 1876, electoral votes from the South were irrelevant—either nonexistent or unnecessary—to Republican victory. It was the loss of Connecticut,

Indiana, and New York in 1876 and 1884, and of those states plus Illinois in 1892, which was critical; had they remained in the Republican column, Democrats would have waited until the twentieth century to claim residence for one of their own in the White House.[2]

What has been charged to timidity might better be credited to prudence. The caution with which Republicans handled the Negro suffrage issue in 1865, 1866, and again in 1868 made political sense. Had the elections of 1866 and 1868 been fought on a platform supporting equal suffrage, who could say with certainty, then or now, that Republicans would have maintained their power?[3] In the state elections of 1867, when Negro suffrage was a major issue, the party took a beating in Connecticut, New York, Pennsylvania, and New Jersey, suffered losses in local elections in Indiana and Illinois, and came within 0.4 per cent of losing the Ohio governorship despite the personal political strength of their candidate Rutherford B. Hayes. In Ohio the issue was clearly drawn, for, in addition to the nationwide commitment to Negro suffrage in the South made by the First Re-

2. For the election of 1868, see Coleman, *Election of 1868*, p. 363. Calculations for the other years are based upon the electoral vote as given in W. Dean Burnham, *Presidential Ballots, 1836–1892* (Baltimore, 1955), 888–89. In 1872 Republicans had 286 electoral votes and would have held a substantial majority without the six Southern states and the two border states which were included in the total. Republicans could have won in 1876 without the 19 contested votes of Florida, Louisiana, and South Carolina had they retained either New York (35 votes) or both Connecticut (6) and Indiana (15). In the elections of 1880, 1884, 1888, and 1892, the Republican candidate gained no electoral votes from any former slave state. In 1884, as in 1876, either the New York vote or a combination of those of Indiana and Connecticut would have won the election for the Republicans. In 1892 the electoral count was 277 Democratic, 145 Republican, and 22 Populist. Republicans needed an additional 78 votes for a majority, which could have come from New York (36), Illinois (24), Indiana (15), and Connecticut (6). The party kept Pennsylvania and Ohio (except for one vote); it had not held New Jersey (10 votes) since 1872.

3. More than a simple majority would have been necessary to retain control of Reconstruction in the face of President Johnson's vetoes and to pass the Fifteenth Amendment. Johnson supporters welcomed Negro suffrage as an issue on which they expected to redress their 1866 defeat.

construction Act of March 1867, the Republican party bore responsibility for a state-wide referendum on behalf of equal suffrage at home. The proposed suffrage amendment to the state constitution went down to defeat with less than 46 per cent of the votes cast. Democrats gained control of both houses of the state legislature, turning a comfortable Republican margin of forty-six into a Democratic majority of eight. Even judged by the gubernatorial vote, Republicans suffered a serious loss of support, for the popular Hayes gained 50.3 per cent of the vote as compared to 54.5 per cent won by the Republican candidate for secretary of state in 1866.

There was nothing exceptional about Ohioans' hostility to Negro suffrage. In Republican Minnesota and Kansas equal-suffrage amendments also went down to defeat in the fall elections of 1867, with a respectable 48.8 per cent of the vote in the former but with less than 35 per cent in the latter despite the fact that Kansas Repubilcans in the 1860's constituted 70 per cent of the electorate. From 1865 through 1869 eleven referendum votes were held in eight Northern states on constitutional changes to provide Negroes with the ballot; only two were successful—those held during the fall of 1868 in Iowa and Minnesota. The Minnesota victory, gained after two previous defeats, has been attributed to trickery in labeling the amendment. The issue was never placed before the white voters of Illinois, Indiana, Pennsylvania, or New Jersey; and this fact probably indicated a higher intensity of race prejudice than in Connecticut, New York, and Ohio, where equal suffrage was defeated.[4] These seven were marginal states of critical importance to the Republicans in national elections. The tenacity of opposition to Negro enfranchisement is well illustrated in New York, where one might have expected to find it minimal since Negroes had always voted in the state although subjected to a discriminatory property qualification since 1821. After a Republican legislature ratified the Fifteenth

4. The other two states where equal suffrage was defeated were Wisconsin and Michigan.

Amendment in April 1869, New Yorkers defeated a similar change in the state constitution, swept the Republicans out of control at Albany and returned a Democratic majority of twenty, which promptly voted to rescind New York's ratification.

In short, Republican sponsorship of Negro suffrage meant flirtation with political disaster in the North, particularly in any one or all of the seven pivotal states where both the prejudice of race and the Democratic opposition were strong. Included among them were the four most populous states in the nation, with corresponding weight in the electoral college: New York, Pennsylvania, Ohio, and Illinois. Negroes were denied equal suffrage in every one of these critically important seven, and only in New York did they enjoy a partial enfranchisement. If Negroes were to be equally enfranchised, as the Fifteenth Amendment directed, it is true that Republicans could count upon support from an overwhelming majority of the new voters. It does not necessarily follow, however, that this prospect was enticing to "shrewd politicians." What simple political computation could add the number of potential Negro voters to be derived from a minority population that reached a high of 3.4 per cent in New Jersey and 2.4 per cent in Ohio, then diminished in the other five states from 1.9 to 1.1 per cent, a population already partially enfranchised in New York and to be partially disenfranchised in Connecticut by the state's nondiscriminatory illiteracy tests; determine and subtract the probable number of white voters who would be alienated among the dominant 96.6 to 98.9 per cent of the population; and predict a balance that would ensure Republican victory?

The impact of the Negro suffrage issue upon the white voter might be softened by moving just after a national election rather than just before one; and this was the strategy pursued in pushing through the Fifteenth Amendment. Yet risk remained, a risk which it is difficult to believe politicians would have willingly assumed had their course been set solely, or primarily, by political arithmetic. Let us, then, consider the nature of the evidence cited to show that Republican policy sprang from narrow party interests.

Since the days of Braxton, historians have used the public statements of public men, straight from the pages of the *Congressional Globe*, not only to document the charge of party expediency but also to prove it by the admission of intent. The frequency with which either Senator Charles Sumner or Thaddeus Stevens has been quoted on the arithmetic of Negro enfranchisement might well have suggested caution in using such oral evidence for establishing motivation. As craftsmen, historians have been alerted against a proclivity to seize upon the discovery of an economic motive as if, to quote Kenneth Stampp, they then were "dealing with reality—with something that reflects the true nature of man." Stampp cites Sumner as an example of the fallacy: ". . . when he argued that Negro suffrage was necessary to prevent a repudiation of the public debt, he may *then* have had a concealed motive—that is, he may have believed that this was the way to convert bondholders to his moral principles." An equal sophistication is overdue in the handling of political motivation. With reference to the Reconstruction legislation of 1867, Sumner did state—frankly, as the cynically inclined would add—that the Negro vote had been a necessity for the organization of "loyal governments" in the South. He continued with equal forthrightness: "It was on this ground, rather than principle, that I relied most. . . ." A man remarkably uncompromising in his own adherence to principle, Sumner obviously did not believe it wise to rely upon moral argument alone to move others. Thaddeus Stevens's belief in the justice of equal suffrage and his desire to see it realized were as consistent and genuine as Sumner's own, but Stevens was a much shrewder practitioner of the art of politics. It is worth noting, then, that Negro suffrage was not the solution to which he clung most tenaciously in order to guarantee "loyal governments" in the South; he looked more confidently to the army and to white disfranchisement. In the last critical stage of battle over Reconstruction policy, it was the moderate Republicans who championed an immediate mandate for Negro suffrage in the South, while Stevens led the fight to delay its advent in favor of an interlude of military rule.

All this suggests the need for a detailed analysis of who said what, when, in arguing that Negro suffrage, South or North, would bring Republican votes and Republican victories. Did the argument have its origin with the committed antislavery men or with the uncommitted politician? Was it used to whet an appetite for political gain or to counter fear of losses? Such a study might start by throwing out as evidence of motivation all appeals to political expediency made after the Fifteenth Amendment was sent to the states for ratification. By that time Republicans were tied to the policy and could not escape the opprobrium it carried; a leadership that used every possible stratagem and pressure to secure ratification in the face of widespread opposition could be expected to overlook no argument that might move hesitant state legislators, particularly one that appealed to party loyalty and interest.

It has been implied that election results in the 1870's and 1880's were evidence of political motivation behind the Fifteenth Amendment. The logic is faulty. Consequences are not linked causally to intentions. Favorable election returns would not constitute proof that decision-making had been dependent upon calculation, nor would election losses preclude the existence of unrealistic expectations. Yet it would be of interest to know the effect of the enfranchisement of Negroes upon Republican fortunes, particularly in the marginal Northern states. Election returns might serve to test the reasonableness of optimistic projections of gain by adding black voters, as against the undoubted risk of losing white voters. If the end result of Negro enfranchisement in the North was one of considerable advantage to Republicans, we may have overestimated the element of political risk. If enfranchisement brought the Republicans little benefit, the case for a careful re-examination of Republican motivation is strengthened. Inquiry can reasonably be restricted to the results of presidential and congressional contests, since these were of direct concern to the Republicans in Congress responsible for the Fifteenth Amendment.[5]

Negro votes in the critical Northern states were not sufficient to ensure victory in three of the six presidential elections following ratification of the Fifteenth Amendment in 1870. For purposes of comparing the "before" and "after" vote, the election of 1872 is unfortunately of no utility. Horace Greeley proved so weak a Liberal Republican-Democratic candidate that in every one of the critical seven states Grant would have won without a single Negro ballot.[6] In the 1876 contest, which affords the best comparison with 1868, the Republican percentage of the vote dropped in every one of the marginal states, four of which were lost to the Democrats. Comparison of the number of Republican losses in the seven states for the three elections before 1872 with those for the three elections after 1872, shows four losses in the earlier period as against nine losses after Negro enfranchisement.[7] Of course, it could be argued that Republicans would have done even worse without the Negro vote and the politicians in 1869 could not have anticipated the depression of 1873. Politicians would have known, however, that Negroes in the North, outside the border states, were too few to constitute a guarantee of victory

5. Local elections did, of course, have consequences for senators, who were elected by state legislatures; and a shift of political fortune in a critical state was always of national interest. However, the Fifteenth Amendment was not generated from local politics. The argument of political expediency implies political profit in national elections.

6. The percentage of Negroes in the population as compared with the percentage margin of victory in 1872 follows: Connecticut, 1.8 per cent with 2.4; New York, 1.2 per cent with 3.1; Pennsylvania, 1.9 per cent with 12.1; New Jersey, 3.4 per cent with 4.4; Ohio, 2.4 per cent with 3.2; Indiana, 1.5 per cent with 3.2; Illinois, 1.1 per cent with 6.2. The Negro percentage is from Gillette's convenient chart, *Right to Vote*, 82; the percentage of the Republican vote was calculated from the election figures in Burnham, *Presidential Ballots*, as was that of 1868 and 1876.

7. Before 1872: New Jersey in 1860 (in part), 1864, and 1868, and New York in 1868. After 1872: Connecticut, New York, and Indiana in 1876 and 1884; New Jersey in 1876, 1880, and 1884.

in the face of any major adversity. In 1880 and 1888, years of success, Republicans might have lost Indiana without the Negro, but they would not have lost the Presidency. The only presidential contest in the nineteenth century in which Negro voters played a critical role was that of 1876, and the voters lived not in the North but in the South. Analysis of ballots in the 1870's and 1880's does not confirm the reasonableness of expectations for a succession of Republicans in the White House as the result of Negro enfranchisement.

As to Congress, Republicans could hope to gain very little more than they already held in 1869. Of thirty-six Democrats seated in the House of Representatives from the seven marginal states, only four came from districts with a potential Negro electorate large enough to turn the Republican margin of defeat in 1868 into a victory.[8] Of the four, Republicans gained just one in 1870, in Cincinnati, Ohio. Their failure to profit from the Negro vote in the Thirteenth District of Illinois, located at the southern tip of the state, is of particular interest. The district had gone Republican in 1866 and had a large concentration of Negro population. In 1868 the Republican share of the vote had been a close 49.1 per cent; in 1870 it actually decreased with the Democratic margin of victory rising from 503 to 1,081. In the two counties with the highest proportion of Negroes to whites, over 20 per cent, a jump in the Republican percentage plus an increase in the actual number of Republican votes cast—unusual in a nonpresidential year—indicate that Negroes exercised their new franchise. How-

8. The four were the Second District in New Jersey, the First in Ohio, the Sixth in Indiana, and the Thirteenth in Illinois. This conclusion is based upon an inspection of election returns as reported in the *Tribune Almanac*, comparing the margin of victory for Democratic winners in 1868 with an approximation of the number of potential Negro voters estimated as one-fifth of the Negro population in the counties comprising each district. Population figures were taken from the *Ninth Census of the United States*, 1870 (Washington, 1872). Districts where Republican candidates were seated as the result of a contest were not counted as Democratic even though a Democratic majority was shown in the *Tribune Almanac* election returns.

ever, this apparently acted as a stimulus for whites to go to the polls and vote Democratic. In three of the five counties in the district where Negroes constituted over 5 per cent of the population, more Democratic votes were recorded in 1870 than in 1868.[9]

The Republicans did better in holding seats won by slim margins in 1868 than in winning new ones. Eighteen congressional districts in the critical seven states had gone to Republicans by a margin of fewer than five hundred votes. Of these, Republicans retained fourteen and lost four to the Democrats in 1870.[10] Three of the four districts lost had a potential Negro electorate large enough to have doubled the Republican margins of 1868. The record of voting in congressional elections from 1860 through 1868 in the fourteen districts retained suggests that half might have remained Republican without any benefit of the Fifteenth Amendment.[11] It is doubtful whether three of the other seven, all districts in Ohio, would have been placed in jeopardy had Negro suffrage not been raised as an issue in 1867 both at home and in Washington, for the margin of victory dropped sharply from 1866

9. That Negroes were responsible for the increase in the Republican vote cannot, of course, be proved but appears highly probable; similarly, the explanation for the larger Democratic vote is inference. The Republican vote in Alexander County with a Negro population of 21.73 per cent rose from 656 to 804 (37.8 to 45.6 per cent); in Pulaski with a Negro population of 27.4 per cent from 543 to 844 (46 to 55.59 per cent). The three counties showing an increase in the number of Democratic votes were Jackson (Republican votes increased there also), Massac, and Pulaski.

10. Districts lost were the Sixteenth Pennsylvania, the Third and Fourth Ohio, and the Seventh Indiana. Districts retained were the Second Connecticut, the Eleventh and Twelfth New York, the Third, Fifth, Tenth, and Thirteenth Pennsylvania, and Fourth New Jersey, the Second, Sixth, Seventh, Fourteenth, and Sixteenth Ohio, and the Fourth Indiana.

11. This tentative conclusion is based upon Republican victories in at least four of the five congressional elections before 1870. The winner in 1860 had to be estimated on the basis of the county vote because district boundaries were changed in 1862. In only one of the seven had the margin of Republican victory in 1866 been less than five hundred. This district, the Fifth in Philadelphia, may have needed Negro votes for victory in 1870 despite its Republican record. Together with it, the Thirteenth in Pennsylvania and the Fourth in Indiana had slim majorities in 1870. In the latter two, however, the margin decreased as compared with 1868, making it unlikely that Negro enfranchisement helped more than it hurt the Republican candidates.

to 1868.[12] One of the remaining four, the Second District in Connecticut, consisted of two counties, Middlesex with a Negro population of 372 and New Haven with 2,734, the largest concentration of Negroes in the state. New Haven had gone Democratic in 1869 (Connecticut elected its congressmen in the spring) by 62 votes, though the Republican won the district; two years later, with Negroes enfranchised, the Democratic margin in New Haven actually increased to 270! Middlesex saved the day for the incumbent, who barely survived by 23 votes. This suggests that the district remained Republican not because of Negro enfranchisement, but despite it. Two seats, one in Pennsylvania and the other in New Jersey, were retained by an increase in the margin of victory larger than the number of potential Negro voters.[13] The last of the fourteen districts, the Eleventh of New York, consisting of Orange and Sullivan counties, may have been saved by Negro voters, although the election results there are particularly difficult to interpret.[14]

If we consider the total picture of the 1870 congressional races, we find that the Republican share of the vote decreased in five of the seven critical states, remained practically constant in Ohio, and increased in New Jersey. The party did best in the two states with the highest percentages of Negroes in their population,

12. In every one of the seven close Ohio districts, the majority vote had been against the state's Negro suffrage amendment in 1867. Their congressmen, however, supported Negro suffrage, all having voted for the First Reconstruction Act of March 1867, and also for Negro suffrage in the District of Columbia on January 18, 1866, and again on December 14, 1866. These men, each of whom served both in the Thirty-ninth and Fortieth Congresses (1865–1869) were Rutherford B. Hayes, Robert C. Schenck, William Lawrence, Reader W. Clarke, Samuel Shellabarger, Martin Welker, and John A. Bingham.

13. The Tenth District in Pennsylvania, made up of Lebanon and Schuylkill counties, had a Negro population of 458, or about 90 potential voters. The Republican margin increased by 404 votes. The Fourth District in New Jersey had a larger Negro population, but the incumbent's margin jumped from 79 to 2,753.

14. The Republican incumbent lost in 1868 by 322 votes but contested the outcome and was seated. In 1870 another Republican won by 500 votes. There were 2,623 Negroes, somewhat more than 500 possible voters, of whom some would have qualified under the old freehold requirement.

Ohio and New Jersey, netting one additional seat in each. However, in the seven states as a whole Republicans suffered a net loss of nine representatives. Democrats gained most in New York and Pennsylvania, almost doubling their congressional delegation in the latter from six to eleven out of a total of twenty-four. Republicans retained control in Congress but with a sharply reduced majority. In short, results of the Northern congressional elections of 1870 suggest that Negro voters may have offset to some extent the alienation of white voters by the suffrage issue, that they did little, however, to turn Republican defeats into Republican victories, and that the impact of the Fifteenth Amendment was in general disadvantageous to the Republican party.

Election returns blanket a multitude of issues, interests, and personalities. In an effort to relate them more precisely to the impact of Negro enfranchisement, we have identified all counties in the seven marginal states in which Negroes constituted a higher-than-average percentage of the population. Using 5 per cent, we found thirty-four such counties.[15] An analysis of the number of Republican voters in 1868 as compared with 1870 and of the changing percentage of the total vote won by Republicans in 1866, 1868, 1870, and 1876 would indicate that Negroes did go

15. One in New York (Queens); three in Pennsylvania (Chester, Delaware, Franklin); eight in New Jersey (Cape May, Cumberland, Salem, Camden, Mercer, Monmouth, Somerset, Bergen); ten in Ohio (Meigs, Gallia, Pike, Ross, Brown, Clinton, Fayette, Clark, Greene, Paulding); five in Indiana (Clark, Floyd, Spencer, Vanderburgh, Marion); and seven in Illinois (Alexander, Jackson, Gallatin, Massac, Pulaski, Randolph, Madison). The three urban centers with the largest aggregate number of Negroes in 1870 did not meet the 5 per cent criterion and are not included. Leslie Fishel has compiled a revealing table showing Negro and foreign-born urban population: Table II, Appendix III-B, "The North and the Negro, 1865–1900: A Study in Race Discrimination" (unpublished Ph.D. dissertation, Harvard, 1954). For the three cities with over 5,000 Negroes, the comparative figures in 1870 were:

	Colored	*Foreign-born*	*Total*
Philadelphia	22,147	183,624	674,022
New York	13,072	419,094	942,292
Cincinnati	5,900	79,612	216,239

to the polls and vote Republican in numbers which more than offset adverse white reaction, but this appears to have been the case in less than half the counties.[16] The net effect upon Republican fortunes was negligible, if not negative. Thus, in the first congressional election after Negroes were given the ballot, three of the thirty-four counties shifted from Democratic to Republican majorities, but another three went from the Republicans to the Democrats. The record was no happier for Republicans in the 1876 presidential election. Again, only six counties changed political alignment as compared with the 1868 balloting. Two were added to the Republican column, and four were lost!

From whatever angle of vision they are examined, election returns in the seven pivotal states give no support to the assumption that the enfranchisement of Northern Negroes would help Republicans in their struggle to maintain control of Congress and the Presidency. This conclusion holds for all of the North. Any hope that may have been entertained of gaining substantial strength in the loyal border states was lacking in realism. It failed to take into account the most obvious of facts—the intensity of hostility to any form of racial equality in communities recently and reluctantly freed from the institution of Negro slavery. Only Missouri and West Virginia had shown Republican strength in 1868; of the ten congressional seats which Republicans then won, half were lost in the elections of 1870. Kentucky had the largest Negro population in the North, but in seven of its nine congressional districts the Democratic margin of victory

16. Twelve counties showed an increase in both the number and percentage of Republican votes in 1870 as compared with 1868; in nine of these, Republicans also made a better showing than in 1866. In 1876 twelve counties had a higher percentage of Republican votes than in 1868. Of these, eight were identical with counties showing marked gains in 1870. The eight, with an indication of their pre-1870 party record, are: in New Jersey, Camden (R), Mercer (D/R), and Somerset (D); in Ohio, Pike (D) and Ross (D/R); in Indiana, Clark (D); in Illinois, Alexander (D) and Pulaski (D/R). The two clear instances of contested counties turning Republican in 1870 and remaining Republican were Mercer in New Jersey and Pulaski in Illinois, the former with a Negro population of 5.1 per cent and the latter with 27.3 per cent.

was so overwhelming that the state could not possibly be won by the Republican opposition, and, in fact, all nine seats remained Democratic in 1870. Although no Republican had won a seat from Maryland in 1868, there the odds were better. The outcome, however, was only a little more favorable. In 1870 Republicans failed to make any gain; in 1872 they were victors in two of the six congressional districts; these they promptly lost in 1874. The pattern of politics in Delaware was similar, consistently Democratic except in the landslide of 1872.

The lack of political profit from the Negro vote in pivotal states of the North reinforces the contention that Republican sponsorship of Negro suffrage in the face of grave political risk warrants a re-examination of motive. There is additional evidence which points to this need. Circumstances leading to the imposition of unrestricted Negro suffrage upon the defeated South are not consistent with an explanation based upon party expediency. Two detailed accounts of the legislative history of the Reconstruction Act of March 2, 1867, have recently been written, one by Brock and the other by David Donald; in neither is there any suggestion that the men responsible for the Negro suffrage provision, moderates led by John A. Bingham, James G. Blaine, and John Sherman, placed it there as an instrument of party advantage. They were seeking a way to obtain ratification of the Fourteenth Amendment, which the Southern states had rejected, and to restore all states to the Union without an indefinite interval of military rule or the imposition of more severe requirements.

The nature of the Fifteenth Amendment also suggests the inadequacy of the view that its purpose was to make permanent Republican control of the South. The amendment did not constitute a guarantee for the continuance of Radical Republican regimes, and this fact was recognized at the time. What it did was to commit the nation, not to universal, but to *impartial* suffrage. Out of the tangle of legislative debate and compromise there had emerged a basic law affirming the principle of nondiscrimination. A number of Republican politicians, South and

North, who measured it in terms of political arithmetic, were not happy with the formulation of the amendment. They recognized that under its provisions the Southern Negro vote could be reduced to political impotence by literacy tests and other qualifications, ostensibly equal.

If evidence of Republican concern for the principle of equal suffrage irrespective of race is largely wanting in histories dealing with Negro enfranchisment, it may be absent because historians have seldom considered the possibility that such evidence exists. With the more friendly atmosphere in which recent scholarship has approached the Radicals of Reconstruction, it has become apparent that men formerly dismissed as mere opportunistic politicians—"Pig Iron" Kelley, Ben Wade, Henry Wilson—actually displayed in their public careers a genuine concern for the equal status of the Negro. It is time to take a fresh look at the Republican party record as a whole. For example, let us reconsider the charge that Republicans were hypocrites in forcing equal suffrage upon the South at a time when Northern states outside New England did not grant a like privilege and were refusing to mend their ways. Aside from disregarding the sequence of events which led to the suffrage requirement in the legislation of 1867, this accusation confuses Republicans with Northerners generally. In the postwar referendums on Negro suffrage, race prejudice predominated over the principle of equality but not with the consent of a majority of Republican voters. Thus the 45.9 per cent of the Ohio vote for Negro suffrage in 1867 was equivalent to 84.6 per cent of the Republican electorate of 1866 and to 89 per cent of the Republicans who voted in 1867 for Rutherford B. Hayes as governor.[17] In truth, Republicans had

17. Republican support in Kansas was the weakest, with the 1867 referendum gaining only 54.3 per cent of the vote for the party's candidate for governor the previous year. In the 1867 defeat for Negro suffrage in Minnesota, the proposal had the support equal to 78.7 per cent of those voting for the Republican governor. The 1865 vote on the constitutional proposal in Connecticut amounted to 64 per cent of the vote for the Republican candidate for governor; that in Wisconsin, to 79 per cent of the Republican gubernatorial

fought many lost battles in state legislatures and in state referendums on behalf of Negro suffrage. What is surprising is not that they had sometimes evaded the issue but that on so many occasions they had been its champion. Even the most cynical of observers would find it difficult to account for all such Republican effort in terms of political advantage. What need was there in Minnesota or Wisconsin or Iowa for a mere handful of potential Republican voters? In these states, as in others, the movement to secure the ballot for Negroes antedated the Civil War and cannot be discounted as a mere maneuver preliminary to imposing Negro suffrage upon a defeated South.

Historians have not asked whether Republicans who voted for the Fifteenth Amendment were acting in a manner consistent with their past public records. We do not know how many of these congressmen had earlier demonstrated, or failed to demonstrate, a concern for the well-being of free Negroes or a willingness publicly to support the unpopular cause of Negro suffrage. The vote in the House of Representatives in January 1866 on the question of Negro suffrage in the District of Columbia offers an example of neglected evidence. The issue was raised before a break had developed between President Johnson and Congress; it came, in fact, at a time when an overwhelming majority of Republicans accepted the President's decision not to force Negro suffrage upon the South, even a suffrage limited to freedmen who might qualify by military service, education, or property holding. In other words, this vote reflected not the self-interest but the conscience of Republicans. They divided 116 for the measure, 15 against, and 10 recorded as not voting. In the next Congress, which passed upon the Fifteenth Amendment, support for that measure came from seventy-two representatives elected from Northern states which had not extended equal suffrage to Negroes. Were these men acting under the compulsion of politics

vote. New York rejected equal suffrage in 1869 with supporters equaling 60 per cent of the 1868 Republican vote for governor and 80 per cent of the party's 1869 vote for secretary of state.

or of conscience? More than half, forty-four in all, had served in the House during the previous Congress. Every one of the forty-four had voted in favor of Negro suffrage for the District of Columbia. Why can they not be credited with an honest conviction, to use the words of a New York *Times* editorial, "that a particular color ought not of itself to exclude from the elective franchise . . . ?"

The motives of congressmen doubtless were mixed, but in a period of national crisis when the issue of equality was basic to political contention, it is just possible that party advantage was subordinated to principle. Should further study rehabilitate the reputation of the Republican party in respect to Negro suffrage, it would not follow that the 1860's were a golden age dedicated to the principle that all men are created equal. During the years of Civil War and Reconstruction, race prejudice was institutionalized in the Democratic party. Perhaps this very fact, plus the jibes of inconsistency and hypocrisy with which Democrats derided their opponents, helped to create the party unity that committed Republicans, and through them the nation, to equal suffrage irrespective of race.

Reconstruction: A Local View

The South Carolina Politicos

by Joel Williamson

World events have seriously undermined American mythology in recent decades, and one of the prominent casualties has been the national image of Reconstruction in the South. Having themselves undertaken to occupy and "reconstruct" Germany and Japan following World War II, Americans could no longer view the Southern experience as unique. Nor did growing knowledge of the usual manner in which victors dealt with vanquished in modern civil wars—whether in Russia, Spain, China, Cuba, or elsewhere—support the contention made by previous generations of American historians that Northern treatment of the South had been harsh beyond measure. The images conjured up by such films as "The Birth of a Nation" or "Gone With the Wind," which portrayed an entire region under the oppressive thumb of rapacious Radical carpetbaggers and bestial freedmen, seem from today's perspective more a product of desire than memory. There never was any Black Reconstruction, *and the notion that "black excesses" turned Radical rule into a nightmare for the South endures largely as a monument to America's national neurosis—racism.*

In light of the Black Revolution of the 1960's which helped produce changing American racial attitudes, changes already well underway in the academic community have undertaken a more thorough and less mythical assessment of the Negro's role during Reconstruction. No longer treating blacks solely as objects of fear and abuse, more sympathetic scholars have begun probing the manner in which Negroes experienced *their new freedom. They have found that although blacks clearly did not dominate Reconstruction, they were much more than merely subservient and unwitting tools of ruling, white politicians. Despite the humble post-emancipation status of most Southern Negroes as landless farmers, the Fifteenth Amendment had promised Constitutional protection for their right to vote. In every Southern state under Radical rule, politicians eagerly competed for their ballots. Local Southerners or Northern emigrants, many of them black, often wrestled for power among themselves in the name of principle, economic privilege, or simple plunder—and all needed votes.*

One of the period's most undeniably tragic aspects concerned the aborted development of a Negro leadership class, particularly in state and local politics. By the time the South had reverted completely to conservative white domination in 1877, the Negro's political leaders had either fled the South or been silenced. In the following selection, Joel Williamson describes the development of such a group and the problem it faced during the Reconstruction period in South Carolina.

The alliance of Negroes with the Republican party was a logical outgrowth of the pursuit by individuals of their own interests. Yet, some allowance must be made for the leadership that focused and organized the political energy of the Negro masses. The men who supplied this leadership and the manner in which they pursued their objectives are the subjects of this chapter.

The traditional story that Radical Republicans in the North dispatched paid organizers to South Carolina to encourage Ne-

From Joel Williamson, *After Slavery: The Negro in South Carolina During Reconstruction, 1861–1877* (Chapel Hill: University of North Carolina Press, 1965), pp. 363–83, 387–92, 394, 416–17. Reprinted by permission; footnotes omitted.

groes to claim their political rights and join the Republican party only after they plotted to pass the first Reconstruction Act is a patent exaggeration. Actually, Republican organization in South Carolina began during the war. As if by deliberate selection, the great majority of Northern civilians and the higher officers of the military who came to the Sea Islands before the surrender were of the Republican persuasion. In 1864, Republicans on the islands were well enough organized to send a delegation to the national convention of the party and in the following year to elect the Radical editor of the Beaufort *Free South,* James G. Thompson, to the otherwise all-Democratic state constitutional convention which met at Johnson's call. Many of these Sea Island Republicans were abolitionists who, after emancipation, passed on to Radicalism. Before 1867, however, most of them were much more avid in pursuing their professions than in organizing potential Negro voters as Republicans.

The tradition also asserts that governmental employees, military officials, and, particularly, the agents of the [Freedmen's] Bureau were hand-picked Republican emissaries. Assuming that subsequent political prominence would mark most such people, this, too, is clearly untrue. Indeed, with the exception of the educational department of the Bureau, less than a dozen Republican leaders emerged from the hundreds thus employed. Albert Gallatin Mackey, Daniel T. Corbin, and Charles P. Leslie were the only federal officials who took leading parts in organizing Republicanism in South Carolina. Mackey, a native Charlestonian and a persistent Unionist, received the choicest post in the state—that of collector of the port of Charleston. Mackey became the very able presiding officer of the convention that drafted the Constitution of 1868. Corbin, a Vermonter who had been a captain of Negro troops during the war, became the federal district attorney after the war. Corbin acted as a legal adviser to the Constitutional Convention of 1868, was a perennial senator from Charleston, and remained an active Republican leader in the state long after Redemption. Leslie came to the state as a collector of internal revenue. By the spring of 1867, however, when he emerged an active Republican, he had already left the service of the treasury department and was eminently unsuccessful as a planter in Barnwell District.

The military was even less political. From early 1866 into the summer of 1867, the commanding general was Daniel Sickles, a close personal friend of Orr. Sickles's relief, E. R. S. Canby, evinced a mild Republicanism which even the native whites found inoffensive. Only two officers in the entire command became active Republicans. One of these, a Colonel Moore who commanded the Sixth Infantry, was relieved after appearing at several political meetings in the Columbia area. The other, A. J. Willard, pursued a peculiar political career. A New York lawyer who came South as the lieutenant-colonel of a Negro regiment, he remained to become a legal adviser to the commanding general. In 1867, he was given the duty of registering voters in the two Carolinas. There is no indication that he was an active Republican until after he was seated on the supreme court bench by the first Republican legislature.

Outside of its educational division, the Bureau was hardly more political. Saxton had never been able to make an abolitionist stronghold out of his various commands. His successor in the Bureau, Scott, became the first Republican governor and laid the Bureau open to the obvious charge. Yet, the Bureau under Scott was as often accused of anti-Republicanism as otherwise. Indeed, his staff seemed to tend away from Republicanism and certainly from Radicalism. "They are often more pro-slavery than the rebels themselves," scandalized Laura Towne, "and only care to make the blacks work. . . ." Leaving aside its educators and Scott, only three Bureau agents were active Republican organizers. R. C. De Large and Martin Delany held minor offices in the Bureau, and J. J. Wright was Scott's legal adviser.

It is true that before the passage of the first Reconstruction Act South Carolina Negroes were not organized by and as Republicans in any significant degree. They were, however, organized *for* Republicanism. They were associated in such a way that when they were enfranchised, the establishment of the party amounted to little more than formalizing a pattern which already existed. The elements most responsible for this pre-conditioning of the Negro voter-to-be were the Bureau schools, the Northern churches, and the native Negro leadership. Moreover, these three sources supplied a ready-made core of chiefs to South Carolina Republicanism.

Many early Republican leaders found their first postwar employment in the educational division of the Bureau. Reuben Tomlinson, a Pennsylvania Quaker who had been among the first experimenters to come to the Sea Islands during the war, was for nearly three years the Bureau's superintendent of education in South Carolina. In the summer of 1868, he took a seat in the first Republican legislature. Two of Tomlinson's assistant superintendents, Whittemore and Randolph, were front rank leaders in the organization of the state's Republicans. Whittemore was particularly influential in the northeastern quarter of the state, represented Darlington in the Constitutional Convention of 1868, and became the first Republican congressman elected in that area. Randolph was active in the vicinity of Orangeburg and was that county's first Republican state senator. A number of Northern-born Negro soldiers also became Bureau teachers and passed into the Republican leadership. London S. Langley and Stephen A. Swails were two who belonged to this class.

In addition, the Bureau recruited as teachers a host of Charleston Negroes (many of whom had been free before the war) and sent them into the hinterland. There they did yeoman work, not only as educators, but in imparting a sense of political awareness to the parents of their scholars. Many of them returned to Charleston as delegates to the Constitutional Convention of 1868. Examples of such cases are numerous and worth close attention because they indicate one means by which Republicanism spread among the Negro population before they actually obtained the vote. These examples also reveal much of the character of what might be called the second echelon of Republican leadership in the state. Henry L. Shrewsbury, twenty-one years old in 1868, a mulatto offspring of the free Negro population of Charleston and well educated, was sent to Cheraw as a Bureau teacher soon after the war. In 1868, he returned to Charleston as Chesterfield's Negro delegate to the Constitutional Convention. Henry E. Hayne, who had also been free before the war and became a sergeant in the First South, was sent to Marion as a Bureau teacher and returned to Charleston in 1868 as the leader of the three-man Negro delegation from that district. William J. McKinlay and T. K. Sasportas went to Orangeburg from Charleston as Bureau teachers. Both were scions of free Negro families which were prominent in the trades. Sasportas was the son of a butcher who had himself owned slaves before the war. Sasportas was educated in Philadelphia, remained there during the war, and was said to be intelligent and very well informed. The work of Randolph, Sasportas, and McKinlay goes far toward explaining the large Negro vote cast for the convention in Orangeburg District in the fall of 1867 and the subsequent development of Orangeburg as the stronghold of Republicanism, Northern Methodism, and Negro education. All three of these educators returned to Charleston in 1868 as delegates to the convention. What these men did in Orangeburg was duplicated by James N. and Charles D. Hayne in Barnwell District. Offspring of the free Negro society of Charleston, the brothers probably came to Barnwell as Bureau teachers and, along with Northern Methodist minister Abram Middleton, formed the core of Republican leadership in that district. James Hayne was apparently the leader of the trio which combined with ex-slave Julius Mayer to represent Barnwell in the Convention of 1868. Interestingly, in the convention, Sasportas voted with Randolph on every recorded vote, and the Negro delegates from Barnwell paralleled Randolph's vote six out of seven times. . . .

Technically all these teachers were employed by private parties, the function of the Bureau being simply to supply the physical materials necessary. Actually, however, as superintendent of education, Tomlinson had a large degree of control over recruiting, assigning, and overseeing the performance of teachers in schools supported by the Bureau.

Also prominent in early Republican organization in South Carolina and in the Constitutional Convention of 1868 were two Negroes who came to the state as the direct agents of the American Missionary Association for the purpose of establishing schools and, hence, were closely associated with the Bureau. These were F. L. Cardozo, who was the principal of the largest Negro school in the state, and J. J. Wright who passed into full Bureau service soon after entering the state.

Of the seventy-four Negroes who attended the Constitutional Convention of 1868, certainly eleven and probably thirteen . . . came by way of their involvement in Negro schools. Even though Tomlinson did not himself attend the convention, he followed the same path into the Republican legislature. It could hardly be denied that this phase of the Bureau's program in South Carolina was politically vital.

Probably as significant in conditioning the Negro population for Republicanism were the labors of religious missionaries from the North. The real meaning of their work was that they taught and practiced a religion which did not discriminate against the freedman because of his race. . . . Many leading ministers did manage to avoid direct political participation. Many others, however, devoted themselves wholeheartedly to promoting the interests of the Republican party.

Northern Methodists were especially prominent politically. French, Whittemore, and Randolph might well be considered politicians rather than ministers, but when formal Republican organization began in the spring of 1867 they moved easily and familiarly among the Northern Methodist congregations of the state. It is no coincidence that the very areas in which Northern Methodism was strongest—Camden, Greenville, Kingstree, Orangeburg, Summerville, Florence, Maysville, Sumter, Darlington,

Aiken, Barnwell, and Charleston—were also areas in which Republican organization proceeded comparatively rapidly and successfully. . . .

At least five of the 124 members of the Constitutional Convention of 1868 were Northern Methodist ministers. At least one delegate—Barney Burton, a forty-year-old ex-slave who had moved to Chester after the war—and perhaps several others were among the 102 local preachers in the conference.

Aside from Bishop Payne nearly every leading minister in the African Methodist Church was also a practicing politician. R. H. Cain was the most successful in both careers, but there were others who were hardly less active than he. William E. Johnston of Sumter was a delegate to the Constitutional Convention of 1868 and later the senator from that county. Richard M. Valentine was an early organizer for the African Church in Abbeville and, although not a delegate to the convention, he sat as a representative in the first Republican legislature. It is virtually a fact that the African Methodists moved their 30,000 members into the Republican party as a solid phalanx.

Individual ministries in other churches were also active politicians. Altogether at least thirteen of the seventy-four Negro delegates who sat in the convention of 1868 were professional or lay ministers.

By 1867 in South Carolina, a numerous resident leadership had already evolved among Negro laymen to make the work of Republican organization easy. The coastal Negro population who had won their freedom before the end of the war supplied a disproportionately large number of top-level leaders for their race. Many of these came directly out of the Union Army to assume prominent places in their communities. At least nine members of the Constitutional Convention of 1868 had been soldiers in the Negro regiments. Three of these had been in South Carolina regiments and became active Republican organizers in the interior districts—H. E. Hayne in Marion, Prince R. Rivers in Edgefield, and Richard Humbird in Darlington. Six were Northerners who had joined the Massachusetts regiments and remained in the coastal area after the war. . . .

Negroes in the interior were not without their natural leaders and some of these appeared in the Constitutional Convention of 1868. W. Beverly Nash, a middle-aged, ex-hotel waiter who had once belonged to William C. Preston, gained national attention in 1866 by his criticism of the Bureau's activities in the middle districts. By 1868, Nash was unquestionably the chief spokesman for the Negro electorate of Richland, a position which he maintained over all rivals throughout Reconstruction. Even in the most remote districts, Negro communities pressed forward a home-grown leadership. . . .

Utilizing the ready-made organization and leadership provided by Bureau schools, churches, and the native Negro community, Republicans in South Carolina rapidly marshaled their powers. Almost simultaneously, in mid-March, organizing meetings were held in Columbia and Charleston. Early in May, Republicans from as far away as Greenville met in Charleston for the purpose of establishing the party on a statewide basis. The Charleston meeting was decidedly not representative, but it did call for a Columbia convention in July and formed a committee to accelerate formal organization in areas not represented. . . . When the referendum on the calling of a constitutional convention was held in November, Republicans were able to present a slate of candidates in each district and to muster some 69,000 votes to secure their election.

Obviously, Republican organization in South Carolina was largely homespun rather than imported as tradition maintains. However, Northern emissaries were not entirely lacking. In March, 1867, heretofore strange Negro ministers from Washington appeared in Charleston and Columbia. In May, Senator Wilson (escorted by Parson French), was circulating through the state, and "Pig Iron" Kelley was expected to follow soon. A white woman residing in Abbeville in August saw some of the lesser lights in the field. "With Rev. Nick Williams's & Armstrong's lecturing our semi-chimpangee brethren at our very doors," she wailed, "God only knows what will come, & I have decided to hide my head." A few of the lesser Northern politicos remained to participate in the constitutional convention. William N. Viney, for instance, was an Ohio-born Negro who came to the state as a paid political organizer and went to the convention as a delegate from Colleton District. . . .

In 1867 and 1868, Union or Loyal Leagues were an important part of Republican activity in the state. Possibly, Leagues had existed in South Carolina in 1865 and 1866, but it was only after the passage of the first Reconstruction Act that the organizational device was widely used. Leagues were used to indoctrinate Negroes with Republicanism, but they were also schools to instruct Negroes in their civic responsibilities. It was perhaps no accident that the first president of the League in South Carolina was Gilbert Pillsbury, a long-time abolitionist who had first headed the military's school system in the Charleston area. Negroes must have found the Leagues entertaining. Visiting his low-country plantation near Adams Run in December, 1867, The Reverend Cornish found that "Sam—the then negro boy that waited on me when I lived at the Hermitage on Edisto Island— . . . is now president of the Loyal Leage [*sic*] & a very influential character among the Negroes—is Sam Small——" Leagues were not always harmless, however. Sometimes they assumed a militant front. Early in January, 1868, the mistress of Social Hall, also near Adams Run, noted that the Negroes in the vicinity were well organized. "The men have weekly meetings for the purposes of drill—fife, fine dinners, uniforms, drum, flags & c. Prince Wright acting Brig. Gen., Ned Ladson (R. knows him) Colonel!" As described above, in the mountain district of Oconee, the threat passed into open violence when members of a League killed a white boy in the course of a riot and proceeded to seize control of the community. Occasionally the whites retaliated. A year after the Oconee riot, Elias Kennedy, a Negro minister living in adjacent Anderson County and well known as a League organizer, was killed while on a League mission in a neighboring Georgia town. Leagues were numerous in South Carolina, but outside of the cities they were not durable. After the heated campaigns of 1867 and 1868, the great mass of Negro voters apparently faded out of the organization. The subsequent character of the League in South Carolina was accurately reflected in the politics of their president, F. L. Cardozo, one of the most conservative Negro politicians in the state.

Far more permanent and effective than the League was the regular party organization, which had developed in the traditional pattern. The grass roots were represented by individual Republicans who met either in township or, frequently, in county conventions to nominate candidates for local offices and to choose delegates to conventions representing larger districts—counties, congressional districts, or the state and nation. Each convention chose its permanent executive committee which, with its chairman, was responsible for carrying on the party's business until relieved by the next convention. At the peak of the pyramid was the state executive committee. After 1870, control of this committee by Negroes gave them important power in the heart and core of Republican politics in South Carolina.

The character of professional Republican politicians in South Carolina during Reconstruction has often been debated. The Redeemers, who wrote most of the history of the period, damned them all. The scalawags were poor whites without character, education, or position. The carpetbaggers—except those with money—were bootless ex-officers of the Union Army and unprincipled adventurers in search of political plunder. And Negro politicians were either Northern-sprung zealots in various stages of mental derangement or ignorant and deluded freedmen who moved directly from the cotton fields into office without so much as a change of clothes. Even a cursory survey of these groups reveals the inaccuracy of such a description.

Actually, scalawags represented—in economic status, education, and, to a large extent, social standing—every phase of Carolina society. The single quality found in the backgrounds of most native white Republican leaders was a spirit of Unionism distinctly deeper than that of their neighbors. Even here, however, scalawags as a group were still in some degree representative of the community, mustering a few first-line fire-eaters in their ranks. Franklin J. Moses, Jr., for instance, had been the secretary of the secession governor and had personally hauled the United States flag down from over Fort Sumter in 1861. Some scalawags were poor. Solomon George Washington Dill of Charleston and Kershaw, by his own report, had always been a poor man and identified himself with the interest of the poor. Others were rich. Thomas Jefferson Robertson, a United States senator throughout the period, was reputedly one of the wealthiest men in the state after the war. Precisely as South Carolina exhibited a high degree of illiteracy in its white population, so too were there ill-educated scalawags. Dill of Kershaw, Allan of Greenville, Owen and Crews of Laurens, and many others apparently possessed only common school educations. On the other hand, many scalawag leaders were at least as erudite as their conservative opponents. Dr. Albert Gallatin Mackey graduated first in his class in Charleston's Medical School, and a Northern correspondent, visiting him in the book-lined study in his Charleston home, found him highly learned. . . . Doubtless some native whites became Republicans out of expediency, but it is also certain that many adopted the party out of principle. John R. Cochran and John Scott Murray of Anderson and Simeon Corley of Lexington, for instance, were Republican leaders whose principles were above reproach even by the opposition. Although none of the self-styled aristocracy became open Republicans, a fair proportion of the scalawag leadership had been accepted in the elite social circle of their own communities before becoming Republicans, and in most cases, apparently they did not immediately lose social prestige by crossing the political divide. . . .

Carpetbaggers exhibited the same degree of variety. . . . The average carpetbagger was rather better educated than his Southern counterpart of the same age and economic background. . . .

Indeed, one seeks in vain among the leading carpetbaggers for one who was ill-educated, and many of those least educated in the formal sense were, like Timothy Hurley, intelligent men of wide experience. Few political carpetbaggers were received socially by the aristocracy, but they obviously remained fully acceptable in their home communities in the North. . . .

The Redeemers' estimate of Northern Negroes in the South was nearly correct—they were zealots. Some, like R. H. Gleaves, came to further their material fortunes by business pursuits. Others, like Whipper and the lawyer class in general, probably saw a chance for personal profit in representing the claims of the newly emancipated. But, most of them came (or, having left the army, remained) primarily as religious, educational, and cultural missionaries, hoping to accomplish an elevation of their racial brothers which was not possible in the restricted and less populous Negro communities in the North. Just as the Massachusetts Negro regiments drew off the cream of young manhood from the Northern Negro population during the war, Reconstruction attracted the cream in peace.

The one thing that most native Negro leaders were not was fresh from the cotton fields. Of the seventy-four Negroes who sat in the Constitutional Convention of 1868, fourteen were Northerners. Of the fifty-nine Negroes who had been born or settled in South Carolina before the war, at least eighteen and probably twenty-one had been free. A dozen of these were Charlestonians. Nearly all had been tradesmen. Roughly two-thirds of this group continued to pursue their trades after the war and at least until the time of the convention. The remainder took service as Bureau teachers. T. K. Sasportas, Henry Shrewsbury, and others had risen to the educational level of the high school graduate in the North. Most possessed the equivalent of a common school education, while several were, apparently, barely literate. F. L. Cardozo, of course, having attended the University of Glasgow and the London School of Theology, was as well educated as any man in the state.

Thirty-eight of the delegates were clearly former slaves. The occupations of twelve of these are not known, but not one was described as an agricultural worker. Twenty-six were trades-, professional, or business men. Eight of the twenty-six were ministers (some being tradesmen as well), four were carpenters, two blacksmiths, two shoemakers, two had been coachmen and the remaining eight included a businessman, a businessman and steamer captain (Smalls), a tanner, a barber, a teacher, a waiter, a servant, and a carriage maker. Most of those who were tradesmen had pursued the same occupation as slaves. For instance, John Chesnut, the barber, was the son of a Camden barber whose father had been freed by the first General James Chesnut. John was born of a slave mother and, hence, was a slave but had been allowed to learn his trade in his father's shop. The degree of education possessed by these freedmen was not high. However, nearly all appeared to be literate in some degree, and a few were amazingly well read. Nash, for example, could quote Shakespeare with apparent ease and obviously read the leading Northern papers. During the war, Robert Smalls had been taught intensively by two professional educators while he was stationed for a year and a half in the Philadelphia Naval Yard. It is true that conservatives had considerable grounds for complaint against the ignorance of their late-slaves become legislators, but their charges of stupidity changed with the political climate. Early in 1866, the Camden press lauded John Chesnut and Harmon Jones as "two intelligent freedmen" for their speeches to the Negroes denying that the government was to give them lands and urging them to return to work. After 1867, when John Chesnut went into Republican politics, became a delegate to the convention which drafted a new constitution, and served thereafter in the Republican legislature, words strong enough to describe Chesnut's lack of talent were not available.

In view of the high degree of natural ability extant among leading Republicans of both races, it is hardly surprising that the higher offices were filled with men who were quite capable of executing their responsibilities.

In the executive area, the abilities of such white office holders as Dr. Ensor as the director of the insane asylum and H. L. Pardee as superintendent of the penitentiary and such Negro office holders as F. L. Cardozo and H. E. Hayne withstood the closest criticism. Although he was frequently overridden by a less careful legislature, Cardozo as treasurer of the state from 1872 until the summer of 1876 (after which his office was virtually nullified by a boycott of white taxpayers) revealed the highest capacities. . . .

Even political opponents generally recognized the capacity of leading Republican legislators. South Carolina's Negro congressmen—Elliott, Rainey, Ransier, De Large, Cain, and Smalls—were usually conceded to be able enough for their posts. Though Democrats in the House scoffed, Elliott's speech to Congress on the Ku Klux was widely celebrated. Capable Negro solons also appeared in the Constitutional Convention of 1868 and in the Republican legislatures which followed. Ransier, Gleaves, and Swails as presiding officers in the Senate and Samuel J. Lee and, again, Elliott as speakers of the house were remarkably effective managers in view of their sudden elevation to their posts. There were others, like Whipper, who were virtually professional legislators and became excellent parliamentarians.

It was inevitable that combinations of intelligence, education, experience, and natural ability were in short supply among Republicans in South Carolina. After all, there were comparatively few Negroes in South Carolina who could claim to possess a high level of education or significant experience in government. In the legislature, and in local offices in many areas, there was obviously a lack of competence among Republican leaders. This absence was usually identified with the presence of the Negro officeholder.

Yet, what one saw in the legislature was obviously determined by what one was conditioned to see. . . . The more astute visitors, however skeptical they may have been of the results, invariably saw something vital in the proceedings of Republican and Negro legislatures in the state. "It is not all sham, nor all burlesque," wrote James Pike after his celebrated visit in the winter of 1873. "They have a genuine interest and a genuine earnestness in the business of the assembly which we are bound to recognize and respect unless we would be accounted shallow critics."

Conservative native whites were distressed by what they saw even before they entered the legislative chambers. . . .

The proceedings of the House particularly offended whites. In August, 1868, an upcountry editor was shocked to find seven "dusky belles" seated on the platform with Speaker Moses. A year later, another observer noted that members frequently defied the chair, conversed with debaters on the floor, and, on one occasion, T. K. Sasportas answered an argument from Representative De Large with his fist. A Northern visitor in 1874 was amazed by the lack of respect accorded to some members by others. As an instance, he noted that Representative Holmes of Colleton called on the speaker for the yeas and nays on a measure, but the speaker refused to recognize him until the vote had been announced. Holmes then rose to a question of privilege and was overruled. He persisted and other members began to cough. Holmes tried to talk over the noise. The coughing grew louder. Finally, E. W. M. Mackey suggested that someone call a doctor and the house roared in amusement, while the exasperated Holmes collapsed in his chair.

Capacity and incompetence frequently traveled side by side in the legislature, but incapacity was often glaringly in evidence among officeholders of the lower echelons. "Our letters are often lost now," wrote a resident of Camden to her son, "Adamson is travelling Agent to distribute the letters and Boswell and Frank Carter, Ned's son, are Postmaster[s] here." The cause, of course, was apparent: "In Columbia and elsewhere, they have negroes in the Post office, and I have no doubt our letters go astray." County and city officers elicited similar complaints. Much distressed, the grand jury of Williamsburg County, in the spring of 1871, charged that the county commissioners permitted the county's prisoners to roam the streets of Kingstree after the jail burned in 1867, kept no records worthy of the name, and had allowed the roads and bridges of the county (some of which had not been worked upon in two years) to become almost impassable. Further, they feared that the county poor farm was "calculated to do more harm to the County than good."

The great problem of the Republican regime in South Carolina, however, was not so much a lack of capacity among its leaders as it was an absence of a sense of responsibility to the whole society, white as well as black. In the idealistic days of the Constitutional Convention of 1868, Republicans often reflected verbally upon the fact that their work was for the benefit of all. Yet, within two months after the close of the convention, election results showed that, willingly or not, the Republican party in South Carolina was the party of the Negro and for the Negro. Within a short time, it also became a party by the Negro. This was a line which the whites themselves had helped to draw. There emerged among Republican leaders a new concept that their first loyalty was due, not to their total constituency, but to that particular Republican and Negro element which had put them into office. This attitude was evident in the inclination of Republicans to drive Democrats and native whites of the conservative persuasion completely out of the government. It was also evident in a certain superciliousness which developed among members of the party in power toward the opposition. In this atmosphere, the protests of the white minority became proper subjects for Republican disdain and, indeed, ridicule. "Please read where I have marked, and judge the class of men which composed the late Taxpayer's convention of South Carolina," Negro Congressman Rainey jeered quietly in a confidential communiqué to President Grant's secretary early in 1874. Three years earlier, while the first taxpayers' convention was in session, A. O.

Jones, the mulatto clerk of the house, suggested to his partner in a corruption-laden ring of public printers that their Republican Printing Company enter a bid for the printing of "Ye Taxpayers." "R. P. C.," he jested, "That's as effective on the State Treasury as the other terrible triad is on Radical office holders—eh?" If the opposition had no political rights, they also had no economic rights. Attacks on the property by heavy taxation and then by the theft of those tax moneys was perhaps within the limits of this new morality.

Among Republican politicos in Reconstruction South Carolina, there is no correlation between intelligence, education, wealth, experience, and competence on the one hand and, on the other, integrity. The thieves included men who claimed all or most of these qualities, as well as men who could claim none. The relationship which did exist was the logical one: among those who did steal, the most successful thieves invariably combined high intelligence and large administrative talents with generous endowments of education, wealth, and experience. Petty frauds were numerous and widespread, but the truly magnificent peculations were conceived and executed by a relatively few men, usually residing in Columbia or Charleston. However, these larger schemes frequently required the purchase of the co-operation of scores of state officers and legislators, and thus corruption was spread.

The first and always the most gigantic steals consisted simply of issuing state bonds in excess of the amounts authorized by the legislature. In the summer of 1868, the legislature sanctioned the issue of one million dollars worth of bonds to pay the interest on the state debt and to re-establish its credit. The financial board, consisting of Governor Scott and the other leading officers in the state government, was authorized to market the bonds through a financial agent, H. H. Kimpton, in New York. The authorized issue was promptly made. Probably under Kimpton's management, another million was clandestinely added. Since Scott had to sign each bond and Treasurer N. G. Parker had to issue them and honor payments of interest, it is certain that they were implicated in the plot, but the involvement of other members of the board is not clear. When the legislature directed the issue of another million dollars in bonds in 1869, the fraud was repeated. After passing and repealing an act to re-finance the debt through London sources, the legislature repudiated about half of the state's twelve-million-dollar debt and converted the remainder into a single loan guaranteed by about six million dollars' worth of "Conversion Bonds." But again the actual issue almost doubled the amount authorized. By flagrantly misrepresenting the state's finances and by buying and selling his own issues, Kimpton kept the bond bubble afloat. To its authors, a part of the appeal of the bond scheme was that it needed the co-operation of the inner few only and did not require the wide-scale bribery of state officials. Indeed, the fewer to profit the better. Moreover, the ring only served its own interest when it encouraged efforts at financial reform and re-establishing the state's credit, because these displays tended to drive up the market price and to prepare the way for further illicit issues. . . .

There were a number of other major "jobs" pushed through the legislature. During the first Scott administration, a group of native white conservative Charleston businessmen combined with several carpetbag politicians to gain, over Scott's veto, a fabulously lucrative monopoly of the mining of phosphates (for fertilizer) from the river beds of the state. Agent for the job was Timothy Hurly, a Boston-born Republican who reportedly came to Columbia carrying a carpetbag containing $40,000 which he used, partly through scalawag Speaker Moses, to win the desired legislation.

The most effective jobber, however, was always Patterson. It appears that the Pennsylvania financier enjoyed legislative bribery as a game. In the fall of 1871, he and his henchman, H. C. Worthington, one-time Nevada congressman, Union general, and minister to Brazil, volunteered to defend Governor Scott from a threatened impeachment. They used $50,000 of the state's money provided by Scott. On the morning before the vote initiating proceedings was taken, Patterson arranged the usual caucus through Rivers, who "was always looked to as a leader of certain members, about fifteen or twenty." As host, Rivers served drinks, "viands," and cigars. Patterson and Worthington attended and spoke against the impeachment. Afterward, only Patterson and Rivers were in the room. "So when Patterson saw me in the room," Rivers later testified, "he just said: 'You go and vote against the impeachment and I'll give you $200;' and I said: 'All right.'" By the same methods, and at the cost of $40,000, Patterson bought himself a seat in the United States Senate and promptly had Worthington appointed collector of the port of Charleston where both doubtless soon earned several times that amount by soliciting bribes from merchants. In the fall of 1873, Senator Patterson again lent his special legislative talents to a friend, Hardy Solomon, and succeeded in getting legislation passed to pay the obligations of the state to that merchant and banker.

There were other patterns of corruption in the legislature. Presiding officers in both houses and their clerks conspired to issue fraudulent pay certificates and to honor claims for legislative expenses which were without justification. Between 1870 and 1874, a steady source of bribe money was the Republican Printing Company, an organization administered and ostensibly owned by the clerks of the two houses, A. C. Jones, a Negro, and Josephus Woodruff, a Charleston and Columbia journalist become scalawag. Through bribery, the clerks patched together enough support to secure the contract for state printing, but actually they were constantly pressed for funds by some legislators as if the company were co-operatively owned by the members and Woodruff and Jones merely the managers. Virtually every election by the legislature elicited a rash of bribery; but there were also other forms of graft. The sumptuous furnishings of Columbia committee rooms somehow seemed to find their way into the homes of members and of attachés in all parts of the state. A committee clerk from Aiken later testified that Speaker Samuel J. Lee, a Negro also from Aiken, during one session furnished rooms for himself and his wife over a Columbia restaurant as a "Committee Room." Later the clerk saw the same "marble-top table, settees, cushioned chairs, sideboards, &c" in the parlor of Lee's Aiken home. John Williams, the sergeant-at-arms for the house, furnished rooms for himself and Prince Rivers in the same way. Williams, too, carried furniture to his Hamburg residence and transferred other pieces so that "a house of ill fame kept by a colored woman named Anna Wells was also furnished."

Corruption at the local level was less spectacular, but it was prevalent enough. In many places, e.g., Beaufort, Negro officers maintained high standards of integrity, but all too often Negroes and whites were knaves together. The grand jury of Williamsburg, looking over the books—such as they were—of the clerk of the county commissioners in the spring of 1874, found that "upon many occasions when money was received, it was forthwith divided out between the members of the board and the clerk." Further, the commissioners had drawn pay for more than the maximum number of days allowed per year; the Negro school commissioner could not account for his funds; and the county treasurer paid only such claims as he chose to honor. By June, 1874, no less than twenty-four county commissioners, three county treasurers, two sheriffs, and one school commissioner had been presented by grand juries, indicted, or convicted. During Moses's gubernatorial term, punishment was neither swift nor certain for the guilty. . . . After 1874, when reform was in the air and public peculation had become precarious, thievery seemed almost entirely halted. . . .

Cities, too, frequently fell victim to the spoilers. Columbia, which underwent an expansion of its boundaries to give the Republicans absolute control and Negro officers from mayor to policeman, suffered an increase in its debt from some $426,000 in 1872 to $620,000 in 1874, and to $677,000 in 1875. Meanwhile, Charleston's debt swelled prodigiously beyond the two-million-dollar mark.

The average Negro officeholder realized very little profit by resorting to rascality. Those who became wealthy by thievery were few, and all the most successful were white—Scott, Parker, Kimpton, Patterson, and, perhaps, Neagle and Woodruff. These were the men who conceived, organized, and directed steals on a statewide basis. Key figures who abetted them in their predatory operations, either as officers of the government or as lobbyists, also received substantial sums—Moses, Hurley, Leslie, Worthington, Whittemore, Elliott, Samuel J. Lee, and Swails—amounting over the entire period from scores of thousands to several hundred thousand dollars each. The average Negro legislator and officeholder, however, found that the wages of sin were pitifully small. There were only four occasions when large sums of money were passed out as bribes; other divisions were made of the printing money, and occasionally some office seeker was willing to buy votes. Senators were usually paid from $500 to $5,000 for their support on such occasions. Members of the House received much less. . . .

The real profits of the corruptionists, large and small, were often much less than quoted. For instance, the bond ring sold its issues to doubtful investors at much less than par value (usually at about sixty cents on the dollar). As more bonds flooded the market and criticism of the government rose, good issues and bad dropped to fractions of their face value. One issue eventually fell to 1 per cent of its nominal value. Blue Ridge Railroad scrip, used to pay the largest bribe bill contracted during the Reconstruction Period, circulated at less than its face value. Legislative pay certificates, whether or not legitimately obtained, were usually sold at a considerable discount by impecunious members of businessmen like Hardy Solomon. Such circumstances existed because the treasury was itself perennially empty and those having claims against it had to await the pleasure or indulgence of the treasurer. While Parker held that position, large sums of tax money were sent North to Kimpton to keep the bond bubble inflated by interest payments on both good and bad issues. Local obligations were very liable to be neglected. After 1872, each claimant had to face the suspicious Cardozo, who soon became the bane of every corruptionist's existence by his miserly management of the treasury. The officers of the Republican Printing Company, to which a generous legislature appropriated $385,000 for the state fiscal year 1873–1874, had the greatest difficulty during the summer of 1874 in squeezing $250 to $300 out of the treasurer every Saturday to meet their minimum operating expenses. Lecturers in history are fond of titillating their classes with the story of how the Negro legislature voted Speaker Moses a gratuity of $1,000 for his services as presiding officer after his having lost that amount to Whipper in a horse race. Yet, Moses probably thought the gesture something less than generous since pay certificates, if the holder were fortunate enough to find any buyer, seldom sold at more than three-fourths of face value. Moreover, Moses probably considered it an ordinary reward for the extra duty demanded by his office, a burden which many legislatures, North and South, customarily eased by voting special compensation.

There *was* plush living in Columbia during Reconstruction. The senators maintained a bar in one of their cloak rooms in the Capitol and fine food, smooth whiskey, and the best Havana cigars were copiously available. The legislative halls, the offices in the Capitol, and the committee rooms located in privately owned buildings (many were in Parker's Hall, often spelled "Haul" by contemporaries) were lavishly furnished. Yet the bar, which was allegedly supported by the senators from their private resources, was closed to other officers except by invitation, and the enjoyment of the accommodations afforded by other rooms were usually limited to those who used them officially.

The average Negro representative came to Columbia on his own money. He roomed and took his meals—usually on credit—in an ordinary boarding house with a dozen or so other legislators, clerks, and legislative attachés. Many could not afford appropriate clothing. Hardy Solomon found one member on the street so ill clad that he took him to his store and fitted him into a suit without requiring a vote in return. Occasionally some affluent Republican might offer the favorite "oyster supper" at a local dining room, or a caucus be held in which refreshments were served; but these were rare events. Such high living as was done by the legislators was done in the barrooms and, typically, on credit. . . .

Far from a jubilee, attending a session of the legislature was for many Negro members a prolonged torture. Occasionally, political excitement ran high, as during the Ku Klux troubles and recurrently during elections. But the typical legislator followed a dull, drab, daily routine. During the mornings, he attended committee meetings or caucuses, stood on the streets or about the Capitol grounds, or remained in his boarding house. Beginning at noon, he attended a three- or four-hour legislative session, most of which were uneventful and, indeed, unimportant. In the late afternoons, he repeated the morning's performances, had his communal dinner at his boarding house, and retired. Throughout the session, he was plagued by a lack of money and by a worrying uncertainty whether he would be able to collect his pay at all, regardless of how much he voted himself, and whether he would realize from his nominal salary enough cash to meet his debts in Columbia and his obligations at home, familial and otherwise. Retrospectively, the life of the Reconstruction Negro legislator was rather monkish when compared to the annual excursions to the capital of his antebellum counterpart. . . .

If, as Chamberlain alleged in the summer of 1874, the mass of Negro voters thought that public peculation was no less wrong than private thievery, the question arises of how the thieves remained in office year after year. The circumstances suggest a series of obvious answers. First, the period of blatant corruption was actually quite short, beginning when the railroad and printing schemes got out of hand in 1870 and ending as reform pressures became increasingly strong in the spring and summer of 1874. Further, the full extent of corruption became known only after

Redemption, if then. Very few Republican officials admitted to any robbery before 1877, and even the conservative native whites, in the Taxpayers' Convention of 1871, certified the soundness of Republican fiscal administration.

Rumors there were of fraud, and probably many Negro voters realized something of the state of affairs, but Republican politicos sagaciously chose to accentuate the positive aspects of their activities and to call the roll of the offenses of the whites. With a fair degree of honesty, Republican campaigners could point with pride to a legislative program dedicated fully to the Negro's economic, educational, and political interests, and the paper pattern had at least some fraction of reality in every county. . . .

During their first dozen years of freedom in South Carolina, Negroes realized a progressive expansion of the meaning of their new liberty. From slaves and quasi-slaves they burgeoned into soldiers, farmers, lawyers, businessmen, and investors; elders and bishops; college students and teachers; jurors, voters, and politicians; family men, Masons, and, even, criminals. In a large measure, this growth was made possible by an outside political power which, early in the period, expanded the basis of that power to include the Negroes themselves. Yet, an irony of the post-Reconstruction history of the Negro is that the very political freedom under which other liberties were early nurtured could not sustain itself in a period in which those liberties continued to grow. Negro losses in the political realm were largely the result of the effectiveness of the Redeemer campaign in vilifying Republicanism in South Carolina. The extravagant charges levied in the report of the Fraud Committee (attested to by scores of witnesses who were confessed participants) seemed ample by its very volume and redundancy to cover the whole body of Republicanism with layers of slime. The numerous indictments against absent Republicans and the apparent ease with which convictions were obtained where the state chose to prosecute was proof enough of the guilt of all. It is hardly surprising that many native white contemporaries convinced themselves and the following generation that Republicanism meant "corruption," and that Negro Republicanism meant "corruption compounded." In time, Northerners accepted the Southern argument as it applied to the South and found in it a certain measure of relief from a sense of guilt for their apostasy. The results were unique; the men who had lost the war in South Carolina had won the peace. Not many vanquished can claim such a victory.

A Selected Modern Bibliography

General Works

Richard Hofstadter, *The American Political Tradition . . .* (New York, 1954)

Ralph H. Gabriel, *The Course of American Democratic Thought . . .* (New York, 1940)

Arthur A. Ekirch, Jr., *The American Democratic Tradition . . .* (New York, 1963)

Louis Hartz, *The Liberal Tradition in America . . .* (New York, 1955)

Arthur A. Ekirch, Jr., *The Decline of American Liberalism* (New York, 1955)

Clinton Rossiter, *Conservatism in America . . .* (2nd edition, New York, 1962)

Daniel J. Boorstin, *The Genius of American Politics* (Chicago, 1953)

Wilfred E. Binkley, *American Political Parties: Their Natural History* (4th edition, New York, 1962)

Herbert Agar, *The Price of Union* (Boston, 1950)

William Nisbet Chambers and Walter Dean Burnham (eds.), *The American Party Systems, Stages of Political Development* (New York, 1967)

Kirk H. Porter and Donald B. Johnson (eds.), *National Party Platforms, 1840–1956* (Urbana, Ill., 1956)
Pendleton Herring, *The Politics of Democracy: American Parties in Action* (New York, 1940)
Clinton Rossiter, *Parties and Politics in America* (Ithaca, N.Y., 1960)
Joseph LaPalombara and Myron Wiener (eds.), *Political Parties and Political Development* (Princeton, 1966)
V. O. Key, Jr., *Politics, Parties, and Pressure Groups* (5th edition, New York, 1964)
Hugh A. Bone, *Party Committees and National Politics* (Seattle, 1958)
Cornelius P. Cotter and Bernard C. Hennessy, *Politics Without Power: The National Party Committees* (New York, 1964)

Frank R. Kent, *The Democratic Party, a History* (New York, 1928)
Henry A. Minor, *The Story of the Democratic Party* (New York, 1928)
Ralph M. Goldman, *The Democratic Party in American Politics* (New York, 1966)
Ronald F. Stinnett, *Democrats, Dinners and Dollars* (Ames, Iowa, 1967)
William T. Cash, *History of the Democratic Party in Florida* (Tallahassee, 1936)
George L. Willis, *Kentucky Democracy* (3 vols., Louisville, Ky., 1935)
Thomas E. Powell, *The Democratic Party of . . . Ohio* (Columbus, 1913)

Malcolm C. Moos, *The Republicans: A History* . . . (New York, 1956)
George H. Mayer, *The Republican Party, 1854–1966* (2nd edition, New York, 1967)
Francis Curtis, *The Republican Party* . . . 1854–1904 (2 vols., New York, 1904)
Charles O. Jones, *The Republican Party* . . . (New York, 1965)
Milton Viorst, *Fall from Grace: The Republican Party and the Puritan Ethic* (New York, 1968)
Paul D. Casdorph, *A History of the Republican Party in Texas* . . . (Austin, 1965)

Eugene H. Roseboom, *A History of Presidential Elections* (New York, 1957)

James W. Davis, *Springboard to the White House: Presidential Primaries . . .* (New York, 1967)

William B. Brown, *The People's Choice: The Presidential . . . Campaign Biography* (Baton Rouge, 1960)

W. Dean Burnham (comp.), *Presidential Ballots, 1836–1892* (Baltimore, 1955)

V. O. Key, *The Responsible Electorate: Rationality in Presidential Voting, 1936–1960* (Cambridge, Mass., 1966)

Lucius Wilmerding, Jr., *The Electoral College* (New Brunswick, N.J., 1958)

Wallace S. Sayre and Judith H. Parris, *Voting for President: The Electoral College . . .* (Washington, D.C., 1971)

George F. Milton, *The Use of Presidential Power, 1789–1943* (Boston, 1944)

Edward S. Corwin, *The President: Office and Powers, 1787–1948 . . .* (3rd edition, New York, 1948)

Morton Borden (ed.), *America's Ten Greatest Presidents* (Chicago, 1961)

Harold J. Laski, *The American Presidency . . .* (New York, 1940)

Sidney Hyman, *The American President* (New York, 1954)

Sidney Hyman (ed.), "The Office of the American Presidency," *Annals of the American Academy of Political and Social Science*, Vol. 307 (September 1956)

Clinton Rossiter, *The American Presidency* (2nd edition, New York, 1960)

Herman Finer, *The Presidency . . .* (Chicago, 1960)

Richard E. Neustadt, *Presidential Power* (New York, 1960)

Wilfred E. Binkley, *The Man in the White House: His Powers and Duties* (rev. edition, New York, 1964)

Carleton Jackson, *Presidential Vetoes, 1792–1945* (Athens, Ga., 1967)

James Hart, *The Ordinance Making Powers of the President . . .* (Baltimore, 1925)

Richard P. Longaker, *The Presidency and Individual Liberties* (Ithaca, N.Y., 1961)

James E. Pollard, *The Presidents and the Press* (New York, 1947)

Rexford G. Tugwell, *The Enlargement of the Presidency* (New York, 1970)

Mary L. Hinsdale, *A History of the President's Cabinet* (Ann Arbor, Mich., 1911)

Richard F. Fenno, Jr., *The President's Cabinet: . . . from Wilson to Eisenhower* (Cambridge, Mass., 1959)
Dorothy G. Fowler, *The Cabinet Politician: The Postmasters General, 1829–1909* (New York, 1943)

Carl Russell Fish, *The Civil Service and the Patronage* (New York, 1905)
Paul P. Van Riper, *History of the United States Civil Service* (Evanston, Ill., 1958)
W. Lloyd Warner *et al., The American Federal Executive* . . . (New Haven, 1963)
Harold Seidman, *Politics, Position and Power: The Dynamics of Federal Organization* (New York, 1971)
Wilfred E. Binkley, *President and Congress* (3rd edition, New York, 1962)
Clinton Rossiter, *The Supreme Court and the Commander in Chief* (Ithaca, N.Y., 1951)
Glendon A. Schubert, Jr., *The Presidency in the Courts* (Minneapolis, 1957)

Ernest S. Griffith, *Congress: Its Contemporary Role* (3rd edition, New York, 1961)
Randall B. Ripley, *Majority Party Leadership in Congress* (Boston, 1969)
Charles O. Jones, *The Minority Party in Congress* (Boston, 1970)
Barbara Hinckley, *The Seniority System in Congress* (Bloomington, Ind., 1971)
Marshall E. Dimock, *Congressional Investigating Committees* (Baltimore, 1929)
Emmy E. Werner, "Women in Congress, 1917–1964," *Review of Politics,* XIX (March 1966)
George H. Haynes, *The Senate of the United States: Its History and Practice* (2 vols., Boston, 1938)
Joseph P. Harris, *The Advice and Consent of the Senate: . . . Confirmation of Appointments* . . . (Berkeley, 1953)
Donald R. Matthews, *U.S. Senators and Their World* (Chapel Hill, 1960)
George B. Galloway, *History of the House of Representatives* (New York, 1961)
H. B. Fuller, *The Speakers of the House* (Boston, 1909)

Robert G. McCloskey, *The American Supreme Court* (Chicago, 1960)
Leo Pfeffer, *This Honorable Court . . .* (Boston, 1965)
John R. Schmidhauser, *The Supreme Court, Its Politics, Personalities, and Procedures* (New York, 1960)
Carl B. Swisher, *The Supreme Court in Modern Role* (rev. edition, New York, 1965)
Conyers Read (ed.), *The Constitution Reconsidered* (New York, 1938)
Robert K. Carr, *The Supreme Court and Judicial Review* (New York, 1942)
Charles G. Haines, *The American Doctrine of Judicial Supremacy* (rev. edition, Berkeley, 1932)
William W. Crosskey, *Politics and the Constitution . . .* (2 vols., Chicago, 1953)
Martin Shapiro, *Law and Politics in the Supreme Court . . .* (Glencoe, Ill., 1964)
Richard Claude, *The Supreme Court and the Electoral Process* (Baltimore, 1970)

Horace B. Davis, "The Occupations of Massachusetts Legislators, 1790–1950," *New England Quarterly*, XXIV (March 1951)
DeAlva S. Alexander, *A Political History of the State of New York* (4 vols., New York, 1906–23)
V. O. Key, *Southern Politics in State and Nation* (New York, 1949)
Perry H. Howard, *Political Tendencies in Louisiana, 1812–1952* (Baton Rouge, 1957)
Jasper B. Shannon, *Presidential Politics in Kentucky, 1824–1948* (Lexington, Ky., 1950)
J. Stephen Turett, "The Vulnerability of American Governors, 1900–1969," *Midwest Journal of Political Science*, XV (February 1971)

Allan G. Bogue, "United States: The 'New' Political History," *Journal of Contemporary History*, III (January 1968)
George M. Belnap, "A Method for Analyzing Legislative Behavior," *Midwest Journal of Political Science*, II (November 1958)
Lee F. Anderson *et al.*, *Legislative Roll-Call Analysis* (Evanston, Ill., 1966)
Robert P. Swierenga, "Ethnocultural Political Analysis: A New Ap-

proach to American Ethnic Studies," *Journal of American Studies*, V (April 1971)

Charles A. McCoy and John Playford, *Apolitical Politics: A Critique of Behavioralism* (New York, 1967)

I *Colonial Politics, 1607–1776*

Jack P. Greene, "Changing Interpretations of Early American Politics," in Ray Allen Billington (ed.), *The Reinterpretation of Early American History* . . . (San Marino, Calif., 1966)

Wesley Frank Craven, *The Colonies in Transition, 1660–1713* (New York, 1968)

James M. Smith (ed.), *Seventeenth-Century America* . . . (Chapel Hill, 1959)

Oliver M. Dickerson, *American Colonial Government* . . . (Cleveland, 1912)

Bernard Bailyn, *Origins of American Politics* (New York, 1968)

Bernard Bailyn, "Political Experience and Enlightenment Ideas in Eighteenth-Century America," *American Historical Review*, LXVII (January 1962)

Michael Kammen, *Deputyes and Libertyes: The Origins of Representative Government in Colonial America* (New York, 1969)

Roy N. Lokken, "The Concept of Democracy in Colonial Political Thought," *William and Mary Quarterly*, XVI (October 1959)

Mary P. Clarke, *Parliamentary Privilege in the American Colonies* (New Haven, 1943)

Leonard W. Labaree, *Conservatism in Early American History* (New York, 1948)

William S. Carpenter, *The Development of American Political Thought* (Princeton, 1930)

Lawrence H. Leder, *Liberty and Authority: Early American Political Ideology, 1689–1763* (Chicago, 1968)

John B. Kirby, "Early American Politics—The Search for Ideology: An Historiographical Analysis . . . ," *Journal of Politics*, XXXII (November 1970)

T. H. Breen, *The Character of the Good Ruler: Puritan Political Ideas in New England, 1630–1730* (New Haven, 1970)

Richard S. Dunn, *Puritans and Yankees: The Winthrop Dynasty of New England* . . . (Princeton, 1962)

Michael Zuckerman, *Peaceable Kingdoms: New England Towns in the Eighteenth Century* (New York, 1970)
Thomas J. Wertenbaker, *The Puritan Oligarchy* (New York, 1947)
Edmund S. Morgan, *The Puritan Dilemma: The Story of John Winthrop* (Boston, 1958)
B. Katherine Brown, "Freemanship in Puritan Massachusetts," *American Historical Review*, LIX (July 1954)
Kenneth A. Lockridge and Alan Kreider, "The Evolution of Massachusetts Town Government, 1640 to 1740," *William and Mary Quarterly*, XXIII (October 1966)
Robert M. Zemsky, ". . . Leadership Patterns in the Massachusetts Assembly, 1740–1755," *William and Mary Quarterly*, XXVI (October 1969)
John A. Schutz, *William Shirley: King's Governor of Massachusetts* (Williamsburg, Va., 1961)
Alan Simpson, "How Democratic Was Roger Williams?" *William and Mary Quarterly*, XIII (January 1956)
Edmund S. Morgan, *Roger Williams: The Church and the State* (New York, 1967)
Charles S. Grant, *Democracy in the Connecticut Frontier Town of Kent* (New York, 1961)
Robert Sklar, "The Great Awakening and Colonial Politics: Connecticut's Revolution in the Minds of Men," *Connecticut Historical Society Bulletin*, XXVIII (July 1963)

Nicholas Varga, "Election Procedures and Practices in Colonial New York," *New York History*, XLI (July 1960)
Milton M. Klein, "Democracy and Politics in Colonial New York," *New York History*, XL (July 1959)
Milton M. Klein, "Politics and Personalities in Colonial New York," *New York History*, XLVII (January 1966)
Jerome R. Reich, *Leisler's Rebellion . . .* (New York, 1953)
Stanley N. Katz, *Newcastle's New York: Anglo-American Politics, 1732–1753* (Cambridge, Mass., 1968)
Lawrence H. Leder, *Robert Livingston . . . and the Politics of Colonial New York* (Chapel Hill, 1961)
Patricia U. Bonomi, "Political Patterns in Colonial New York City . . . ," *Political Science Quarterly*, LXXXI (September 1966)
Bruce M. Wilkenfeld, "The New York City Common Council, 1689–1800," *New York History*, LII (July 1971)

Jerome J. Nadelhaft, "Politics and the Judicial Tenure Fight in Colonial New Jersey," *William and Mary Quarterly*, XXVIII (January 1971)
Joseph E. Illick, *William Penn the Politician* . . . (Ithaca, N.Y., 1965)
Mary M. Dunn, *William Penn: Politics and Conscience* (Princeton, 1967)
Edwin B. Bronner, *William Penn's "Holy Experiment": The Founding of Pennsylvania, 1681–1701* (New York, 1962)
Gary B. Nash, *Quakers and Politics: Pennsylvania, 1681–1726* (Princeton, 1968)
Roy N. Lokken, *David Lloyd, Colonial Lawmaker* (Seattle, 1959)
Joan de Lourdes Leonard, "Elections in Colonial Pennsylvania," *William and Mary Quarterly*, XI (July 1954)
G. B. Warden, "The Proprietary Group in Pennsylvania, 1754–1764," *William and Mary Quarterly*, XXI (July 1964)
William S. Hanna, *Benjamin Franklin and Pennsylvania Politics* (Stanford, Calif., 1964)

Jack P. Greene, *The Quest for Power: The Lower Houses of Assembly in the Southern Royal Colonies* . . . (Chapel Hill, 1963)
Donald M. Owings, *His Lordship's Patronage: Offices of Profit in Colonial Maryland* (Baltimore, 1953)
Aubrey C. Land, *The Dulanys of Maryland* . . . (Baltimore, 1955)
Robert L. Morton, *Colonial Virginia* (2 vols., Chapel Hill, 1960)
Sigmund Diamond, "From Organization to Society: Virginia in the Seventeenth Century," *American Journal of Sociology*, LXIII (March 1958)
Thomas J. Wertenbaker, *Torchbearer of the American Revolution: The Story of Bacon's Rebellion* . . . (Princeton, 1940)
Wilcomb E. Washburn, *The Governor and the Rebel: A History of Bacon's Rebellion in Virginia* (Chapel Hill, 1957)
John C. Rainbolt, "The Alteration in the Relationship Between Leadership and Constituents in Virginia, 1660 to 1720," *William and Mary Quarterly*, XXVII (July 1970)
Leonidas Dodson, *Alexander Spotswood, Governor of Colonial Virginia, 1710–1722* (Philadelphia, 1932)
Carl Bridenbaugh, *Seat of Empire: The Political Role of Eighteenth-Century Williamsburg* (Williamsburg, Va., 1950)
Desmond Clarke, *Arthur Dobbs Esquire* . . . *Governor of North Carolina* (Chapel Hill, 1957)

M. Eugene Sirmans, *Colonial South Carolina: A Political History . . .* (Chapel Hill, 1966)

M. Eugene Sirmans, "The South Carolina Royal Council," *William and Mary Quarterly*, XVIII (July 1961)

Richard P. Sherman, *Robert Johnson, Proprietary & Royal Governor of South Carolina* (Columbia, S.C., 1966)

Robert L. Middlekauff, "The American Continental Colonies in the Empire," in Robin W. Winks (ed.), *The Historiography of the British Empire–Commonwealth . . .* (Durham, N.C., 1966)

Leonard W. Labaree, *Royal Government in America . . .* (New Haven, 1930)

Alison G. Olson and Richard Maxwell Brown (eds.), *Anglo-American Political Relations, 1675–1775* (New Brunswick, N.J., 1970)

Carl Ubbelohde, *The American Colonies and the British Empire . . .* (New York, 1968)

Michael Kammen, *Empire and Interest: The American Colonies and the Politics of Mercantilism* (Philadelphia, 1970)

Lawrence A. Harper, *The English Navigation Laws . . .* (New York, 1940)

I. K. Steele, *Politics of Colonial Policy: The Board of Trade . . . 1696–1720* (New York, 1968)

Michael G. Hall, *Edward Randolph and the American Colonies, 1676–1703* (Chapel Hill, 1960)

Michael G. Kammen, *A Rope of Sand: The Colonial Agents, British Politics, and the American Revolution* (Ithaca, N.Y., 1968)

Jack M. Sosin, *Agents and Merchants: British Colonial Policy and the Origins of the American Revolution, 1763–1775* (Lincoln, Nebr., 1965)

Thomas C. Barrow, *Trade and Empire: The British Customs Service in Colonial America . . .* (Cambridge, Mass., 1967)

Louis B. Namier, *The Structure of Politics at the Accession of George III* (London, 1929)

Louis B. Namier, *England in the Age of the American Revolution* (London, 1930)

Herbert Butterfield, *George III and the Historians* (rev. edition, New York, 1959)

Max Savelle, *Seeds of Liberty: The Genesis of the American Mind* (New York, 1948)

Clinton Rossiter, *Seedtime of the Republic: The Origin of the American Tradition of Political Liberty* (New York, 1953)
Bernard Bailyn, *The Ideological Origins of the American Revolution* (Cambridge, Mass., 1967)
Edmund S. Morgan, *The Birth of the Republic, 1763–1789* (Chicago, 1956)
Bernhard Knollenberg, *Origin of the American Revolution . . .* (New York, 1960)
Lawrence Henry Gipson, *The Coming of the Revolution . . .* (New York, 1954)
Randolph G. Adams, *Political Ideas of the American Revolution . . .* (3rd edition, New York, 1958)
Charles M. Andrews, *Colonial Background of the American Revolution* (New Haven, 1924)
Robert C. Newbold, *The Albany Congress and Plan of Union* (New York, 1955)
Edmund S. and Helen M. Morgan, *The Stamp Act Crisis . . .* (Chapel Hill, 1953)
Robert J. Chaffin, "The Townshend Acts of 1767," *William and Mary Quarterly*, XXVII (January 1970)
Oliver M. Dickerson, *The Navigation Acts and the American Revolution* (Philadelphia, 1951)
R. Coupland, *The Quebec Act . . .* (Oxford, England, 1925)
Arthur M. Schlesinger, *Prelude to Independence: The Newspaper War on Britain, 1764–1776* (New York, 1957)
Ira D. Gruber, "The American Revolution as a Conspiracy: The British View," *William and Mary Quarterly*, XXVI (July 1969)
Carl L. Becker, *The Declaration of Independence* (New York, 1922)
John M. Head, *A Time to Rend: An Essay on the Decision for American Independence* (Madison, Wisc., 1968)

Jere R. Daniell, *Experiment in Republicanism: New Hampshire Politics and the American Revolution, 1741–1794* (Cambridge, Mass., 1970)
Richard D. Brown, *Revolutionary Politics in Massachusetts: The Boston Committee of Correspondence . . .* (Cambridge, Mass., 1970)
John C. Miller, *Sam Adams: Pioneer in Propaganda* (Boston, 1936)
Benjamin W. Labaree, *The Boston Tea Party* (New York, 1964)

Alan and Katherine Day, "Another Look at the Boston 'Caucus,'" *Journal of American Studies,* V (April 1971)

David S. Lovejoy, *Rhode Island Politics and the American Revolution . . .* (Providence, 1958)

Mack E. Thompson, "The Ward–Hopkins Controversy and the American Revolution in Rhode Island," *William and Mary Quarterly,* XVI (July 1959)

Oscar Zeichner, *Connecticut's Years of Controversy, 1750–1776* (Chapel Hill, 1949)

Carl L. Becker, *The History of Political Parties in the Province of New York, 1760–1776* (Madison, Wisc., 1909)

Bernard Mason, *The Road to Independence: The Revolutionary Movement in New York . . .* (Lexington, Ky., 1966)

Don R. Gerlach, *Philip Schuyler and the American Revolution in New York* (Lincoln, Nebr., 1964)

Roger Champagne, "New York's Radicals and the Coming of Independence," *Journal of American History,* LI (June 1964)

Bernard Friedman, "The Shaping of the Radical Consciousness in Provincial New York," *Journal of American History,* LVI (March 1970)

Donald L. Kemmerer, *Path to Freedom: The Struggle for Self-Government in Colonial New Jersey, 1703–1776* (Princeton, 1940)

Theodore Thayer, *Pennsylvania Politics and the Growth of Democracy, 1740–1776* (Harrisburg, Pa., 1953)

Dietmar Rothermund, *The Layman's Progress; Religious and Political Experience in Colonial Pennsylvania, 1740–1770* (Philadelphia, 1961)

Richard Bauman, *For the Reputation of Truth: Politics, Religion, and Conflict Among the Pennsylvania Quakers, 1750–1800* (New Haven, 1971)

David L. Jacobson, *John Dickinson and the Revolution in Pennsylvania, 1764–1776* (Berkeley, 1965)

Charles A. Barker, *The Background of the Revolution in Maryland* (New Haven, 1940)

James Haw, "Maryland Politics on the Eve of the Revolution . . . ," *Maryland Historical Magazine,* LXV (Summer 1970)

Lucille Griffith, *The Virginia House of Burgesses, 1750–1774* (rev. edition, University, Ala., 1970)

Thad W. Tate, "The Coming of the Revolution in Virginia . . . ," *William and Mary Quarterly*, XIX (July 1962)

George E. Frakes, *Laboratory for Liberty: The South Carolina Legislative Committee System, 1719–1776* (Lexington, Ky., 1971)

Robert M. Weir, ". . . Pre-Revolutionary South Carolina Politics," *William and Mary Quarterly*, XXVI (October 1969)

Richard Walsh, *Charleston's Sons of Liberty* . . . (Columbia, S.C., 1959)

Richard Maxwell Brown, *The South Carolina Regulators* . . . (Cambridge, Mass., 1963)

W. W. Abbott, *The Royal Governors of Georgia, 1754–1775* (Chapel Hill, 1959)

II *The Revolutionary Struggle, 1776–1789*

Jack P. Greene, "The Reappraisal of the American Revolution in Recent Historical Literature," in Greene (ed.), *The Reinterpretation of the American Revolution* . . . (New York, 1968)

R. R. Palmer, *The Age of the Democratic Revolution: A Political History of Europe and America, 1760–1800* (2 vols., Princeton, 1959–64)

J. R. Pole, *Political Representation in England and the Origins of the American Republic* (London, 1966)

Forrest McDonald, *E Pluribus Unum: The Formation of the American Republic 1776–1790* (Boston, 1965)

Gordon S. Wood, *The Creation of the American Republic, 1776–1787* (Chapel Hill, 1969)

Thad W. Tate, "The Social Contract in America, 1774–1787 . . . ," *William and Mary Quarterly*, XXII (July 1965)

Merrill Jensen, "Democracy and the American Revolution," *Huntington Library Quarterly*, XX (August 1957)

Cecilia M. Kenyon, "Republicanism and Radicalism in the American Revolution," *William and Mary Quarterly*, XIX (April 1962)

Richard Buel, Jr., "Democracy and the American Revolution . . . ," *William and Mary Quarterly*, XXI (April 1964)

Elisha P. Douglass, *Rebels and Democrats: The Struggle for Equal Political Rights and Majority Rule* (Chapel Hill, 1961)

J. R. Pole, "Historians and the Problem of Early American Democracy," *American Historical Review*, LXVII (April 1962)

Philip Davidson, *Propaganda and the American Revolution* . . . (Chapel Hill, 1941)

Edmund C. Burnett, *The Continental Congress* (New York, 1941)

Lynn Montross, *The Reluctant Rebels . . . the Continental Congress* (New York, 1950)

Jackson Turner Main, *The Upper House in Revolutionary America, 1763–1788* (Madison, Wisc., 1967)

Jackson Turner Main, "Government by the People: The American Revolution and the Democratization of the Legislatures," *William and Mary Quarterly*, XX (July 1966)

Allan Nevins, *The American States During and After the Revolution* (New York, 1924)

Richard Upton, *Revolutionary New Hampshire . . .* (Hanover, N.H., 1936)

Robert E. Brown, *Middle-Class Democracy and the Revolution in Massachusetts . . .* (Ithaca, N.Y., 1955)

David Syrett, "Town-Meeting Politics in Massachusetts, 1776–1786," *William and Mary Quarterly*, XXI (July 1964)

Ellen E. Brennan, *Plural Office-Holding in Massachusetts 1760–1780 . . .* (Chapel Hill, 1945)

Robert J. Taylor, *Western Massachusetts in the Revolution* (Providence, 1954)

Christopher Collier, *Roger Sherman's Connecticut: Yankee Politics and American Revolution* (Middletown, Conn., 1971)

Thomas J. Wertenbaker, *Father Knickerbocker Rebels: New York City During the Revolution* (New York, 1948)

J. Paul Selsam, *The Pennsylvania Constitution of 1776 . . .* Philadelphia, 1936)

Philip A. Crowl, *Maryland During and After the Revolution . . .* (Baltimore, 1942)

Robert E. and B. Katherine Brown, *Virginia, 1705–1786: Democracy or Aristocracy?* (East Lansing, 1964)

Robert L. Ganyard, "Radicals and Conservatives in Revolutionary North Carolina . . . ," *William and Mary Quarterly*, XXIV (October 1967)

Kenneth Coleman, *The American Revolution in Georgia . . .* (Athens, Ga., 1958)

C. H. Van Tyne, *Loyalists in the American Revolution* (New York, 1902)

William H. Nelson, *The American Tory* (Oxford, 1961)
Wallace Brown, *The King's Friends* (Providence, 1966)
North Callahan, *Flight from the Republic* . . . (Indianapolis, 1967)
Julian P. Boyd, *Anglo-American Union: Joseph Galloway's Plans To Preserve the British Empire* . . . (Philadelphia, 1941)
Lawrence Henry Gipson, *American Loyalist: Jared Ingersoll* (New Haven, 1920)
L. F. S. Upton, *The Loyal Whig: William Smith of New York and Quebec* (Toronto, 1969)
Robert O. DeMond, *Loyalists in North Carolina* . . . (Durham, N.C., 1940)

Richard B. Morris, "The Confederation Period and the American Historian," *William and Mary Quarterly*, XIII (April 1956)
Merrill Jensen, *The Articles of Confederation* . . . (Madison, Wisc., 1940)
Merrill Jensen, *The New Nation* . . . 1781–1789 (New York, 1950)
E. James Ferguson, *The Power of the Purse* . . . 1776–1790 (Chapel Hill, 1961)
Jackson Turner Main, *Political Parties Before the Constitution* (New York, 1971)
Irwin H. Polishook, *Rhode Island and the Union, 1774–1795* (Evanston, Ill., 1969)
Ernest W. Spaulding, *New York in the Critical Period* . . . (New York, 1932)
Richard P. McCormick, *Experiment in Independence: New Jersey in the Critical Period* . . . (New Brunswick, N.J., 1950)
Jackson Turner Main, "Sections and Politics in Virginia, 1781–1787," *William and Mary Quarterly*, XII (January 1955)
James R. Morrill, *The Practice and Politics of Fiat Finance: North Carolina in the Confederation* . . . (Chapel Hill, 1969)
W. W. Abbot, "The Structure of Politics in Georgia: 1782–1789," *William and Mary Quarterly*, XIV (January 1957)
Marian L. Starkey, A *Little Rebellion* [Shays'], (New York, 1955)
Robert A. Feer, "Shays' Rebellion and the Constitution: A Study in Causation," *New England Quarterly*, XLII (September 1969)
Stanley Elkins and Eric McKitrick, "The Founding Fathers: Young Men of the Revolution," *Political Science Quarterly*, LXXVI (June 1961)

Max Farrand, *The Framing of the Constitution* . . . (New Haven, 1913)

Charles Warren, *The Making of the Constitution . . .* (Boston, 1928)
Clinton Rossiter, *1787: The Grand Convention* (New York, 1966)
John P. Roche, "The Founding Fathers: A Reform Caucus in Action," *American Political Science Review*, LV (December 1961)
Edward M. Burns, *James Madison: Philosopher of the Constitution* (New Brunswick, N. J., 1938)
Arthur N. Holcombe, "The Role of Washington in the Framing of the Constitution," *Huntington Library Quarterly*, XIX (August 1956)
Staughton Lynd, "The Compromise of 1787," *Political Science Quarterly*, LXXXI (June 1966)
Paul Eidelberg, *The Philosophy of the American Constitution . . .* (New York, 1968)
Douglass Adair, ". . . David Hume, James Madison and the Tenth Federalist," *Huntington Library Quarterly*, XX (August 1957)
Charles A. Beard, *An Economic Interpretation of the Constitution* (new edition, New York, 1935)
Forrest McDonald, *We the People: The Economic Origins of the Constitution* (Chicago, 1958)

Gottfried Dietze, *The Federalist . . .* (Baltimore, 1960)
Charles W. Roll, Jr., "We, Some of the People: Apportionment in the Thirteen State Conventions Ratifying the Constitution," *Journal of American History*, LVI (June 1969)
Cecilia M. Kenyon, "Men of Little Faith: the Anti-Federalists . . . ," *William and Mary Quarterly*, XII (January 1955)
Jackson T. Main, *The Anti-Federalists* (Chapel Hill, 1961)
Hamilton M. Bishop, *Why Rhode Island Opposed the Federal Constitution* (Providence, 1950)
Linda Grant De Pauw, *The Eleventh Pillar: New York State and the Federal Constitution* (Ithaca, N.Y., 1966)
Staughton Lynd, *Anti-Federalism in Dutchess County, New York . . .* (Chicago, 1962)
Louise I. Trenholme, *Ratification . . . in North Carolina* (New York, 1932)
Robert A. Rutland, *The Birth of the Bill of Rights . . .* (Chapel Hill, 1955)

III *Foundations for a New Politics, 1789–1824*

James Hart, *The American Presidency in Action, 1789* (New York, 1948)

Ralph V. Harlow, *History of Legislative Methods . . . Before 1825* (New Haven, 1917)

Richard R. Beeman, "Unlimited Debate in the Senate: The First Phase," *Political Science Quarterly*, LXXXIII (September 1968)

Patrick J. Furlong, "The Origins of the House Committee of Ways and Means," *William and Mary Quarterly*, XXV (October 1968)

J. R. Saylor, "Creating the Federal Judiciary," *Baylor Law Review*, VIII (Summer 1956)

John C. Miller, *The Federalist Era . . .* (New York, 1960)

Jacob E. Cooke, "The Compromise of 1790," *William and Mary Quarterly*, XXVII (October 1970)

Leland D. Baldwin, *Whiskey Rebels: The Story of a Frontier Uprising* (Pittsburgh, 1939)

Stanley D. Rose, "Alexander Hamilton and the Historians," *Vanderbilt Law Review*, XI (June 1958)

Gerald Stourzh, *Alexander Hamilton and the Idea of Republican Government* (Stanford, Calif., 1970)

Edward Handler, *America and Europe in the Political Thought of John Adams* (Cambridge, Mass., 1964)

John R. Howe, Jr., *The Changing Political Thought of John Adams* (Princeton, 1966)

Stephen G. Kurtz, "The Political Science of John Adams . . . ," *William and Mary Quarterly*, XXV (October 1968)

Stephen G. Kurtz, *The Presidency of John Adams . . .* (Philadelphia, 1957)

Samuel F. Bemis, *Jay's Treaty . . .* (rev. edition, New Haven, 1962)

Jerald A. Combs, *The Jay Treaty: Political Battleground of the Founding Fathers* (Berkeley, 1970)

Alexander DeConde, *The Quasi-War: The Politics and Diplomacy of the Undeclared War with France, 1797–1801* (New York, 1966)

John A. Munroe, *Federalist Delaware, 1775–1815* (New Brunswick, N.J., 1954)

Charles S. Sydnor, *Gentlemen Freeholders: Political Practices in Washington's Virginia* (Chapel Hill, 1952)

Roy F. Nichols, *The Invention of the American Political Parties* (New York, 1967)

Joseph Charles, *The Origins of the American Party System* (Williamsburg, Va., 1956)

William N. Chambers, *Political Parties in a New Nation . . .* (New York, 1963)

Morton Borden, *Parties and Politics in the Early Republic . . .* (New York, 1967)

Harry Ammon, "The Genêt Mission and the Development of American Political Parties," *Journal of American History,* LII (March 1966)

Charles A. Beard, *Economic Origins of Jeffersonian Democracy* (New York, 1915)

Manning J. Dauer, *The Adams Federalists* (Baltimore, 1953)

David Hackett Fischer, *The Revolution of American Conservatism: The Federalist Party in the Era of Jeffersonian Democracy* (New York, 1965)

Linda K. Kerber, *Federalists in Dissent: Imagery and Ideology in Jeffersonian America* (Ithaca, N.Y., 1970)

Shaw Livermore, Jr., *The Twilight of Federalism: The Disintegration of the Federalist Party . . .* (Princeton, 1962)

Anson E. Morse, *The Federalist Party in Massachusetts to the Year 1800* (Princeton, 1909)

James M. Banner, Jr., *To the Hartford Convention: The Federalists and the Origins of Party Politics in Massachusetts, 1789–1815* (New York, 1969)

Robert Ernst, *Rufus King: American Federalist* (Chapel Hill, 1968)

Lisle A. Rose, *Prologue to Democracy: The Federalists in the South, 1789–1800* (Lexington, Ky., 1968)

Norman K. Risjord, "The Virginia Federalists," *Journal of Southern History,* XXXIII (November 1967)

U. B. Phillips, "The South Carolina Federalists," *American Historical Review,* XIV (April–July 1909)

John R. Howe, Jr., "Republican Thought and the Political Violence of the 1790's," *American Quarterly*, XIX (Summer 1967)

Leonard W. Levy, *Freedom of Speech and Press in Early American History* . . . (New York, 1963)

James Morton Smith, *Freedom's Fetters: The Alien and Sedition Laws* . . . (Ithaca, N.Y., 1956)

James Morton Smith, "Grass Roots Origins of the Kentucky Resolutions," *William and Mary Quarterly*, XXVII (April 1970)

Adrienne Koch and Harry Ammon, "The Virginia and Kentucky Resolutions . . . ," *William and Mary Quarterly*, V (April 1948)

Donald H. Stewart, *The Opposition Press of the Federalist Period* (Albany, 1969)

Marshall Smelser, *The Democratic Republic, 1801–1815* (New York, 1968)

Merrill D. Peterson, *Thomas Jefferson and the New Nation* (New York, 1970)

Dumas Malone, *Jefferson the President: First Term, 1801–1805* (Boston, 1970)

Charles O. Lerche, Jr., "Jefferson and the Election of 1800: A Case Study of the Political Smear," *William and Mary Quarterly*, V (October 1948)

Raymond Walters, Jr., *Albert Gallatin* . . . (New York, 1957)

Sidney H. Aronson, *Status and Kinship in the Higher Civil Service: Standards of Selection in the Administrations of John Adams, Thomas Jefferson, and Andrew Jackson* (Cambridge, Mass., 1964)

Carl E. Prince, "The Passing of the Aristocracy: Jefferson's Removal of the Federalists, 1801–1805," *Journal of American History*, LVII (December 1970)

Thomas P. Abernethy, *The Burr Conspiracy* (New York, 1954)

Adrienne Koch, *Jefferson and Madison: The Great Collaboration* (New York, 1950)

Irving Brant, *The Fourth President: A Life of James Madison* (Indianapolis, 1970)

Francis Harrold, "The Upper House in Jeffersonian Political Theory," *Virginia Magazine of History*, LXXVIII (July 1970)

Joseph Cooper, "Jeffersonian Attitudes Toward Executive Leadership and Committee Development in the House of Representatives," *Western Political Quarterly*, XVIII (March 1965)

Paul Goodman, "Social Status of Party Leadership: The House of

Representatives, 1797–1804," *William and Mary Quarterly*, XXV (July 1968)
James Sterling Young, *The Washington Community, 1800–1828* (New York, 1966)

Richard E. Ellis, *The Jeffersonian Crisis: Courts and Politics in the Young Republic* (New York, 1971)
Caleb P. Patterson, *The Constitutional Principles of Thomas Jefferson* (Austin, 1953)
Leonard W. Levy, *Jefferson and Civil Liberties . . .* (Cambridge, Mass., 1963)
Donald O. Dewey, *Marshall versus Jefferson: The Political Background of Marbury* v. *Madison* (New York, 1970)
C. Peter Magrath, *Yazoo: Law and Politics in the New Republic* (Providence, 1966)

Ronald F. Banks, *Maine Becomes a State: The Movement To Separate Maine from Massachusetts, 1785–1820* (Middletown, Conn., 1970)
Dixon Ryan Fox, *The Decline of Aristocracy in the Politics of New York, 1801–1840* (New York, 1919)
Alvin Kass, *Politics in New York State, 1800–1830* (Syracuse, N.Y. 1965)
Howard L. McBain, *DeWitt Clinton and the Origins of the Spoils System in New York* (New York, 1907)
Walter R. Fee, *The Transition from Aristocracy to Democracy in New Jersey . . .* (Somerville, N.J., 1933)
Stanford W. Higginbotham, *The Keystone in the Democratic Arch: Pennsylvania Politics, 1800–1816* (Harrisburg, Pa., 1952)
Willey E. Hodges, "The Theoretical Basis of Anti-Governmentalism in Virginia, 1789–1836," *Journal of Politics*, IX (August 1947)
Thomas P. Abernethy, *From Frontier to Plantation in Tennessee: A Study in Frontier Democracy* (Chapel Hill, 1932)
Alfred B. Sears, *Thomas Worthington: Father of Ohio Statehood* (Columbus, 1958)

Noble E. Cunningham, Jr., *The Jeffersonian Republicans . . .* (2 vols., Chapel Hill, 1957–63)
Leonard D. White, *The Jeffersonians: A Study in Administrative History* (New York, 1951)

W. A. Robinson, *Jeffersonian Democracy in New England* (New Haven, 1916)

Paul Goodman, *The Democratic-Republicans of Massachusetts* . . . (Cambridge, Mass., 1964)

Alfred F. Young, *The Democratic Republicans of New York: The Origins, 1763–1797* (Chapel Hill, 1967)

Ray W. Irwin, *Daniel D. Tompkins: Governor of New York and Vice-President of the United States* (New York, 1968)

Carl E. Prince, *New Jersey's Jeffersonian Republicans* . . . (Chapel Hill, 1967)

Norman K. Risjord, *The Old Republicans: Southern Conservatism in the Age of Jefferson* (New York, 1965)

Harry Ammon, "The Richmond Junto, 1800–1824," *Virginia Magazine of History* . . . , LXI (October 1953)

Delbert H. Gilpatrick, *Jeffersonian Democracy in North Carolina* (New York, 1931)

John H. Wolfe, *Jeffersonian Democracy in South Carolina* (Chapel Hill, 1940)

Lowell H. Harrison, *John Breckinridge, Jeffersonian Republican* (Louisville, Ky., 1969)

Louis M. Sears, *Jefferson and the Embargo* (Durham, N.C., 1927)

Norman K. Risjord, "1812: Conservatives, War Hawks, and the Nation's Honor," *William and Mary Quarterly*, XVIII (April 1961)

Reginald Horsman, *Causes of the War of 1812* (Philadelphia, 1962)

Roger H. Brown, *The Republic in Peril: 1812* (New York, 1964)

Victory A. Sapio, *Pennsylvania and the War of 1812* (Lexington, Ky., 1970)

Myron F. Wehtje, "Opposition in Virginia to the War of 1812," *Virginia Magazine of History*, LXXVIII (January 1970)

George Dangerfield, *The Era of Good Feelings* (New York, 1951)

Charles S. Sydnor, "The One-Party Period of American History," *American Historical Review*, LI (April 1946)

Harry Ammon, *James Monroe* (New York, 1971)

Norris W. Preyer, "Southern Support of the Tariff of 1816—a Reappraisal," *Journal of Southern History*, XXV (August 1959)

Vincent J. Capowski, "The Era of Good Feelings in New Hampshire . . . ," *Historical New Hampshire*, XXI (Winter 1966)

Philip S. Klein, *Pennsylvania Politics, 1817–1832: A Game Without Rules* (Philadelphia, 1940)

James A. Kehl, *Ill Feeling in the Era of Good Feeling: Western Pennsylvania Political Battles, 1815–1825* (Pittsburgh, 1956)

Thomas P. Abernethy, *The Formative Period in Alabama, 1815–1828* (Montgomery, 1922)

Lonnie J. White, *Politics on the Southwestern Frontier: Arkansas Territory, 1819–1836* (Memphis, 1964)

Lynn L. Marshall, "Genesis of Grass-Roots Democracy in Kentucky," *Mid-America*, XLVII (October 1965)

Edward S. Corwin, *John Marshall and the Constitution* (New Haven, 1920)

Robert K. Faulkner, *The Jurisprudence of John Marshall* (Princeton, 1968)

Gerald T. Dunne, *Justice Joseph Story* (New York, 1971)

Donald G. Morgan, *Justice William Johnson, the First Dissenter* (Columbia, S.C., 1954)

William G. North, "The Political Background of the Dartmouth College Case," *New England Quarterly*, XVIII (June 1945)

Harold J. Plous and Gordon E. Baker, "McCulloch *v.* Maryland . . . ," *Stanford Law Review*, IX (July 1957)

Maurice G. Baxter, *Daniel Webster and the Supreme Court* (Amherst, Mass., 1966)

Robert J. Steamer, "Congress and the Supreme Court During the Marshall Era," *Review of Politics*, XXVII (July 1965)

R. Kent Newmyer, *The Supreme Court Under Marshall and Taney* (New York, 1968)

IV *Jacksonian Politics in Action, 1824–1848*

Everett S. Brown, "The Presidential Election of 1824–1825," *Political Science Quarterly*, XL (September 1925)

Paul C. Nagel, "The Election of 1824 . . . ," *Journal of Southern History*, XXVI (August 1960)

Charles Sellers, "Jackson Men with Feet of Clay," *American Historical Review*, LXII (April 1957)

Samuel Flagg Bemis, *John Quincy Adams and the Union* (New York, 1956)

George A. Lipsky, *John Quincy Adams: His Theory and Ideas* (New York, 1950)
Robert V. Remini, *The Election of Andrew Jackson* (Philadelphia, 1963)

Chilton Williamson, *American Suffrage from Property to Democracy . . .* (Princeton, 1960)
Marchette Chute, *The First Liberty: A History of the Right To Vote . . .* (New York, 1969)
J. R. Pole, "The Suffrage in New Jersey, 1790–1807," *New Jersey History*, LXXI (January 1953)
J. R. Pole, "Representation and Authority in Virginia from the Revolution to Reform," *Journal of Southern History*, XXIV (February 1958)
George F. Taylor, "Suffrage in Early Kentucky," *Register of the Kentucky Historical Society*, LXI (January 1963)
George D. Luetscher, *Early Political Machinery in the United States* (Philadelphia, 1903)
William G. Morgan, ". . . the Congressional Nominating Caucus," *Proceedings of the American Philosophical Society*, CXIII (April 1969)
James S. Chase, "Jacksonian Democracy and the Rise of the Nominating Convention," *Mid-America*, XLV (October 1963)

Richard Hofstadter, *The Idea of a Party System: The Rise of Legitimate Opposition in the United States, 1780–1840* (Berkeley, 1969)
Michael Wallace, "Changing Concepts of Party in the United States: New York, 1815–1828," *American Historical Review*, LXXIV (December 1968)
David P. Peltier, "Party Development and Voter Participation in Delaware, 1792–1811," *Delaware History*, XIV (October 1970)
Homer C. Hockett, *Western Influences on Political Parties to 1825* (Columbus, 1917)
Richard P. McCormick, *The Second American Party System: Party Formation in the Jacksonian Period* (Chapel Hill, 1966)
Ronald P. Formisano, "Political Character, Antipartyism, and the Second Party System," *American Quarterly*, XXI (Winter 1969)

Brian G. Walton, "The Second Party System in Arkansas, 1836–1848," *Arkansas Historical Quarterly*, XXVIII (Spring 1969)

Ronald P. Formisano, "A Case Study of Party Formation: Michigan, 1835," *Mid-America*, L (April 1968)

Rodney O. Davis, ". . . Party Divisions in the Illinois Legislature, 1834–1841," in Robert P. Swierenga (ed.), *Quantification in American History* . . . (New York, 1970)

Charles Sellers, "Andrew Jackson versus the Historians," *Mississippi Valley Historical Review*, XLIV (March 1958)

Alfred A. Cave, *Jacksonian Democracy and the Historians* (Gainesville, Fla., 1964)

Frederick Jackson Turner, *The United States: 1830–1850* (New York, 1935)

Glyndon G. Van Deusen, *The Jacksonian Era, 1828–1848* (New York, 1959)

Arthur M. Schlesinger, Jr., *The Age of Jackson* (Boston, 1946)

Edward Pessen, *Jacksonian America: Society, Personality and Politics* (Homewood, Ill., 1969)

John William Ward, *Andrew Jackson: Symbol for an Age* (New York, 1955)

Robert V. Remini, *Andrew Jackson* (New York, 1966)

Erik M. Erikson, "The Federal Civil Service Under President Jackson," *Mississippi Valley Historical Review*, XIII (March 1927)

Norman A. Graebner, "James K. Polk: A Study in Federal Patronage," *Mississippi Valley Historical Review*, XXXVII (March 1952)

Richard P. McCormick, "New Perspectives on Jacksonian Politics," *American Historical Review*, LXV (January 1960)

Samuel R. Gammon, *The Presidential Campaign of 1832* (Baltimore, 1922)

Donald B. Cole, "The Presidential Election of 1832 in New Hampshire," *Historical New Hampshire*, XXI (Winter 1966)

Chauncey S. Boucher, *The Nullification Controversy* . . . (Chicago, 1916)

William W. Freehling, *Prelude to Civil War: The Nullification Controversy* (New York, 1966)

Charles M. Wiltse, *John C. Calhoun* . . . (3 vols., Indianapolis, 1944–51)

Gerald M. Capers, *John C. Calhoun, Opportunist* . . . (Gainesville, Fla., 1960)

Richard P. Longaker, "Andrew Jackson and the Judiciary," *Political Science Quarterly*, LXXI (September 1956)
William S. Hoffman, "Andrew Jackson, State Rightist: The Case of the Georgia Indians," *Tennessee Historical Quarterly*, XI (December 1952)
Joseph C. Burke, "The Cherokee Cases: A Study in Law, Politics, and Morality," *Stanford Law Review*, XXI (February 1969)
Carl B. Swisher, *Roger B. Taney* (New York, 1935)
Stanley I. Kutler, *Privilege and Creative Destruction: The Charles River Bridge Case* (Philadelphia, 1971)
Michael A. Conron, "Law, Politics and Chief Justice Taney . . . ," *American Journal of Legal History*, XI (October 1967)
John P. Frank, *Justice [Peter V.] Daniel Dissenting . . .* (Cambridge, Mass., 1964)
Francis P. Weisenburger, *The Life of John McLean: A Politician on the . . . Supreme Court* (Columbus, 1937)

Bray Hammond, *Banks and Politics in America from the Revolution to the Civil War* (Princeton, 1957)
Ralph C. H. Catterall, *The Second Bank of the United States* (Chicago, 1903)
Thomas P. Govan, *Nicholas Biddle: Nationalist and Public Banker . . .* (Chicago, 1959)
Robert V. Remini, *Andrew Jackson and the Bank War* (New York, 1967)
Frank Otto Gatell, ". . . Van Buren, the Albany Regency, and the Wall Street Conspiracy," *Journal of American History*, LIII (June 1966)
Lynn L. Marshall, "The Authorship of Jackson's Bank Veto Message," *Mississippi Valley Historical Review*, L (December 1963)
Frank Otto Gatell, "Spoils of the Bank War: Political Bias in the Selection of Pet Banks," *American Historical Review*, LXX (October 1964)
John M. McFaul, *The Politics of Jacksonian Finance* (Ithaca, N.Y., 1972)
James Roger Sharp, *The Jacksonians versus the Banks: Politics in the States After the Panic of 1837* (New York, 1970)

Alden Whitman, *Labor Parties, 1827–1834* (New York, 1943)
Edward Pessen, "The Workingmen's Movement of the Jacksonian

Era," *Mississippi Valley Historical Review*, XLIII (December 1956)

Walter Hugins, *Jacksonian Democracy and the Working Class . . .* (Stanford, Calif., 1960)

Carl N. Degler, "The Loco-Focus: Urban 'Agrarians,'" *Journal of Economic History*, XVI (September 1956)

William A. Sullivan, "Did Labor Support Andrew Jackson?" *Political Science Quarterly*, LXII (December 1947)

Edward Pessen, *Most Uncommon Jacksonians: The Radical Leaders of the Early Labor Movement* (Albany, 1967)

Reginald C. McGrane, *The Panic of 1837 . . .* (Chicago, 1924)

William G. Carleton, "Political Aspects of the Van Buren Era," *South Atlantic Quarterly*, L (April 1951)

William Trimble, "Diverging Tendencies in New York Democracy in the Period of the Locofocos," *American Historical Review*, XXIV (April 1919)

James C. Curtis, *The Fox at Bay: Martin Van Buren and the Presidency . . .* (Lexington, Ky., 1970)

Max M. Mintz, "The Political Ideas of Martin Van Buren," *New York History*, XXX (October 1949)

Robert G. Gunderson, *The Log-Cabin Campaign* [1840], (Lexington, Ky., 1957)

Arthur B. Darling, *Political Changes in Massachusetts, 1824–1848 . . .* (New Haven, 1925)

Lee Benson, *The Concept of Jacksonian Democracy: New York as a Test Case* (Princeton, 1961)

Frank Otto Gatell, "Money and Party in Jacksonian America: A Quantitative Look at New York City's Men of Quality," *Political Science Quarterly*, LXXII (June 1967)

The Jacksonian Heritage, *Pennsylvania Politics, 1833–1848* (Harrisburg, Pa., 1958)

Howard Braverman, "The Economic and Political Background of the Conservative Revolt in Virginia," *Virginia Magazine of History*, LX (April 1952)

William S. Hoffman, *Andrew Jackson and North Carolina Politics* (Chapel Hill, 1958)

Robert V. Remini, *Martin Van Buren and the Making of the Democratic Party* (New York, 1959)

Leonard D. White, *The Jacksonians . . .* (New York, 1954)

Marvin Meyers, *The Jacksonian Persuasion: Politics and Belief* (Stanford, Calif., 1957)
Russel B. Nye, *George Bancroft, Brahmin Rebel* (New York, 1945)
John A. Garraty, *Silas Wright* (New York, 1949)
Charles H. Ambler, *Thomas Ritchie* (Richmond, 1913)
William N. Chambers, *Old Bullion [Thomas Hart] Benton . . .* (Boston, 1956)

Donald B. Cole, *Jacksonian Democracy in New Hampshire . . .* (Cambridge, Mass., 1970)
Arthur B. Darling, "Jacksonian Democracy in Massachusetts," *American Historical Review*, XXIX (January 1924)
Robert V. Remini, "The Albany Regency," *New York History*, XXXIX (October 1958)
Jerome Mushkat, *Tammany: The Evolution of a Political Machine, 1789–1865* (Syracuse, N.Y., 1971)
Mark H. Haller, "The Rise of the Jackson Party in Maryland," *Journal of Southern History*, XXVII (August 1962)
W. Wayne Smith, "Jacksonian Democracy on the Chesapeake . . . ," *Maryland Historical Magazine*, LXII (December 1967), LXIII (March 1968)
Constance M. Green, "The Jacksonian 'Revolution' in the District of Columbia," *Mississippi Valley Historical Review*, XLV (March 1959)
Clarence C. Norton, *The Democratic Party in Ante-Bellum North Carolina . . .* (Chapel Hill, 1930)
Arthur W. Thompson, *Jacksonian Democracy on the Florida Frontier* (Gainesville, Fla., 1961)
Edwin A. Miles, *Jacksonian Democracy in Mississippi* (Chapel Hill, 1960)
Robert E. Shalhope, "Jacksonian Politics in Missouri . . . ," *Civil War History*, XV (September 1969)
Harry R. Stevens, *The Early Jackson Party in Ohio* (Durham, N.C., 1957)

E. Malcolm Carroll, *Origins of the Whig Party* (Durham, N.C., 1925)
Lynn L. Marshall, "The Strange Stillbirth of the Whig Party," *American Historical Review*, LXXII (January 1967)
Edwin A. Miles, "The Whig Party and the Menace of Caesar," *Tennessee Historical Quarterly*, XXVII (Winter 1968)

Glyndon G. Van Deusen, "Some Aspects of Whig Thought and Theory in the Jacksonian Period," *American Historical Review,* LXIII (January 1958)

George R. Poage, *Henry Clay and the Whig Party* (Chapel Hill, 1936)

Glyndon G. Van Deusen, . . . *Henry Clay* (Boston, 1937)

Clement Eaton, *Henry Clay* . . . (Boston, 1957)

Norman D. Brown, *Daniel Webster and the Politics of Availability* (Athens, Ga., 1969)

Albert D. Kirwan, *John J. Crittenden* . . . (Lexington, Ky., 1962)

Glyndon G. Van Deusen, *Thurlow Weed: Wizard of the Lobby* (Boston, 1947)

Henry R. Mueller, *The Whig Party in Pennsylvania* (New York, 1922)

Charles M. Thompson, *The Illinois Whigs* . . . (Urbana, Ill., 1915)

Arthur C. Cole, *The Whig Party in the South* (Washington, D.C., 1913)

Charles Sellers, "Who Were the Southern Whigs?" *American Historical Review,* LIX (January 1954)

Henry H. Simms, *Rise of the Whigs in Virginia* . . . (Richmond, 1929)

Max R. Williams, "The Foundations of the Whig Party in North Carolina . . ." *North Carolina Historical Review,* XLVII (April 1970)

Paul Murray, *The Whig Party in Georgia* . . . (Chapel Hill, 1948)

Herbert J. Doherty, Jr., *The Whigs of Florida* . . . (Gainesville, Fla., 1959)

Thomas B. Alexander *et al.*, "Who Were the Alabama Whigs?" *Alabama Review,* XVI (January 1963)

Randolph Campbell, "The Whig Party of Texas . . . ," *Southwestern Historical Quarterly,* LXXIII (July 1969)

John Vollmer Mering, *The Whig Party in Missouri* (Columbia, Mo., 1967)

V *The Politics of Slavery, 1820–1860*

Glover Moore, *The Missouri Controversy, 1819–1821* (Lexington, Ky., 1953)

Philip F. Detweiler, "The Congressional Debate on Slavery . . . 1819–1821," *American Historical Review,* LXIII (April 1958)

Richard M. Brown, "The Missouri Crisis, Slavery, and the Politics of Jacksonianism," *South Atlantic Quarterly*, LXV (Winter 1966)
Philip J. Staudenraus, *The African Colonization Movement* (New York, 1961)
Robert J. Clarke, *The Road from Monticello: . . . the Virginia Slavery Debate of 1832* (Durham, N.C., 1941)
Gerald S. Henig, "The Jacksonian Attitude Toward Abolitionists in the 1830's," *Tennessee Historical Quarterly*, XXVIII (Spring 1969)
Leonard L. Richards, *"Gentlemen of Property and Standing": Anti-Abolition Riots . . . in the 1830's* (New York, 1970)
James M. McPherson, "The Fight Against the Gag Rule . . . ," *Journal of Negro History*, XLVIII (July 1963)
Russel B. Nye, *Fettered Freedom: Civil Liberties and the Slavery Controversy . . .* (East Lansing, 1949)

Robert J. Morgan, *A Whig Embattled: The Presidency Under John Tyler* (Lincoln, Nebr., 1954)
James C. N. Paul, *Rift in the Democracy* (Philadelphia, 1951)
Charles Sellers, *James K. Polk . . .* (2 vols., Princeton, 1957–66)
Charles A. McCoy, *Polk and the Presidency* (Austin, 1960)
James J. Horn, "Trends in Historical Interpretation: James K. Polk," *North Carolina Historical Review*, XLII (October 1965)
Norman A. Graebner, *Empire on the Pacific: A Study in American Continental Expansion* (New York, 1955)
John Hope Franklin, "The Southern Expansionists of 1846," *Journal of Southern History*, XXV (August 1959)
Chaplain W. Morrison, *Democratic Politics and Sectionalism: The Wilmot Proviso Controversy* (Chapel Hill, 1967)
Eric Foner, "The Wilmot Proviso Revisited," *Journal of American History*, LVI (September 1969)
Peter T. Harstad and Richard W. Resh, "The Causes of the Mexican War: A Note on Changing Interpretations," *Arizona and the West*, VI (Winter 1964)

Kinley J. Brauer, *Cotton versus Conscience: Massachusetts Whig Politics and Southwestern Expansion . . .* (Lexington, Ky., 1967)
Arthur M. Mowry, *The Dorr War: Or, the Constitutional Struggle in Rhode Island* (Providence, 1901)
H. D. A. Donovan, *The Barnburners . . .* (New York, 1925)

Edgar A. Holt, *Party Politics in Ohio, 1840–1850* (Columbus, Ohio, 1931)
Floyd B. Streeter, *Political Parties in Michigan, 1837–1860* . . . (Lansing, Mich., 1918)
Robert M. Ireland, "Aristocrats All: The Politics of County Government in Ante-Bellum Kentucky," *Review of Politics*, XXXII (July 1970)
Stanley Siegel, A *Political History of the Texas Republic, 1836–1845* (Austin, 1956)

Theodore C. Smith, *The Liberty and Free Soil Parties in the Northwest* (New York, 1897)
Betty Fladeland, *James Gillespie Birney* . . . (Ithaca, N.Y., 1955)
Ralph L. Morrow, "The Liberty Party in Vermont," *New England Quarterly*, II (April 1929)
Joseph G. Rayback, "The Liberty Party Leaders of Ohio . . . ," *Ohio Historical Quarterly*, LVII (April 1958)
Eric Foner, "Politics and Prejudice: The Free Soil Party and the Negro . . . ," *Journal of Negro History*, L (October 1965)
Edward C. Schriver, "Antislavery: Free Soil . . . in Maine . . . ," *New England Quarterly*, XLII (March 1969)
Richard H. Sewell, *John P. Hale and the Politics of Abolition* (Cambridge, Mass., 1965)
Frank Otto Gatell, *John Gorham Palfrey and the New England Conscience* (Cambridge, Mass., 1963)
Frederick J. Blue, "Ohio Free Soilers . . . ," *Ohio History*, LXXXVI (Winter 1967)

Allan Nevins, *Ordeal of the Union* . . . (2 vols., New York, 1947)
Jesse Macy, *Political Parties* . . . *1846–1861* (New York, 1900)
Dean L. Yarwood, "Legislative Persistence: A Comparison of the United States Senate in 1850 and 1860," *Midwest Journal of Political Science*, XI (May 1967)

Holman Hamilton, *Prologue to Conflict: The Crisis and Compromise of 1850* (Lexington, Ky., 1964)
Holman Hamilton, *Zachary Taylor* . . . (2 vols., Indianapolis, 1941–51)
Frank H. Hodder, "The Authorship of the Compromise of 1850," *Mississippi Valley Historical Review*, XXII (March 1936)
Major L. Wilson, ". . . Webster and His Critics in the Crisis of 1850," *Civil War History*, XIV (December 1968)

Robert R. Russel, "What Was the Compromise of 1850?" *Journal of Southern History*, XXII (August 1956)

Larry Gara, "The Fugitive Slave Law: A Double Paradox," *Civil War History*, X (September 1964)

Stanley W. Campbell, *The Slave Catchers: Enforcement of the Fugitive Slave Law . . .* (Chapel Hill, 1970)

Larry Gara, *The Liberty Line: The Legend of the Underground Railroad* (Lexington, Ky., 1961)

Horatio T. Strother, *The Underground Railroad in Connecticut* (Middletown, Conn., 1962)

Norman L. Rosenberg, "Personal Liberty Laws and Sectional Crisis . . ." *Civil War History*, XVII (March 1971)

Roy F. Nichols, "The Kansas-Nebraska Act: A Century of Historiography," *Mississippi Valley Historical Review*, XLIII (September 1956)

Robert R. Russel, "The Issues in the Congressional Struggle over the Kansas-Nebraska Bill," *Journal of Southern History*, XXIX (May 1963)

James C. Malin, *The Nebraska Question, 1852–1854* (Lawrence, Kans., 1953)

Alice Nichols, *Bleeding Kansas* (New York, 1954)

James A. Rawley, *Race and Politics: "Bleeding Kansas" and the Coming of the Civil War* (Philadelphia, 1969)

Samuel A. Johnson, *Battle Cry of Freedom: The New England Emigrant Aid Company in the Kansas Crusade* (Lawrence, Kans., 1954)

Ray A. Billington, *The Protestant Crusade, 1800–1860* (New York, 1938)

David Brion Davis, "Some Themes of Counter-Subversion: An Analysis of Anti-Masonic, Anti-Catholic, and Anti-Mormon Literature," *Mississippi Valley Historical Review*, XLVII (September 1960)

William G. Bean, "Puritan versus Celt, 1850–1860," *New England Quarterly*, VII (March 1934)

Larry A. Rand, "The Know-Nothing Party of Rhode Island . . . ," *Rhode Island History*, XXIII (October 1964)

Carroll J. Noonan, *Nativism in Connecticut, 1829–1860* (Washington, D.C., 1938)

Louis D. Scisco, *Political Nativism in New York State* (New York, 1901)

Warren F. Hewitt, "The Know-Nothing Party in Pennsylvania," *Pennsylvania History*, II (April 1935)

Evangeline Thomas, *Nativism in the Old Northwest* (Washington, D.C., 1936)

George M. Stephenson, "Nativism in . . . the Mississippi Valley," *Mississippi Valley Historical Review*, IX (December 1922)

W. Darrell Overdyke, *The Know-Nothing Party in the South* (Baton Rouge, 1950)

Mary S. McConville, *Political Nativism in . . . Maryland . . .* (Washington, D.C., 1928)

Leon C. Soulé, *The Know Nothing Party in New Orleans . . .*(Baton Rouge, 1961)

Ralph A. Wooster, ". . . the Texas Know-Nothings," *Southwestern Historical Quarterly*, LXX (January 1967)

Wallace B. Turner, "The Know-Nothing Movement in Kentucky," *Filson Club Historical Quarterly*, XXVIII (July 1954)

Avery O. Craven, *The Growth of Southern Nationalism, 1848–1861* (Baton Rouge, 1953)

Douglas Bowers, "Ideology and Political Parties in Maryland, 1851–1856," *Maryland Historical Magazine*, LXIV (Fall 1969)

Avery O. Craven, *Edmund Ruffin, Southerner . . .* (New York, 1932)

J. G. DeRoulhac Hamilton, *Party Politics in North Carolina, 1835–1860* (Durham, N.C., 1916)

Ralph A. Wooster, *The People in Power: Courthouse and Statehouse in the Lower South, 1850–1860* (Knoxville, Tenn., 1969)

Harold S. Schultz, *Nationalism and Sectionalism in South Carolina, 1852–1860 . . .* (Durham, N.C., 1950)

Horace Montgomery, *Cracker Parties* (Baton Rouge, 1950)

Lewy Dorman, *Party Politics in Alabama from 1850 to 1860* (Wetumpka, Ala., 1935)

Thomas B. Alexander *et al.*, "The Basis of Alabama's Ante-Bellum Two-Party System," *Alabama Review*, XIX (October 1966)

Donald M. Rawson, "Democratic Resurgence in Mississippi, 1852–1853," *Journal of Mississippi History*, XXVI (February 1964)

Ralph A. Wooster, "Membership in Early Texas Legislatures, 1850–1860," *Southwestern Historical Quarterly*, LXIX (October 1965)

Eugene H. Berwanger, *The Frontier Against Slavery: Western Anti-Negro Prejudice and the Slavery Extension Controversy* (Urbana, Ill., 1967)

Loomis M. Ganaway, *New Mexico and the Sectional Controversy* . . . (Albuquerque, 1944)

William H. Ellison, A *Self-Governing Dominion: California, 1849–1860* (Berkeley, 1950)

Robert W. Johannsen, *Frontier Politics and the Sectional Conflict: The Pacific Northwest* . . . (Seattle, 1956)

Roy F. Nichols, *The Democratic Machine, 1850–1854* (New York, 1923)

Joel H. Silbey, "The Southern National Democrats, 1845–1861," *Mid-America*, XLVII (July 1965)

Andrew W. Crandall, *Early History of the Republican Party* . . . (Boston, 1930)

Eric Foner, *Free Soil, Free Labor, Free Men: The Ideology of the Republican Party Before the Civil War* (New York, 1970)

Ruhl J. Bartlett, *John C. Fremont and the Republican Party* (Columbus, 1930)

Edward P. Brynn, "Vermont . . . and the Emergence of the Republican Party," *Vermont History*, XXXVIII (Spring 1970)

Martin B. Duberman, ". . . Beginnings of the Republican Party in Massachusetts," *New England Quarterly*, XXXIV (September 1961)

David Donald, *Charles Sumner and the Coming of the Civil War* (New York, 1960)

Jeter A. Isely, *Horace Greeley and the Republican Party* (Princeton, 1947)

Michael F. Holt, *Forging a Majority: The Formation of the Republican Party in Pittsburgh* . . . (New Haven, 1969)

Roger H. Van Bolt, "Rise of the Republican Party in Indiana . . . ," *Indiana Magazine of History*, LI (September 1955)

David S. Sparks, "Birth of the Republican Party in Iowa . . . ," *Iowa Journal of History*, LIV (January 1956)

Morton M. Rosenberg, "The First Republican Election Victory in Iowa," *Annals of Iowa*, XXXVI (Summer 1962)

Victor B. Howard, "Cassius M. Clay and the Origins of the Republican Party [in Kentucky]," *Filson Club Historical Magazine*, XLV (January 1971)

Roy F. Nichols, *Disruption of American Democracy* (New York, 1948)

Philip S. Klein, *President James Buchanan* . . . (University Park, Pa., 1962)

Vincent C. Hopkins, *Dred Scott's Case* (New York, 1951)

Robert W. Johannsen, "Stephen A. Douglas, Popular Sovereignty and the Territories," *The Historian*, XXII (August 1960)

Robert W. Johannsen, "Stephen A. Douglas and the South," *Journal of Southern History*, XXXIII (February 1967)

Kirk Jeffrey, Jr., "Stephen Arnold Douglas in American Historical Writing," *Illinois State Historical Society Journal*, LXI (Autumn 1968)

Harry V. Jaffa, *Crisis of the House Divided . . . the Lincoln–Douglas Debates* (Garden City, N.Y., 1959)

Allan Nevins, *The Emergence of Lincoln* . . . (2 vols., New York, 1950)

Don E. Fehrenbacher, *Prelude to Greatness: Lincoln in the 1850's* (Stanford, Calif., 1962)

Stephen B. Oates, *To Purge This Land with Blood: A Biography of John Brown* (New York, 1970)

Keith Sutherland, "The Structure of Congress as a Factor in the Legislative Crisis of 1860," *Mid-America*, LI (October 1969)

Thomas J. Pressly, *Americans Interpret Their Civil War* (Princeton, 1954)

Thomas N. Bonner, "Civil War Historians and the 'Needless War' Doctrine," *Journal of the History of Ideas*, XVII (April 1956)

John S. Rosenberg, "Toward a New Civil War Revisionism," *American Scholar*, XXXVIII (Spring 1969)

James G. Randall, "The Blundering Generation," *Mississippi Valley Historical Review*, XXVII (June 1940)

Avery Craven, *The Civil War in the Making* . . . (Baton Rouge, 1959)

David M. Potter, *The South and the Sectional Conflict* (Baton Rouge, 1968)

George H. Knoles (ed.), *The Crisis of the Union, 1860–1861* (Baton Rouge, 1965)

Norman A. Graebner (ed.), *Politics and the Crisis of 1860* (Urbana, Ill., 1961)

Reinhard D. Luthin, *The First Lincoln Campaign* (Cambridge, Mass., 1944)

Frederick C. Luebke (ed.), *Ethnic Voters and the Election of Lincoln* (Lincoln, Nebr., 1971)
Ollinger Crenshaw, *The Slave States in the Presidential Election of 1860* (Baltimore, 1945)
Seymour Martin Lipset, "The Emergence of the One Party South—The Election of 1860," in Lipset, *Political Man* . . . (New York, 1960)
Frank H. Heck, "John C. Breckinridge in the Crisis of 1860–1861," *Journal of Southern History*, XXI (August 1955)
Arthur C. Cole, "Lincoln's Election an Immediate Menace to Slavery . . . ?" *American Historical Review*, XXVI (July 1931)

VI *Division and Forced Reunion, 1860–1877*

Ralph A. Wooster, "The Secession of the Lower South: . . . Changing Interpretations," *Civil War History*, VII (June 1961)
William J. Donnelly, ". . . the Historiography of the Support for Secession," *North Caroline Historical Review*, XLII (January 1965)
Dwight L. Dumond, *The Secession Movement* . . . (New York, 1931)
Ralph A. Wooster, *The Secession Conventions of the South* (Princeton, 1962)
Henry T. Shanks, *The Secession Movement in Virginia* . . . (Richmond, 1934)
Joseph C. Sitterson, *The Secession Movement in North Carolina* (Chapel Hill, 1939)
Stephen A. Channing, *Crisis of Fear: Secession in South Carolina* (New York, 1970)
Clarence P. Denman, *The Secession Movement in Alabama* (Montgomery, 1933)
Percy L. Rainwater, *Mississippi: Storm Center of Secession* . . . (Baton Rouge, 1938)
Charles B. Dew, "Who Won the Secession Election Louisiana?" *Journal of Southern History*, XXXVI (February 1970)
Wallace B. Turner, "The Secession Movement in Kentucky," *Register of the Kentucky Historical Society*, LXVI (July 1968)
Mary Scrugham, *The Peaceable Americans of 1861* (New York, 1921)
Robert G. Gunderson, *Old Gentlemen's Convention: The Washington Peace Conference of 1861* (Madison, Wisc., 1961)
Kenneth M. Stampp, *And the War Came: The North and the Secession Crisis* . . . (Baton Rouge, 1950)

John S. Tilley, *Lincoln Takes Command* (Chapel Hill, 1941)
David M. Potter, *Lincoln and His Party in the Secession Crisis* (New Haven, 1942)
Richard N. Current, *Lincoln and the First Shot* (Philadelphia, 1963)

Benjamin P. Thomas, *Portrait for Posterity: Lincoln and His Biographers* (New Brunswick, N.J., 1947)
David M. Potter, *The Lincoln Theme and American National Historiography* (Oxford, England, 1948)
James G. Randall, *Lincoln the President* (4 vols., New York, 1945–55)
Benjamin P. Thomas, *Abraham Lincoln* (New York, 1952)
Harry J. Carman and Reinhard Luthin, *Lincoln and the Patronage* (New York, 1943)
Benjamin Quarles, *Lincoln and the Negro* (New York, 1962)
John Hope Franklin, *The Emancipation Proclamation* (New York, 1963)
Mark M. Krug, "The Republican Party and the Emancipation Proclamation," *Journal of Negro History*, XLVIII (April 1963)
Forrest G. Wood, *Black Scare: The Racist Response to Emancipation and Reconstruction* (Berkeley, 1968)

Clarence E. Macartney, *Lincoln and His Cabinet* (New York, 1931)
Burton J. Hendrick, *Lincoln's War Cabinet* (Boston, 1946)
Glyndon G. Van Deusen, *William Henry Seward* (New York, 1967)
Benjamin P. Thomas and Harold M. Hyman, *Stanton: . . . Lincoln's Secretary of War* (New York, 1962)

Leonard P. Curry, *Blueprint for Modern America: Nonmilitary Legislation of the First Civil War Congress* (Nashville, Tenn., 1968)
Allan G. Bogue, "Bloc and Party in the United States Senate: 1861–1863," *Civil War History*, XIII (September 1967)
Hans L. Trefousse, "The Joint Committee on the Conduct of the War . . . ," *Civil War History*, X (March 1964)

David M. Silver, *Lincoln's Supreme Court* (Urbana, Ill., 1956)
James G. Randall, *Constitutional Problems Under Lincoln* (rev. edition, Urbana, Ill., 1951)
Frank L. Klement, *The Limits of Dissent: Clement L. Vallandigham and the Civil War* (Lexington, Ky., 1970)

Joseph G. Gambone, "Ex Parte Milligan . . . ," *Civil War History*, XVI (September 1970)

William F. Zornow, *Lincoln and the Party Divided* (Norman, Okla., 1954)

Sidney Kaplan, "The Miscegenation Issue in the Election of 1864," *Journal of Negro History*, XXXIV (July 1949)

Grady McWhiney (ed.), *Grant, Lee, Lincoln and the Radicals* (Evanston, Ill., 1964)

T. Harry Williams, *Lincoln and the Radicals* (Madison, Wisc., 1941)

H. J. Eckenrode and Bryan Conrad, *George B. McClellan: The Man Who Saved the Union* (Chapel Hill, 1941)

Wood Gray, *The Hidden Civil War: The Story of the Copperheads* (New York, 1942)

Frank L. Klement, *The Copperheads in the Middle West* (Chicago, 1960)

William B. Hesseltine, *Lincoln and the War Governors* (New York, 1948)

Edith Ellen Ware, *Political Opinion in Massachusetts During Civil War and Reconstruction* (New York, 1916)

John Niven, *Connecticut for the Union* (New Haven, 1965)

Stewart Mitchell, *Horatio Seymour of New York* (Cambridge, Mass., 1938)

James A. Rawley, *Edwin D. Morgan . . .* (New York, 1955)

Erwin S. Bradley, *The Triumph of Militant Republicanism: . . . Pennsylvania and Presidential Politics, 1860–1872* (Philadelphia, 1964)

William Dusinberre, *Civil War Issues in Philadelphia . . .* (Philadelphia, 1965)

Harold Hancock, *Delaware During the Civil War* (Wilmington, 1961)

Richard O. Curry, *A House Divided: A Study of Statehood Politics . . . in West Virginia* (Pittsburgh, 1964)

George H. Porter, *Ohio Politics During the Civil War* (New York, 1911)

Kenneth M. Stampp, *Indiana Politics During the Civil War* (Indianapolis, 1949)

William E. Parrish, *Turbulent Partnership: Missouri and the Union* (Columbia, Mo., 1963)

Charles R. Lee, Jr., *The Confederate Constitutions* (Chapel Hill, 1963)
Ralph Richardson, "The Choice of Jefferson Davis as Confederate President," *Journal of Mississippi History*, XVII (May 1955)
Hudson Strode, *Jefferson Davis* . . . (3 vols., New York, 1955–65)
Rudolph Von Abele, *Alexander H. Stephans* . . . (New York, 1946)
Robert W. Patrick, *Jefferson Davis and His Cabinet* (Baton Rouge, 1944)
Robert D. Meade, *Judah P. Benjamin* . . . (New York, 1943)
Ulrich B. Phillips, . . . *Robert Toombs* (New York, 1913)
Wilfred B. Yearns, *The Confederate Congress* (Athens, Ga., 1960)
Richard E. Beringer, "A Profile of the Members of the Confederate Congress," *Journal of Southern History*, XXXIII (November 1967)
Frank L. Owsley, *State Rights in the Confederacy* (Chicago, 1925)
Curtis A. Amlund, *Federalism in the Southern Confederacy* (Washington, D.C., 1966)
May S. Ringold, *The Role of the State Legislatures in the Confederacy* (Athens, Ga., 1966)
Bernard H. Nelson, "Legislative Control of the Southern Free Negro, 1861–1865," *Catholic Historical Review*, XXXII (April 1946)
David M. Potter, "Jefferson Davis and the Political Factors in Confederate Defeat," in David Donald (ed.), *Why the North Won the Civil War* (Baton Rouge, 1960)
Robert D. Little, "Southern Historians and the Downfall of the Confederacy," *Alabama Review*, IV (January 1951)

Herman Belz, *Reconstructing the Union: Theory and Policy During the Civil War* (Ithaca, N.Y., 1969)
William B. Hesseltine, *Lincoln's Plan for Reconstruction* (Chicago, 1967)
Wilbert H. Ahern, "The Cox Plan of Reconstruction: . . . Ideology and Race Relations," *Civil War History*, XVI (December 1970)
John G. Sproat, "Blueprint for Radical Reconstruction," *Journal of Southern History*, XLV (December 1958)

W. E. B. DuBois, *Black Reconstruction* . . . (New York, 1935)
John Hope Franklin, *Reconstruction* . . . (Chicago, 1961)
Kenneth M. Stampp, *The Era of Reconstruction* . . . (New York, 1965)

Rembert W. Patrick, *The Reconstruction of the Nation* (New York, 1967)
David Donald, *The Politics of Reconstruction* . . . (Baton Rouge, 1965)

Albert Castel, "Andrew Johnson: His Historiographical Rise and Fall," *Mid-America*, XLV (July 1963)
Eric L. McKitrick, *Andrew Johnson and Reconstruction* (Chicago, 1960)
LaWanda and John Cox, *Politics, Principle and Prejudice: . . . 1865–1866* (Glencoe, Ill., 1963)
W. R. Brock, *An American Crisis: Congress and Reconstruction, 1865–1867* (New York, 1963)
Michael Perman, "The South and Congress's Reconstruction Policy, 1866–1867," *Journal of American Studies*, IV (February 1971)
Theodore B. Wilson, *The Black Codes of the South* (University, Ala., 1965)
Joe M. Richardson, "The Florida Black Codes," *Florida Historical Quarterly*, XLVII (April 1969)
Martha M. Bigelow, "Public Opinion and . . . the Mississippi Black Codes," *Negro History Bulletin*, XXXIII (January 1970)

Larry Kincaid, "Victims of Circumstance: . . . Changing Attitudes Toward Republican Policy Makers and Reconstruction," *Journal of American History*, LVII (June 1970)
John G. Clark, "Historians and the Joint Committee on Reconstruction," *Historian*, XXIII (May 1961)
Richard N. Current, *Old Thad Stevens* . . . (Madison, Wisc., 1942)
Fawn M. Brodie, *Thaddeus Stevens* . . . (New York, 1959)
David Donald, *Charles Sumner and the Rights of Men* (New York, 1970)
Hans L. Trefousse, *The Radical Republicans* . . . (New York, 1968)
George R. Bentley, *A History of the Freedmen's Bureau* (Philadelphia, 1955)
William S. McFeeley, *Yankee Stepfather: General O. O. Howard and the Freedmen* (New Haven, 1968)
Jacobus TenBroek, *The Antislavery Origins of the Fourteenth Amendment* (Berkeley, 1951)
Joseph B. James, *The Framing of the Fourteenth Amendment* (Urbana, Ill., 1956)

George P. Smith, "Republican Reconstruction and Section Two of the Fourteenth Amendment," *Western Political Quarterly*, XXIII (December 1970)

Alfred H. Kelly, "The Congressional Controversy over School Segregation, 1867–1875," *American Historical Review*, LXIV (April 1959)

James E. Sefton, "The Impeachment of Johnson: A Century of Writing," *Civil War History*, XIV (June 1968)

Bertram Wyatt-Brown, "The Civil Rights Act of 1875," *Western Political Quarterly*, XVIII (December 1965)

Ronald B. Jager, "Charles Sumner . . . and the Civil Rights Act of 1875," *New England Quarterly*, XLII (September 1969)

J. David Hoeveler, Jr., "Reconstruction and the Federal Courts: The Civil Rights Act of 1875," *Historian*, XXXI (August 1969)

Charles O. Lerche, Jr., "Congressional Interpretations of the Guarantee of a Republican Form of Government . . . ," *Journal of Southern History*, XV (May 1949)

Stanley I. Kutler, *Judicial Power and Reconstruction Politics* (Chicago, 1968)

Harold M. Hyman, *Era of the Oath: Northern Loyalty Tests . . .* (Philadelphia, 1954)

David Montgomery, *Beyond Equality: Labor and the Radical Republicans . . .* (New York, 1967)

LaWanda and John H. Cox, "Negro Suffrage and Republican Politics: The Problem of Motivation in Reconstruction Historiography," *Journal of Southern History*, XXXIII (August 1967)

Charles H. Coleman, *The Election of 1868* (New York, 1933)

Leslie H. Fishel, Jr., "Northern Prejudice and Negro Suffrage, 1865–1870," *Journal of Negro History*, XXXIX (January 1954)

Glenn M. Linden, ". . . Negro Suffrage and Republican Politics," *Journal of Southern History*, XXXVI (August 1970)

Edgar A. Toppin, ". . . The Negro Suffrage Issue in Post-Bellum Ohio Politics," *Journal of Human Relations*, XI (Winter 1963)

G. Galin Berrier, "The Negro Suffrage Issue in Iowa . . . ," *Annals of Iowa*, XXXIX (Spring 1968)

Robert R. Dykstra and Harlan Hahn, "Northern Voters and Negro Suffrage: The Case of Iowa, 1868," *Public Opinion Quarterly*, XXXII (Summer 1968)

William Gilette, *The Right To Vote: Politics and the Passage of the Fifteenth Amendment* (Baltimore, 1965)

Everette Swinney, "Enforcing the Fifteenth Amendment . . . ," *Journal of Southern History*, XXVIII (May 1962)

George R. Woolfolk, *The Cotton Regency: The Northern Merchants and Reconstruction* . . . (New York, 1958)

Frank B. Evans, *Pennsylvania Politics, 1872–1877* . . . (Harrisburg, Pa., 1966)

Felice A. Bonadio, *North of Reconstruction: Ohio Politics, 1865–1870* (New York, 1970)

Richard O. Curry (ed.), *Radicalism, Racism, and Party Realignment: The Border States During Reconstruction* (Baltimore, 1969)

Allen W. Trelease, "Who Were the Scalawags?" *Journal of Southern History*, XXIX (November 1963)

Jack P. Maddex, Jr., *The Virginia Conservatives, 1867–1879: A Study in Reconstruction Politics* (Chapel Hill, 1970)

W. McKee Evans, *Ballots and Fence Rails: Reconstruction on the Lower Cape Fear* (Chapel Hill, 1967)

Francis B. Simkins and Robert H. Woody, *South Carolina During Reconstruction* (Chapel Hill, 1947)

Olive H. Shadgett, *The Republican Party in Georgia, from Reconstruction through 1900* (Athens, Ga., 1964)

Elizabeth S. Nathans, *Losing the Peace: Georgia Republicans and Reconstruction* . . . (Baton Rouge, 1968)

David Donald, "The Scalawag in Mississippi Reconstruction," *Journal of Southern History*, X (November 1944)

William C. Harris, "A Reconsideration of the Mississippi Scalawag," *Journal of Mississippi History*, XXXII (February 1970)

Howard A. White, *The Freedmen's Bureau in Louisiana* (Baton Rouge, 1970)

W. C. Nunn, *Texas Under the Carpetbaggers* (Austin, 1962)

Thomas B. Alexander, *Political Reconstruction in Tennessee* (Nashville, Tenn., 1950)

Robert Cruden, *The Negro in Reconstruction* (Englewood Cliffs, N.J., 1969)

Samuel D. Smith, *The Negro in Congress, 1870–1901* (Chapel Hill, 1940)

Alrutheus A. Taylor, *The Negro in the Reconstruction of Virginia* (Washington, D.C., 1926)

Joel Williamson, *After Slavery: The Negro in South Carolina During Reconstruction* . . . (Chapel Hill, 1965)

Okon Edet Uya, *From Slavery to Public Service: Robert Smalls . . .* (New York, 1971)

Edward F. Sweat, "Francis L. Cardozo: . . . Integrity in Reconstruction Politics," *Journal of Negro History*, XLVI (October 1961)

E. Merton Coulter, *Negro Legislators in Georgia During the Reconstruction Period* (Athens, Ga., 1968)

Joe M. Richardson, *The Negro in the Reconstruction of Florida . . .* (Tallahassee, 1965)

Vernon L. Wharton, *The Negro in Mississippi, 1865–1877* (Chapel Hill, 1947)

Melvin I. Urofsky, "Blanche K. Bruce: United States Senator, 1875–1881," *Journal of Mississippi History*, XXIX (May 1967)

John Hope Franklin (ed.), . . . *The Autobiography of John Roy Lynch* (Chicago, 1970)

Charles Vincent, "Negro Leadership and Programs in the Louisiana Constitutional Convention of 1868," *Louisiana History*, X (Fall 1969)

Agnes S. Grosz, "The Political Career of P. B. S. Pinchback," *Louisiana Historical Quarterly* (April 1944)

Alrutheus A. Taylor, *The Negro in Tennessee, 1865–1880* (Washington, D.C., 1944)

William B. Hesseltine, "Economic Factors in the Abandonment of Reconstruction," *Mississippi Valley Historical Review*, XXII (September 1935)

Patrick W. Riddleberger, "The Radicals' Abandonment of the Negro During Reconstruction," *Journal of Negro History*, XLV (April 1960)

Alfred B. Williams, *Hampton and His Red Shirts: South Carolina's Deliverance in 1876* (Charleston, 1935)

Garnie W. McGinty, *Louisiana Redeemed: The Overthrow of Carpetbag Rule, 1876–1880* (New Orleans, 1941)

C. Vann Woodward, *Reunion and Reaction: The Compromise of 1877 . . .* (2nd edition, Garden City, N.Y., 1956)

Vincent P. DeSantis, *Republicans Face the Southern Question . . .* (Baltimore, 1959)

Stanley P. Hirshon, *Farewell to the Bloody Shirt: Northern Republicans and the Southern Negro . . .* (Bloomington, Ind., 1962)